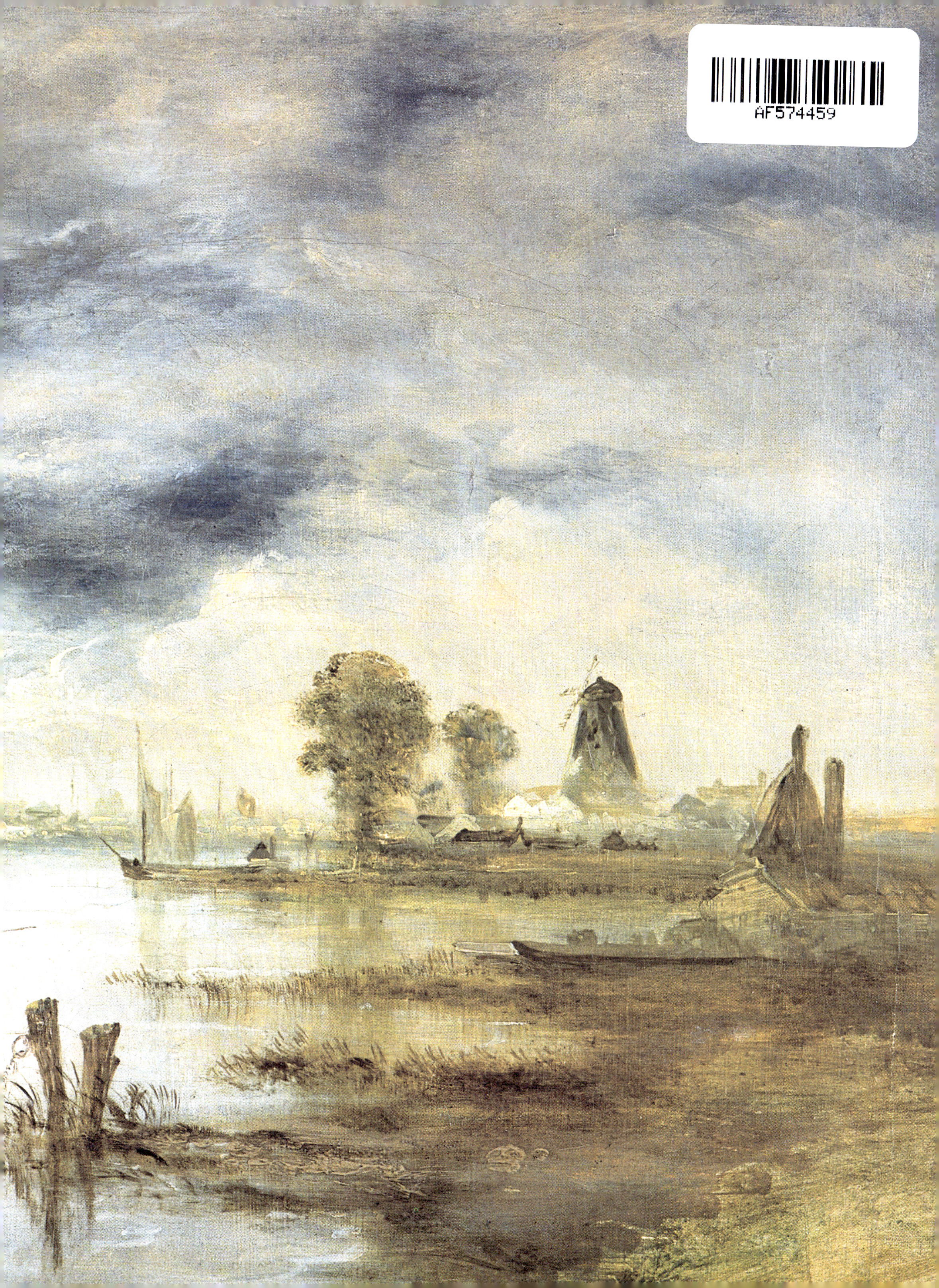

Art and Artists of the

NORWICH SCHOOL

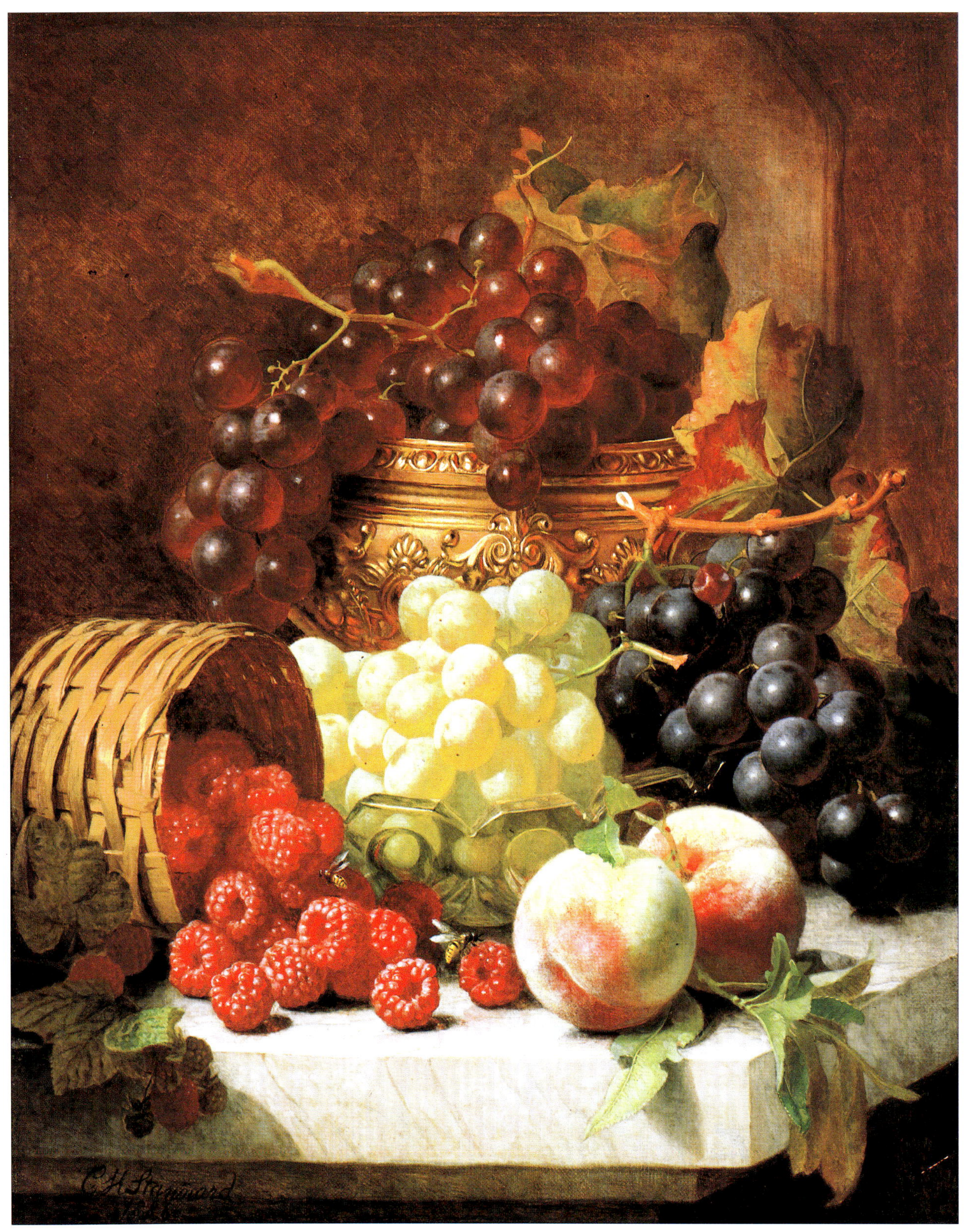

Eloise Harriet Stannard, Still-life with Fruit, 1886, 17½in x 14 in

'In the winter I put the gold in my pictures'

Art and Artists of the
NORWICH SCHOOL

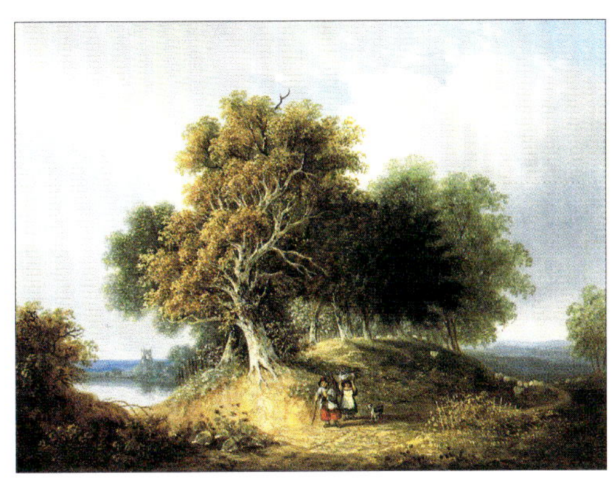

Josephine Walpole

ANTIQUE COLLECTORS' CLUB

First published 1997

ISBN 1 85149 261 5

British Library Cataloguing-in-Publication Data
A catalogue record for this book is available from the British Library

---

Title page illustration: *Samuel David Colkett, By the River Yare, oil on panel, 14 in x 18 in*

Published and printed in England
by the Antique Collectors' Club Ltd., Woodbridge, Suffolk IP12 1DS
on Consort Royal Era Satin paper from Donside Mill, Aberdeen, Scotland

ACKNOWLEDGEMENTS

Although intermittently, I have for many years made a study of the Norwich School and its painters and spent many happy hours in Norwich Castle Museum. Now that the opportunity has arisen to turn a large miscellany of notes, thoughts, illustrations and quotations into a reasonably coherent whole, the time has also come to express my thanks for all the help I have received.

I am especially grateful to Geoffrey and John Allen of Mandell's Gallery, Norwich, who have been so generous in sharing not only their wealth of knowledge but also in permitting me to illustrate a number of works that have passed through their hands or become part of their collection. I am grateful also to Norma Watt together with some of her predecessors and colleagues at Norwich Castle Museum and to Norfolk Museums Service for permission to reproduce works from their Collection, to several private collectors who have requested anonymity, to Peter and the late Oscar Johnson, Harold Day, restorers John and Jennifer Oliver-Budd, the late Stuart Somerville, the late Leonard Squirrell, engraver Joe Lubbock, Rosamund Strode, Michael Webber, photographer Peter Williams, Barbara Husk, Anne Paterson-Wallace, Sotheby's, Phillips, the Norfolk and Suffolk Record Offices, English Heritage, the Heather Newman Gallery, and the Parker Gallery, London.

Obviously I am indebted to earlier writers, particularly Derek Clifford, Andrew Moore, Marjorie Allthorpe-Guyton and Dr Miklos Rajnai. While I am familiar with much of his earlier work, I purposely refrained from reading Andrew Moore's recent book (1996) until my own text was complete, although it is no secret that we, in company with all contemporary writers on the Norwich School, have shared the same source material to some extent – we all owe an inestimable debt to the late James Reeve and his dedication to collecting the work and perpetuating the memory of the Norwich School of Painters.

I must also acknowledge the help given by other Museums and Galleries: the British Museum; Ipswich Museums, particularly Sally Dummer, registrar; Alex Robertson, Keeper of Art, Leeds City Art Gallery; David Scrase, Keeper of Drawings, Paintings and Prints, Fitzwilliam Museum, Cambridge; the National Gallery of Scotland, Edinburgh; the National Gallery of Ireland, Dublin; the Ashmolean Museum, Oxford; the Guildhall Gallery, Aldermanbury, London; Art Gallery and Museum, Glasgow; Abbot Hall, Kendal, Cumbria; the National Portrait Gallery, London; Walker Art Gallery, Liverpool; York City Art Gallery; Birmingham Museum and Art Gallery; Castle Museum, Nottingham; Great Yarmouth Museums; Derby Museum and Art Gallery; Manchester Art Gallery; Grundy Art Gallery, Blackpool; Rochdale Art Gallery; Bolton Museum and Art Gallery; Victoria Art Gallery, Bath; Bury (Lancashire) Art Gallery; Bristol Museums and Art Gallery; the Royal Albert Memorial Museum and Art Gallery, Exeter; Doncaster Art Gallery; Southampton Art Gallery.

I am most grateful, too, to Lady Albemarle for her foreword and for acknowledging the fact that the family ancestry gives her a more positive connection with the old Norwich Society than anyone else I know – in spite of the nobleman in question *not* always being a family favourite!

J. W.

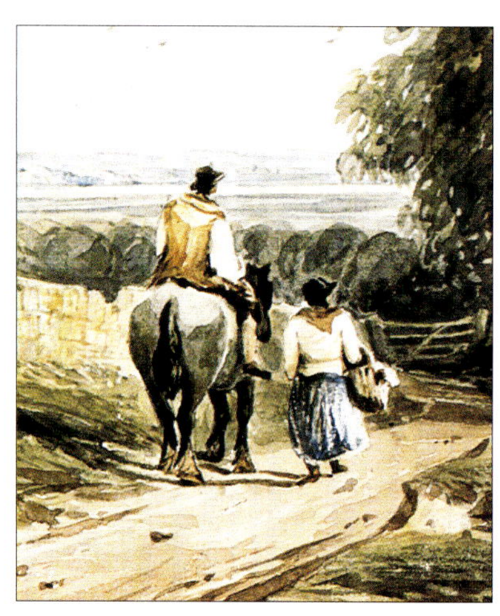

In grateful memory of Sister Catherine Joan, S.N.D.,
my Norwich mentor.

requiescat in pace

CONTENTS

FOREWORD

It is with great pleasure that I write this foreword to Josephine Walpole's fascinating book on the Norwich School. Ever since 1931, when I first came to live in East Anglia, my love for these lovely indigenous landscape paintings has deepened. This book should make the Norwich School painters better known and appreciated and will help us to understand the indefinable bond that informs their work.

I have another reason for my interest in the book. My late husband's great, great grandfather - William Charles, 4th Earl of Albemarle - was one of the earliest supporters of the Norwich Society and became its Patron in 1818, thereby contributing to the stability and continuity of the Society at a time of economic uncertainty. There is a certain irony in this because the family always resented his having to sell thirty of the best pictures from Quidenham Hall to pay off his racing debts! I feel he redeemed himself by his patronage of the Norwich Society.

Research for this book has shown that the works of these artists are well represented in Great Britain and in parts of the United States, but the cream and the bulk of them are in Norwich Castle Museum. To honour the terms of the major bequest from the late Russell Colman there they must remain; they are not available for external exhibition. May this book encourage lovers of landscape painting to hasten to Norwich and to spend a few days beneath the wide skies of Norfolk with its villages, churches and wooded groves.

Diana Albemarle

The Countess of Albemarle

INTRODUCTION

A long time ago when the East Anglian School for girls, now amalgamated with the boys' East Anglian School at Culford Hall, first opened its doors at Bury St. Edmunds, its four Houses were designated Gainsborough, Constable, Cotman and Crome. I was assigned to Gainsborough House whose members, I am able to report, showed up extremely well in inter-house matches and among speech day prizewinners.

It was these House names that ignited my first flickering spark of interest in East Anglian painters, fuelled no doubt by my aptitude for and enjoyment of drawing and painting. Some years later my parents moved to the outskirts of Norwich where I spent much of my time, including many hours in Norwich Castle Museum. The spark had kindled into an encouraging flame by then and my artistic interest became very much focused on the Norwich School of Painters. Excursions to London galleries offering a wider field usually ended up at Lowndes Lodge where Oscar and Peter Johnson enthusiastically promoted East Anglian art, particularly the Norwich Painters.

Although from time to time the fire has simply had to smoulder, over the years I have studied, written about and talked of many individual artists, many single facets of the Norwich School. Now the time has come to pull it all together, to write my own history of an important School which, though for too long underrated, is attracting more and more attention as the years go by and receiving some of the recognition it so richly deserves.

Gainsborough and Constable were not, of course, of the Norwich School but very near neighbours who, as individuals, have had greater prominence than a group might expect. To those four artists who gave their names to the Houses of a girls' public school, this old girl for one owes a debt she is trying in some measure to repay.

J.W.

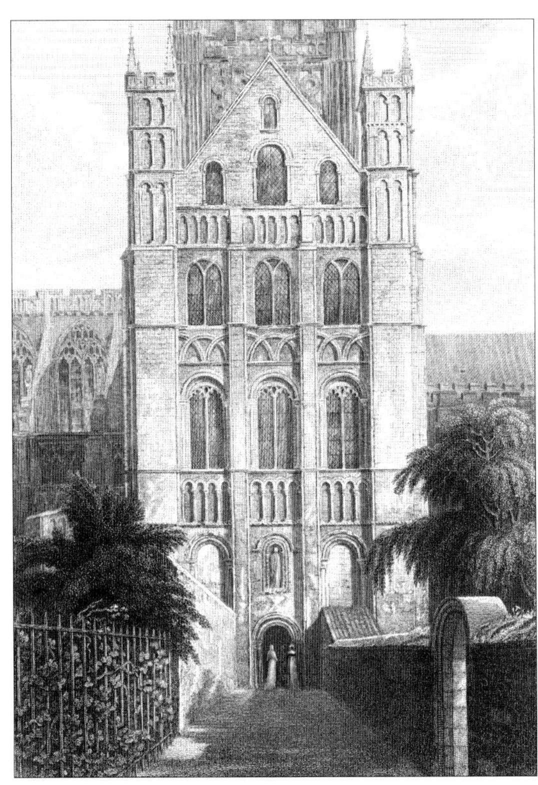

Chapter 1

IN THE BEGINNING . . .

The Norwich School has the distinction of being the only School of Painting in England which takes its name, and drew its nurture, from a definite city and neighbourhood, like the earlier schools of Italy. Artists in this country are little prone to group themselves under the banner of a watchword or theory, as artists of Latin race delight to do. The incurable individualism of the English nature prevents such associations for the furtherance of a closer union from being very effective; personal difference asserts itself, and the bonds become loose. The Norwich artists formulated no theory and adopted no war cry. But there is a deep unconscious bond between them, so that many a painting, though we may be at a loss to attribute it to a particular artist, is unmistakably recognised to belong to the Norwich School.

Laurence Binyon

Norwich Cathedral Church, View of the North Transept, engraving by James Lewis from a drawing by E. Mackenzie for Britton's History &c. of Norwich Cathedral, *published 1816*

Of all the many attempts that have been made concisely to explain or define the phenomenon of the Norwich School, that of Laurence Binyon must surely be the most succinct. That 'deep unconscious bond', itself so unique, so indefinable, makes the Norwich School the only provincial school of painting not only to have stood the test of time but to have increased in stature and significance as the years have gone by. There are no hard and fast dates of its beginning or its end or even, at the fringes, who did or did not belong. Yet, as Binyon says, a Norwich School painting has its own hallmark although that hallmark often defies logical description.

It has to be said that the background was ready made. For many years before the birth of the Norwich Society, Norwich itself had been, after London, a significant cultural centre in the country and the focus of many intellectual groups and societies. Members of these societies were generally appreciative of the various other cultural activities around them; well before there existed a society for the visual arts, Norwich had a Philosophical Society, a Speculative Society, a flourishing theatre and a wide variety of musical activities. Suitably qualified members of the various intellectual and artistic gatherings frequently lectured to the others, they attended each

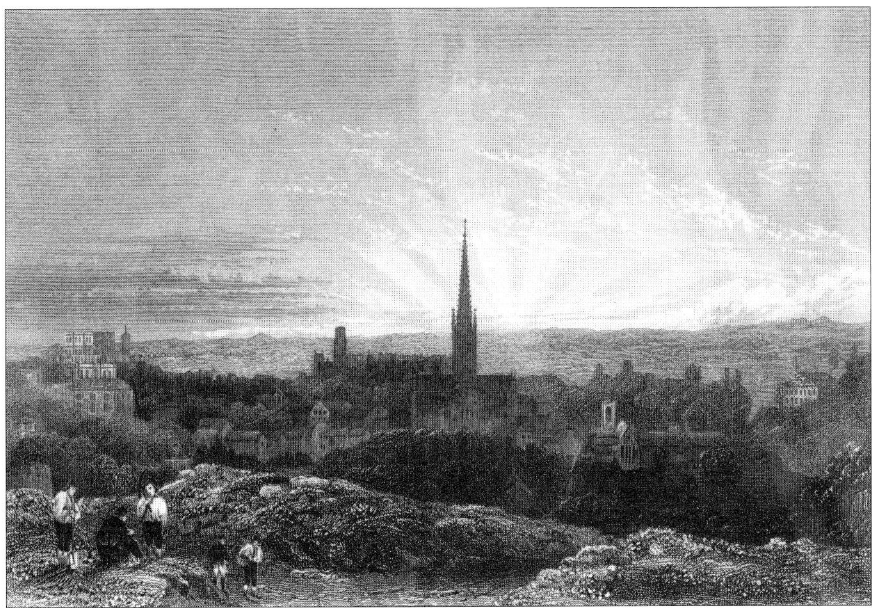

Norwich Cathedral from the East Hill, mid-19th century engraving by B. Winkles

other's meetings and the cross fertilisation of cultures gave Norwich an academic prestige that was unique in the provinces.

Back-tracking even further to the 12th and 13th centuries, when the population of East Anglia, and of Norwich in particular, was the densest outside London, many artists and craftsmen lived and worked in Norwich. There was an enormous wealth of churches in the city and an extraordinary number, approximately 200, of monasteries and convents in the county of Norfolk. Consider the craftsmanship and artistry involved in every one of these glorious buildings, the wonderful architecture, the elaborate wood carving and stonework, the monumental brasses, the wall paintings and illumination and the magnificent stained glass. Dr Woodforde, who wrote *The Norwich School of Glass Painting in the 15th Century*, claimed that some 60 glass painters worked in Norwich between the mid-13th century and the Reformation; it is quite feasible that some of these artists may have been the forefathers of Norwich School painters. The ancient arts and crafts certainly provided good breeding ground.

The Reformation halted the ecclesiastical artistic activities to some extent but by this time Norwich had established a reputation that was there to stay. During the 18th century a number of important national figures came to Norwich to paint, often outstaying their original intention. Joseph Brown, 'the Norwich Claude' 1720-1801, Charles Catton 1728-1798, a founder member of the Royal Academy and born in Norwich, his son Charles Catton 1756-1819, Joseph Farington 1747-1821, Thomas Rowlandson 1756-1827, William Capon 1757-1827, and Williams of Norwich fl. 1758-1795, all painted Norfolk and Norwich subjects, while the German painter, John Theodore Heins 1697-1757, who settled in Norwich, painted some impressive portraits of the city's civic dignitaries. The Academician William Beechey was very attracted to Norwich and his famous portrait of Horatio Nelson is an important feature of the civic collection.

There were also a number of local resident artists painting, teaching and dealing in the city and the periodic exhibitions held drew others from a wide area. There were wealthy merchants and bankers, too, educated people who appreciated the arts in all their forms and could afford to indulge their fancies. Thomas Harvey of Catton, master weaver and banker, was an enthusiastic collector. Dawson Turner, the Yarmouth banker, not only collected paintings but wrote books on architecture, travel and local history for which he needed illustrators. The Beauchamps, the Gurneys and other great Norfolk families were also collectors and many of them employed artists as drawing masters for the ladies. The ground was well prepared for the formation of an artists' society and such painters as Wilson, Gainsborough and Constable were introducing and fostering the taste for rural landscapes for which Norfolk could provide unlimited material.

One prominent and public spirited pillar of Norwich society, also the founder of the

Speculative Society and a collector and connoisseur of works of art, was Dr Edward Rigby by whom, when he left school, John Crome was engaged as general assistant and errand boy. Dr Rigby soon discovered the boy's interest in art and recognised a budding talent, so it is quite feasible to assume that, when the Norwich Society of Artists was formed, ostensibly by John Crome and Robert Ladbroke, the good doctor was the brain behind the venture. Neither Crome nor Ladbroke had much formal education to help with the business and regulatory side of forming a society but both were enthusiastic amateur artists. No doubt it was Dr Rigby who drew up the aims of the society and decided on the best way of running it; it would be surprising if he did not supply financial assistance as well.

The Norwich Society was formed in 1803 'for the purpose of an Enquiry into the Rise, Progress and present state of Painting, Architecture and Sculpture with a view to point out the Best Methods of Study to Attain to Greater Perfection in these Arts'. Initially there was a President to be elected annually by three-quarters of the members present, while the President chose his own Vice-President and Secretary. Potential members, having proved their suitability, were also elected by three quarters of members present at which ever fortnightly meeting applied. These meetings were initially held in a small room in Little Cockey Lane (so called because the stream from Swine Market, via Back of the Inns, crossed it) and individual members were entitled to suggest the subject for discussion at the next meeting. Members built up a collection of books, prints and paintings and, with the President's consent, could use the room at any time. As time went on the number and duties of officials increased and, in 1818, patrons were introduced including Dr Rigby himself, the Earl of Albemarle, Lord Stafford and other influential Norfolk citizens. As time went yet further on, donors and subscribers were added to boost membership and finances, and prestige was added by the introduction of Honorary Members in the form of Royal Academicians, including the President Sir Martin Archer Shee, and other important artists. Oddly enough a number of Norwich School painters never joined the Society as members but availed themselves of the opportunities for exhibiting their work.

The first exhibition was held in 1805 in Sir Benjamin Wrenche's Court, of which Norwich Castle has an interesting drawing by Henry Ninham. The exhibition was so successful that it was decided to repeat it annually; the fact that the exhibitors, both professional and amateur, were local people painting the local countryside appealed to those whose appetites had been whetted by Constable, Gainsborough and the Dutch landscape painters already collected by Harvey of Catton and other wealthy Norwich art lovers. Dr Miklos Rajnai tells us that there were 223 works in this first exhibition from 18 exhibitors including five drawing masters and eight professional artists. It has to be said that the Norwich painters were strongly instrumental in establishing the British taste for landscape painting which persists today throughout the country alongside the many styles and fashions that have come and gone. In the early 19th century trouble on the international scene and economic anxiety at home made collectors particularly appreciative of these restful pictures that brought into their own homes the natural Norfolk landscape they knew and loved.

Membership of the Society increased* for there were many artists, drawing masters and illustrators in the city and those who moved away continued to exhibit as the prestige of the exhibitions grew. Norwich itself was proud of the fact that it was the only provincial city to enjoy an organised annual exhibition of paintings modelled on, it believed, the Royal Academy. By the same token members and exhibitors alike took themselves seriously and exerted every effort to make the exhibitions as successful as possible. In 1816 there was trouble in the ranks when a difference blew up between Crome and Ladbroke, the founder members. Various reasons, often conflicting, have been given for this but there seems no certain known answer even from the Norwich press of the day. Whatever the cause, it was either a serious rift or one blown up out of proportion. Ladbroke broke away entirely accompanied by, among others, James Sillett and John Thirtle, both Society officials. They formed an alternative society – the Norfolk and

* During its 30 or so years the Society had 79 formal members, 50 full, 29 honorary, reaching its peak in 1830 (Rajnai).

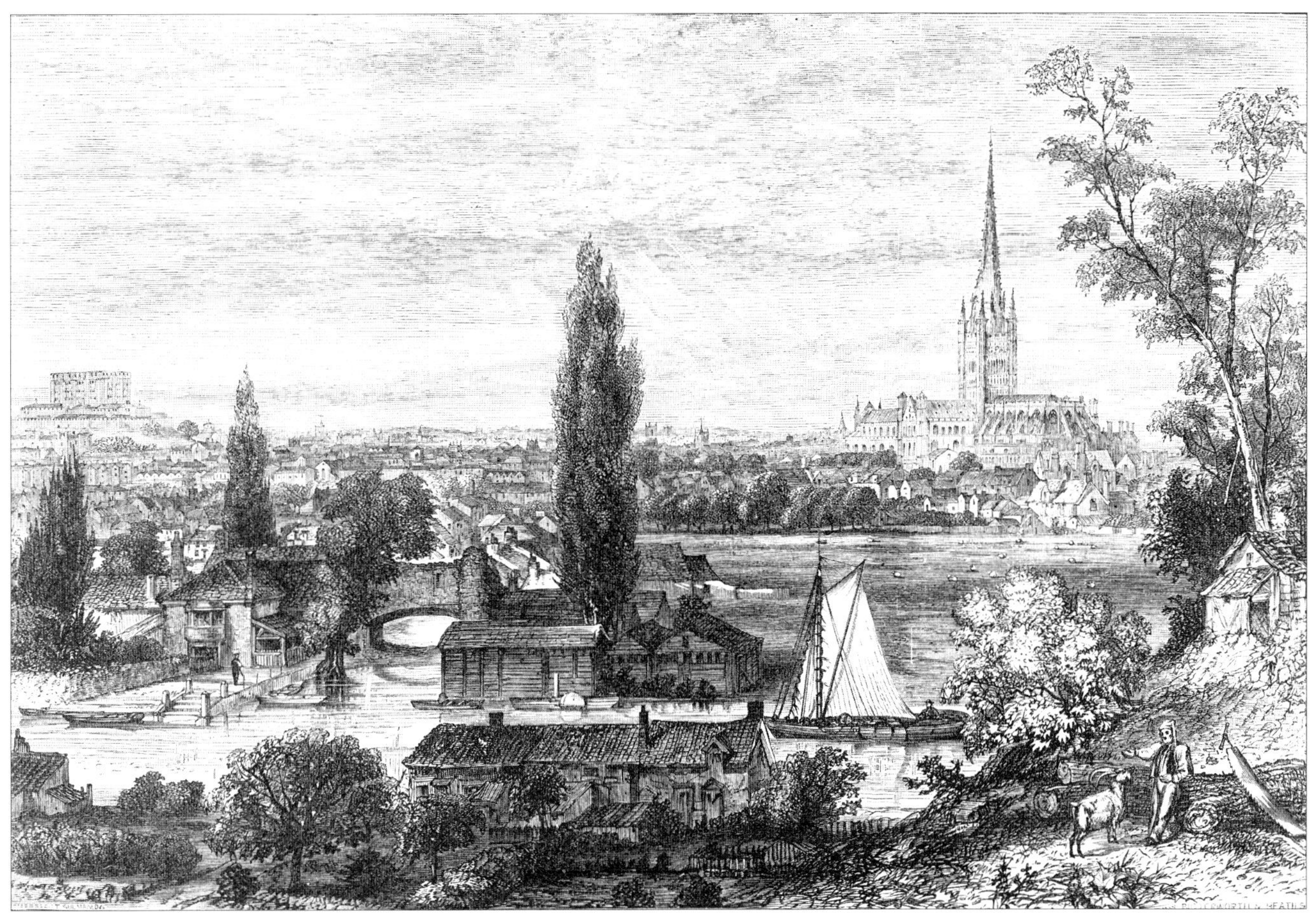

Norwich from the Meadows, early 19th century engraving by Butterworth & Heath

Norwich Society of Artists – and mounted their own exhibition independently in a room on Theatre Plain; some of the local artists took advantage of the dual opportunity and showed with both societies. Both considered themselves to be the mainstream Society and consequently, in the years 1816, 1817 and 1818, there were two catalogues numbered 12, 13 and 14. The secession petered out after the third exhibition and gradually most of the seceding artists returned to the parent society as exhibitors if not members.

In the years 1826/7 there were no exhibitions owing to the demolition of Sir Benjamin Wrenche's Court; the building was in such a bad state of repair that it was decided the only option was to knock it down. A new Corn Exchange was being built where a room would be made available for the Norwich Society but, while building was in progress, no exhibitions could take place. They were restarted in 1828 in a much more dignified setting.*

The annual exhibitions continued until 1833, an unprecedented continuity which says much for the collective identity of the Norwich painters and for Norwich itself as a city of culture. By the 1830s, however, not only was the number of artists diminishing but the walls of even the wealthiest collectors must almost have reached saturation point. But above all the economic situation and the unstable political climate acted against luxury spending except for the very rich. Although the interest was still there, the entrance charge to the exhibitions along with very limited sales were not enough to keep the Society going. Loan exhibitions of old masters and other works of special interest, even a small grant from the City Council, failed to provide adequate back-up funds. Nevertheless the 30 year record and the quality of work established the Norwich Society, considered to have been the foundation stone of the Norwich School of Painters which continued well after 1833, as an extremely important contribution to British painting, in particular the natural landscape. It has been said that Norwich produced more significant painters than any other city. There was, too, the magic ingredient, that indefinable 'unconscious bond' referred to by Laurence Binyon that has established for the Norwich School a unique place in the History of Art.

* In the 1826/7 pause it was decided to change the name of the Society to the Norfolk and Norwich Institute for the Promotion of the Fine Arts but, to this day, it continues to be most frequently referred to as the Norwich Society.

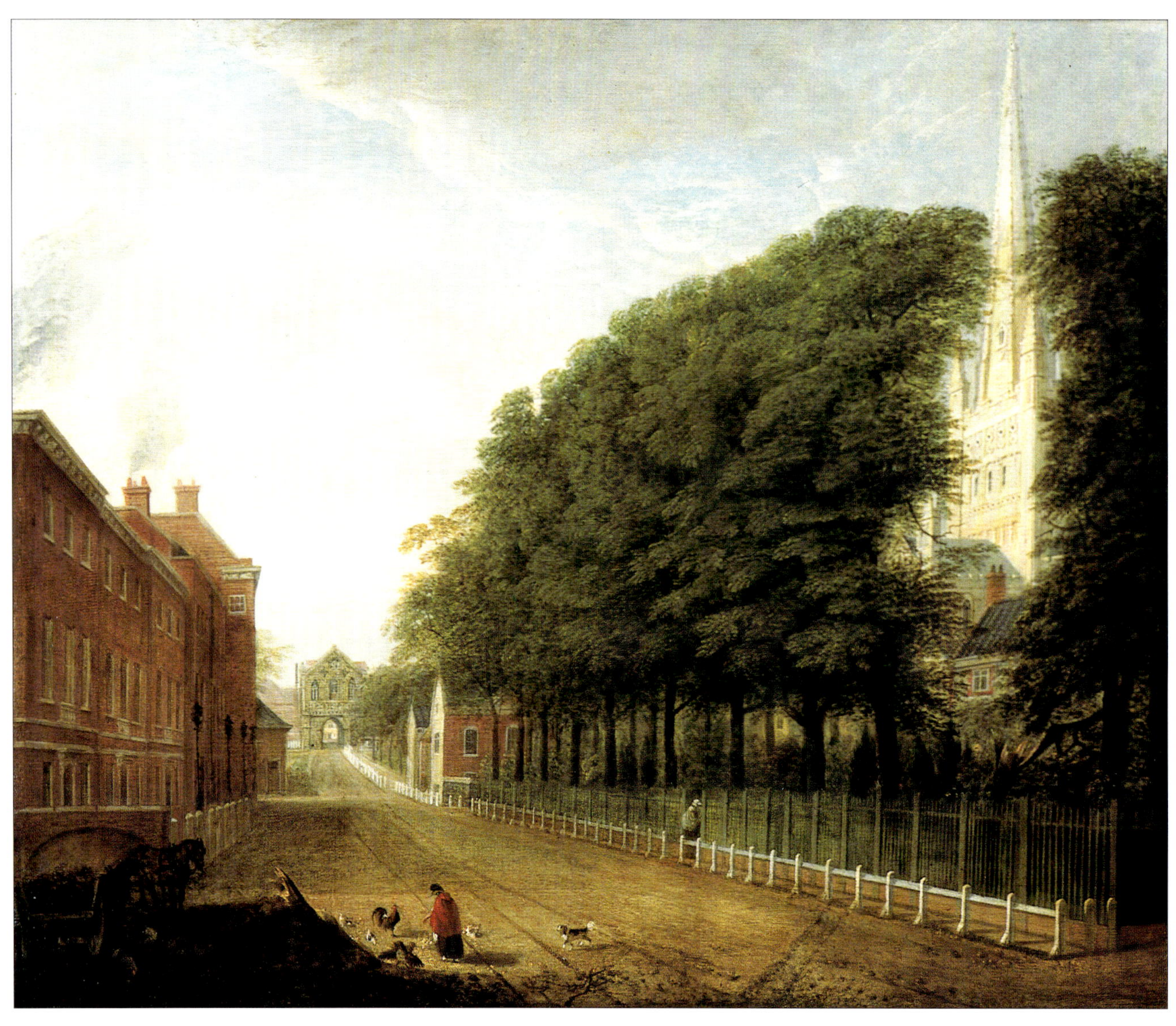

Robert Ladbroke, The Lower Close, Norwich, looking towards St. Ethelbert's Gate, oil on canvas, 25 in x 30 in

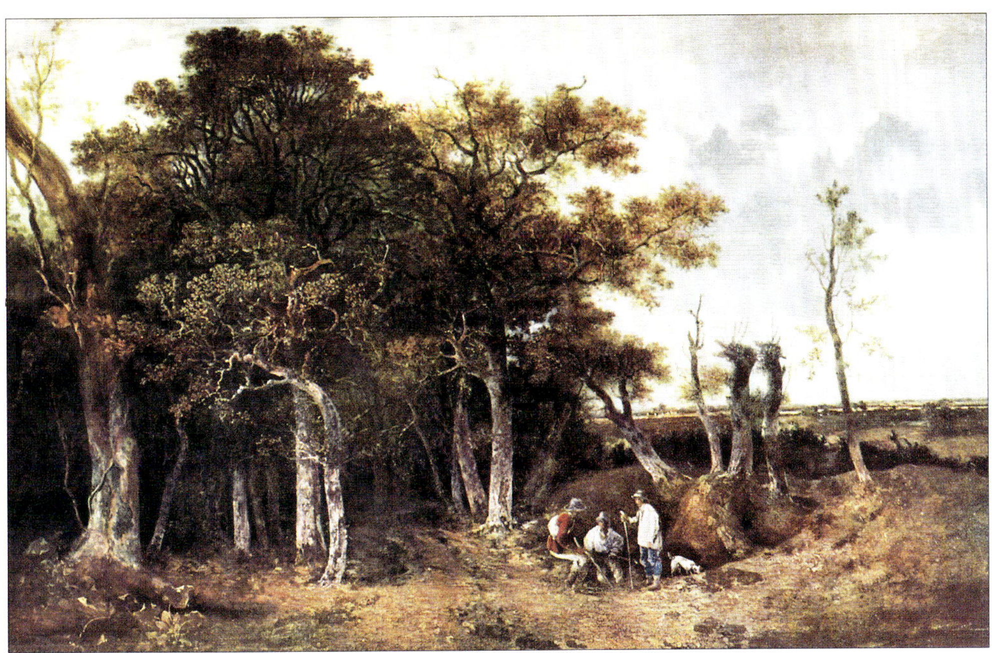

John Crome, The Beaters, oil on canvas, 21½ in x 33½ in

Chapter 2

CROME AND LADBROKE

> . . . the little man with the brown coat and the top boots, whose name will one day be considered the chief ornament of the old town [Norwich] and whose works will at no distant period rank among the proudest pictures of England – thy master . . . Crome.
>
> *George Borrow,* Lavengro

It is probably true to say that without **John Crome** (1768-1821) there would have been no Norwich School. It is doubtful whether the Norwich Society would ever have come into being without Crome's patience and determination and it was this Society that drew together the artists of the city and beyond into that 'deep unconscious bond' that became the Norwich School. But there is more to Crome than that and his character as much as his painting was behind the extraordinary flowering of the Norwich art scene.

Too much of the 'local lad made good' attitude has been applied to Crome. Certainly he was of fairly humble origins. His father was keeper of the Griffin Inn at the time of his birth until 1770, but later became a journeyman weaver, and his son's education seems to have been rudimentary. This son's intellect, however, was above his perceived station and his capacity for absorbing knowledge, together with an appealing personality, largely compensated. Crome was a determined individual also; having set himself a goal, he worked tenaciously at achieving that goal in his quiet, persevering way. He had none of the temperamental excesses of John Sell Cotman or, for that matter, certain of his own followers, neither had he the wanderlust that seemed to attack many of his contemporaries. Much has been written of Crome's genius, but although he had less inherent talent than John Sell Cotman, he achieved greater material success in his own lifetime largely by sheer hard work and diligent application.

As we have seen when Crome was 12 years old, he went to work for Dr Rigby, a prominent city physician who, in spite of the boyish pranks indulged in by his young errand boy,* not only liked him but recognised in him an ambition and drive that was likely to stand him in good stead given the right sort of encouragement. Dr Rigby was a patron of the arts and his extensive personal collection was Crome's first introduction to the wonderful world of art.

* Dr Rigby's medical students shared Crome's high spirits and capacity for pranks. When Crome discovered the practice skeleton tucked up in his bed, he threw it from the window into the street below to the apparent consternation of passers by!

After about two years, Crome left Dr Rigby and became apprenticed for a seven-year term to a coach painter and sign maker called Whisler. Again this was a propitious step in his career, for with Whisler he first learned a great deal about paint, grinding and mixing colours being one of his first duties. It was important in this business to study the the durability of paints, permanence of colours and their reaction to grounds; many artists' work could have benefited from a rather more scientific study of their materials. Whisler soon recognised in his apprentice a natural ability to draw and to create a picture, which meant that Crome was soon allowed out painting signs in addition to the more routine work. It may well have been the discipline of creating a design within a limited space that enabled him in later years to isolate a complete picture within a broader landscape and to ignore anything that went on around his chosen, contained, composition. Care and accuracy in drawing would have been helped by the strictures of heraldry and sign writing, and the people he met during these assignments, from landlords of the taverns to dukes, would certainly have encouraged his natural aptitude for getting on with people and mixing in any society.

It was during his apprenticeship that Crome met Robert Ladbroke who was himself apprenticed to a printer and who, like Crome, had artistic aspirations and a flair for drawing. Together the two took a garret studio and spent almost all their spare time either working there or sketching in the countryside around Norwich. They scraped and saved on the meagre wages of apprentices to buy materials and sometimes good prints for copying, notably, in Crome's case, those of Rembrandt. It was not long before they started making a little pocket money, Ladbroke offering portrait heads for 5s. and Crome selling a few landscapes when and where he could.

Crome had kept in touch with Dr Rigby who seems to have taken an interest in both boys' work and introduced Crome to another amateur painter, Thomas Harvey of Catton. Harvey was a man of means and a keen collector of paintings – Wilson, Gainsborough, Constable and the Dutch masters (his wife was Dutch) Hobbema, Cuyp, Ruysdael, Fyt and the van der Veldes. He readily allowed Crome access to his collection, to copy whatever he liked so that he could apply what he had learnt to the natural Norfolk landscape. Crome improved his painting technique enormously in this way; he had the intelligence to absorb not only the influence of these painters but to reconstruct the methods and understand the effects the artists were aiming to achieve.

He made other friends through Harvey and also, through him and Dr Rigby, acquired most of his early patrons. One of these introductions was to Sir William Beechey, R.A., who gave Crome, in his London studio, some very constructive lessons belying William Gunn's sardonic description of the 'poor lad who laid the foundations of his celebrity cleaning brushes for Beechey'. The fact that Beechey knew Richard Wilson well and was able, with authority, to discuss his work with Crome was another bonus, for Crome had greatly admired and learnt much from the Wilsons in Harvey's collection. The distinguished portrait painter John Opie was another one of Beechey's circle who was introduced to Crome; in later years Opie painted Crome's portrait when Opie had married a Norwich lady, the writer Amelia Alderson.*

Years later Beechey wrote:

> Crome when I first met him must have been about twenty years old and was a very awkward, uninformed country lad, but extremely shrewd in all his remarks on Art though he wanted words and terms to express his meaning. As often as he came to town he never failed to call on me and to get what information I was able to give him upon the subject of that particular branch of Art which he had made his study. His visits were very frequent and all his time was spent in my painting room when I was not particularly engaged. He improved so rapidly that he delighted and astonished me. He always dined and spent his evenings with me.

At the end of his apprenticeship, Crome made ends meet partly by continuing with some of the work he had trained for with Whisler, taking on any jobs offered within the artistic arena and

* The portrait by Opie of Amelia, described as 'one of the loveliest and most gifted women of her day', is in the National Portrait Gallery, London. Opie's portraits of some Norfolk dignitaries are in Blackfriars Hall, Norwich.

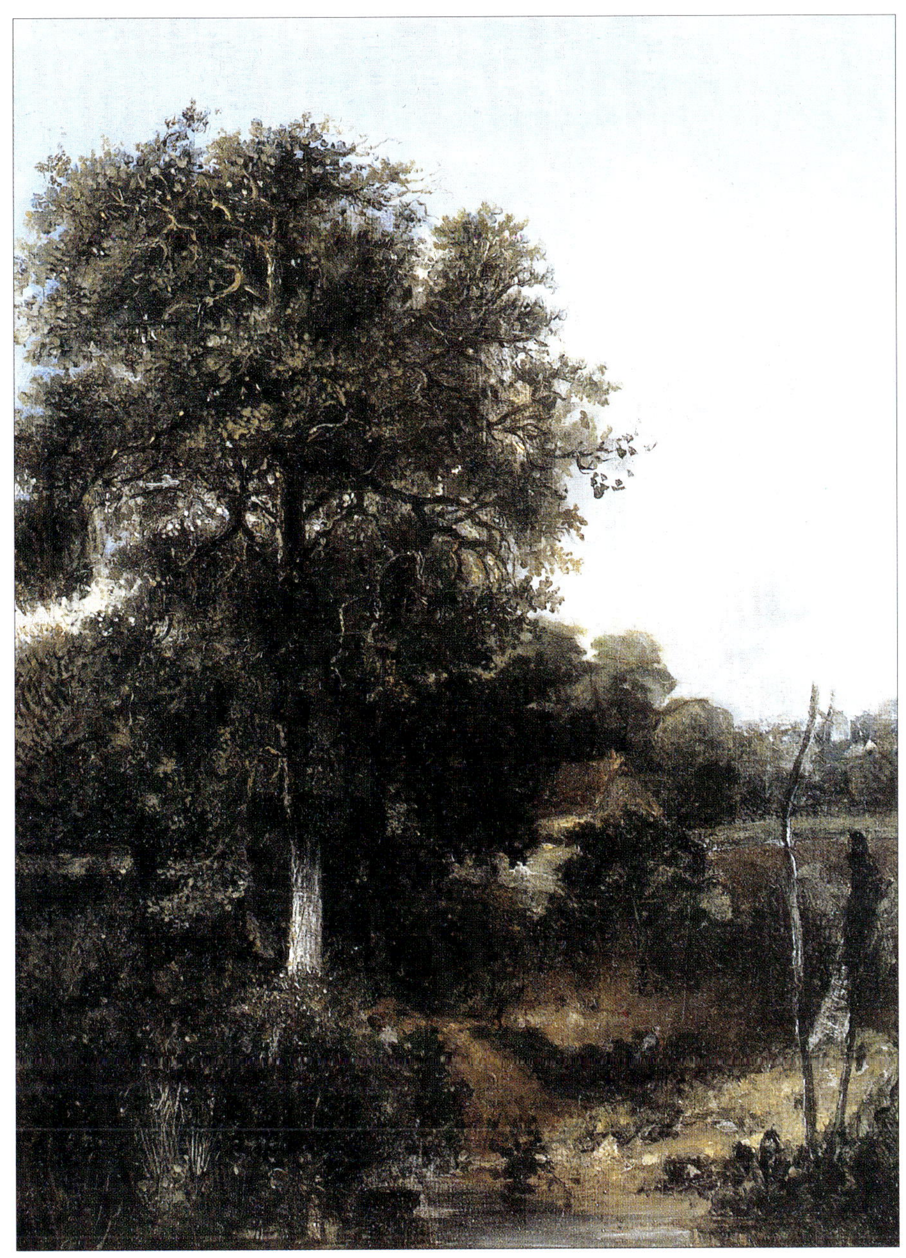

John Crome,
Landscape with an Oak,
oil on panel, 9 in x 6¾ in

An exceptionally small Crome but one of the finest of his known works. The silver light gives the painting a magical quality and the diversity of green tones within such a tiny painting epitomises his consummate skill

accepting occasional commissions for drawing and painting. He was selling a few paintings, too, and had become so confident in his draughtsmanship that he was soon giving lessons in drawing at one guinea the half year.

These proved so successful that, with the help of the generous Rigby and Harvey, Crome established his own drawing practice. This was the first of many subsequently set up in the city which gave Crome the advantage of being well established before the advent of competition. He is reputed to have had an inspiring manner of teaching and to have shown such a genuine interest in and concern for his students and their progress that the practice developed rapidly; his two sponsors were able to give him introductions to some of the more affluent Norfolk families who could afford to pay well for the tuition of their sons and daughters. Again fate smiled on John Crome – the two most fortuitous introductions were to Dawson Turner, the Yarmouth banker, and the Gurneys of Earlham, also important bankers and the cream of Norwich society.

Crome was not just a drawing master to these families but became a real friend. His natural charm of manner and pleasing personality endeared him to all sorts and conditions of men and women and must have helped significantly in the furtherance of his career. When the Gurneys

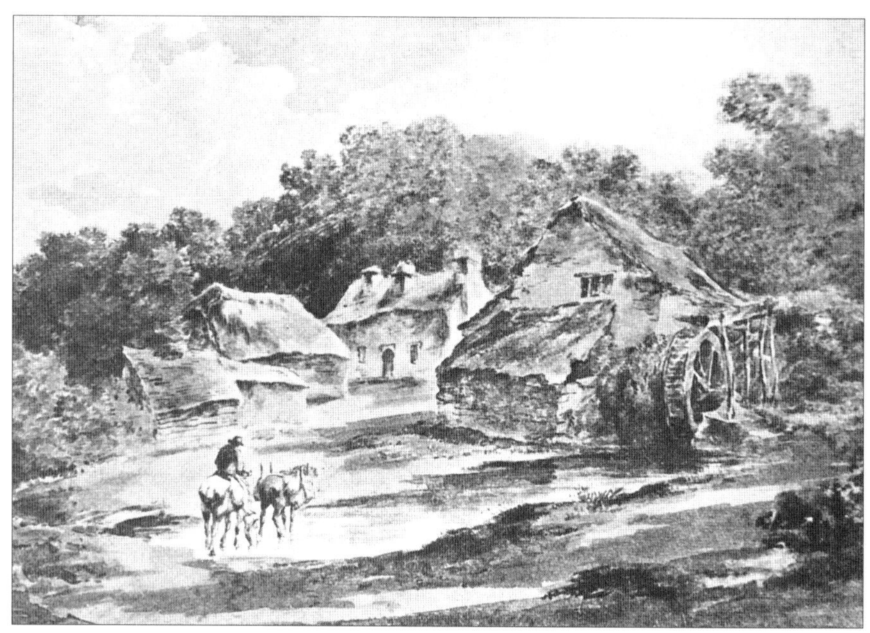

John Crome,
The Mill Wheel, watercolour,
c.1795, 11½ in x 16¼ in

visited the Lake District early in the 19th century, Crome was also invited; later they took him to Wales and on a second trip to the Lakes, all of which gave him opportunities of working in parts of the country well away from Norfolk, opportunities he might not otherwise have had. Crome's only other significant travel was a visit to Paris in 1814 with Daniel Coppin and William Barnes Freeman. The Napoleonic Wars were over and all three were interested in viewing the new treasures of the Louvre and other important French collections. Crome must have spent some time sketching as, from then on, French subjects continued to crop up in his painting from time to time.

In 1792 when Crome was 24 and the drawing practice was starting to bring in a more secure income, he married Phoebe Berney, a year before Ladbroke married her sister Mary. Their daughter, Abigail, was born a month later but died before reaching her second birthday; this was a difficult period for Crome who spent two spells in the Norfolk and Norwich hospital suffering from hydrocele.

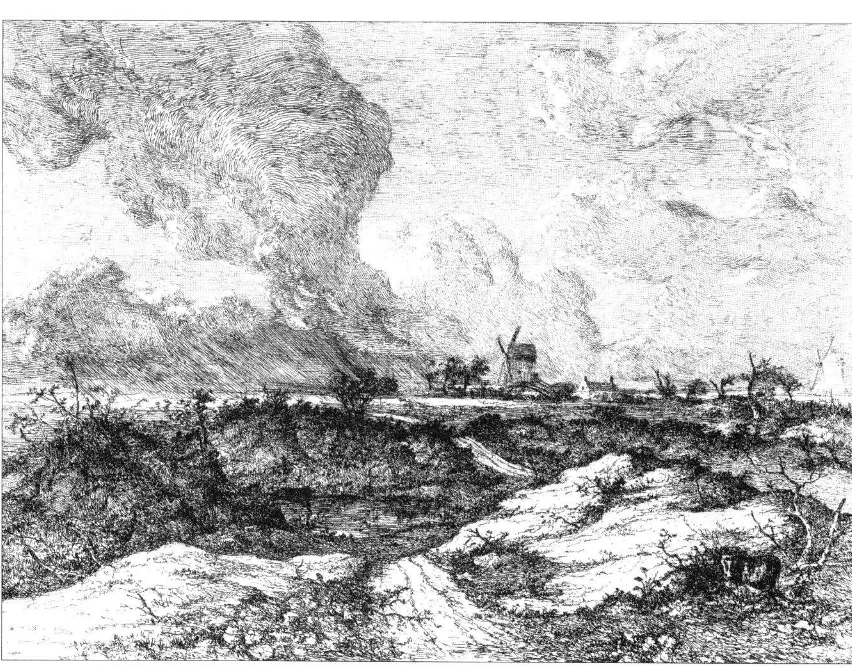

John Crome,
Mousehold Heath, Norwich,
etching, c.1810, 9 in x 12 in

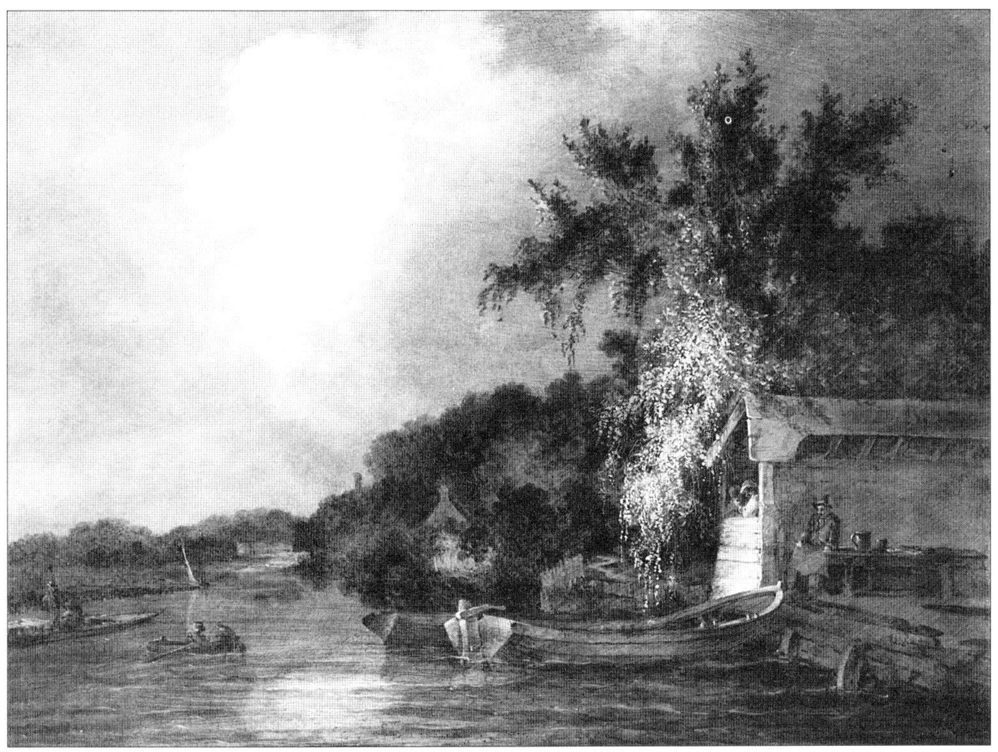

John Crome,
The Yare at Thorpe,
oil on panel, c.1806,
16½in x 22¼in

As we have seen in Chapter 1, it was in 1803 that Crome and Ladbroke formed the Norwich Society of Artists, a group of young artists initially including Dixon, Hodgson, Coppin, Stark, Vincent and Thirtle; these young men took themselves and their art extremely seriously and worked very hard to promote their ideals. The first exhibition in 1805 in effect was the beginning of the history of Norwich School. In this first exhibition 18 exhibitors showed 223 works in oil and watercolour and its perhaps unexpectedly great success inspired the Society to make it an annual event. With one or two hiccups along the way, these exhibitions continued until 1833 although, as economic conditions worsened following the Napoleonic Wars, the exceptional successes of the earlier years were not consistently maintained. The secession was, of course, a minor setback in that patronage which was, for three years, spread over two exhibitions.

The early successes of the Society's exhibitions put Norwich very much on the artistic map as the only provincial city to have a society with its own annual exhibition after the London fashion. It did much, also, to enhance Crome's personal prestige in the city and he became more and more in demand as drawing master and commissioned artist. He was appointed art teacher at Norwich Grammar School under Dr Valpy and many of the later members of the Norwich School had been taught either by him or by John Sell Cotman after the latter's return to the city in 1807. As well as being the first in the field as teacher of drawing in Norwich and the instigator of the city's exhibitions, Crome enhanced his position and raised his personal profile not only by joining other academic societies and working extremely hard on behalf of his own, but also by staying in Norwich almost all of his life. He and Phoebe lived in what is now 83 and 85 St. George's Street, Ancient Guildengate, for nearly 30 years bearing 11 children of whom seven survived. Everybody knew 'Old Crome' and he seemed to become part of the fabric of his city; he was a Freemason, a Liberal voter and regularly attended the Baptist Church. Crome's work never degenerated but continued to advance up to the time of his death in 1821 while still at the height of his powers. Mercifully his final illness lasted only seven days.

Crome is sometimes classed as self taught but this is only partly true: as well as Beechey, Opie and contemporary teachers, he could claim as his masters Hobbema, Cuyp and Ruysdael, Wilson Gainsborough and Constable. His apprenticeship with Whisler was, of course, all part of the learning process, not least as far as the properties of paints and glazes were concerned, and this technical knowledge has undoubtedly contributed to the lasting quality of his paintings.

Even discounting the time spent copying Rembrandt and other painters' work in the garret

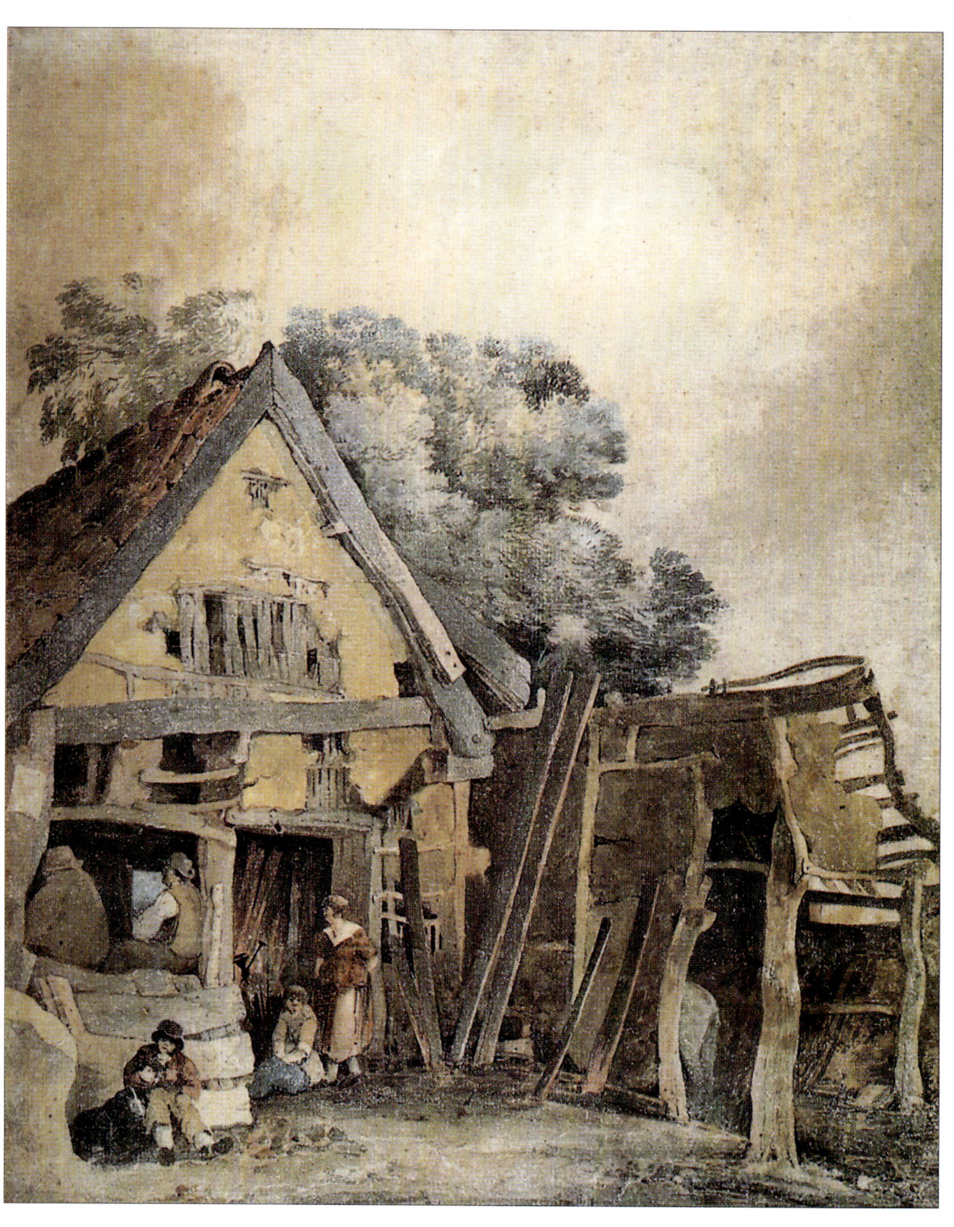

John Crome,
The Blacksmith's Shop, Hingham, Norfolk,
watercolour, c.1795

studio, Crome was exceptionally fortunate in the people who came into his life and made available access to some first class collections. Of English paintings, he particularly admired Wilson's work from which he learnt a great deal about light and atmosphere and how to introduce contrast into his landscapes. Crome himself acknowledged his debt to Hobbema and, again, much of his early work showed a decidedly Dutch influence exemplified at Norwich Castle Museum by the paintings 'St. Martin's Gate' and 'Back of the New Mills'. Along with the Suffolk painters Gainsborough and Constable, he provides part of the important bridge between the 17th century Dutch landscape painters and the artists of rural East Anglia. Sir John Rothenstein with astute perception has written: 'To claim for Crome that he added the comprehensiveness which the tradition of Hobbema and Ruysdael needed in order to fulfil itself, that he completed what the Dutchman had begun, is not to rate his achievement too high.'

Crome's real strength lay in his ability, after much studying, copying and absorbing the methods and results of painters he admired, to translate all that he had gleaned into a portrayal of his beloved Norfolk landscape. He developed, in his own way, out of all the various influences coupled with his own natural talent, a very personal style. Importantly Crome had his own way

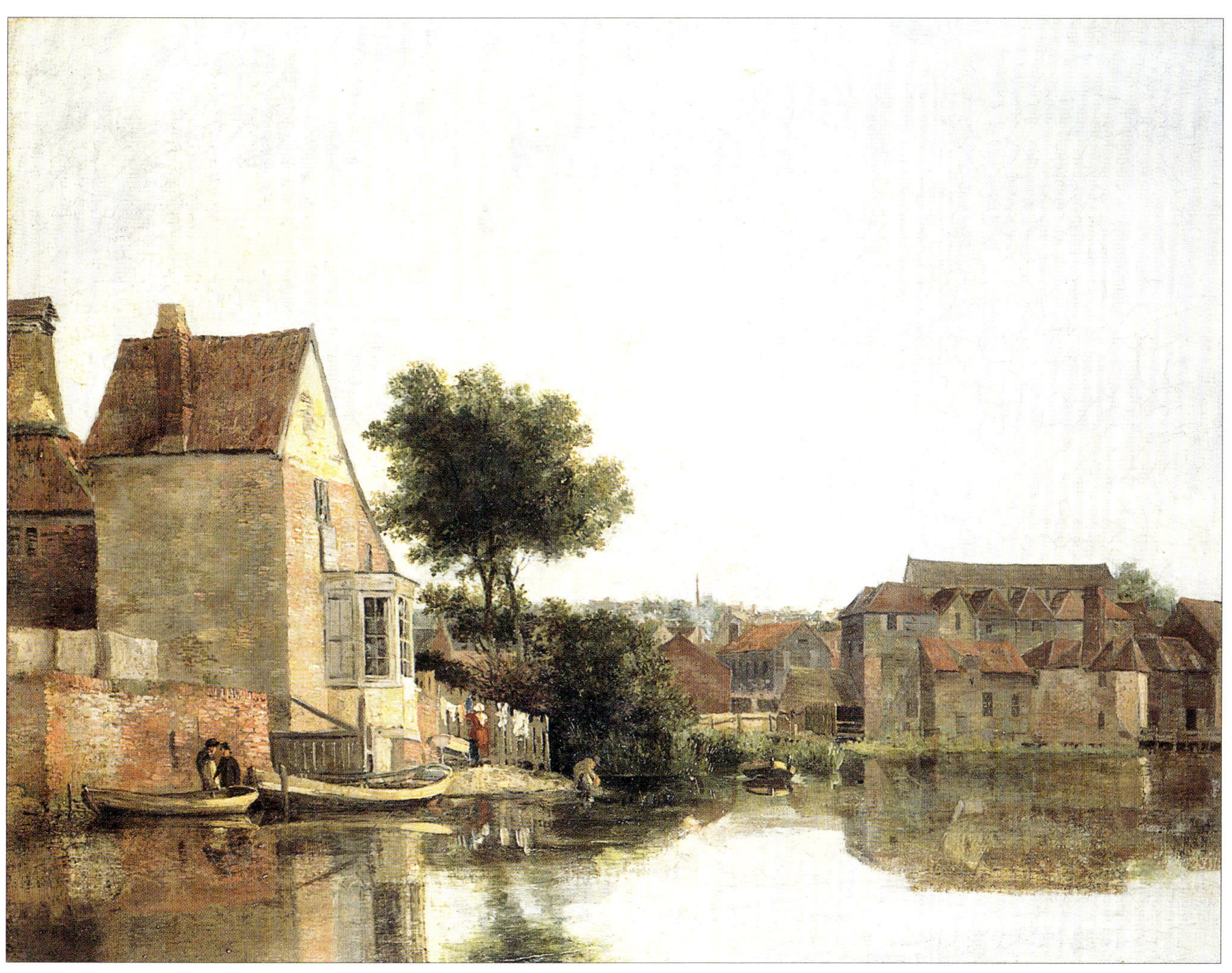

John Crome,
"Back of the New Mills"
c.1814-17. Oil on canvas,
16¼ in x 21¼ in

of seeing, of selecting a section or corner of the landscape and turning it into a picture divorced from all that went on around it. This must not suggest an enclosed, almost enveloping, approach, for Crome always emphasised and impressed on his pupils the importance of breadth: '... breadth implied both the suppression of detail and the creation of pictorial effect through the arrangement of light, shade and colour in a discernible compositional structure.'* He was clever enough to combine the one with the other in a way that few, if any, of his successors have managed to emulate.

The development of his brushwork was entirely his own and has sometimes been the deciding factor in difficult attributions. Whereas the Dutch painters carefully stroked on their paint, Crome tended to 'place' it on the canvas in a calculated manner and in considered conjunction with a more conventional brushing. It is probably this light, slightly impasto, effect that gives such life and character to his trees, the focal parts of so many of his most attractive works. It adds, too, to the unique harmony of his colouring and was used for those almost elusive touches of dancing light.

Over the years there have been many problems of attribution with Crome's work, aggravated by his tendency not to sign, to paint a subject many times over and to give pupils his own work to copy. Inevitably in later years there were fakes and bad copies, some even with false signatures but, as Rajnai emphatically points out, he was *not* the 'perpetrator of the many indifferent or downright awful canvases which over the years carelessly or unscrupulously have become attached to his name'. Even at a higher level, a reassessment about 15 years ago of some works in the Paul Mellon collection identified several 'Cromes' as by Stark and Hodgson. There hangs in Norwich Castle Museum Crome's 'Study of Burdock,' c.1813, and beside it a copy, 'after Crome', by an unknown hand. It is a reasonable copy but no serious student of Crome's work could be deceived.

* The words have been attributed to John Crome but have a rather more scholarly ring than one would expect from the writer of the letter reproduced on page 35.

Nevertheless it serves as an object lesson of the point that has so frequently been made about the attribution of Crome's work. And not all copyists acknowledge as 'after' Crome!

Although not generally considered a watercolour painter, Crome did produce some interesting pieces in that medium although, in a way, in the more finished examples, he employed rather a similar technique to that used for his oils – carefully composed, beautifully drawn, but with a wealth of detail not generally synonymous with pure watercolour. Paradoxically, for this is looking at his work from a more modern viewpoint, in his own time the critics sometimes maligned certain of his paintings as appearing 'unfinished' – the *Norfolk Chronicle* in 1820 commented on one of his French subjects that it would have received greater acclaim had he not 'lost half the praise he would have got had he but discreetly bestowed a little more pains on the finishing of it'. Yet Crome himself wrote to one of his pupils that 'trifles in Nature must be overlooked that we may have our feelings roused by seeing the whole picture at a glance, not knowing how or why we are so charmed'.

It seems likely that most of Crome's watercolours were executed during the early years of the 19th century, sometimes no doubt within his teaching practice. To some extent the same might be said of his monochrome wash drawings for these can be of great value in teaching students the use of tonal values within a single neutral colour. Some of these, however, are genuine works of art rather than simply teaching aids, indicating that this was a medium he may well have enjoyed for its own sake. Derek Clifford is of the opinion that 'these delicate grey wash drawings contain at times more of the essential genius of Crome than his full watercolours and his oils. Their combination of strength and fragility make them seem like delicate fragments from an early Chinese scroll painting.' I quote Clifford to support what some might call my bias towards this particular genre. Equally I find many of John Sell Cotman's monochromes particularly satisfying and, jumping 150 years, those of the late Leonard Squirrell. Crome's 'Whitlingham' and 'Near Lakenham' in the Castle Museum are outstanding examples, as is 'View of Carrow Abbey', although this is slightly less expressive.

As far as 'finished' watercolours are concerned, only a few appear to have survived and these are coloured or tinted drawings rather than watercolour in the more modern idiom introduced by John Sell Cotman. By far the best known are 'The Mill Wheel' and (overleaf) 'The Blacksmith's Shop at Hingham', both charming studies, although 'The Mill Wheel' was originally a grey wash drawing coloured in at a later date.

Crome also revived the art of original etching, probably inspired by his early study of Rembrandt. Thirty-three of his etchings survive; using the soft ground technique, he worked in the medium largely between 1809 and 1813. He issued a prospectus in 1812 obviously intending to publish some or all if he could find enough subscribers. Publication eventually took place in 1834 at the instigation of Mrs Crome, with a short appreciation by Dawson Turner who remained a friend even after John Crome had, as it were, handed over the teaching of Turner's daughters to John Sell Cotman. Travelling to Yarmouth became too time consuming when he had so many activities in and around Norwich; furthermore Crome had outgrown the need to work under such strictures as Dawson Turner's antiquarian requests imposed.

The outstanding feature of all Crome's work, oils, watercolours or etchings, was an absolute truth to nature and truth to himself; he put down what he saw with no pretension but with a keen observation of the Norfolk landscape. Out of all that he had learnt by patient study of earlier great artists, all that he had learnt of paints and glazes, he evolved a style that was entirely and unequivocably his own. It seemed that, as well as a perfected technique and manner of handling his paint, of using light and shade and co-ordinating the colours of his low-toned palette, he imbued his work with his own sincerity, the one ingredient that none of his followers or imitators could copy.

Restoration was another form of art undertaken by John Crome; one sometimes wonders if

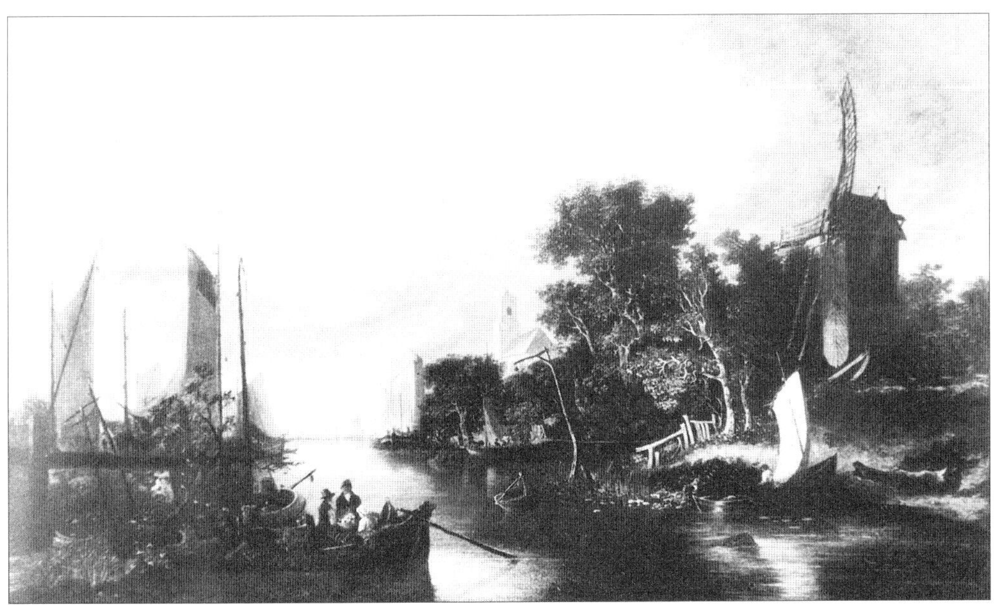

John Crome,
View of Bruges River looking towards Ostend, oil on canvas, 14 in x 72¼ in

these Norwich artists had discovered the art of slipping a few extra hours into the day! He is known to have cleaned and restored the civic portraits in St. Andrew's Hall and probably also took on some private work. For all the sensitivity in his painting, Crome had a very practical streak and within the field of artistry would take on anything that paid for itself, even dabbling, from time to time, in a bit of dealing.

Crome always maintained a keen interest in the work of other artists he admired and, inspired by Harvey's collection, started his own – all too soon. Finding himself in financial difficulties, he held a three day sale in 1812 which, although less productive than he might have hoped, brought in enough to put things back on an even keel. As he became more financially secure, he again started to collect – paintings, books, engravings, anything that appealed to his (artistic) magpie instinct. The time came when 'people were crazy for his pictures', his teaching practice and work at the Grammar School were productive, and there were always the incidental commissions and sideline opportunities. By the time of his death, he had accumulated a substantial and quite valuable collection and was living in comparative prosperity.

In his obituary, after commenting that his funeral was attended by 'a numerous attendance of artists and other gentlemen, an immense concourse of people', R. M. Bacon* wrote: 'Crome had achieved in his own lifetime considerable local esteem and a growing metropolitan repertoire with an oeuvre of paintings and etchings which remain a signal contribution to the history of British landscape painting.'

Although recognised as the co-founder of the Norwich Society, **Robert Ladbroke** (1769-1842), is a much more shadowy figure than Crome. Little is known of his early life and upbringing before the association with Crome while apprenticed to a Mr. White, printer and engraver. It would appear that he had some artistic inclination by virtue of the nature of the apprenticeship, but his connection with Crome gave him more prominence than he might otherwise have achieved.

Initially he seemed inclined to portraiture during the garret studio days with Crome; after some practice he was selling portrait heads for 5s, but he seems not to have continued with that particular interest. Out of the 230 exhibits listed by Day, only a very few are portrait subjects.

Like Crome, Ladbroke established a teaching practice but, lacking Crome's more outgoing personality, it failed to achieve the same prestige. The early friendship between the two, their joint interest in the promotion of the Norwich Society, and their marriages to the Berney sisters maintained a certain bond between them until the secession in 1816. The real reason for their disagreement has never been fully clarified. Dr Rajnai claims that it was caused by 'an agitation by the artists who were not drawing masters to exclude amateurs from membership of the Society'. Some say it was over the way the Society's finances were administered, others that

* Robert MacKenzie Bacon, Editor *Norwich Mercury*

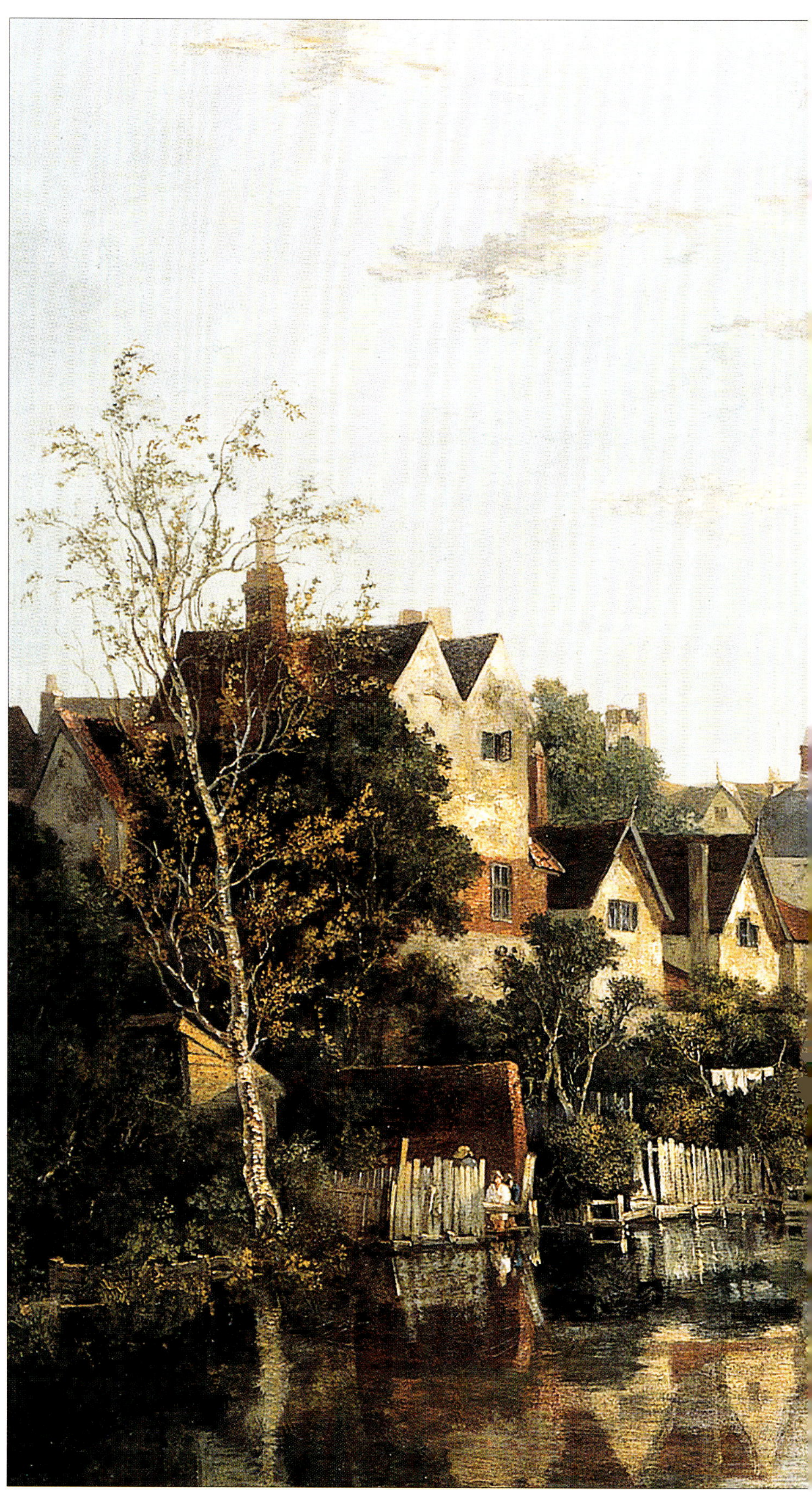

John Crome, Norwich River: Afternoon, oil on canvas, c.1819, 28 in x 40½ in

This important painting was acquired by Norwich Castle Museum in 1994, a wonderful acquisition and the most splendid example of Crome's work to become available for many years

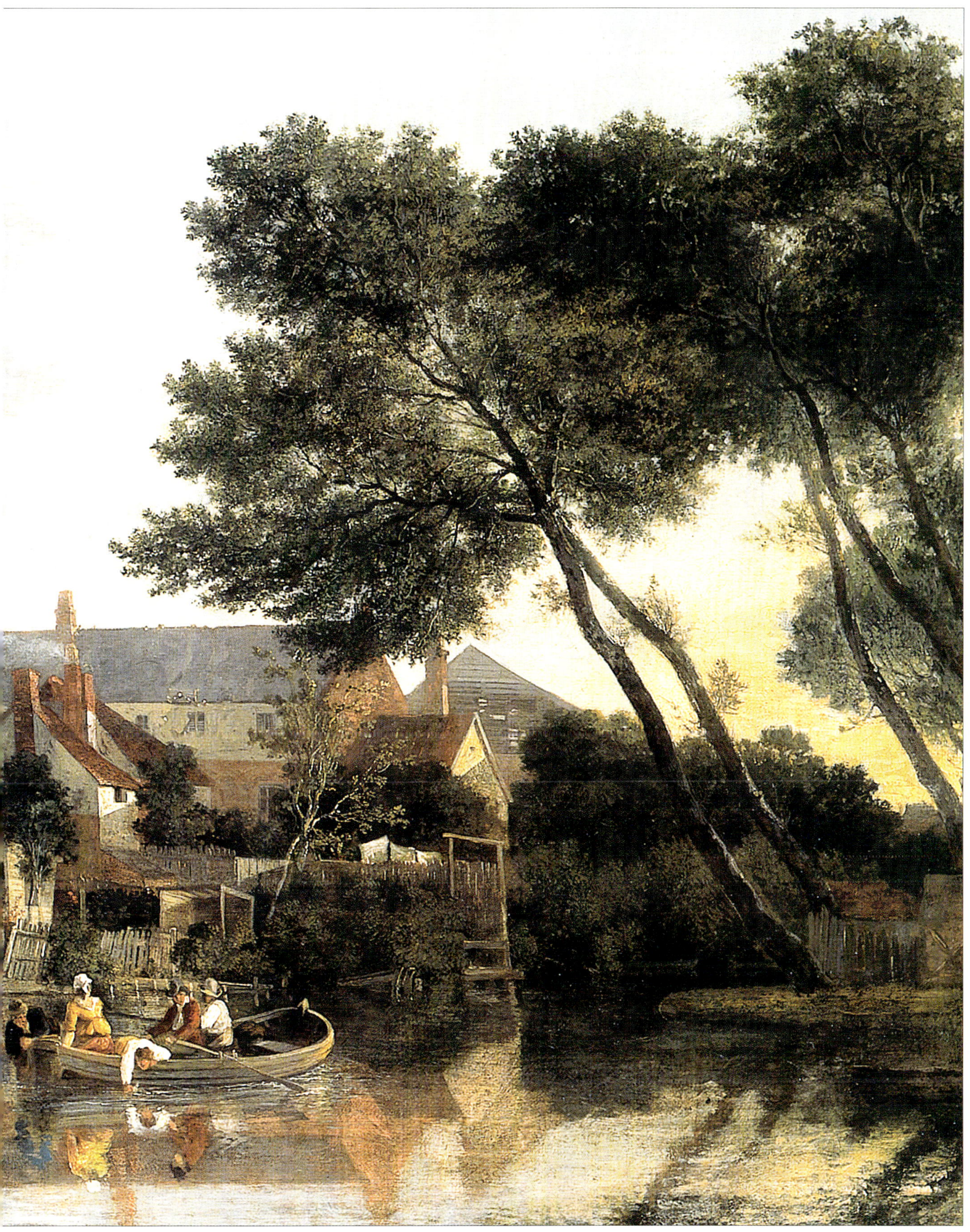

Ladbroke objected to the appointment of Sillett as President, which seems unlikely as Sillett joined Ladbroke along with Joseph Stannard, John Thirtle and Ladbroke's sons in the breakaway group which formed the alternative society, holding exhibitions in a hall on Theatre Plain.

There could also have been an element of jealousy which may well have been festering over a period of time. Ladbroke is said to have been a dour, unprepossessing individual, often excluded from the company that welcomed the more outgoing and sociable Crome. Crome's paintings were proving more saleable, he had numerically more and more promising pupils, and he was accepted into a world wherein Ladbroke felt out of place. Although the *Norwich Mercury* in its obituary in 1842 wrote that he was 'of a cheerful and kindly disposition, respected by all who knew him', it did not necessarily follow that he was a popular personality.

Ladbroke certainly knew sadness in his life. His first wife, Mary, died in 1807 and his second wife in 1825. After that he became something of a recluse. He had at last made his peace with Crome, albeit on the latter's death-bed, and he had the grace in 1824 to exhibit once more with the original Society after six years of self-imposed exile. Most of the other seceding artists had drifted back. Some had, in fact, exhibited with the two societies when both were operating. It seems that the central dispute, whatever the reason, was between Crome and Ladbroke.

Of the two, Ladbroke was the less dedicated painter and, as time went on, he developed other interests. It may be he had come into an inheritance or had made money in some other way, for on his death he left substantial real estate. He did a certain amount of dealing in old pictures and at some stage opened a shop from which to operate and where he set up a picture framing business. This he handed over to his eldest son Robert, who also became a carver and gilder. He made over the teaching practice to his artist sons in 1822, presumably to devote more time to what he considered to be a major project. He had decided to make drawings of all the churches in Norfolk as a basis for a series of nearly 700 lithographs. These drawings were lithographed by his son, John Berney but, unfortunately, not published until after Ladbroke senior's death. Maybe in a way it was just as well for, apart from any documentary value, the result of his labour had little to recommend it. The drawing was apparently indifferent and John Berney Ladbroke was not, at that time, particularly experienced in lithography; the printing, to quote Dickes, was 'execrable'.

A totally diverse move was the purchase of the Shakespeare Tavern. He is also said to have brought a property on Ber Street not long before he died. Dealing in property as well as paintings may have been a source of income.

There is a major mystery attached to Robert Ladbroke's paintings – where have they all gone? It is not easy to appraise his works; there are too few to see and a fair amount of guesswork has been used in some of the attributions. Because of their parallel early years, it was inevitable that his work should be compared to that of Crome but Ladbroke has usually suffered by comparison – a pity because, on its own merit, some of his work has character of its own. He was susceptible to various influences; the *Norwich Mercury* once remarked on his pictures 'in the manner of Claude and Poussin', and certainly there was another stage when the Dutch element was very much in evidence. Perhaps he was lacking in a great deal of imagination for he enjoyed copying other artists' works, even exhibiting some as 'after the manner of'. His son, Henry, dubbed him 'the best copyist in East Anglia'. Often his subjects overlapped with Crome's; probably, when they were sketching together, Crome decided on the subjects. Two Yarmouth views of 1810 point to the major difference in the two styles; Crome's painting has a much softer approach and is more coherent as well as more lively. Ladbroke's is a model of correctness but with much less personality. He had a more classical bent than Crome, some of his paintings even appearing to be the products of an earlier age.

In the main Ladbroke's oils were characterised by a very heavy, sometimes even gloomy, approach accentuated by an unusual use of black. Often he achieved his effects by contrasting heavy impasto, usually on his trees, with thinly painted areas, even to the extent of glaze over

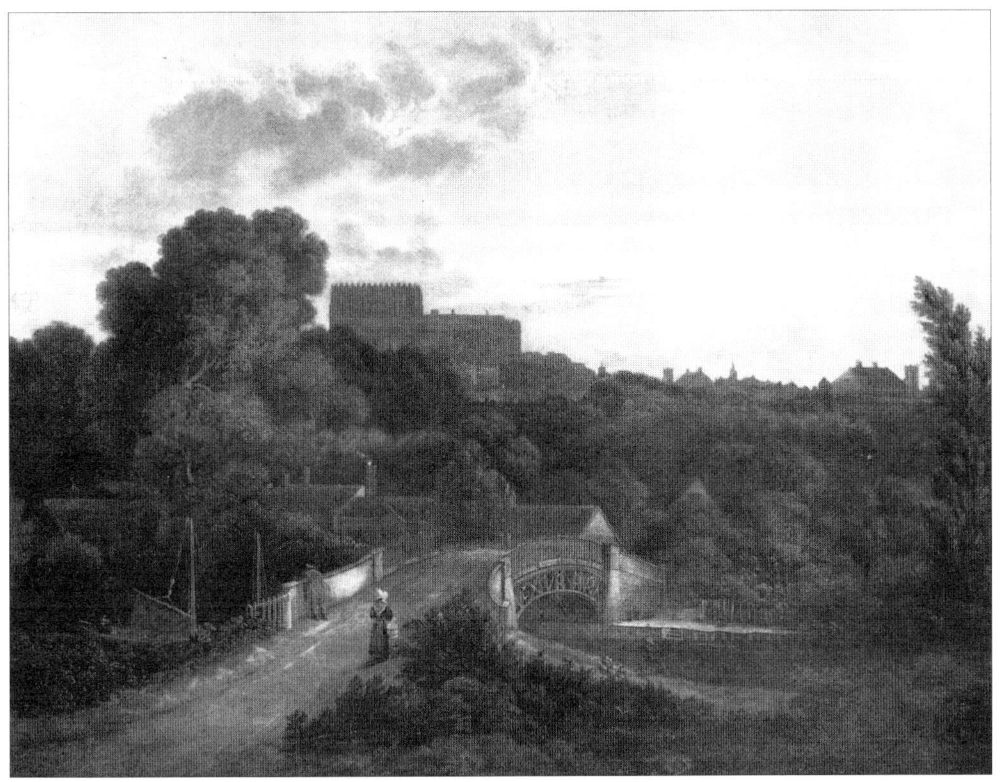

Robert Ladbroke, Foundry Bridge, oil on canvas, c. 1815, 26¼in x 38¼in

ground. When he let himself go a little with more colour and light some of the weight lifts and his paintings become more attractive. Possibly more interesting work has yet to come to light; over 200 exhibits plus such commissions as he had undertaken and work for his own pleasure, means that we are not really in a position to judge the overall quality of his work from the small quantity known. Most of his painting seems to have been done early in his career and to have declined somewhat after the failure of the secession.

An interesting feature of Ladbroke's work, as we know of it, seems to have been the small, on the spot, oil sketches that were sold on his death. His obituary in the *Art Union Monthly* of 1842 commented on the 'numerous sketches painted on the spot and dispersed by auction shortly after his death and which, for simplicity and truth, have very rarely been surpassed.' Certainly the four known survivors in the Castle Museum have far more appeal and spontaneity than his dark, heavy compositions but, again, we need to see more. Who is to say that the spaciousness and light that characterises these sketches was not also a feature of some finished oils no art historian has yet been able to see?

I personally know of very few watercolours of Robert Ladbroke's although he certainly used the medium and even received favourable comment from the critical *Norwich Mercury** in 1809. Derek Clifford, one of the country's foremost authorities on watercolour painters, has written:

> Crome's brother-in-law, Robert Ladbroke, is scarcely known as a watercolourist at all which is a great pity because the few of his drawings that have been recognised suggest an original talent. He is sometimes Crome-like but usually darker in tone and coarser in handling than the master. It may well be that Ladbroke was capable of greater range than we can yet attribute to him.

Not only are Ladbroke's missing paintings one of the greatest mysteries of the Norwich School but so is the man himself. An able painter, yes, but overshadowed by Crome and, later, by some of the younger Norwich artists when he seemed almost to have given up painting seriously. At the time when he and Crome shared their garret studio, money was obviously scarce yet he died leaving money, land and property. By no means a prepossessing personality, his introversion denied him social contacts readily available to the charming and ebullient Crome yet, many years before his death, he seemed in a position to hand over various business activities to his sons and concentrate on what appears to have been a mediocre collection of drawings for a project he never saw completed. Maybe one day some of the answers will emerge from some unlikely source.

* The Old Water-colour Society's Annual Volume 1966.

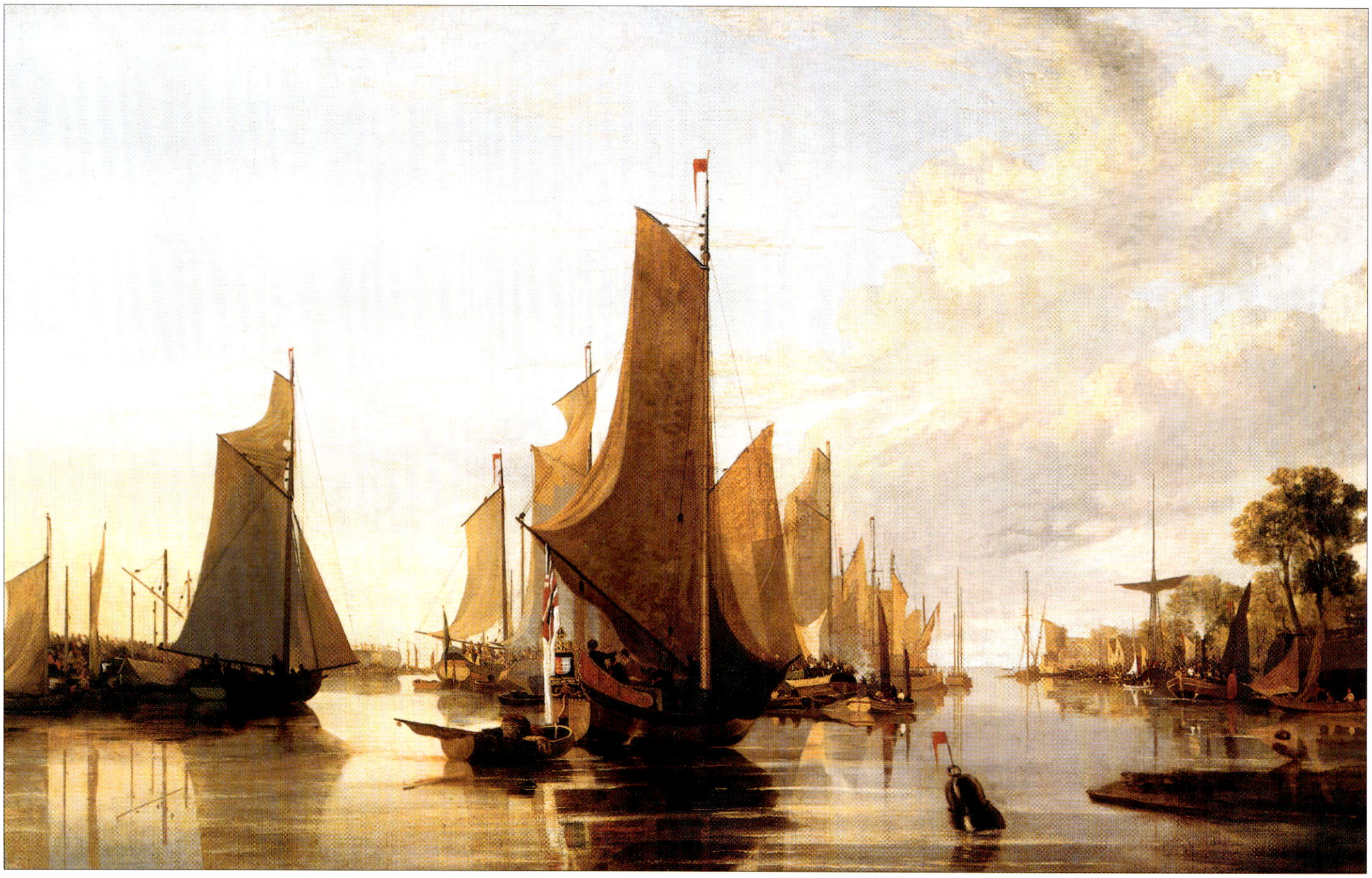

John Crome & John Berney Crome, "The Yarmouth Water Frolic, Evening" c.1821. Oil on canvas, 41 in x 68 in

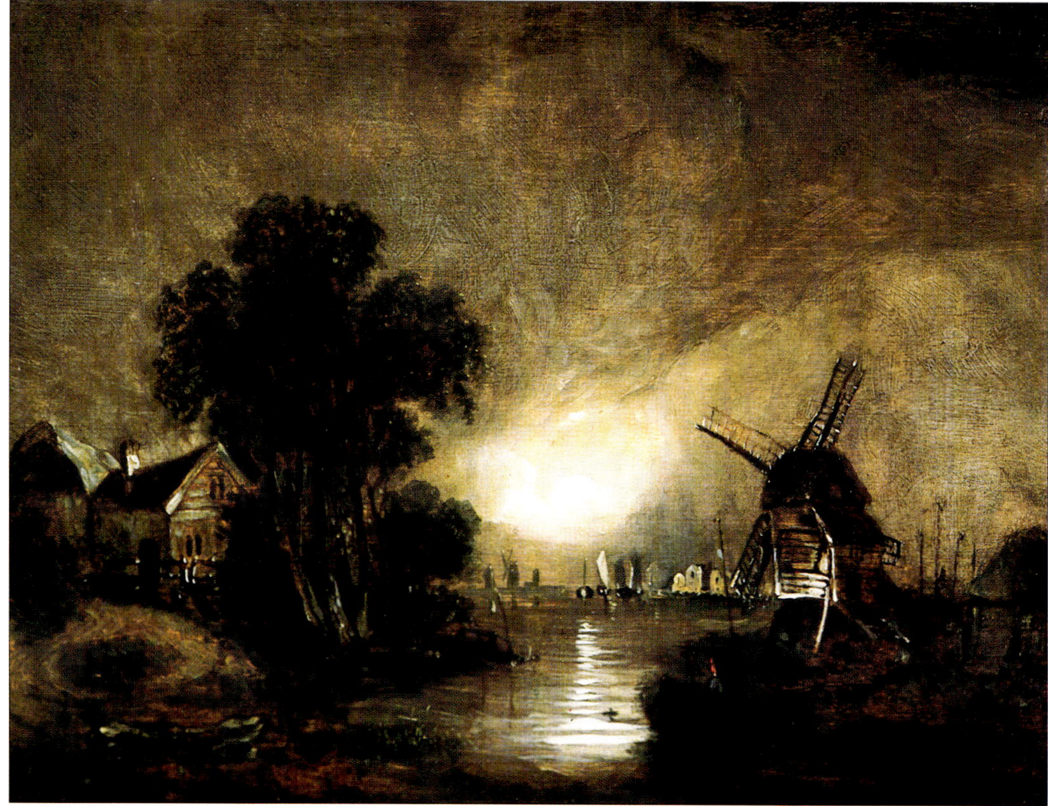

John Berney Crome, Moonlit River Scene, oil on panel, 9 in x 11 in

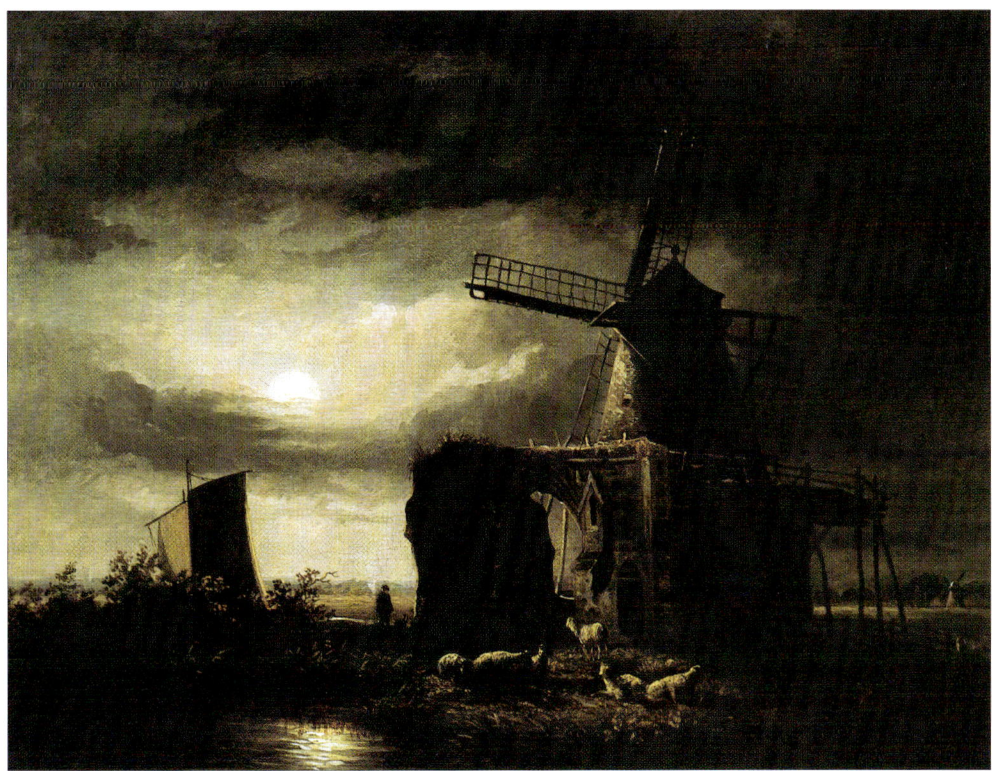

John Berney Crome, St. Benet's Abbey, oil on canvas

Chapter 3

FOLLOWERS OF CROME AND LADBROKE

Immediate followers of John Crome, at least from a family stand-point, were the three of his own sons who became painters. The eldest, **John Berney Crome** (1794-1842), in many ways did his father great credit and obeyed the latter's dying injunction – 'John my boy, paint, but paint for fame; and if your painting is only a pigsty – dignify it.' In spite, however, of promise of a brilliant future, it could be said that John Berney destroyed himself.

It was at a very early age that John Berney Crome came under the influence and thereby the teaching of his father. In 1806 at the tender age of 12 he first exhibited with the Norwich Society and again in 1808; his work was hung in the Royal Academy in 1811 when he was only 17 and he continued to exhibit extensively. In 1818 he became President of the Norwich Society, the youngest ever to hold the post, and one to which he was subsequently re-elected more frequently than any other member. He certainly did more than anyone for the Society as an institution especially by his fund raising activities and efforts to encourage patronage; his poor health and early death probably hastened its seemingly inevitable demise in 1833.

John Berney Crome was not just an extremely able painter; as a pupil of Norwich Grammar School he distinguished himself academically, particularly as a classicist. In 1813 he became School Captain and delivered a Latin oration on Guild Day in front of the Mayor of Norwich. This gift for public speaking stayed with him. Like his father he joined the Norwich Philosophical Society to whom he lectured on 'Remarks on Painting as connected with Poetry', from which no doubt spawned his 'Essay on Painting and Poetry' of which Norwich Castle Museum holds the complete text. His prominence in Norwich cultural circles, his success in the art world and his, albeit somewhat honorary, appointment as Landscape Painter to H.R.H. the Duke of Sussex, gave John Berney Crome a standing which he felt the need to live up to even to the extent of living beyond

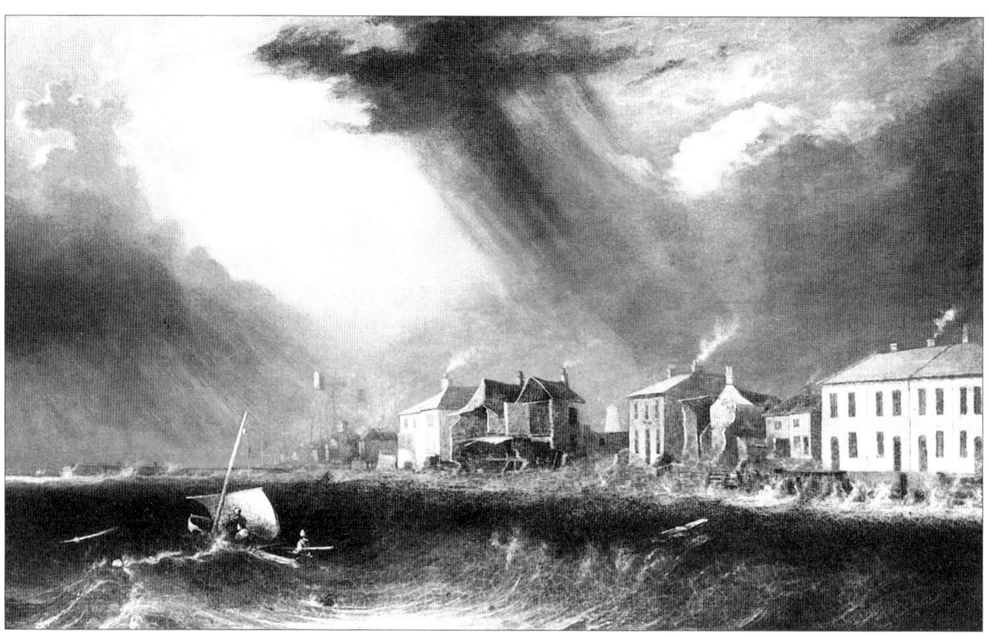

John Berney Crome, Great Gale at Yarmouth on Ash Wednesday, 1836, oil on canvas, 21 in x 34¼ in

his means. His was obviously an outgoing, popular personality which encouraged extravagance in his entertaining and general life style. His first wife, sadly, died within three years of their marriage but in 1830 he married secondly one Sarah Ann Clipperton. It was in the early 1830s that the economic recession really started to bite, pupils became scarce to the extent that on one occasion he is said to have travelled 70 miles for just three pupils. People were less able to afford paintings and anxiety about the general situation started John Berney drinking to excess and falling into debt. On the first occasion he appeared in court, the gift of a fine painting bailed him out but, later, he had to sell up his home and was declared bankrupt in 1834. Worry and drink were playing havoc with his health. His personal prestige in Norwich had been such that he could not face up to the shame and moved to Yarmouth. Both his health and his skills deteriorated and he died a few years later, a tragic end to a career that gave so much early promise.

It has been said that John Berney Crome was an uneven painter fluctuating between the exceptionally brilliant and downright bad. This many be true up to a point but it was only in his later years that the quality of his work more frequently suffered. Even his drawing which, though perhaps not so immaculate as his father's, had been strong and vigorous became weak and out of character. It would be too cruel to dismiss him as an erratic painter on the strength of his later unfortunate efforts; at his best he could hold his own with any of his contemporaries even, at times, his father. He is best known, as his sobriquet 'Moonlight Crome' implies, for his moonlight landscapes and seascapes, many of which are wonderfully striking and superbly painted. A good 'selling line' it may have been but it produced some splendid pictures and this feeling for dramatic effect was quite obviously part of his personality and not just commercialism.

In 1816 John Berney visited France and Holland with George Vincent. He was singularly unmoved by the French painters but impressed by the Dutch whose influence, particularly that of Hobbema and Cuyp, frequently shows in his more traditional landscapes. The propensity for moonlight scenes may well have been inspired by van Neer. He painted a number of French subjects after the visit, even though he deprecated the French style, but Norfolk landscapes, the sort of wooded corners beloved of his father, also appealed to him. To some people many of these appear heavy with their dominant browns and greens but I do not find this a problem, tending rather to admire the feeling of dimension and texture created by one who could certainly handle his paint. In the early works, particularly landscapes, his father's influence shows strongly and at times they worked together on a painting. One very famous joint effort for which the composition and sketch were largely the work of the father, the painting completed by the son after John Crome's death, was 'Yarmouth Water Frolic, Evening,' c.1821, a very large (41¾ in x 68 in) and impressive piece now in the permanent collection in Kenwood House (see page 28). A very different water scene but an extraordinary and highly skilled exercise in craftsmanship is John

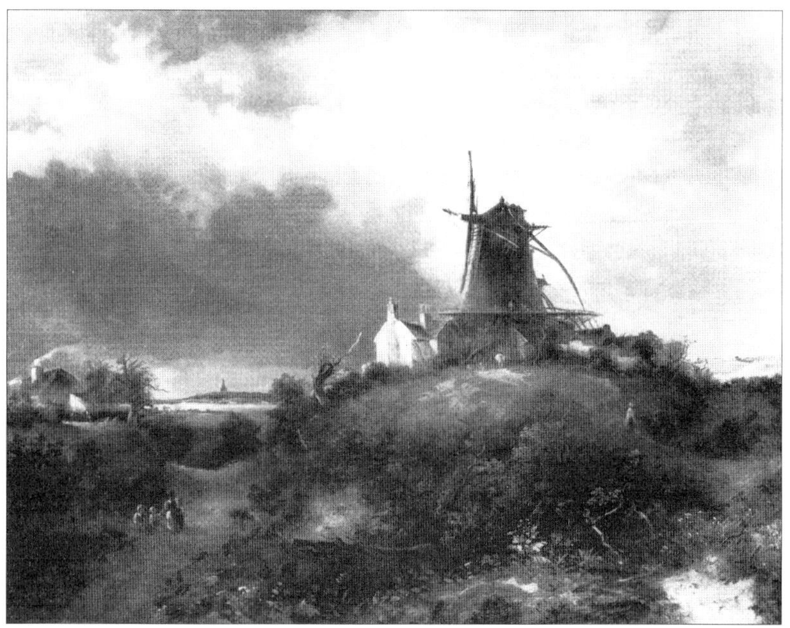

William Henry Crome, View near Norwich, oil on canvas, 24¼ in x 29¼ in

Berney's 'Great Gale at Yarmouth on Ash Wednesday, 1836'. This was a gale of almost hurricane force which caused disastrous flooding from the wild seas and horrendous destitution as the waves crashed through the houses nearest the sea. Furniture and other effects floated on the water or were tossed about on the enormous breakers as though they were toys. The general terrifying devastation and horror lent itself perfectly to the artist's sense of atmosphere and feeling for the drama of the situation. It is this feeling for atmosphere that plays such an important part in his moonlit land and seascapes and gives a magnetic sensation of drawing the spectator into the picture. John Berney exhibited at least 70 moonlit landscapes with the Norwich Society alone – how many others, one wonders, went to such other venues as London, Manchester, Hull, Liverpool and even Scotland?

Certainly John Berney Crome was an industrious worker. On his return from the Continent in 1816, he joined his father as assistant in the family teaching practice taking care of the outlying areas – Bungay, Beccles, Yarmouth or wherever he was needed, while his father concentrated on the city. After John Crome's death he continued with the teaching practice from 1821, assisted by his brother Frederick. The *Norwich Mercury* commented that 'he emulates the industry and promises to surpass the talents of his father, for he is trained to art by a liberal education.' As well as spending much more time teaching while continuing to paint and exhibit, his patient work for the Norwich Society went on. Soon after his father's death, during a further stint as President, he wrote individually to all the seceding artists to try and persuade them back into the mainstream Society. That he was successful is proved by their gradual return and, eventually, that of Robert Ladbroke himself in 1824. Unfortunately John Berney Crome was too ill and too far off to use his former strong influence when the next and final crisis took over.

His obituary stated: 'He had an elegant and classical turn of mind and deserved a better future'. Although at the end he suffered greatly from 'an incurable disease', to some extent he seems to have been the victim of his own success.

Little is known of **Frederick James Crome** (1796-1832) who has no particular reputation as a painter in his own right but, after his father's death, helped John Berney to keep the teaching practice going. He is known to have exhibited with the Norwich Society while still quite young but went on to employment as a bank clerk in Yarmouth through the good offices of Dawson Turner. Undoubtedly he had some skill as a draughtsman, being best known for his etchings which require a high standard of drawing. His early death no doubt precluded any great advancement.

Emily Crome (1801-1840) specialised in still-life painting, a break from the landscape tradition of the rest of the family. She exhibited regularly with the Norwich Society from the age of 15 and her work has been compared to that of Emily Coppin (Mrs Joseph Stannard) but in no way did it reach a comparable standard.

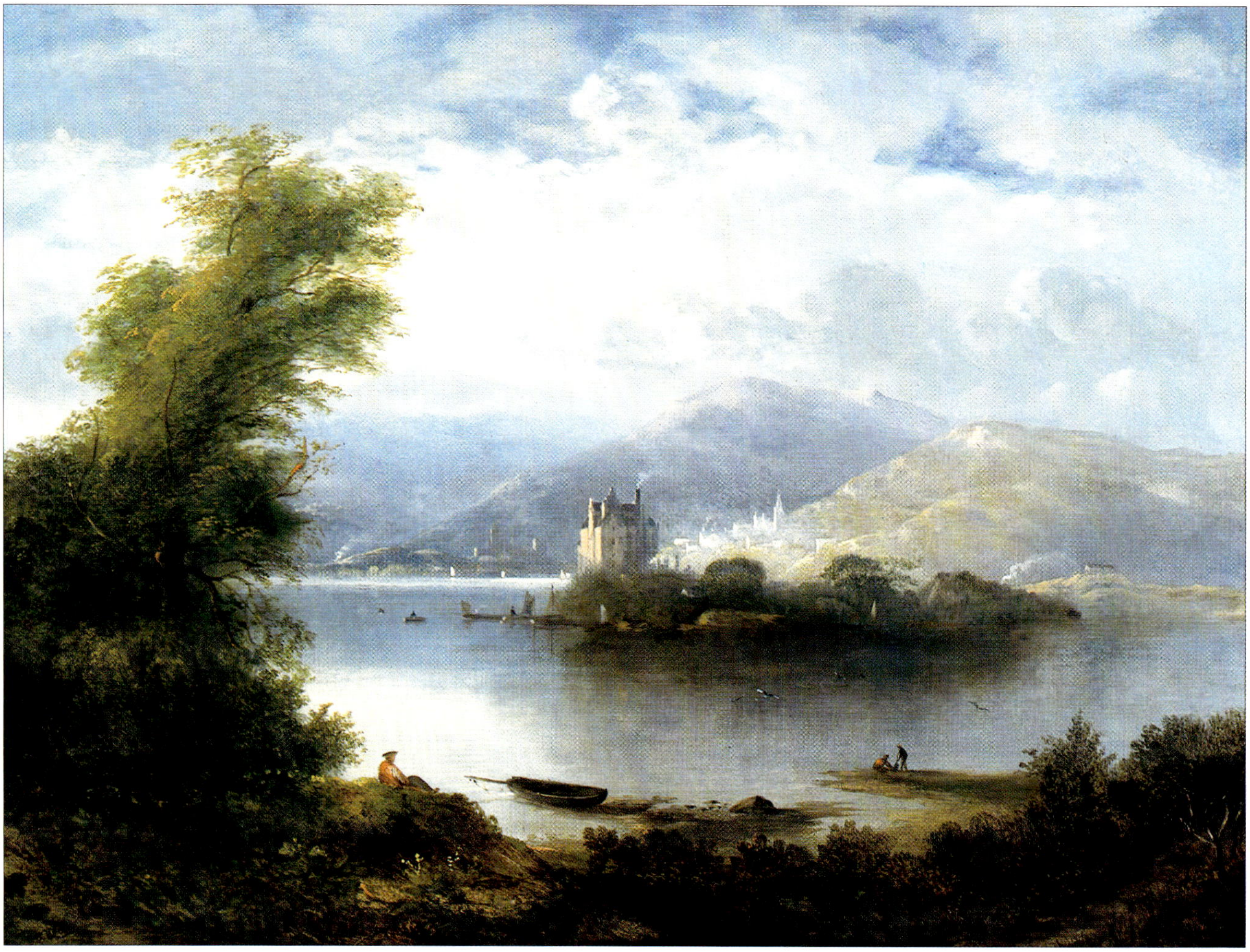

William Henry Crome, A Castle in a Scottish Loch, oil on canvas, 18 in x 24 in

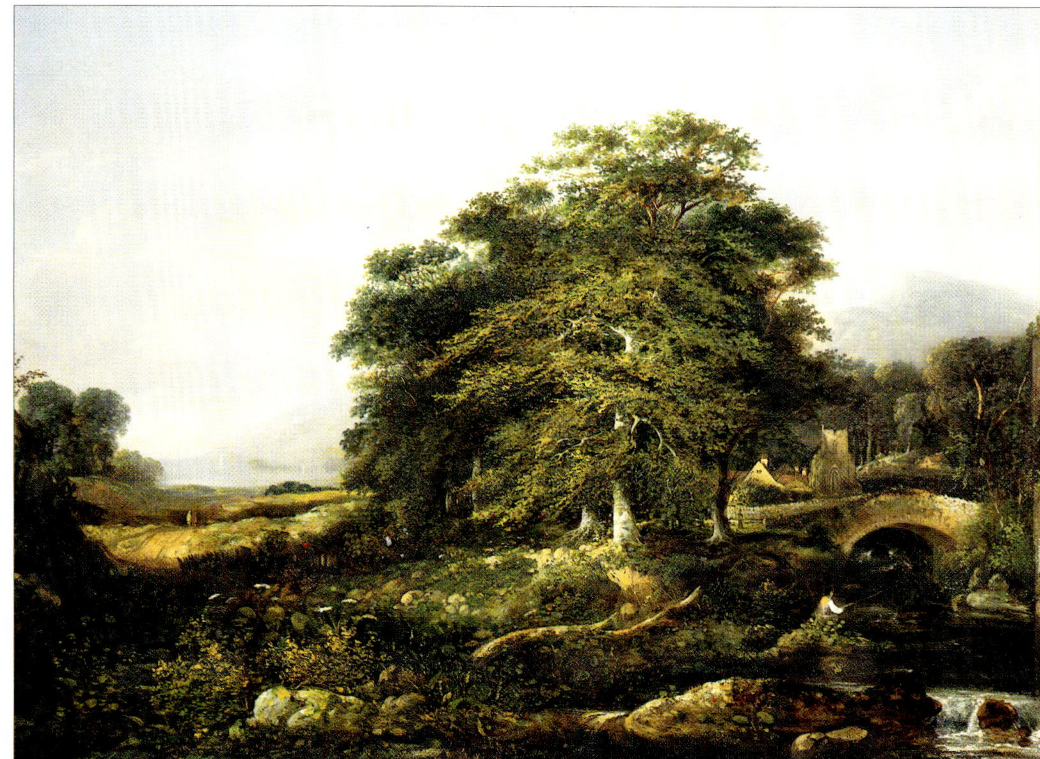

William Henry Crome, "Green" Landscape with Bridge and Man fishing, 1843. Oil on panel, 26¼ in x 37¼ in

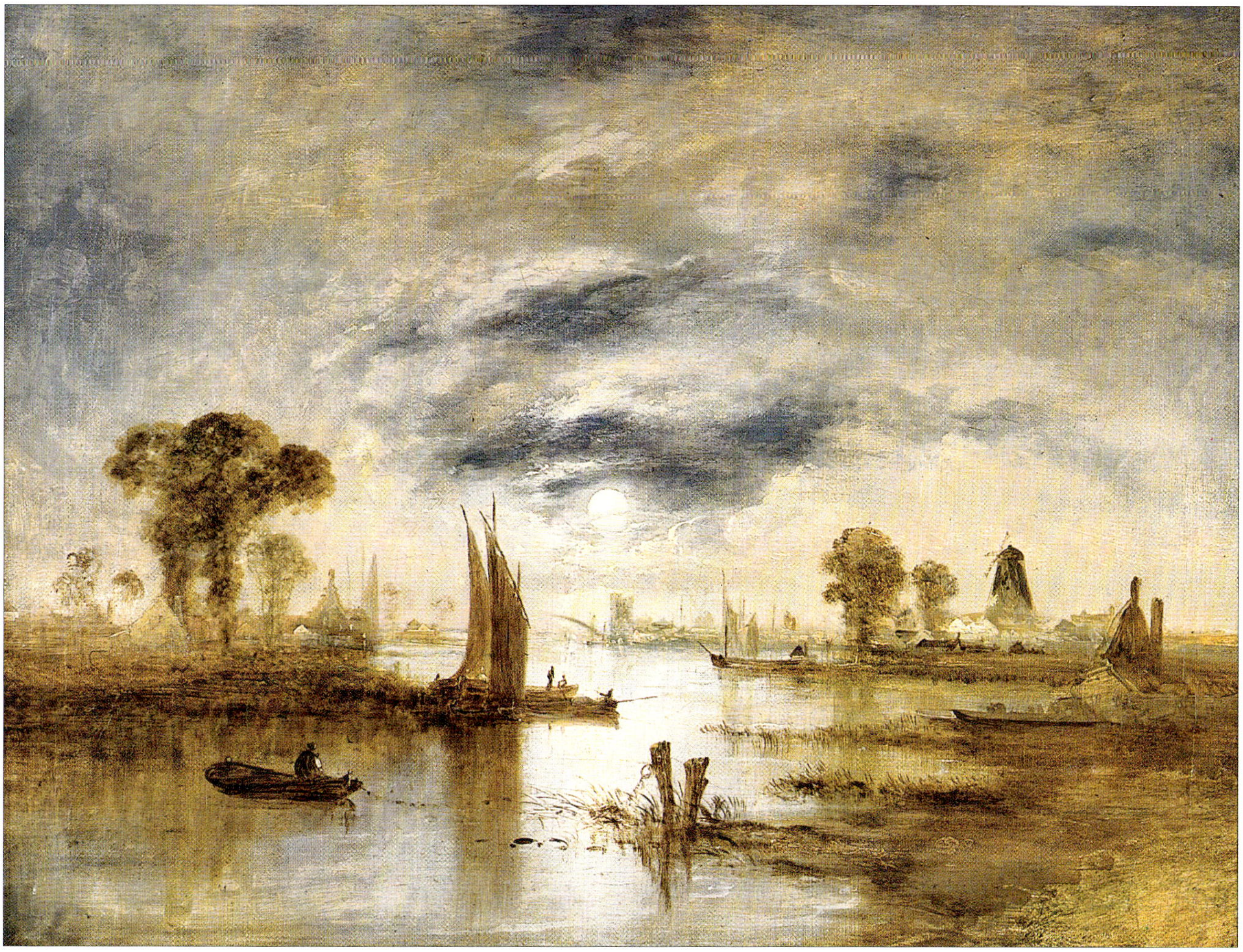

William Henry Crome,
Moonlight on the Yare,
oil on canvas,
17½ in x 23¾ in

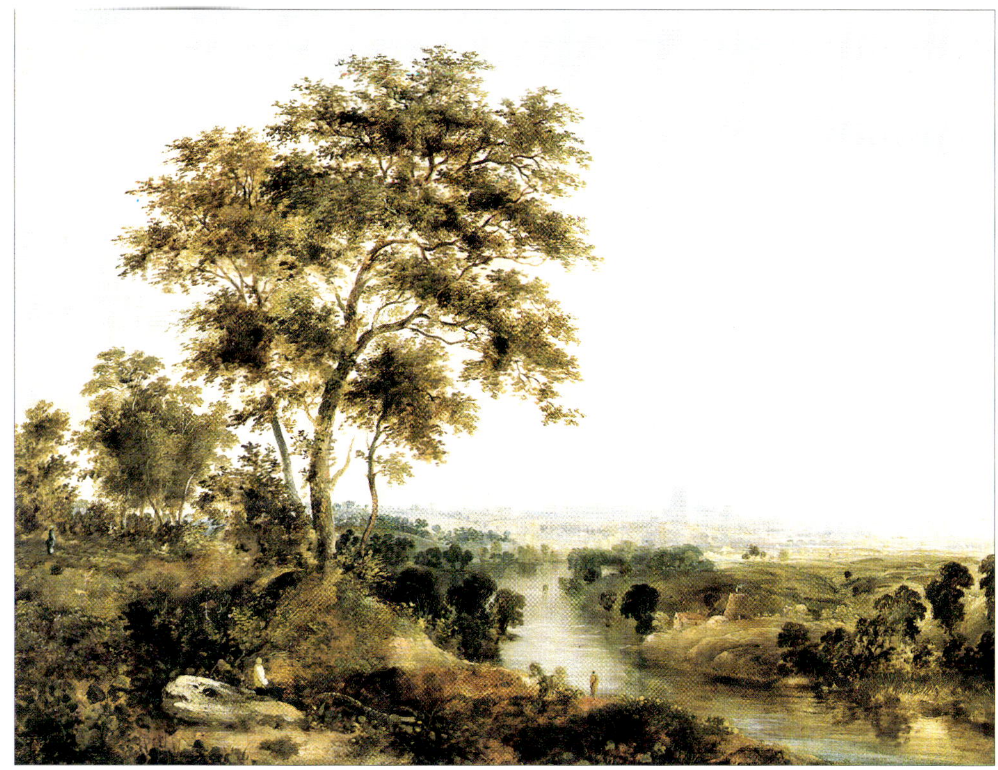

William Henry Crome,
View of Ripon, oil on panel,
27 in x 36 in

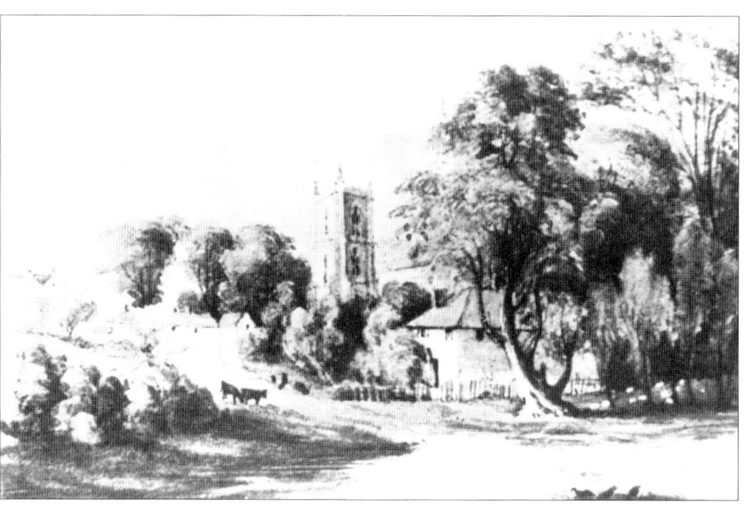

William Henry Crome, untitled watercolour

John Crome's third son, **William Henry Crome** (1806-1867) was only 15 when his father died and was thereby excluded from the extensive period of paternal teaching, help and encouragement available to John Berney which gave him such a flying start. Nevertheless William Henry made his own way quite successfully and it is a shame that he has been so underrated, maybe because he too broke away from the family tradition.

William Henry was certainly painting quite well by his early teens and had undoubtedly absorbed much of the artistic atmosphere surrounding his childhood. Initially he was more influenced by his brother, John Berney, than his father as evinced by a few early woodland scenes by moonlight, but soon he started looking back to Claude Lorraine and coming under his spell. Claude's beautiful blues obviously appealed to him and provided the inspiration for what can be termed a 'blue period'. His Scottish views in particular responded to this blue bias and lent themselves to William Henry's skilful treatment of distant perspective (see p. 32). The detailed close landscape looking over a further secondary scene was a favourite approach of William Henry's, and in his more local subjects he found some romantic corners around Norwich offering broad vistas over the city, usually framed in trees and sometimes bathed in a gentle mist with the cathedral spire somewhere on the horizon. The 'blue', also rather Italian, period of the early 1820s gave way to a spell of more traditional colour work although his subjects were always given a more romantic, slightly more imaginative, treatment than those of his father and brother. Around the 1840s he was inspired by a particular green, the impetus for moving into a 'green period' during which he produced some really beautifully painted landscapes both of Norfolk and further afield. As he grew older, a sort of browny sienna seemed to take over but the 'blue' and 'green' periods are most significant. I find no problem with this predominant colour approach although some critics have considered it idiosyncratic – surely a painter's privilege! Whatever his colour William Henry handled it well and it is certainly no more unorthodox than some combinations used by John Joseph Cotman or, for that matter, John Sell.

William Henry Crome is known to have died in London in adverse circumstances but there are few details of his later years. In a letter to Dawson Turner after the break-up of the Norwich Society, John Sell Cotman, who had been a friend of John Berney Crome, while relating the Crome family's misfortunes, wrote of William Henry: 'William has already left Norwich, for no one to know where, in wretchedness and I am afraid, insane – and so considered by his family.'

William Henry had one son, Vivian, who was also a painter specialising in flowers and animals and who moved with his mother to Birmingham after the death of his father. It was from there that he wrote to the *Norwich Mercury* reporting his mother's death some years later. Vivian himself died in London in 1926.

Nearest to Crome artistically were **James Stark** (1794-1859) and George Vincent, both important pupils who have been considered the bulwarks of the Norwich School after the death of Crome. James Stark was the youngest son of a Scots dyer, originally from Fife and a clever and cultivated man. Stark attended the Norwich Grammar School where he made friends with John Berney Crome who no doubt encouraged any artistic leanings. When his ambition to become a farmer

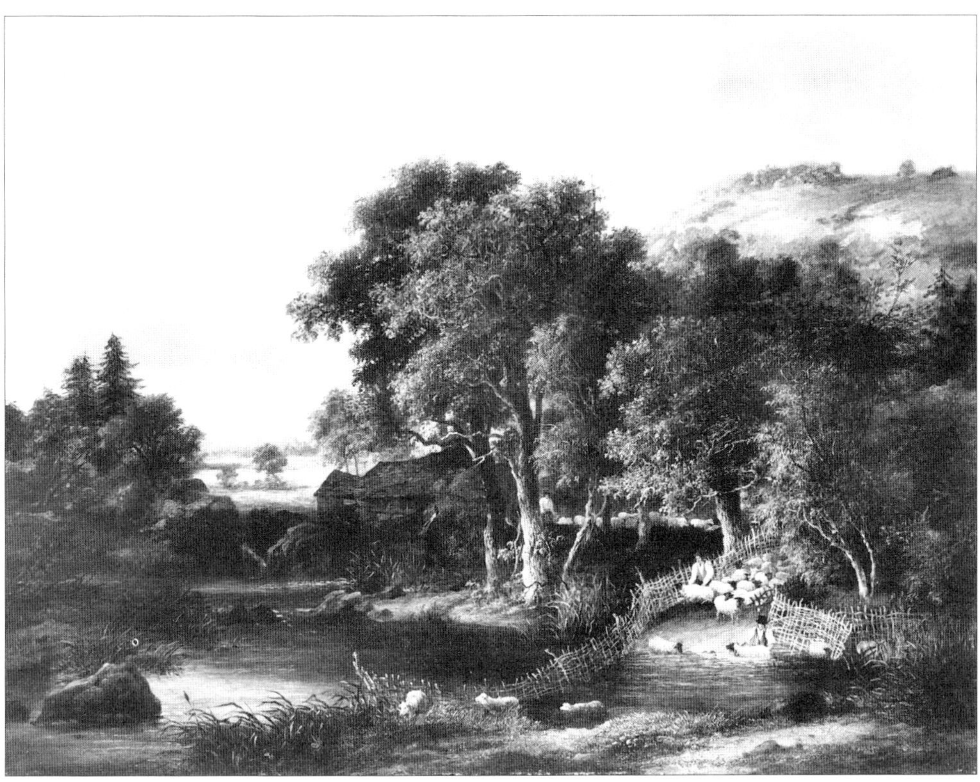

James Stark,
Sheep Washing, oil on panel,
24¼ in x 32¼ in

was thwarted on account of his delicate health, he turned his sights towards an artistic career.

In 1811 Stark was articled to John Crome and studied with him for three years. From all accounts he was a responsive and industrious pupil and Crome obviously thought a great deal of him. All or part of one of Crome's few surviving letters (probably there were only a few bearing in mind his lack of academic education and his dreadful spelling and grammar), has been quoted by most writers on the Norwich School; many will be familiar with it but I make no apology for repeating it for the benefit of those who are not, for it is an important reflection of the master/pupil relationship, or perhaps, more correctly, the relationship of friends:

> Friend James,
> I received your kind letter and feel much pleased at your approval of my picture. I fear you will see too many errors for a painter of my long practice and at my time of life: however, there are parts in it you like, I have no doubt, so I am happy. You are likely to visit us (but mum is the order of the day about that concern). I wish it might be so; we shall be happy to see you in Norwich.
>
> In your letter you wish me to give you my opinion of your picture. I should have liked it better if you had made it more of a whole, that is, the trees stronger, the sky running from them in shadow up to the opposite corner; that might have produced what I think it wanted, and have made it a much less too picture effect. I think I hear you say, this fellow is very vain, and that nothing is right that does not suit his eye. But be assured what I have said I thought on the first sight, it strengthened me in that opinion every time I looked at it. (Honesty, my boy!). So much for what it wanted; but how pleased I was to see so much improvement in the figures, so unlike our Norwich School; I may say they were good. Your boat was too small for them (you see I am at it again), but then the water pleased me, and I think it would not want much alteration in the sky. I cannot let your sky go off without some observation. I think the character of your clouds too affected, that is, too much of some of our modern painters, who mistake some of our great masters because they sometimes put in some of these round characters of clouds, they must do the same; but if you look at any of their skies, they either assist in the composition or make some figure in the picture, nay, sometimes play the first fiddle. I have seen this in Wouvermans and many others I could mention.
>
> Breath [Breadth] must be attended to, if you paint but a muscle, give it breath. Your doing the same by the sky, making parts broad and of a good shape, that they may come in with your composition, forming one grand plan of light and shade, this must always please the eye and keep the attention of the spectator and give delight to everyone. Trifles in Nature must be overlooked that we many have our feelings raised by seeing the whole picture at a glance, not knowing how or why we are so charmed. I have written you a long rigmarole story about giving dignity to what ever you paint – I fear so long that I should be scarcely able to understand what I mean myself; you will, I hope, take the word for the deed, and at the

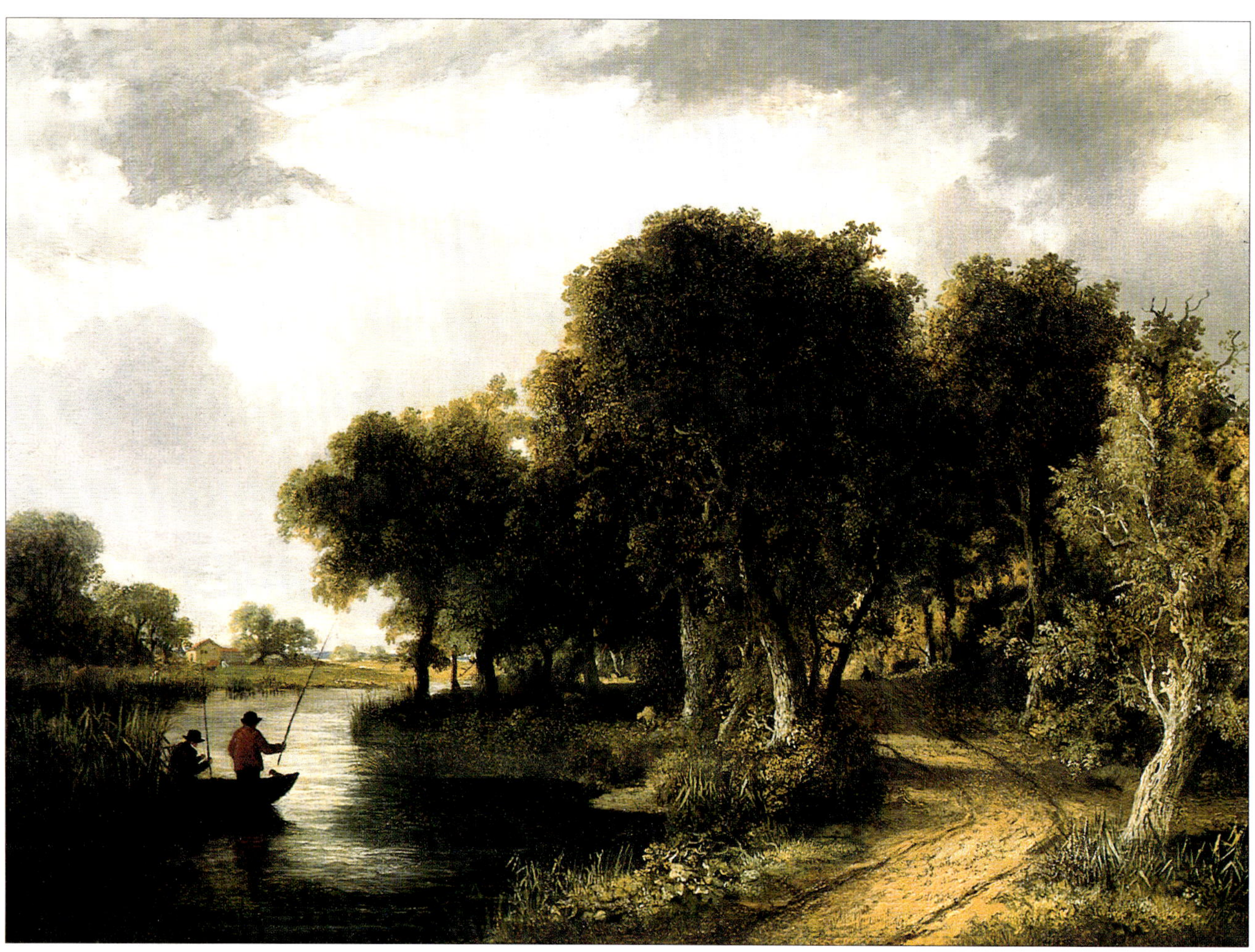

James Stark,
Anglers on the Yare,
oil on panel, 18 in x 25½ in

Painted while Stark was still under the influence of John Crome and the Norfolk countryside. It is in his Norfolk subjects that Stark seems to have been most at ease with himself.

same time forgive all faults of diction, grammar, spelling, etc., etc., etc.,

We have heard from John; I believe he is not petrified from having seen the French School. He says in his letter something about Tea Tray painters. I believe most of those who visit them whistle the same note. So much for the French Artists.

I hope they will arrive safe. Our happiness would be made complete 'if your tongue could be heard amongst us.' 'Parley vous,' my boy, will be echoed from garret to cellar in my house. I think I hear Vincent say to John, 'Why, John, what d...d Franch rascal was that passed us just now? Why, look at his whiskers; why, he must be a Don Cossack.' They had a charming voyage over Vincent belching as a steam packet much to the discomfiture of some of the other passengers. John did not say how Steel* was in the passage, but I believe they were all bad alike.

Sunday night – I put this last in my smooth paper epistle – that the boys are by my fireside going to take a glass of wine, quite well and happy. I wish you were with us. I have nothing more to say, only wishing you health and comfort.

Believe me, dear James,
Yours etc., etc.
John Crome

There is so much warmth and the gentle criticism, both given and received, is kind and constructive; one senses a very happy relationship between John Crome, his son and the two favourite pupils who are seen as his successors in the hierarchy of the Norwich School. Stark joined the Norwich Society in 1813, became Vice-President in 1828/9 and President in 1829/30.

In 1815, Stark moved on to the Royal Academy Schools where he made further significant progress. He had been exhibiting in Norwich some time before leaving the city and soon started exhibiting successfully in London. In 1818 the Directors of the British Institute, the Marquis of Stafford and the Earl of Aberdeen, awarded him a prize of £50, quite a substantial sum at that time (the recipient of a similar prize was Sir Edwin Landseer). In those early days Stark acquired some extremely influential patrons. In 1815 at the British Institute exhibition he had sold to the

* A surgeon who married one of Crome's daughters.

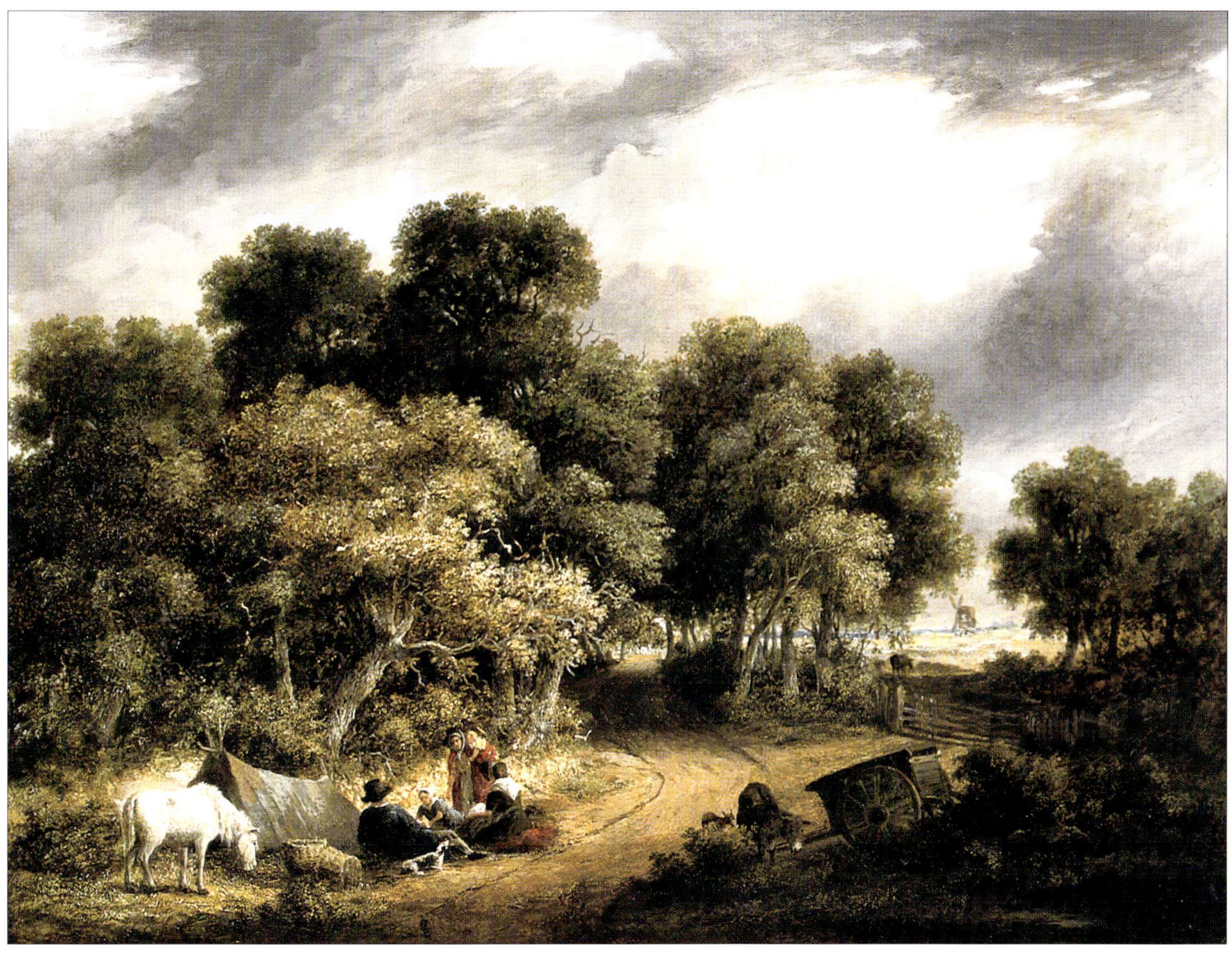

James Stark,
Track Through the Forest with Cottage and Travellers,
oil on panel, 16 in x 13 in

An excellent example of Stark's feeling for trees

Dean of Windsor, his first major triumph, and in 1818 the Marquis of Sheffield bought 'Penning the Flock', one of his several versions of that subject,* a favourite of the Norwich artists, and the Countess de Gray claimed 'Lambeth, Looking Towards Westminster Bridge' now in the Paul Mellon Collection. Crome had recommended the Lambeth area as the source of good subjects and must have been gratified to have his advice so soon and so effectively vindicated! Other early patrons included Sir John Egerton, Lord Northwich, several Royal Academicians and the governors of the Edinburgh Royal Institute.

In 1821 James Stark married Elizabeth Dinmore of King's Lynn and for a short while they lived in Great Yarmouth. Soon, however, they moved back to Norwich, to a house next to Stark's father where his two daughters were born. During 1822/3 he suffered a prolonged spell of poor health; although he stopped exhibiting for a time, he continued to paint with results I shall discuss later. Gradually he recovered and restarted the round of exhibiting. Then, in 1827, he embarked on a series of studies of 'Scenery of the Rivers of Norfolk from pictures painted by James Stark', later to be engraved and published in a volume of 35 subjects with text by J.W. Robberds. The publication was ready in 1834 and achieved modest success.

Arthur James Stark and his father were drawn very close following the death of James' wife in 1834, and they greatly helped and supported each other until James' death. As Arthur James grew up, he developed, not unnaturally, a talent for drawing and painting in which he was greatly encouraged by his father; later they worked side by side, obviously happy with each other's company. In 1839 they moved to Windsor where Stark senior painted many forest scenes which he sent regularly to all the important London exhibitions. Always solicitous for his son, in 1849 when Arthur James reached the age of 18 his father decided it was time to return to London thereby giving Arthur the opportunity of attending the Royal Academy Schools. James continued

* There are examples in both Norwich and Ipswich Museums.

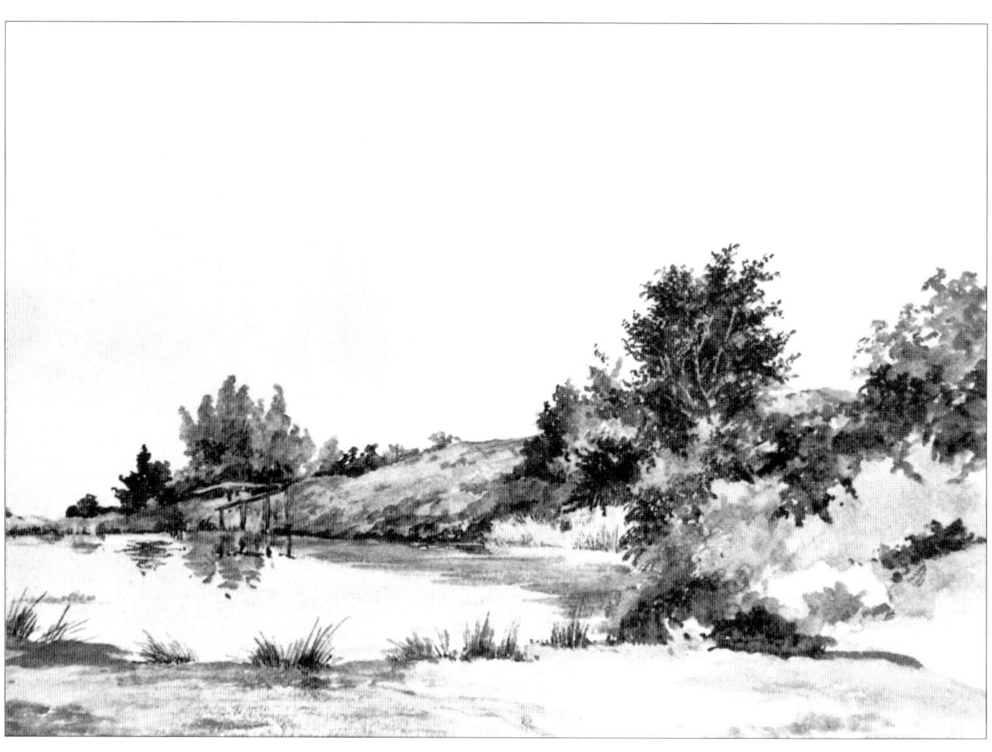

James Stark,
Keston Pond,
pencil and watercolour, c.1830

to paint large, impressive canvases despite fluctuations in health. Father and son still spent periods in Norwich from time to time for James Stark retained a great affection for the city that had given him his start in artistic life. When his health deteriorated to the stage that he needed constant care, his devoted son nursed him until his death while painting and selling as much as possible to keep them housed, clothed and fed. For whatever reason, in spite of the earlier successes, they had become very poor. One can only think that it was the inevitable disaster for artists of the economic recession of the 1830s and 1840s and the expense of James' illnesses. Living in London in any event has never been cheap. His remains were returned to Norwich where he is buried in the Rosary Cemetery.

Returning to Stark's painting career, this followed a somewhat erratic course in spite of the illustrious start when the critics were forecasting a reputation that would go further than that of Crome. Certainly his early works showing the unmistakable influence of Crome were, although typical of the Norfolk landscapes beloved of the Norwich artists, given his own identity by a very personal brushwork particularly evident in his fulsome and remarkably realistic trees. When he went to study in London, he made friends with William Collins who also knew Linnell and Constable; to a certain extent he absorbed something from all three of them but used it, again, in his own way to create a style which, as his distinguished patronage suggests, was greatly admired.

A great deal of adverse criticism has been levelled at his work of the early 1820s, but it must be remembered that it was at this time that his health was at a particularly low ebb. He was already beginning to evince a certain influence from the Dutch Hobbema and, to a lesser extent, Ruysdael, and the first of the succession of leafy glades in the Dutch idiom passed without undue comment. However as these pictures, generally entitled simply 'Landscape', followed in a steady stream, popularity waned and the critics became quite severe in their judgements. Hemingway quotes from one London review: 'We must object to the iteration of subject; a practice that shows he is more conversant with Hobbema than with nature . . . If there is but one subject there is also but one system of colour management . . . what he has done is good but he has as yet painted but one picture.' Others were even more critical and later writers have puzzled at the change from his early natural landscapes, often on a par with Crome himself, to these repetitive, comparatively poorly painted, pseudo copies. As they were later to admit, this dismal period gave way to better things, the *Norwich Mercury* acknowledging that his landscapes had again become 'brilliant with beauty and light. The exchange from Hobbema to nature is indeed a marvellous

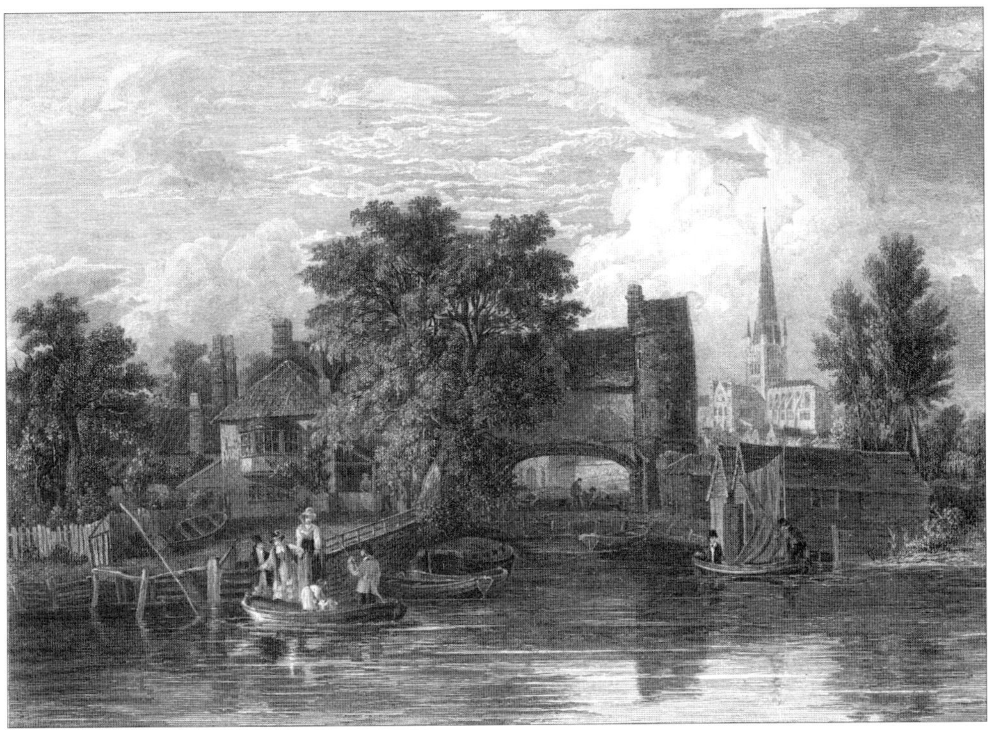

James Stark,
The Ferry (Close, Norwich),
engraved by W. R. Smith

improvement.' Personally I see no need for puzzlement. It seems to me that while Stark was so ill, probably unable to go out and look at nature and finding it difficult to imagine a scene out of context, he pressed on with minor variations on a theme which, initially, had seemed successful. In the absence of an identity, they could only be just 'Landscape'. He may well have been too tired to consider things rationally, perhaps he should not have been attempting to paint at all at this time, but I know of several contemporary artists who, placed in a similar situation, have narrowly missed losing their reputation by insisting on continuing to paint without the necessary stamina and inspiration, believing that constant practice must be maintained at all costs – if you don't use it, you might lose it. A dread that the hand and eye might lose their cunning keeps them pressing on with, often, calamitous results. I am convinced that this happened to James Stark; the symptoms are only too evident. Binyon once wrote of Stark that 'his reputation has suffered from the frequent attribution of his works to Crome and from the attributions to him of inferior works of the Norwich School.' The period of Hobbema glades was no doubt at the root of most of these misattributions.

He had virtually recovered when he decided to undertake the Rivers of Norfolk enterprise; in fact this may have been a deliberate antidote to what hindsight told him was a mistake. Sketching or painting *in situ* again made all the difference to the construction of the pictures and the actual handling of his materials regained much of the confidence and skill sapped by illness, pressure and consequent fatigue. By the time of the move to Windsor, although his work had inevitably changed and progressed, it had regained its former quality.

The thick paint and stroking accents of the Norwich Crome era and the distorted colour and synthetic cauliflower trees of the Hobbema 1820s gave way to a lighter approach showing something of the influence of Collins, more in tune with London fashion of the time. His acute powers of observation had reasserted themselves and the great trees of Windsor Forest became almost portraits in their natural realism. He was at that time, along with his friend John Berney Crome, exhibiting as widely as Glasgow, Edinburgh, Liverpool, Manchester, Newcastle, Birmingham, Bath, Exeter, Dublin and Southampton as well as London and Norwich.

To my mind insufficient attention is paid to Stark's skill as a watercolourist, possibly because few have been seen actually hanging but have spent most of their lives in portfolio collections in Norwich and other museums. It seems possible that watercolour came into his sphere of influence at the time of his preparatory work for the Rivers of Norfolk, another way of breaking out of the previous self-imposed but regrettable phase. There are very few 'pure' watercolours

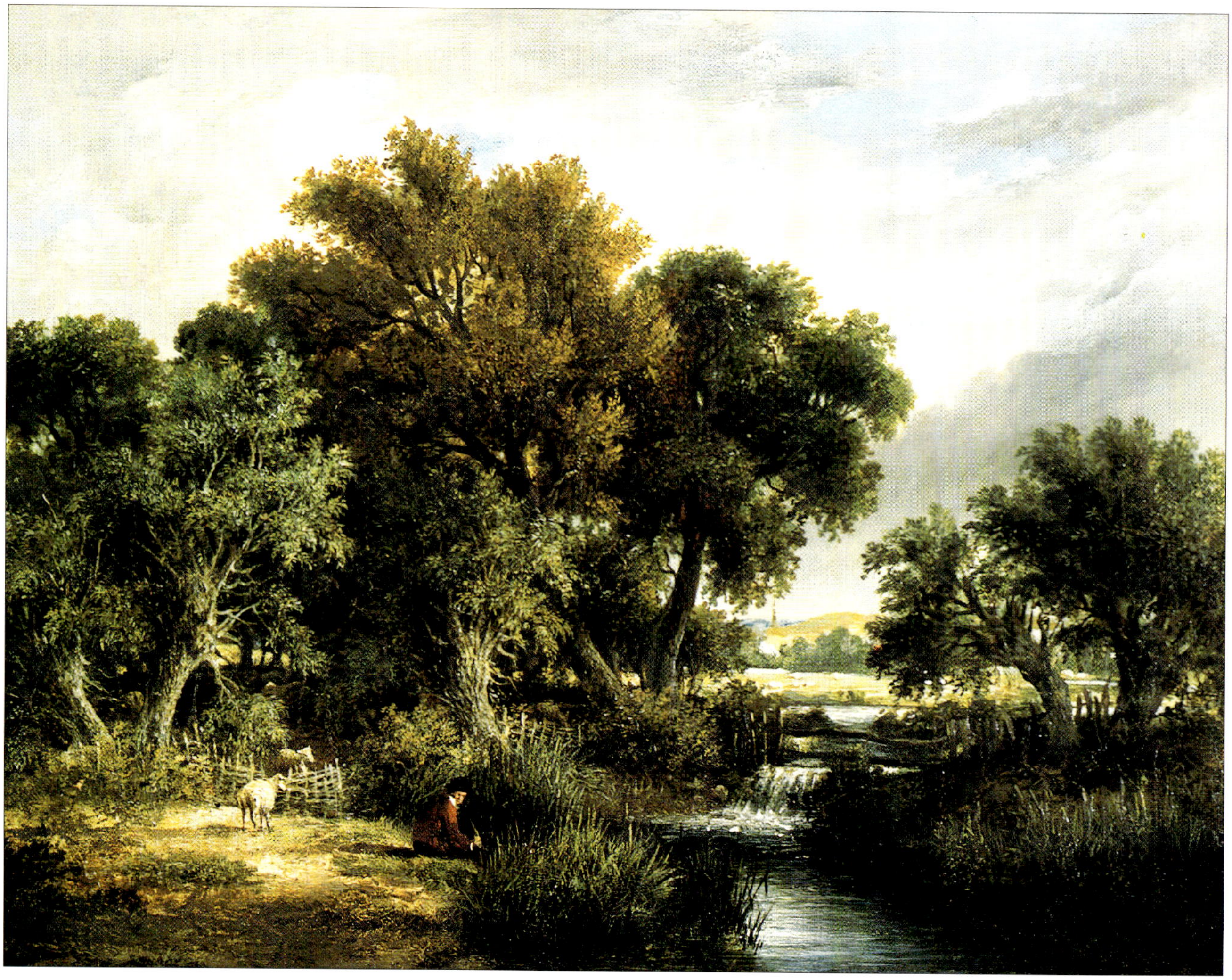

James Stark,
Landscape Looking Towards Norwich, oil on panel, 12¼ in x 16½ in

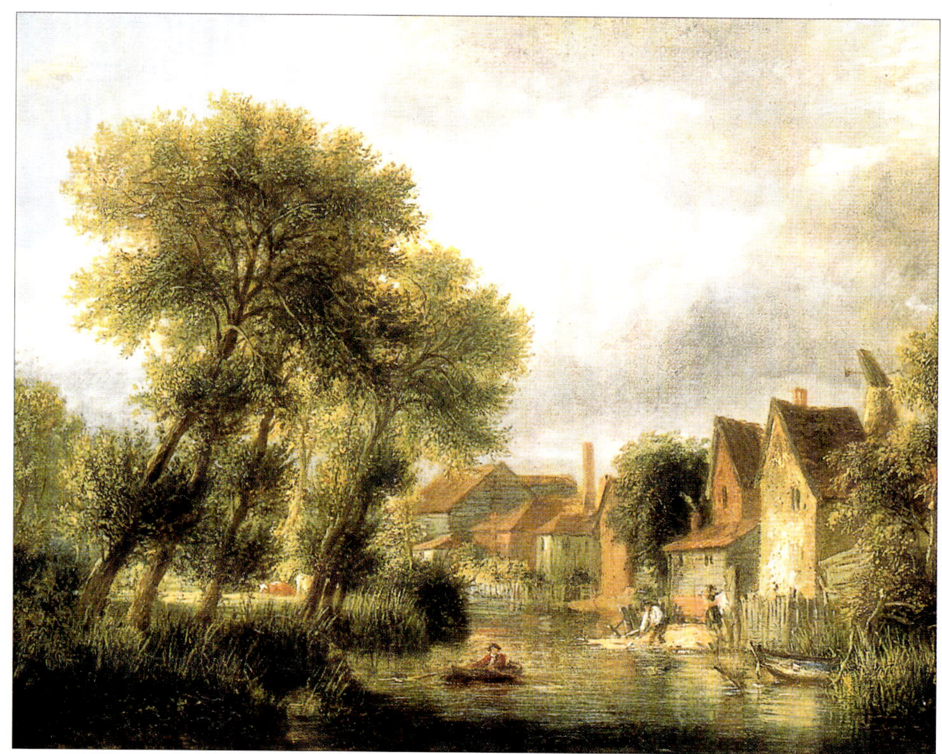

James Stark,
A View of the Old Mills, oil on panel, 10¼ in x 13¼ in

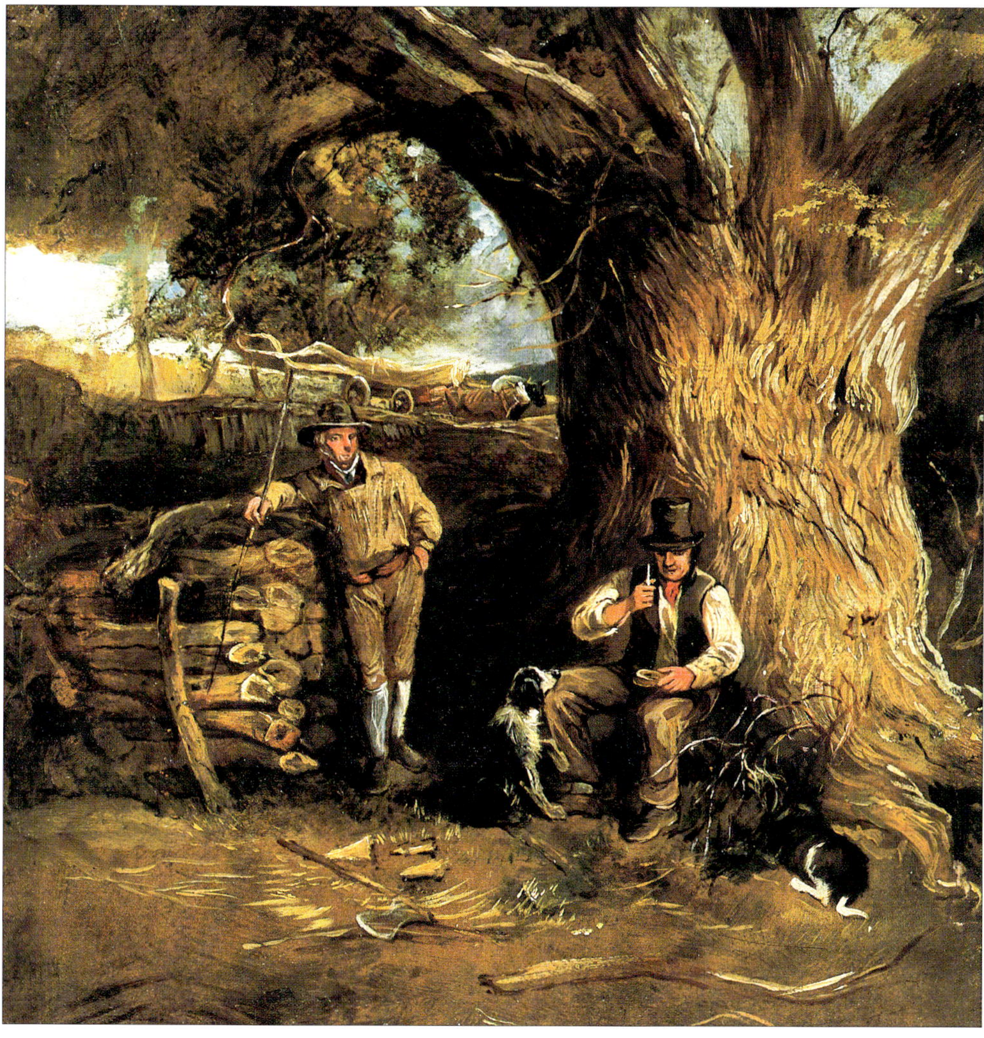

Arthur James Stark, The Woodcutters Resting, oil on canvas, 18 in x 10 in

documented although of the two I have seen there is much that is admirable and Stark's handling is both sensitive and controlled. With many of his sketches, probably on the spot preliminaries in most cases, there is a wonderful spontaneity; bold drawing over which he has used just a few broad washes indicative of the general colour effect portray a great deal with a minimum of painting. They show quite a different side of Stark; even though some are unfinished their keynote is sincerity and truth with a feeling for atmosphere never quite achieved even in the best of his heavier, more highly finished oils. The later oils, using a lighter and altogether more modern approach, tend to confirm the assumption that these little gems of drawing and watercolour surfaced between the Hobbema and Windsor phases; they give the impression of being less laboured. More open skies, broader vistas, except for the more enclosed forest scenes, sparkling light and a more sparing use of paint are all indicative of a maturing outlook. It is said that figures and animals were often added by his son.

Like so many offspring of the famous, **Arthur James Stark** (1831-1902), for many years overshadowed by his father, is more recently becoming appreciated in his own right. Not only did he inherit many of his father's talents but added others that were quite his own. Notwithstanding this, as I have mentioned, father and son became very close. Both have the name for being kindly souls; after all how many young men in their twenties would take on the job of nursing a dying father while keeping house and making a living, however meagre, for them both?

Arthur Stark as a painter was given every possible encouragement and teaching from his father who helped him particularly in the sphere of landscape while recognising that his true métier

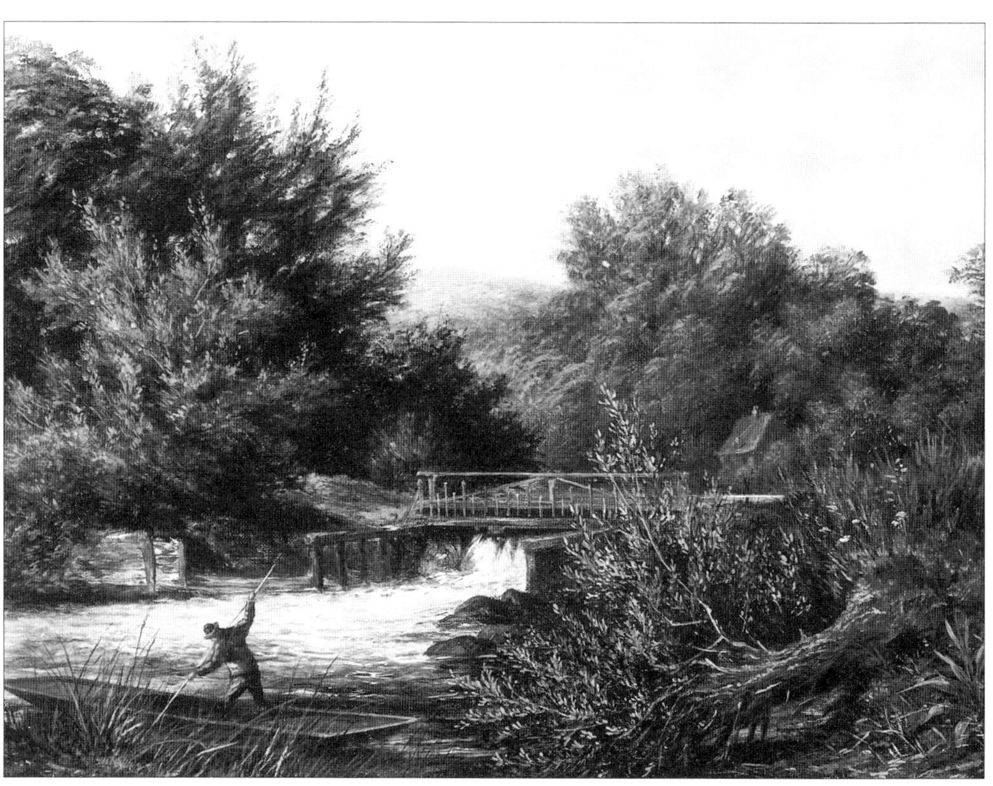

Arthur James Stark, Wooded River Landscape with a Punt by a Weir, oil on canvas, 12¼ in x 16½ in

was as a painter of animals. His father wrote in a letter to his friend, the engraver of Rivers of Norfolk, E.W. Cooke, R.A. :

> I am most anxious to get to London on Arthur's account, as he is to be an animal painter it is absolutely necessary that he should draw and study in the Academy. He is losing time now. I believe Careys to be the best plan to prepare him. He has painted 2 horses in Norfolk and done them capitally but he wants the stimulus which mixing with lads of his own age and persuits would give him.

This, I feel, provides an important insight into James Stark's care and concern for his son which was obviously reciprocated when his own need came.

Quite naturally Arthur Stark's early landscapes were modelled on his father's style of the time, that is the Windsor period. It was the addition on his own volition of animals that made his father aware of the potential talent for the subject and determined that it should be nurtured. While his landscapes in oil are much more than competent (see above), Arthur James was quite a master in his handling of watercolour and deserves much greater recognition. His earlier works were carefully drawn and detailed but, as time went on, he became much broader and freer and his invariably tiny watercolours achieved a moving, almost lyrical, quality that has great charm. Many of his watercolours and most of his oils have animals somewhere in the composition, always completely true to life and displaying a grasp of anatomy and structure as well as a feeling for the beauty of his four-footed friends. His own son wrote in the catalogue of a posthumous exhibition: 'Art to him was a natural religion, its practice an ennobling worship. The passionate love of it was so deep in him, a feeling at once so real and vital, and yet so tender and intimate that he never spoke of it.'

Arthur James exhibited at the Royal Academy, the British Institute and other venues; at 17 his first Royal Academy exhibit was hung in line with that of Sir Edwin Landseer, which must have pleased him greatly, not to mention his father. During his time in London Arthur James was permitted to study and draw horses in the stables of a firm of carriers; later on he hired for three years a studio at Tattersall's with a view to completing his studies and perfecting his drawings and paintings of horses. He was subsequently offered the post of animal painter to Queen Victoria which, though honoured, he turned down feeling that it would be too restrictive to his future development.

Arthur Stark kept up his association with Norfolk where he found many of his subjects, both

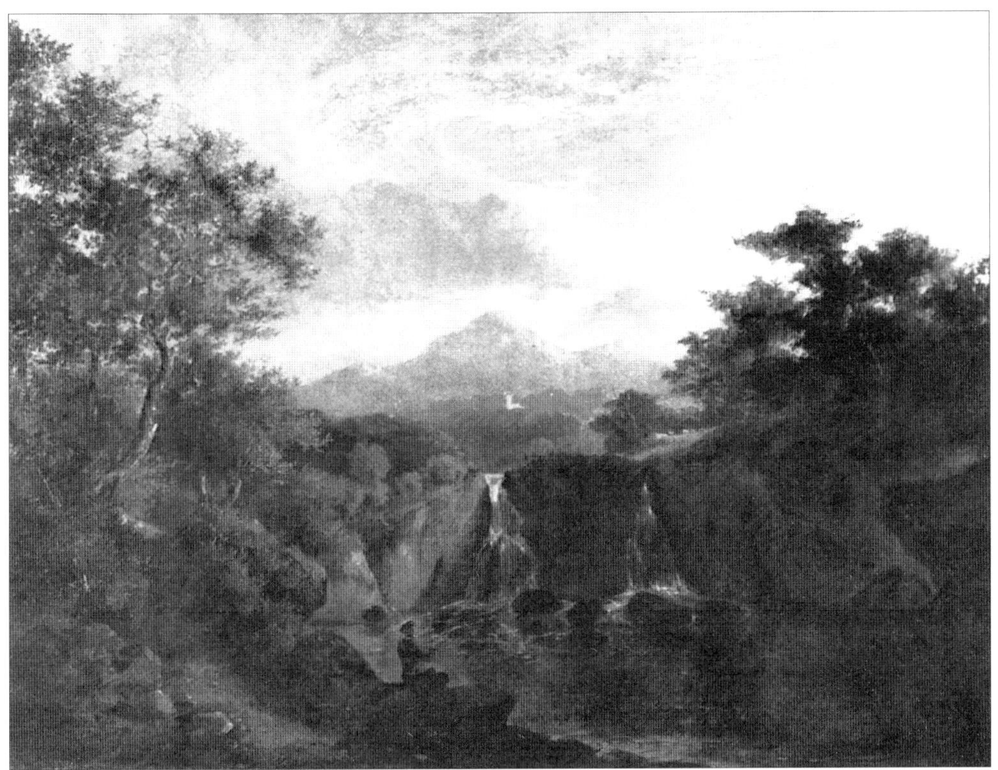

George Vincent,
View in the Highlands,
oil on canvas, 18 in x 24 in

landscape and animals or a combination of both. He travelled widely in this country after his father's death and his subjects were found in many counties. In 1878 he settled down and married Rosa Isabella Kent, daughter of the Chairman of the House of Lords committees; they had a son and a daughter.

Although not always considered to be part of the Norwich School, he was very much part of his father's life and lays some claim to being at least a fringe member. His work can be seen in Norwich Castle Museum as well as the British Museum and the Victoria and Albert, London.

George Vincent (1796–c.1835) jointly with Stark Crome's most illustrious pupil, had a short and very chequered life which meant that he was unable fully to exploit the prodigious talent and promise inherent in his early works. His father, James Vincent, was a Norwich cloth manufacturer who would certainly have known James Stark's father by virtue of their connected trades. By the same token the sons, both attending Norwich Grammar School and friends with the young Cromes, would have been close associates so, with a common interest and talent, it seems quite natural that Vincent, like Stark, should have been articled to John Crome.

As we have seen, he visited France in 1816 with John Berney Crome but only one French subject is known. This is a remarkable example of his early work displaying Vincent's ability, even when so young, to work out a complex composition and find ways of adding as much variety as possible within one, still coherent, painting. Here the fascinating old buildings of Rouen are beautifully painted, in the distance the mountain landscape indicates the charm of the setting, the judiciously placed urban trees give a balancing of colour, while people and animals go about their business in thoroughly life-like fashion.

Vincent was two years younger than James Stark but, after his period of training with Crome, joined his friend in London in 1817 moving into the next door house in Newman Street. Having first exhibited with the Norwich Society in 1811, he now started exhibiting in London, at the Royal Academy and the British Institute where the inveterate collector the Marquis of Stafford bought his work along with that of Stark. Vincent continued to exhibit in Norwich and both local and London critics praised his work highly. In 1819, when Stark's health had forced his return to Norwich, Vincent went on his first trip to Scotland finding ample material for his original style of painting. Less than two years later both ex-pupils attended Crome's funeral in

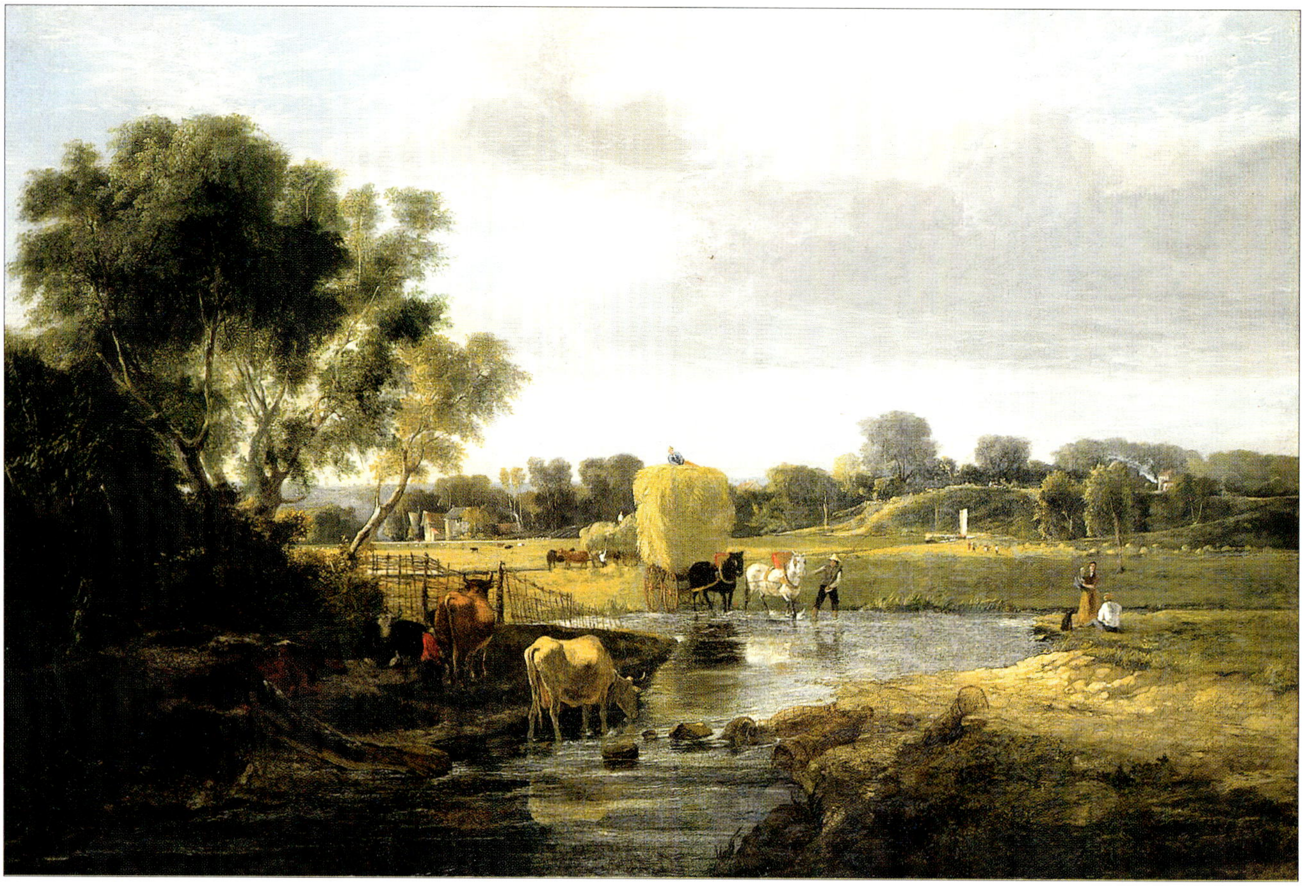

George Vincent,
Trowse Meadows
near Norwich,
oil on canvas,
1828,
28¾ in x 43 in

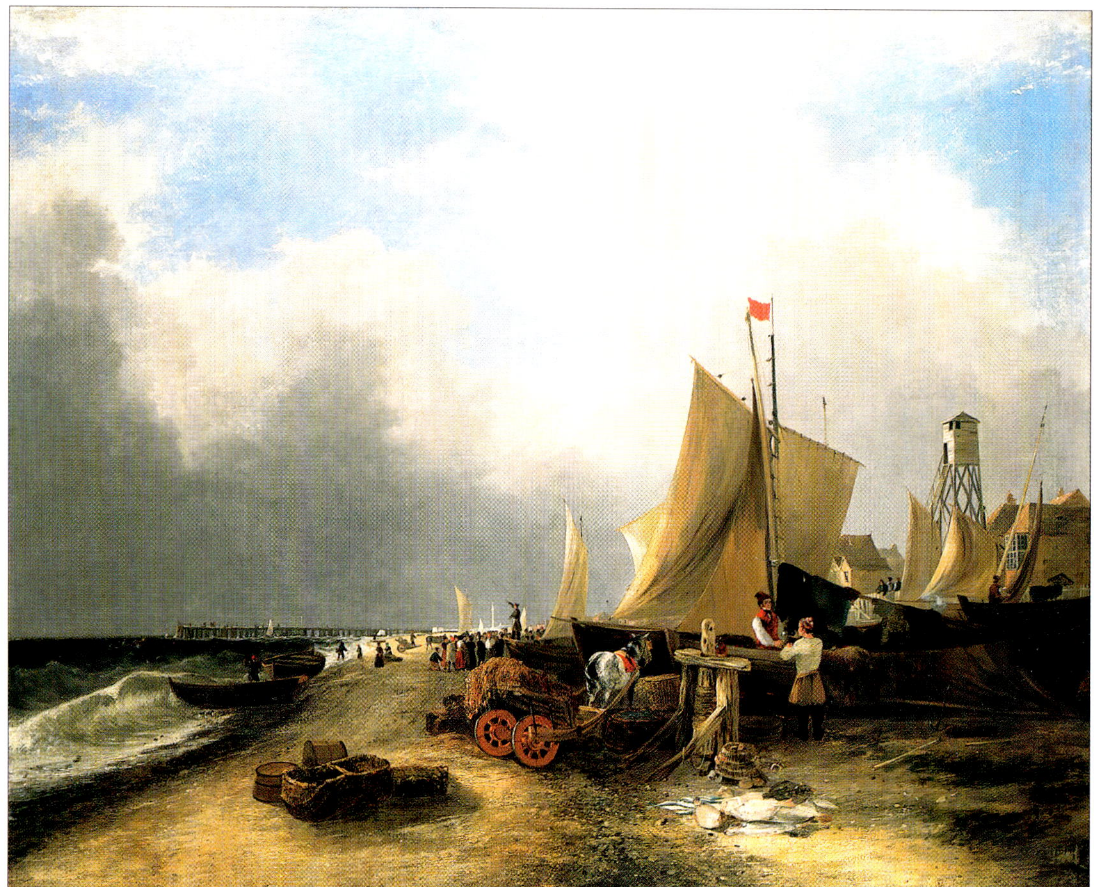

George Vincent,
The Fish Auction,
Yarmouth,
oil on canvas,
1827,
40¼ in x 50½ in

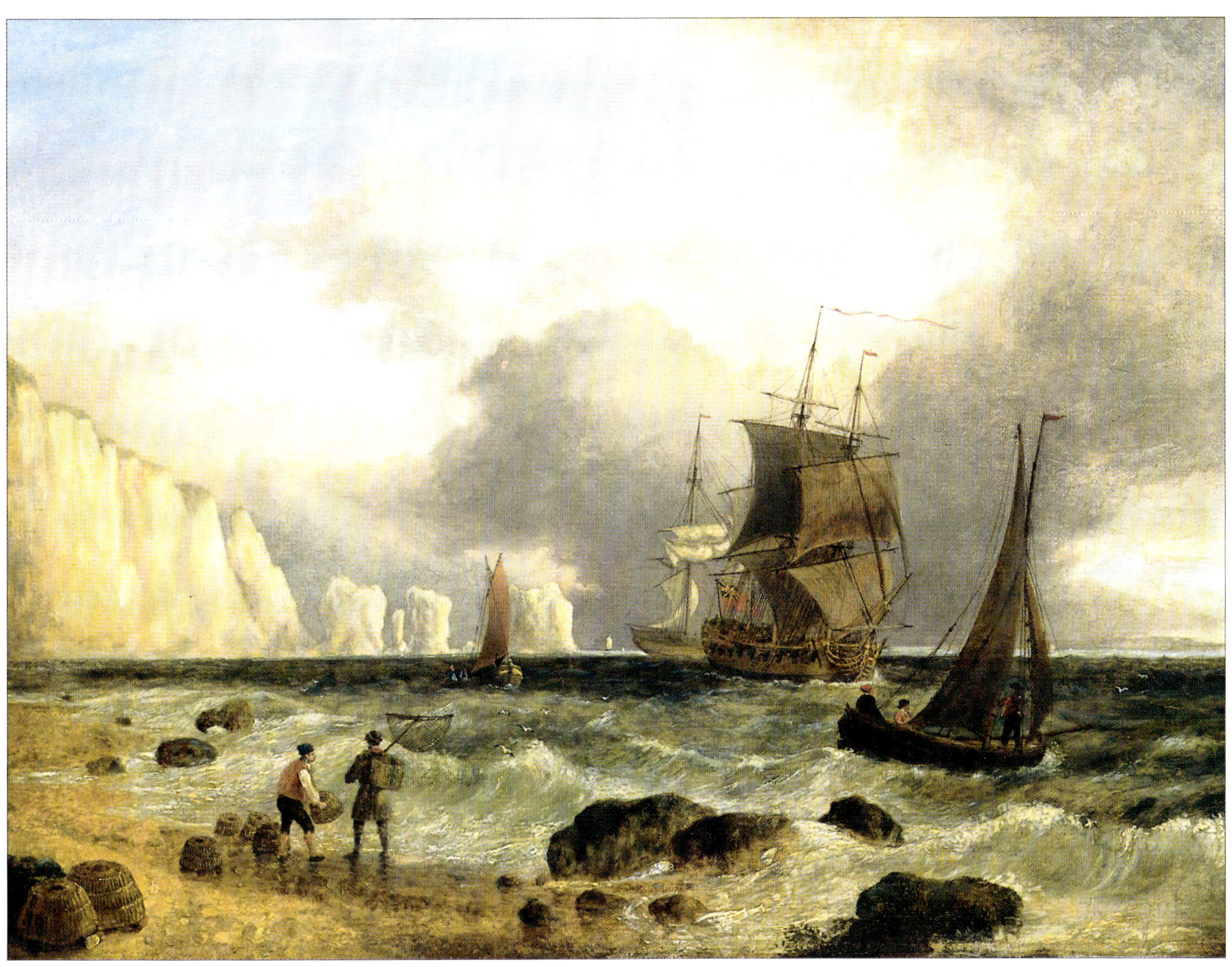

George Vincent, Alum Bay, Isle of Wight, oil on canvas, 12½ in x 16 in

This exceptional example of the work of Crome's pupil, George Vincent, illustrates how difficult identification can be. (Reproduced by kind permission of R. L. Bradbeer, Esq.)

Norwich; Vincent, whose own health at the time was indifferent to say the least, appeared considerably saddened by this event and, when considering his life, it seems that it was without the steadying influence of Crome that his misfortunes began.

In 1822 he married a lady who was reputed to be very wealthy. Encouraged by this, Vincent bought a house in Camden Town which was well beyond his means; whether his wife had no intention of sharing her money or whether she had put about rumours of wealth to attract her future husband we shall probably never know. The plain fact is that, having already got himself into debt, Vincent had to sell up and start all over again in a more modest environment. Even then he had to paint hard to keep going and an increasing tendency to drink too much only aggravated the situation. Some strange and unpleasant rumours abounded, probably some true and some fabricated as with all rumours, and there is mention in a letter from him to a Norwich associate in which he refers to a 'past folly' without going into detail. Apparently it caused a split with his parents, his father already being anxious about his intemperance which may well have contributed to the 'folly'. Whatever it was, it added to the burden of debt and even good sales of paintings were inadequate to get him out of trouble.

The result of all this was committal to Fleet Prison in 1824. Early in his sentence Vincent was allowed to visit Norwich in the company of a keeper in an attempt to sell some paintings quickly and cheaply. It seems that a number were left, hopefully, for future exhibitions. While in Norwich he met James Stark but his old friend took the same disapproving stance as Vincent's parents. Stark, like Crome, was so patently honest himself, he would have been unlikely to condone unseemly behaviour even in his friends.

Vincent spent three years in prison where, to his great relief, he was allowed his painting

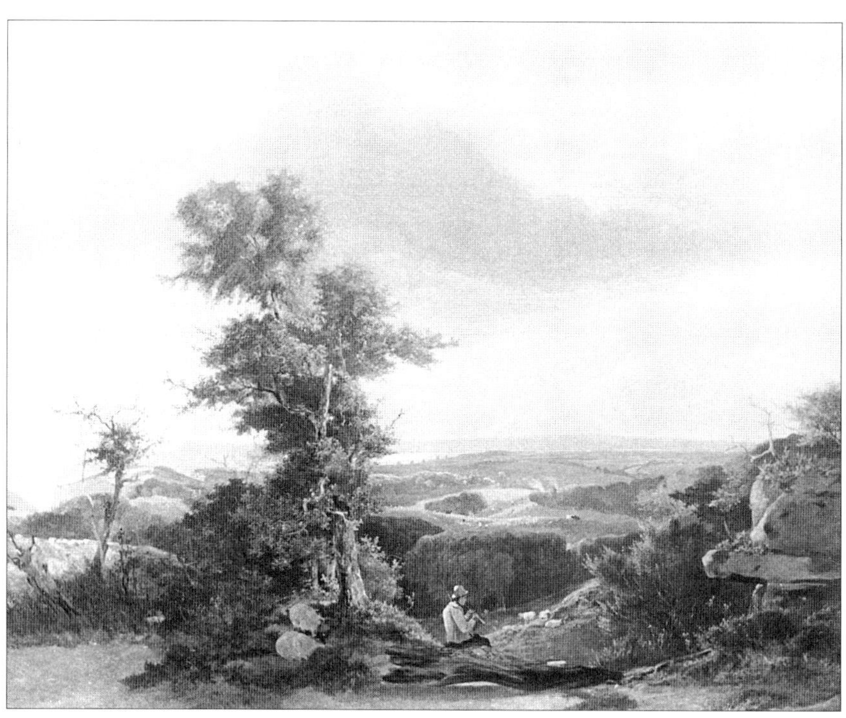

George Vincent, View near Pevensey Bay, Sussex, with Shepherd and Sheep, oil on canvas, 25½ in x 31½ in

materials and produced several small pieces – not his best. Being allowed to paint must have eased the frustration to some extent but his health was not good and the whole affair was something of an ordeal. It must have been a tremendous relief to be greeted on his release with news of a major and highly priced commission from James Wadmore.

Probably on the strength of this he made a second trip to Scotland, drawn by the attractive subject matter combined with the urge to get right away from painful associations and unpleasant memories. The last years of Vincent's life are shrouded in mystery, even the exact date and circumstances of his death are questionable. Quite likely he kept a low profile and moved around to escape his creditors; his health was not good and made worse by the burden of debt and the demon drink. It has even been suggested that he may have become so depressed that he took his own life.

Most authorities give his date of death as 1831, a painting having been exhibited the following year as by 'G. Vincent (deceased)'. Harold Day argues that this cannot be true having examined documents in the British Museum which state that George Vincent inherited part of his father's estate in 1833. Certainly he lived at most a couple of years after that but, if he had money at his disposal, the suicide theory seems unlikely. Another source says that he died in Bath; maybe it was his legacy that prompted the move. However, much of this is speculation. It is worth mentioning that Vincent himself discounted longevity; in the same letter of 1824 that referred to his 'past folly', he stated: 'I believe from the sufferings my mind experiences and has done for the last two years, that my stay in this world will not be for a very long duration.' Premonition or intention?

Whatever the circumstances of Vincent's death, it was yet another waste of tremendous talent and what should have been a productive and satisfying life. Vincent, understandably, was an uneven painter but, particularly in his early work, his best bore the hallmark of genius. To begin with his work strongly indicated the influence of John Crome but, as time went on, he developed a more original style which had something of John Constable whom he greatly admired, and even a flavour of Turner, different as these two were. One of his most ambitious oils shown at the British Institute in 1824, 'Distant view of Pevensey Bay, the Landing Place of King William the Conqueror,' had an unmistakably Turneresque sky although it must be said that, in his own right, Vincent was clever at making his skies, with unusual cloud formations, balance the rest of his pictures if a complicated composition needed help. David Hodgson wrote that George Vincent was 'a dashing painter and equal in his glorious depiction of ether to any other artist.'

His large oils are always the most impressive, the compositions good, the colour varied but harmonious including a judicious use of black unusual in the Norwich men; in spite of intricate

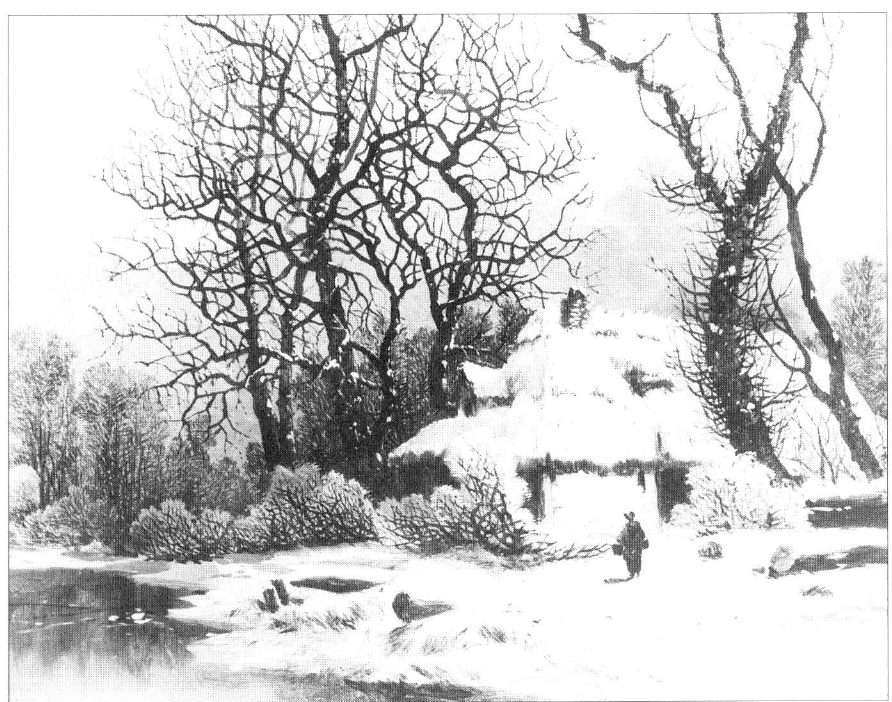

John Berney Ladbroke, Winter Scene, Norfolk, with Cottage and Figures, oil on canvas, 11 in x 15 in

detail, they somehow escape 'busyness'. He had paid attention to Crome's insistence on breadth which is possibly the explanation; sometimes his trees give the impression of every leaf having an identity yet they come together in a mass of glorious foliage in every conceivable natural green. At the time of his first visit to Scotland, Vincent was at the height of his powers and the Scottish paintings are, in the main, absolutely magnificent. The colour and texture of the rugged mountainous scenery, the beautiful reflective water and Vincents' ability to create mood and atmosphere all combine to make impressive works of art. A moonlit scene showing salmon poachers in the Highlands is wonderfully dramatic – his friend John Berney Crome must have envied the subject! Into his rural scenes, mainly Norfolk, Vincent contrives to pack an extraordinary variety of subject matter, figures, animals, changes in middle and distant landscape to accommodate water and boats or interesting features, without clutter; he seems to have delighted in the challenge of making the most complex compositions he could imagine but they are carefully thought out and well constructed. The same could be said of a number of coastal scenes with a variety of shipping painted, mainly, in the Yarmouth area. One personal attribute mentioned by many who have studied his work was his ability to paint amazingly quickly with great verve and panache in spite of the minute detail and intricate construction of his work. This ability must have been a godsend when selling paintings to finance pressing debts was all important.

The variation in quality which later manifested itself was obviously the result of ill health, stress and alcohol. While from time to time some of the old magic surfaced, Vincent never again reached the heights of the early 1820s. His colour sometimes became dark and almost menacing, its life and sparkle gone, no doubt reflecting his mood of the time. His second Scottish trip produced nothing with the drama, vision and intensity of the earlier tour. Some of his rare watercolours were painted at this time; perhaps he hoped to work them up later or perhaps they imposed less effort in their execution. The British Museum has eight late Scottish drawings but they are inconsistent and appear to lack the sort of concentration he had once been giving; in a strange way one would almost rather they were not there. It was a merciful Providence that spared John Crome the last ten years of his star pupil's life.

As John Crome and Robert Ladbroke married sisters it is hardly surprising that two of their sons should bear their mother's maiden name. Contemporary with John Berney Crome we have **John Berney Ladbroke** (1803-1879) Ladbroke's middle (painting) son, by far the best known and certainly the most prolific. One could not say categorically that as a painter he was better than his father but, and to the modern eye, his work suggests a more popular appeal.

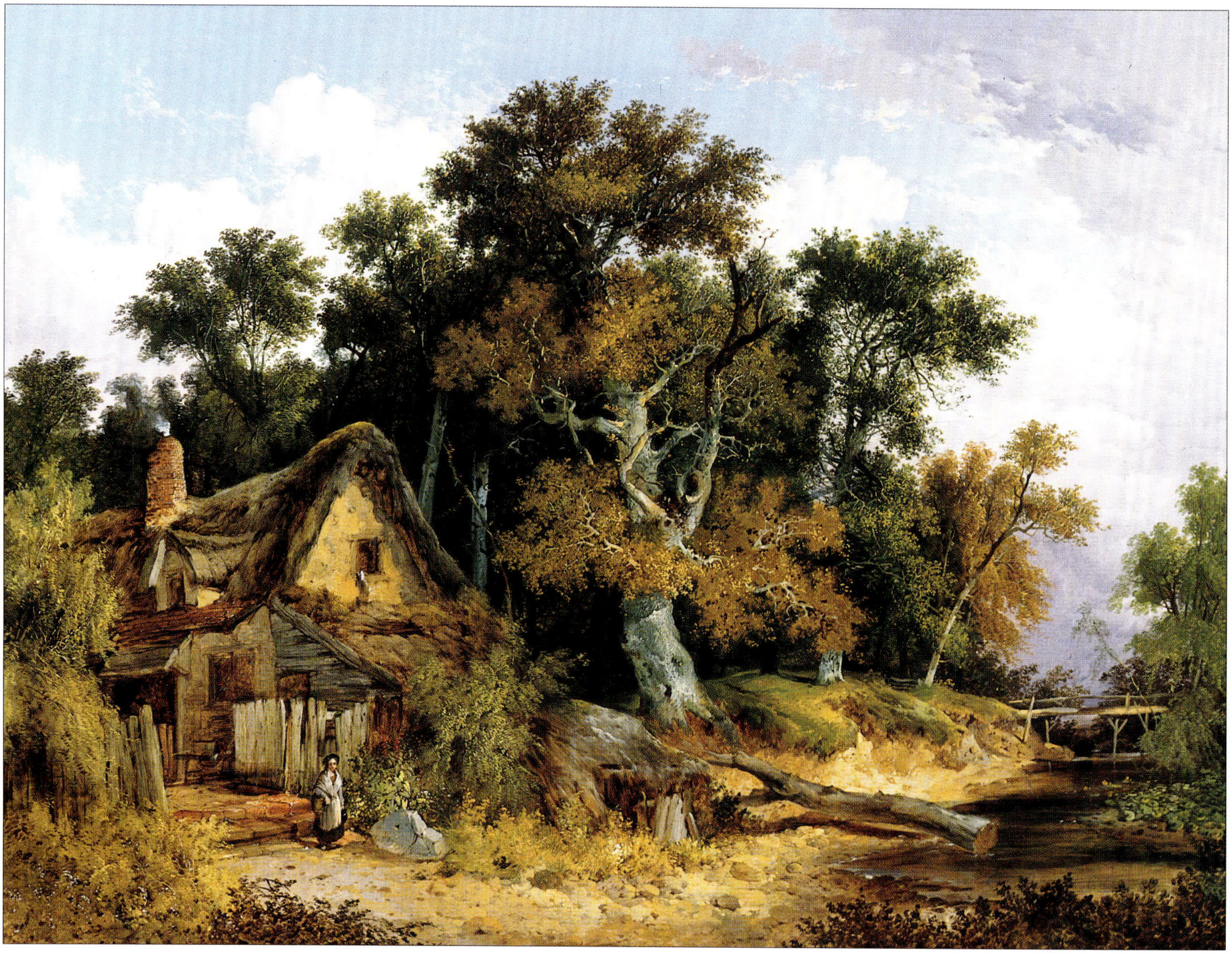

John Berney Ladbroke, "Cottage in a Wooded Landscape". Oil on canvas, 30 in x 40 in

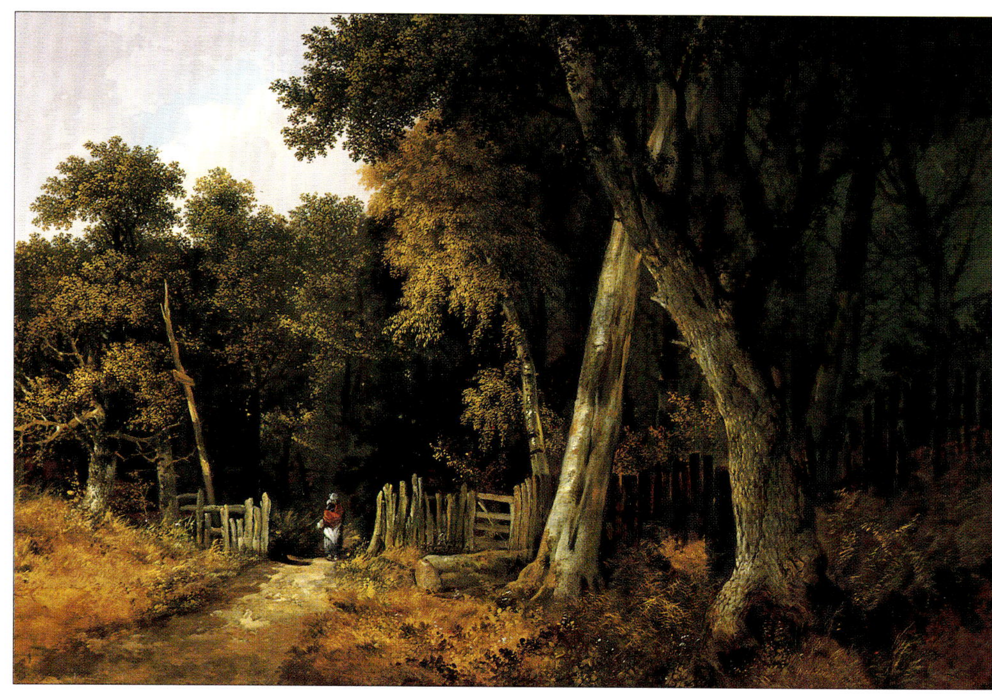

John Berney Ladbroke, Near Kimberley Park, oil on canvas, 1877, 24 in x 36 in

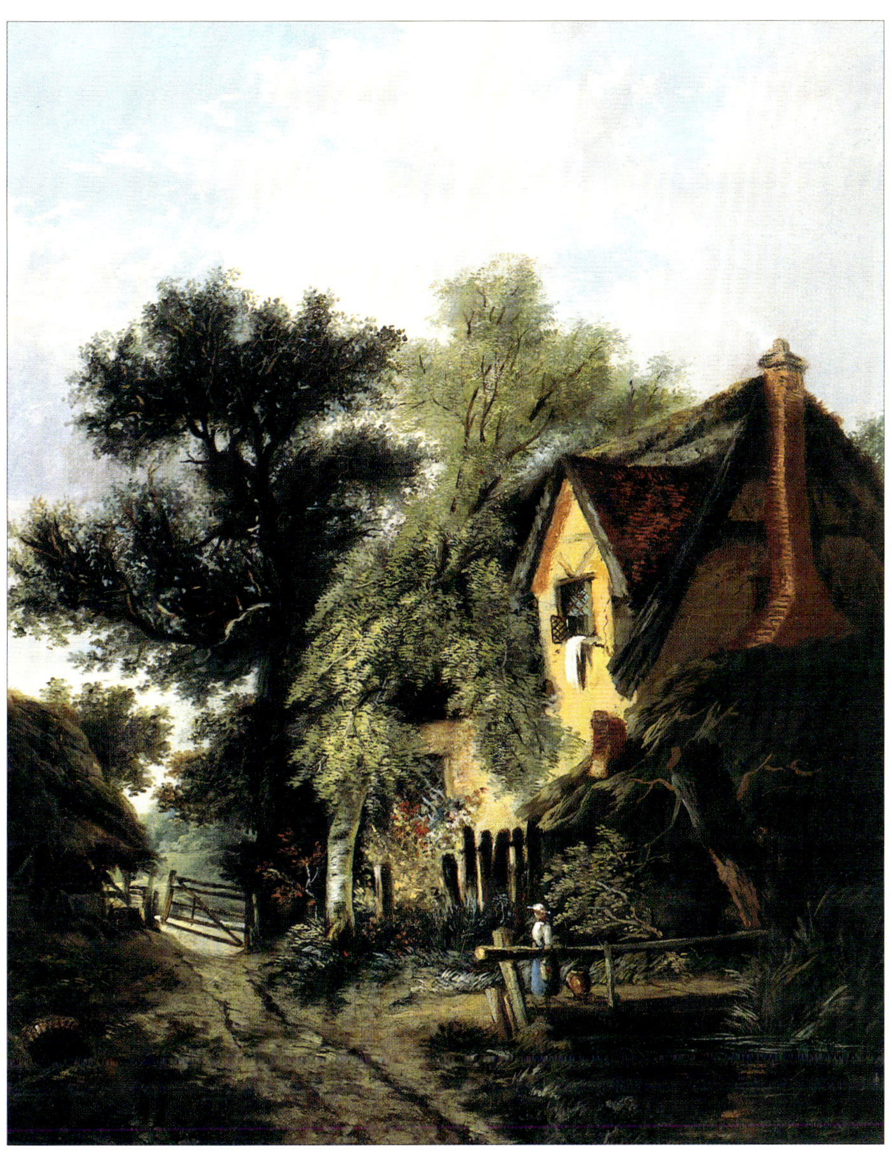

John Berney Ladbroke, Wooded Landscape with Farmhouse by Lane, oil on canvas, 20 in x 16 in

John Berney Ladbroke, whose mother died when he was very young, attended Norwich Grammar School after which his father, as well as giving a certain amount of tuition himself, placed him for about a year with his uncle, John Crome, presumably just before the secession. He exhibited with the seceded society at quite an early age and, in 1818, showed seven works with the Norwich Society, thereafter exhibiting regularly in Norwich and London for most of his life. He joined his father's teaching practice and, with his brother Henry, took over a number of the established pupils as well as new recruits. Always he let it be known that he was prepared to travel around Norfolk giving private tuition in student's homes or at country schools. He appears to have been a popular teacher, including among his pupils John Middleton, William Barnes Freeman and his niece, Maria Margitson.

As well as advertising himself as landscape painter and drawing master, he also offered tuition in lithography in which he had, to some extent, trained himself in order to help his father with the latter's mammoth project depicting all 700 Norfolk churches. He installed a lithographic press in his father's house, Scole's Green, Norwich, and, although at the time he still needed much practice himself, his technique rapidly improved; no doubt adding the extra subject to the teaching repertoire was to help pay for the press. Father and son must both have spent many hours on this collection and it must have seemed sad to John Berney that it was not actually published until a year after Robert Ladbroke's death.

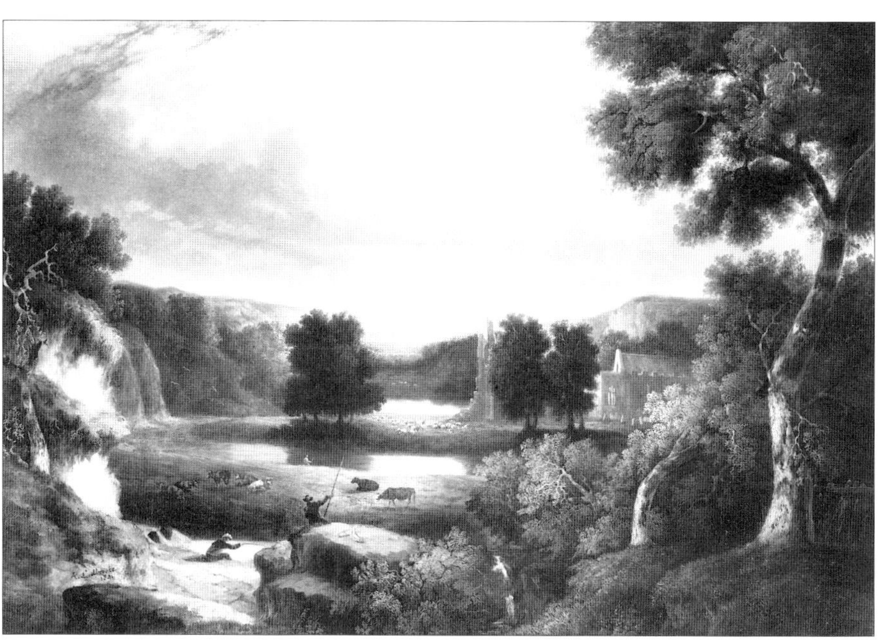

Henry Ladbroke, Bolton Abbey, oil on canvas, 36 in x 51 in

A typical example of Henry Ladbroke's slightly stylistic approach but, nevertheless, a very beautiful and well composed picture

Travelling around Norfolk with his father on the church project and to the various pupils living outside the city introduced him to a wide range of local subjects. He also visited the North of England with Henry *c.*1840 and, on occasion, Scotland, Wales and the Lake District, all of which provided good painting material. Although he visited France and Holland, he preferred British subjects.

Certainly Norfolk landscapes show John Berney Ladbroke at his best, perhaps because there he felt most at home and more receptive to the influence of Crome. In his earlier years he ventured into still-life from time to time, thereby influencing his niece, Maria Margitson, to take the subject further, but landscape was his first love. Wooded landscapes had a strong appeal and certainly he was clever with trees; he had a way of using greens with a soft, silvery light, in fact his use of light and good sense of tone is a particular feature of his work. His eye for a good composition never left him, nor did his attention to detail often enhanced by a sensitive use of impasto. The fact that he is sometimes accused of 'prettiness' is due largely to his choice of subjects, the cottage in a country landscape touch, but I feel he was simply being true to what he saw and conforming partly to the fashion of his time. He was in many ways a more capable artist than his father and, at his peak, often far outshone him. His skill with animals was a further asset; the notoriously difficult cow presented him with no problem and he patently had a soft spot for donkeys.

As he grew older, maybe owing to failing or changing eyesight, his colour changed, becoming darker and less harmonious. Sometimes rather strange combinations creep in giving otherwise well composed work a slightly artificial appearance. Nevertheless he obviously made a success of his life and had his retirement home built to his own specification on a plot of land he had bought on Mousehold Heath. The property, known as Kett's Castle Villa, stood fairly high and the central feature was a small tower giving wonderful views over the city. A slightly more individual but idiosyncratic touch was the incorporation of his personal monogram into the archway over the entrance gate, on one of the back walls, over a fireplace inside and cast in a stained glass window. He continued painting in this haven almost until the time of his death.

The second son of Robert Ladbroke (the eldest did not paint) was **Henry Ladbroke** (1800-1869) who, in spite of his artist father and uncle and one of his school teachers, Charles Hodgson, wanted to enter the Church when he finished school. He must have shown some artistic talent for his father brought pressure to bear on him to follow in his own footsteps. Henry, therefore, was taught primarily by his father and had a short period of tuition under his uncle, John Crome. By the age of 15 he was exhibiting with the Norwich Society; in 1818 he exhibited with the seceding society but was back with the main Norwich Society by 1821. This was well before his father's return but the younger generation felt less strongly about the original disagreement. Initially Henry was painting small works covering a wide variety of subjects but soon graduated to larger landscapes which were very competently executed.

He developed a style that was quite personal to him and it has been said, although it might be hard to prove, that he was the most detailed of all the Norwich painters. He complained in his 'dottings' that his father's training had involved more copying than properly studying from nature, suggesting that this passion for closely observed detail was always with him. Trees were important to him and he must have spent many hours in their execution, putting in every minute feature of the bark and abundant but almost individual leaves. Equally detailed were the man-made additions to his wooded landscapes, and every incidental down to the hedgerows and even grasses was obediently observed. Although all this did give much of his work a slightly stylised appearance, at best his painting is really beautiful in terms of fine craftsmanship. There is a classical feel about his compositions, a romantic classicism rather in the Italian mould with emphasised light and shade.

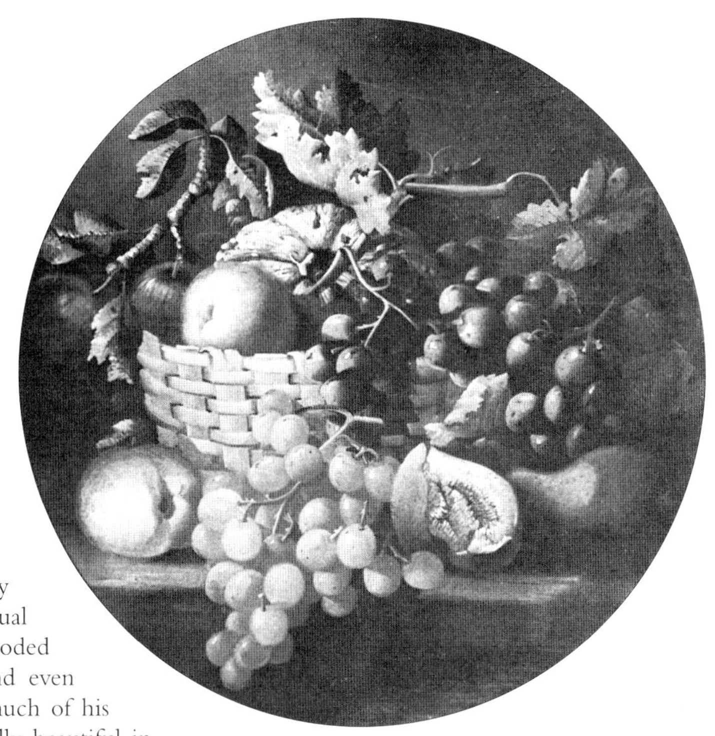

Maria Margitson, 1860, niece of J. B. Ladbroke, Still-life, oil on canvas, 14 in dia.

Henry, as we know, visited Yorkshire with his brother *c.*1840 and he exhibited several Yorkshire subjects in Norwich. Like his brother he became very involved with his father's teaching practice and his circuit included Cromer, North Walsham, King's Lynn, Dereham and Bury St. Edmunds as well as a number of Norfolk villages. As a result of many hours spent travelling and teaching and the time-consuming detail of his paintings, his output was necessarily limited and this explains the reason for his work not having the recognition it deserves. He is known to have had a tolerant and pleasing manner which obviously endeared him to an ever increasing band of pupils. In his teaching days in Norwich, he advertised himself as a teacher of writing as well as drawing but with what results seems not to be known. His own 'dottings', a collection of often quite pungent anecdotes about his father, uncle and other Norwich painters, was published in the *Eastern Daily Press* as recently as 1921. He had much to say about John Sell Cotman who he obviously admired; his statement that 'his [Cotman's] genius was of a much higher cast – infinitely more elegant and classical', suggests that perhaps Cotman was at least in part the inspiration behind his own classical approach.

After living for a time in North Walsham, Henry moved to King's Lynn although he actually died in Norwich having returned to be with his daughter.

Frederick Ladbroke (1810-1865) the youngest son of Robert, deviated completely from the family tradition. Although he did produce some indifferent landscapes, he became by profession a portrait painter, establishing himself in Bury St. Edmunds quite early in his career. Although few portraits are recorded, they suggest that he was competent in his chosen sphere. According to Henry Ladbroke's daughter, it was uncle Frederick who put the figures in her father's pictures. The one likeness I have seen of Frederick Ladbroke indicates a kindly and contented personality; compared to the unfortunate younger Cromes, the second generation of painting Ladbrokes appear to have led happier and more successful lives although blessed with no greater talent or early opportunity.

Maria Margitson (1832-1896) was John Berney Ladbroke's niece who trained partly with her uncle, assisting him for a time in his teaching practice, and there is one shared painting on record.

She was inspired by her uncle's few early examples of still-life painting and went on to take some lessons with Eloise Harriet Stannard, something of an honour, for that lady was usually too busy to have a need for pupils. Maria's paintings of fruit and flowers are of high quality and well composed. It would be hard for anyone to reach the exceptional standard of 'E.H.' but the best of Miss Margitson can hold its own well in the sphere of 19th century still-life painting.

She rarely exhibited outside Norwich and little is known of her personal life.

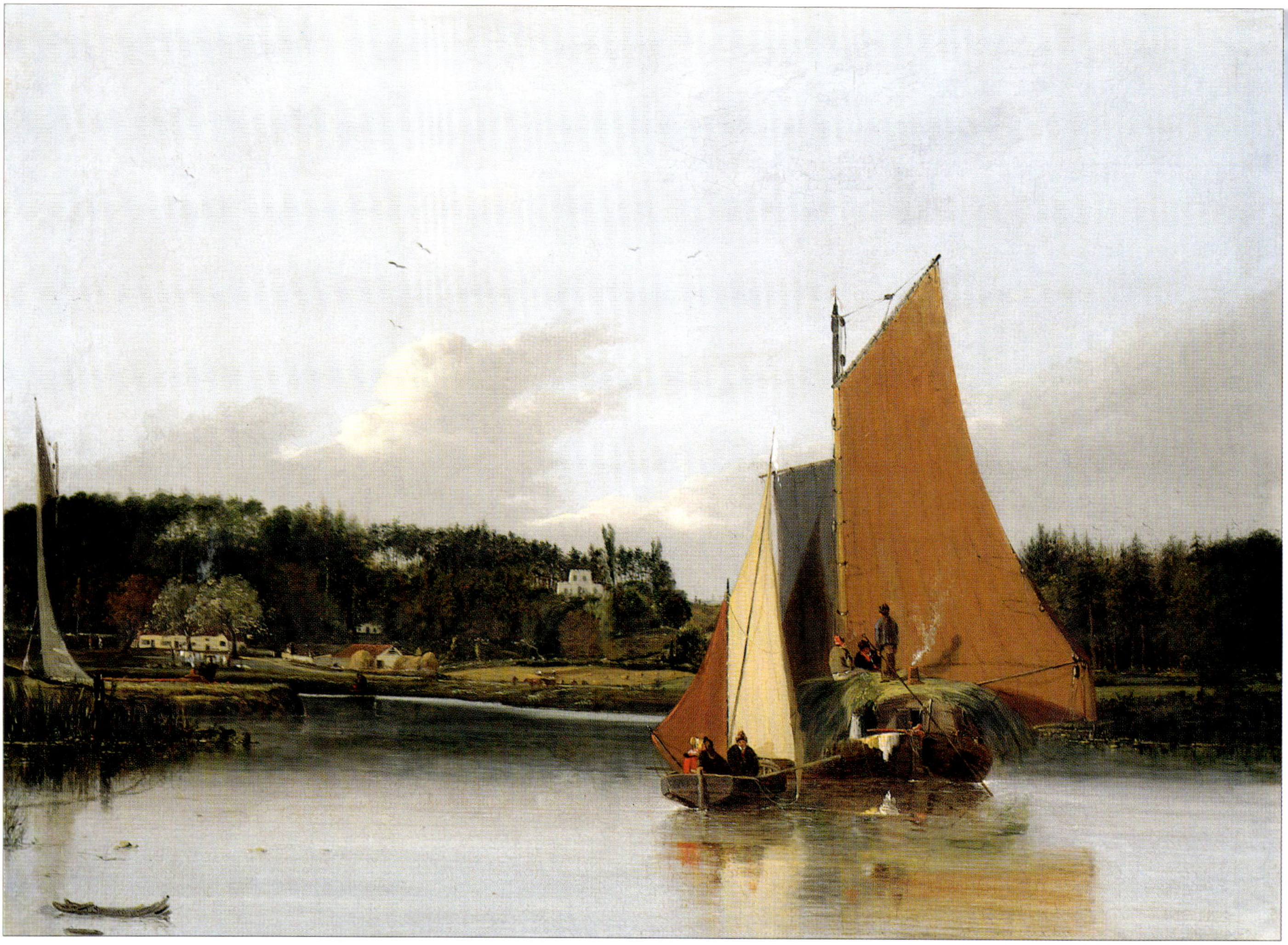

Joseph Stannard,
Boats on the Yare near
Bramerton, Norfolk.
Oil on wood,
18⅛ in x 25½ in

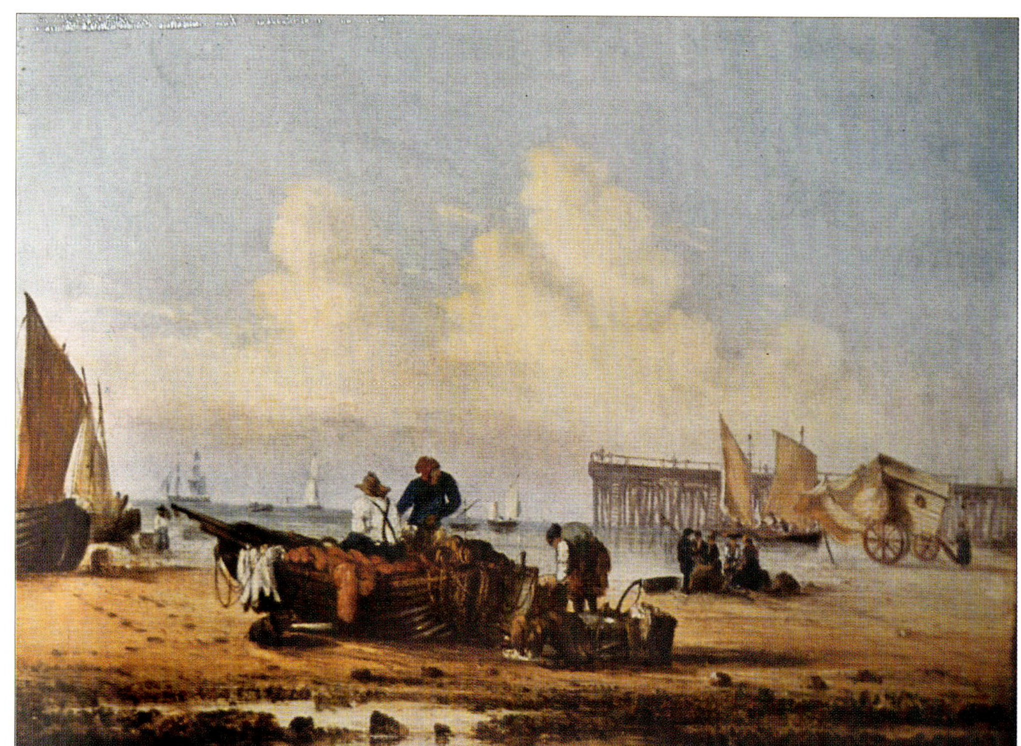

Joseph Stannard,
Fishermen by Yarmouth
Jetty, oil on canvas,
14 in x 18 in

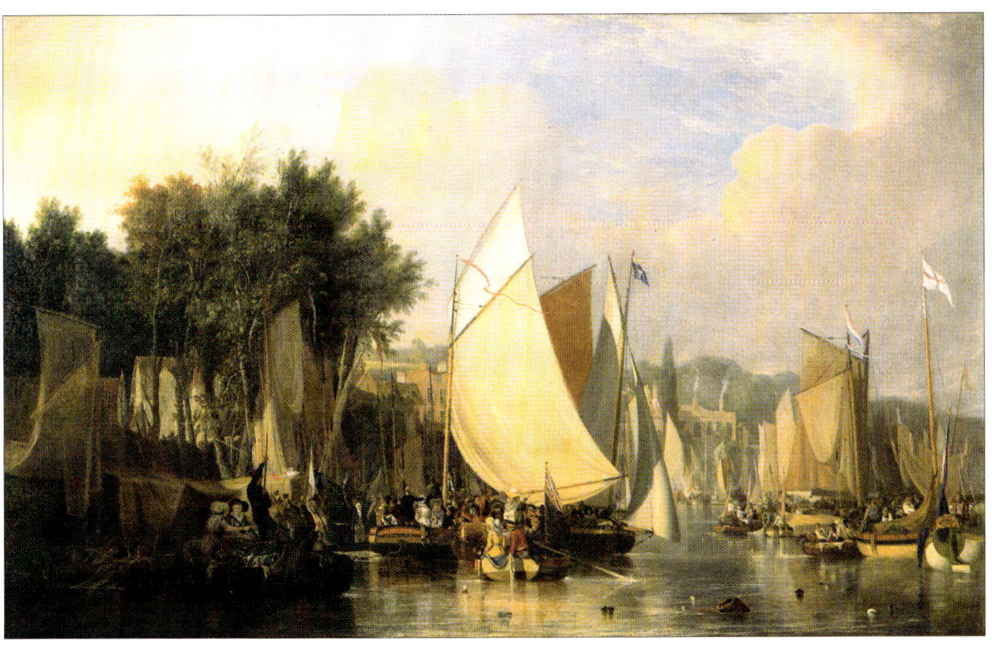

Joseph Stannard,
Thorpe Water Frolic, Afternoon
1824, oil on canvas,
43¼in x 69¼in

Chapter 4

THE STANNARD FAMILY

After Crome and Cotman, **Joseph Stannard** (1797-1830) would generally be classed as the most important member of the Norwich School and, by any standards, a most distinguished painter. His premature death at the age of only thirty-three was no less than a tragedy for British painting.

Joseph Stannard attended Norwich Grammar School and showed such a genuine aptitude for drawing and painting that, at the age of 16, his parents tried to apprentice him to John Crome, the most important Norwich artist at the time. Crome asked such an extortionate fee that it was beyond the means of the Stannard parents; undoubtedly Crome was a busy man and would probably only have considered pupils who could make it well worth his while financially. The Stannards, however, took it as something of a slight and apprenticed their son to Robert Ladbroke who had already been giving him some informal teaching. Ladbroke's teaching was considered far from the level of Crome's but he was a stickler for good drawing and undoubtedly gave Stannard a good grounding in draughtsmanship. His pupil was so gifted in his own right that this was ideal; from the basis of well taught drawing, he was perfectly capable of developing on his own. It has been said that Ladbroke was so impressed by the sheer genius of this young student that he waived any tuition fees, even offering him £10 a year to stay and work in his master's studio.

Joseph Stannard had a pronounced flair for portraiture as well as the talent shown in the landscapes and seascapes for which he is best known. By 1818 he was taking on portrait commissions as well as executing character studies of his own. Perhaps the best known of these is the famous 'Norwich Ratcatcher', but others, such as 'Old Lying Plummer', 'Old Peter the Huntsman', 'Old Blind Dan', and 'Joe Doe the Butcher's Porter', have the same characteristic feeling of identity. One early exhibit, 1819, was entitled 'Scene in a Norwich Alehouse' depicting some familiar Norwich figures which made it something of a talking point. Joseph himself was not a drinking man but the inns provided good subject matter.

Joseph Stannard was born in the parish of St. Andrew, Norwich, the elder son of a musician, Abraham Stannard. He never left the city for long and most of his landscapes are local views. He enjoyed exploring the surrounding countryside and the Norfolk coast in search of congenial

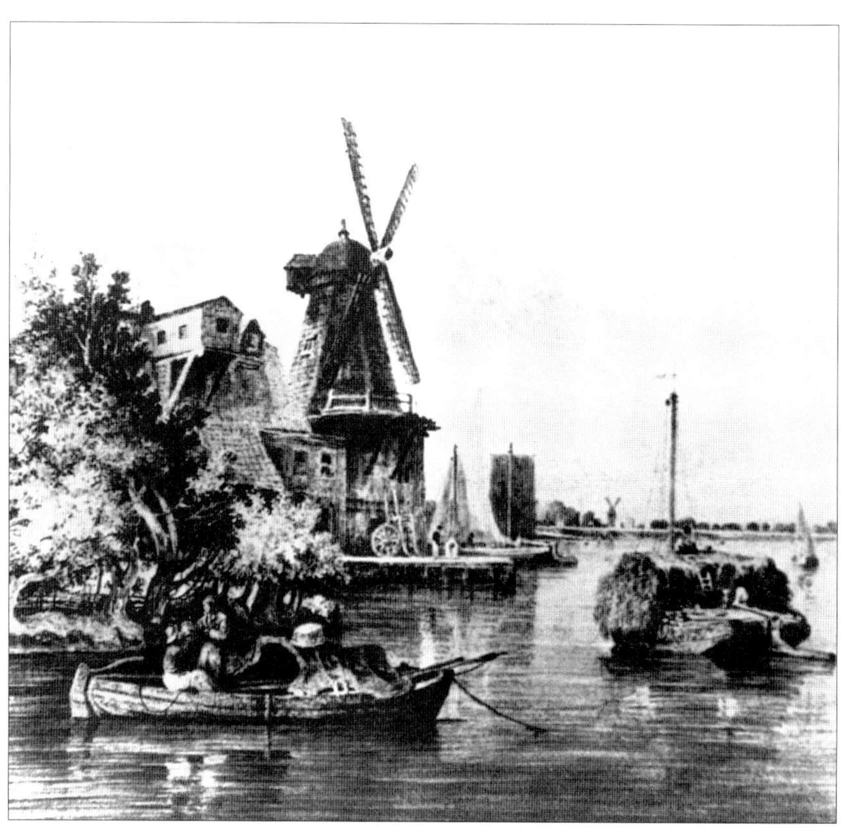

Joseph Stannard,
On the Thames, watercolour,
8¾ in x 8¾ in

subjects. Most of his accomplished pencil drawings would have been done *in situ* and later often used as the basis for larger oil paintings although some of the small oils have the spontaneity of having been completed on the spot. In 1821 Joseph visited Holland, a visit which had a profound and lasting effect on his work. He made many pencil and crayon sketches of the Dutch rivers and coastline, later to be worked up into those magnificent marine oils which owe much more to the influence of the Dutch masters than his mentors of the Norwich School. From the time of his stay in Holland, the sea and ships had taken over as his chosen subjects. His intense love of all things nautical combined with his inherent skill and devastating honesty to produce some of the most poetic and sensitive sea paintings of all time. At last these are being given the recognition they richly deserve. The main reason Joseph Stannard appears to have been neglected lies in the relative scarcity of his work. His declining health and early death naturally limited his output; those paintings in private collections tend to stay where they are and it is only comparatively recently that the public has found it easier to visit the great collections.

Around 1820, probably at meetings of the Norwich Society with whom Joseph Stannard exhibited as well as with the seceded group, he met Emily Coppin whose father was a past President of the Society. Emily had visited Holland with her father and been much influenced by the techniques of the Dutch painters particularly, for her, the flower painters. No doubt it was *chez* Coppin that Joseph Stannard was inspired to visit Holland himself, the home of these wonderful artists, and assimilate all he could from their example. He was principally inspired by Berchem and the van der Veldes, making reference copies of their work in the Rijksmuseum but, to quote Andrew Hemingway on Stannard's own work: 'He achieved more natural illusion of light than they usually did and painted in a far brighter range of colours'.

Following the visit to Holland, Stannard's interest in seascapes and river scenes continued to grow and, in spite of his all too short painting career, he left some extremely powerful examples – sadly, as I have said, they are rarely seen outside important public and private collections. His own importance in the sphere of marine painting is such that he is almost the most significant British marine painter, well outside the Norwich School. Even leaving aside the Dutch influence and any use made of the techniques he imported from Holland, Joseph Stannard's oils have a personality, a charisma, belonging to him alone. The complete confidence of his brushwork and

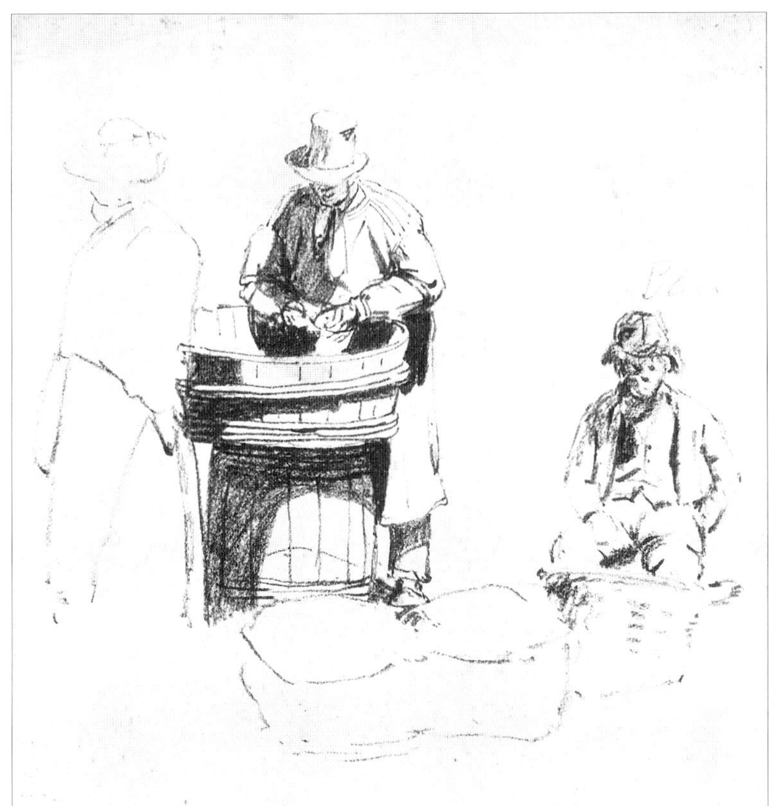

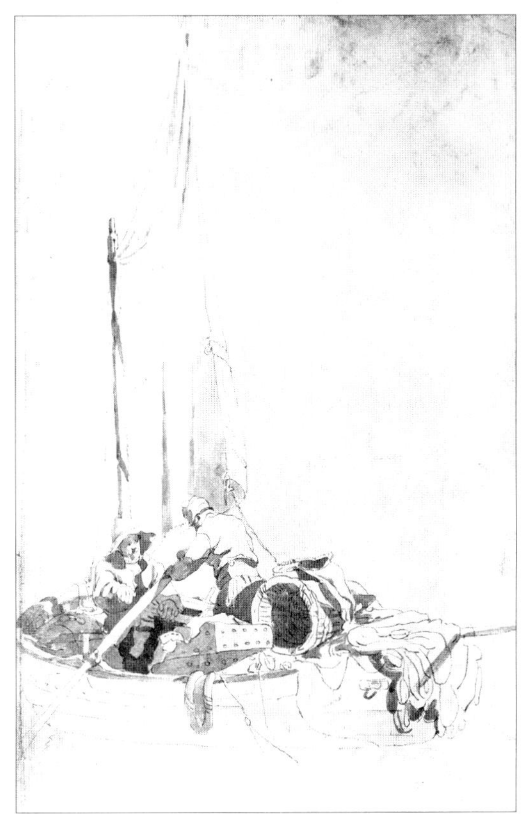

Joseph Stannard, Man at a Swill Tub, chalk, 7 in x 6½ in

Joseph Stannard, Fishing Boat with Fishermen, pencil and wash, 14½ in x 9 in

his impeccable colour sense, the clever tonal valuation and colour coordination, the complex glazes and the effective but sparing use of impasto, all add to their authority but still there is an intangible magic. Thinking later of John Middleton, one cannot help but wonder if such painters are given a special blessing to compensate, in a way, for their cruelly shortened lives.

Perhaps Stannard's most important commission, certainly the best known, came from Colonel John Harvey in 1823; he requested a large painting, 'the finest picture you can', of the Thorpe Water Frolic. This amazing work, now in Norwich Castle Museum, is packed with interest and activity. Hundreds of figures are involved, including musicians with their various instruments, while innumerable boats of all sorts and sizes jostle with each other on the shimmering, reflective water. Joseph's own boat (he was an accomplished oarsman and this boat won honours in the 1825 Frolic) is depicted on the right and Colonel Harvey himself appears as an important figure on his boat, *Sylph,* centre left. The whole scene is beautifully set with the elegant trees to the left and the misty silhouettes of the city in the distance. The *Norwich Mercury,* invariably favourably disposed towards Joseph Stannard's work, commented on the manner in which 'truth and fiction were so nicely blended'.

Months of labour went into this masterpiece to Joseph's cost. It had taken precedence over all other work but, during this time, the general post-Napoleonic war economic situation had worsened and Colonel Harvey found himself unable to meet his obligation. Joseph was left extremely short of money. It was at this time that he started exhibiting extensively in London in order to keep his head above water. Successful sales and the fact that by 1825 Colonel Harvey had claimed his picture meant that he could return to Norwich with an easy mind and attend to local commissions that were again starting to come in.

In January 1826, having made some financial recovery, he married Emily Coppin and they moved to a little house at the end of St. Giles' Terrace, Norwich, which is still standing. Sadly, only two years later, Joseph's health started to deteriorate and he died of tuberculosis in 1830. His devoted wife spared nothing, trying many doctors and many treatments, but all to no avail.

Reverting to Joseph's Stannard's work, which in many minds is dominated by those all powerful seascapes, it may come as a surprise to know that, as well as the numerous marine subjects drawn as preparatory sketches for oils, there are some 50 recorded drawings of figures and animals. Most of these are in the British Museum and Norwich Castle, beautifully and

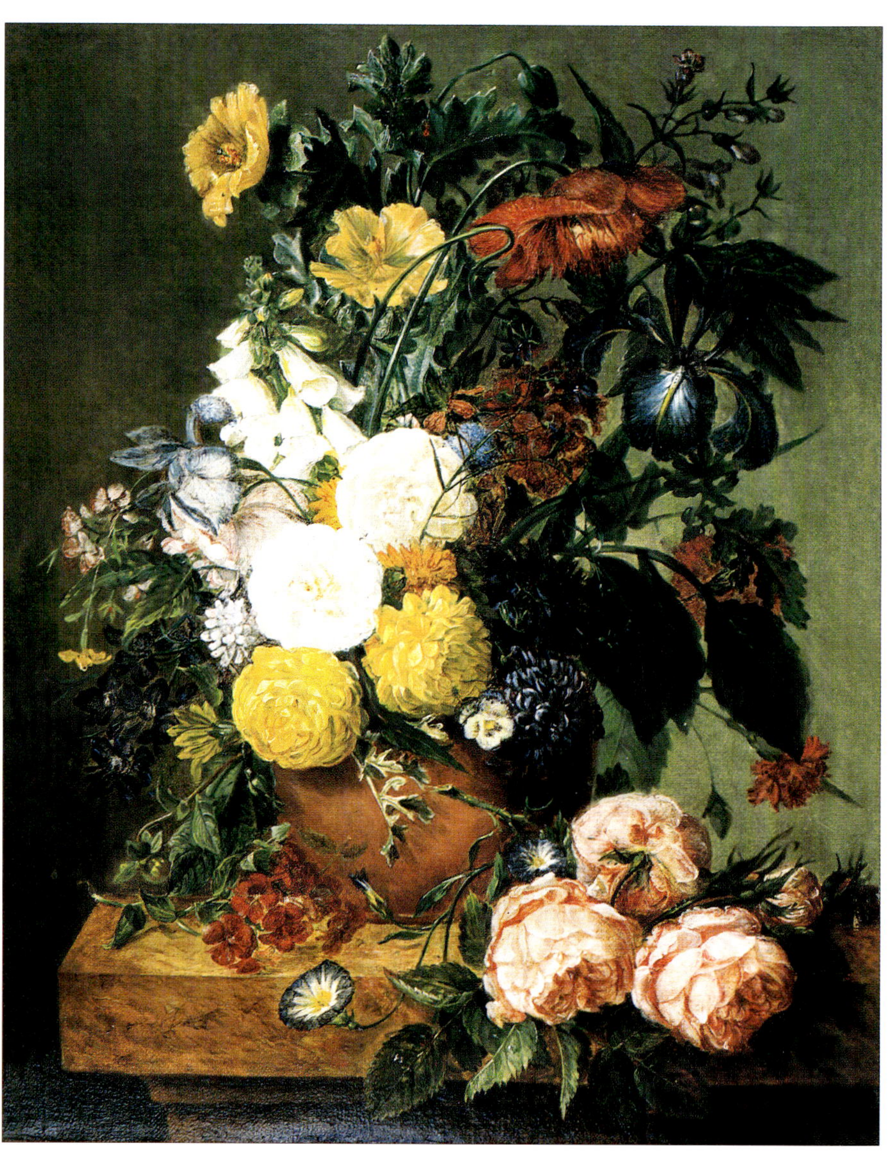

Emily (Mrs Joseph) Stannard, Mixed Summer Flowers in an Urn on a Marble Ledge, oil on canvas, 15 in x 11 in

sympathetically rendered in pencil, crayon and charcoal, sometimes with a light watercolour wash; there are also 34 drawings of Norwich churches in the Castle Museum. Virtually no suggestion of Ladbroke's influence shows in Joseph's oil painting, but certainly Ladbroke's early teaching in the basic skills of draughtsmanship paid handsome dividends. One is struck by the supreme confidence of Joseph's line work and the consummate skill of his shading. With a simple pencil he could produce seemingly infinite tone values and he unerringly placed his shadows where they would produce the right contrasting notes to bring every nuance to life. While many of the pencil drawings were early studies, towards the end of his life when he became too weak to cope with large canvases he worked in crayon to great effect. Simplicity was always the keynote but combined with the masterly skill that gave the required result with the minimum of fuss. He has appropriately been called the master of line. Crayon is a more difficult medium than many realise and an artist needs a good colour sense and a refined taste to obviate a feeling of crudeness. Joseph Stannard had both in good measure and the sensitive little works in the Victoria & Albert Museum as well as in Norwich show that physical weakness detracted not one whit from Stannard's high ideals.

Watercolour, although sometimes used with pencil drawing in carefully controlled washes or, in a different context, to add significant touches of colour, was not really a Stannard medium. However, as with many good draughtsmen, etching became a small part of his repertoire. These etchings are very rare but, as might be expected, of superb quality and to many, even of his

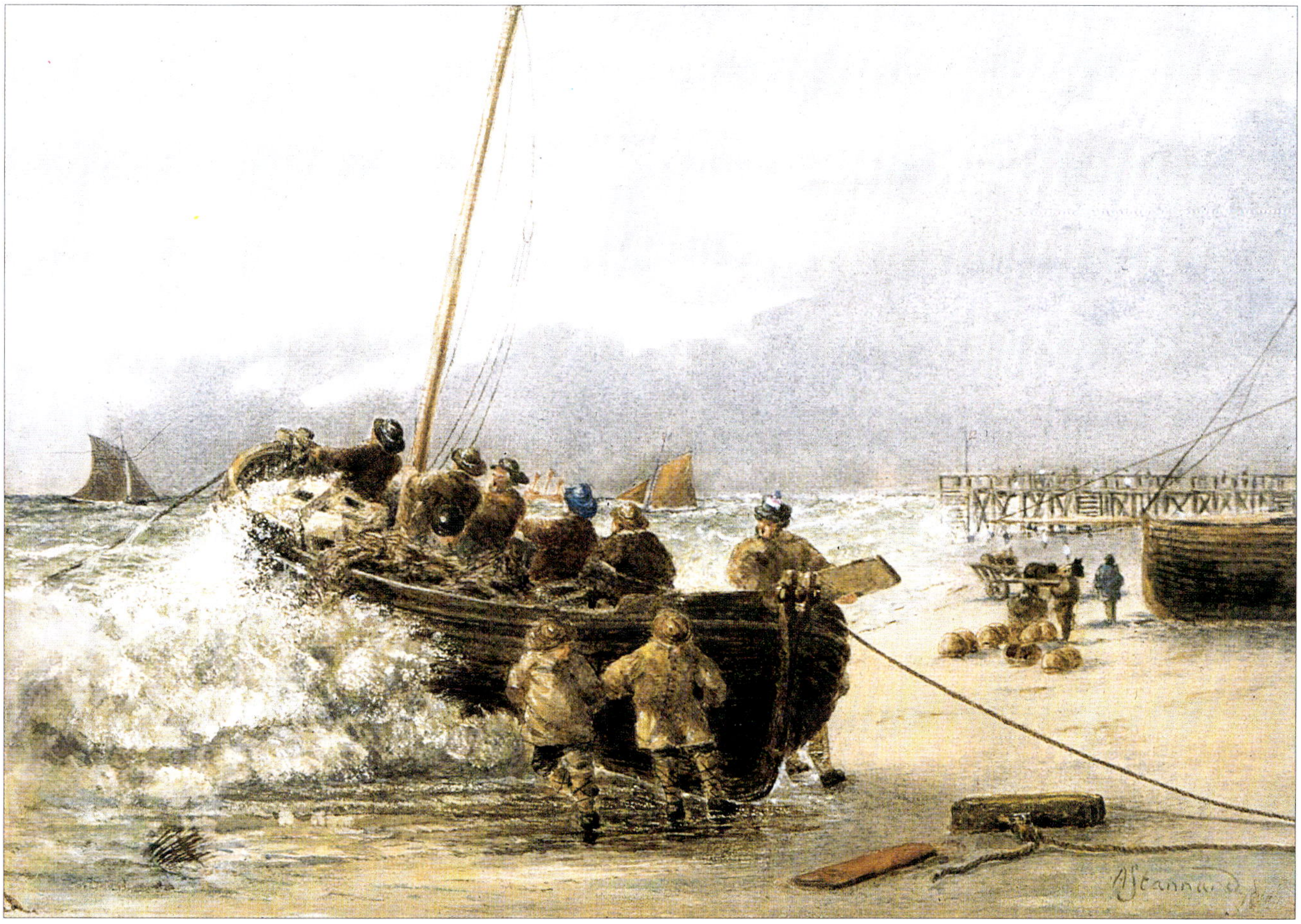

Alfred Stannard, Launching Fishing Boats – Windy Weather off Great Yarmouth, oil on panel, 27 in x 39 in

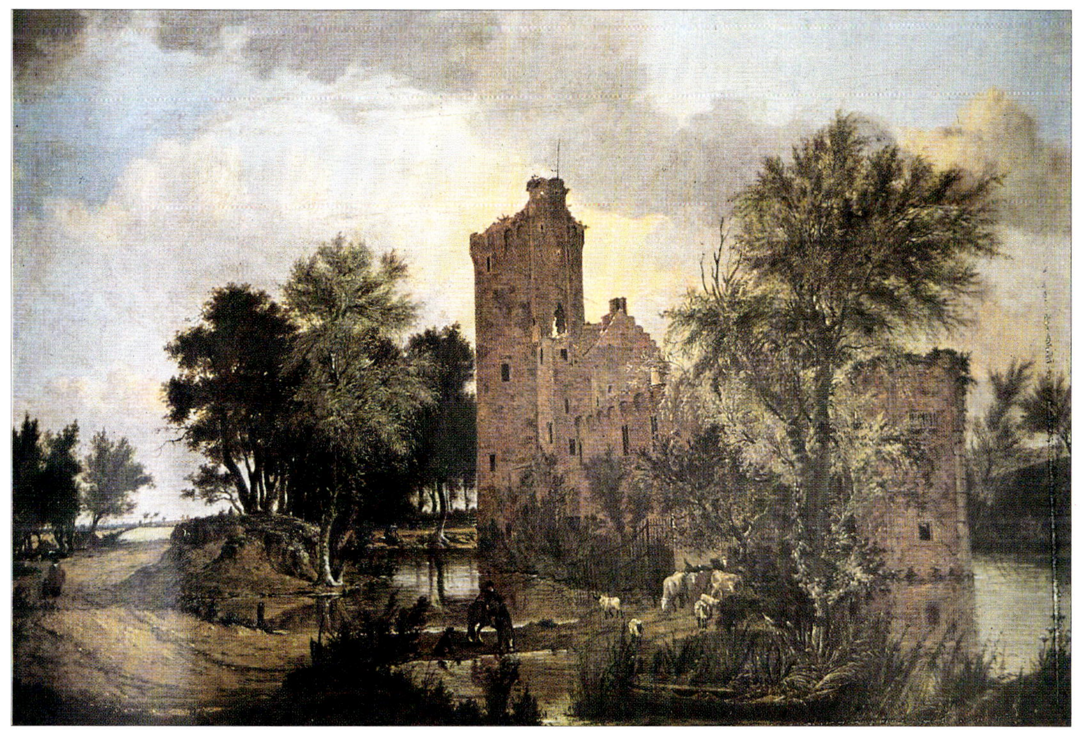

Alfred Stannard, Caistor Castle, Norfolk, oil, 30 in x 40 in

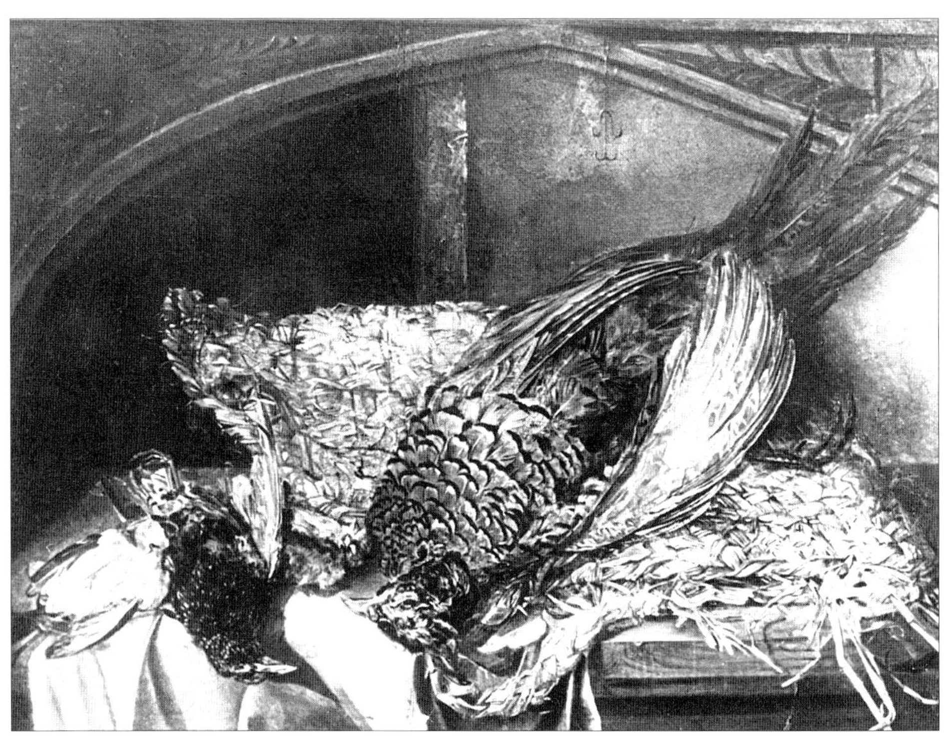

Emily (Mrs Joseph) Stannard, Still-life of Dead Game with Rush Basket on a Wooden Ledge, oil on panel, 12 in x 17 in

admirers, unknown. Eleven executed between 1820 and 1827 were published in book form after his death; copies can be seen in the British Museum and Norwich Castle Museum. Stannard also taught etching to the Rev. E.T. Daniell whose reputation rests largely on this particular art form.

The fact that Joseph Stannard was an expert sailor and oarsman has already been mentioned – a boat was essential to him for getting the angles he wanted on many of his subjects and a means of close observation of detail. He was also a brilliant skater, a different artistry into which he was probably initiated during his stay in Holland. There were some good skating winters in the early 19th century and Joseph became the source of much admiration in Norwich. Numerous people turned out to watch the handsome and stylish young skater; this may well have led to an increased interest in his painting as admirers sought out more information about their idol. Harold Day quotes from an exhibition catalogue printed years after the artist's death:

> His taste was elegant and it was not only displayed in his Art but very forcibly alike in his boating and skating. He was the most elegant skater of his day in that time when the present railway station and the meadows surrounding it were wont to be the resort of the city in the old fashioned winters of years gone by. There Joe Stannard used to take his sport on a piece of ice a few yards square and excite the admiration of all by elegance and perfection by which he 'cut' all the difficult figures of which the art was capable.

After Joseph's death **Emily Stannard** (1803-1885), or Mrs Joseph Stannard as she liked to be called and even sometimes signed her pictures, continued painting for over 50 years until well into her eighties. Both the Coppin parents had been good amateur painters giving her an artistic background even before she met Joseph Stannard and before the visit to Holland in 1820 where she copied the work of van Huysum and others and closely studied their work in the Rijksmuseum. She became a highly skilled painter of flowers and still-life after the Dutch manner; at 17 she was awarded the Gold Medal of the Society of Arts for an original flower painting, again in 1821 for a painting of fruit and in 1828 for one of game. She was made an Honorary member of the Norwich Society in 1831, an honour long overdue for the *Norwich Mercury* had commented in 1823: 'She is an honour to art, an honour to the city, and an honour to her sex, by the taste, industry, and knowledge her beautifully disposed and elaborated pictures display. Can we say more? Ought we to have said less?'

Her beautiful flower paintings certainly have real quality largely due to her painstaking study of the Dutch and Flemish masters combined with a natural talent and an impeccable colour

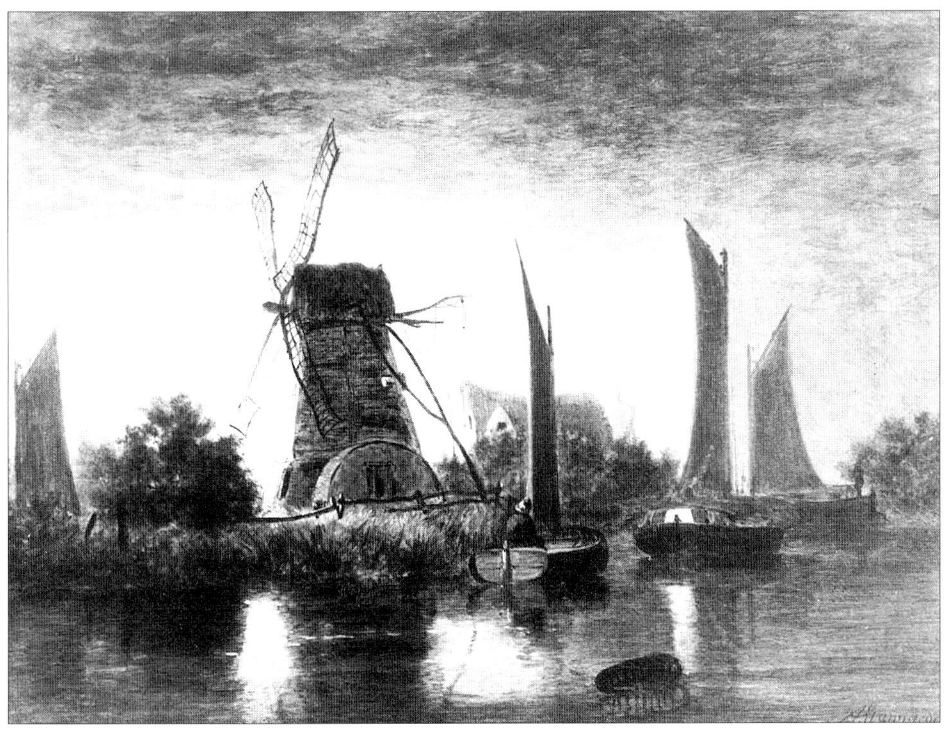

Alfred Stannard,
A Mill by the Norfolk Broads with Wherries, oil on canvas, 12 in x 16 in

sense. It is no exaggeration to say that she was easily the greatest British woman still-life painter of her time, a distinction which was to be handed down to her niece, Eloise Harriet. While I particularly enjoy the flower paintings, I can only admire the quality and realism of the game. I admit to finding the subject distasteful.

Joseph and Emily's daughter **Emily Stannard** (1827-1894) was born just two years before her father's death. She had some artistic talent and was trained by her mother. The senior Emily supplemented her own income by teaching as well as painting for exhibition and in this she was later assisted by her daughter The younger Emily continued for a while after her mother's death but died herself only nine years later.

Alfred Stannard (1806-1889) was born nine years after his brother Joseph but the two became very close, eventually sharing a studio and even working on the same painting. Alfred naturally learned a great deal from early lessons with his brother; it has been said that Alfred's work is comparatively pedestrian but too much has been made of the difference between them by making such comparisons. Without such a shining example before him, Alfred's reputation might well have been much greater today; albeit in a different way, he was a fine painter in his own right. It was towards the end of Joseph's life that they most frequently shared the same work and Alfred's sea paintings were undoubtedly influenced by his brother partly, one suspects, because of a shared passion for the sea and ships and for sailing. Alfred's landscape work is much more individual and although he may not have shared the intangible magic of his brother's work, his own was certainly more than merely competent painting. He was exhibiting as early as 14 years old and in 1827 the *Norwich Mercury* reported (in respect of a small family exhibition held while the Norwich Society awaited the completion of their new exhibition rooms) that Alfred Stannard's work 'does credit to his instructor [Joseph] and evinces a studious application of ability to the purposes of professional improvement . . . that bids fair for future excellence', adding of a particular picture that it was felt to 'bespeak the unsung genius of the artist'.

Unlike his brother, Alfred enjoyed good health and his painting career spanned 70 years; he died in 1889 aged 83. Alfred, like his brother, produced some accomplished drawings, usually in chalk, and tried his hand at etching but without conspicuous success. Eight recorded examples exist dated 1828/9 but in no way do they reach the quality of those produced by Joseph's other pupil, the Rev. E.T. Daniell. Alfred invented a type of crayon of his own which he claimed gave

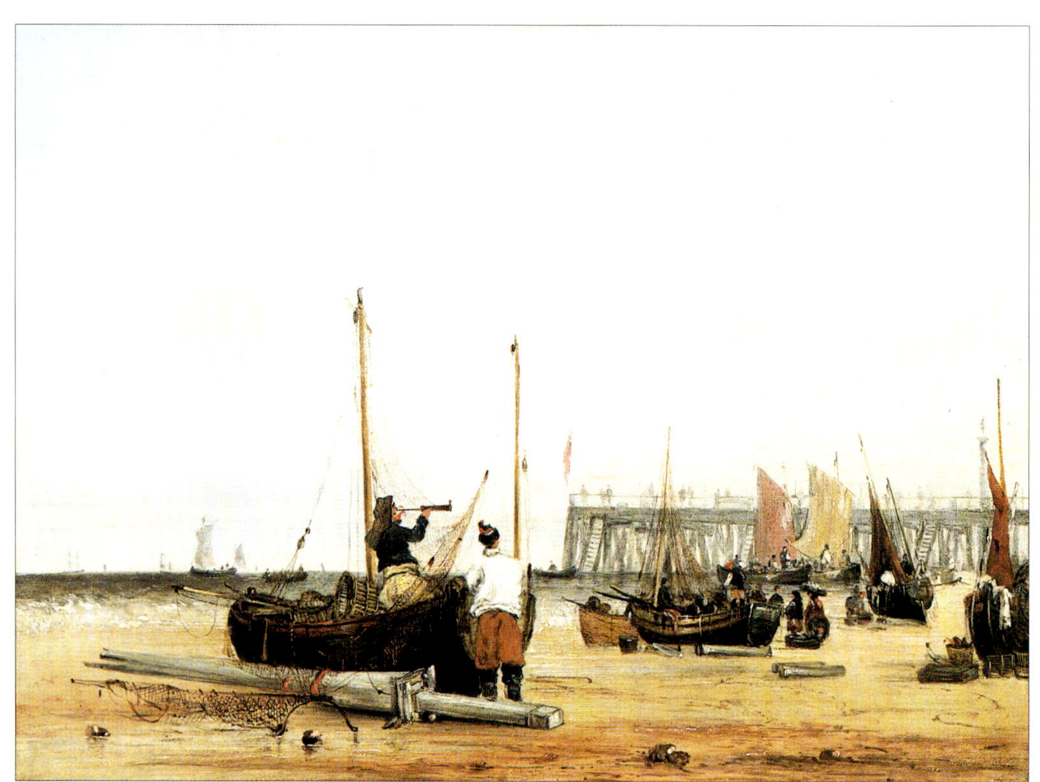

Alfred George Stannard, Fishing Boats off the Jetty at Great Yarmouth, oil on canvas, 14¼ in x 19½ in

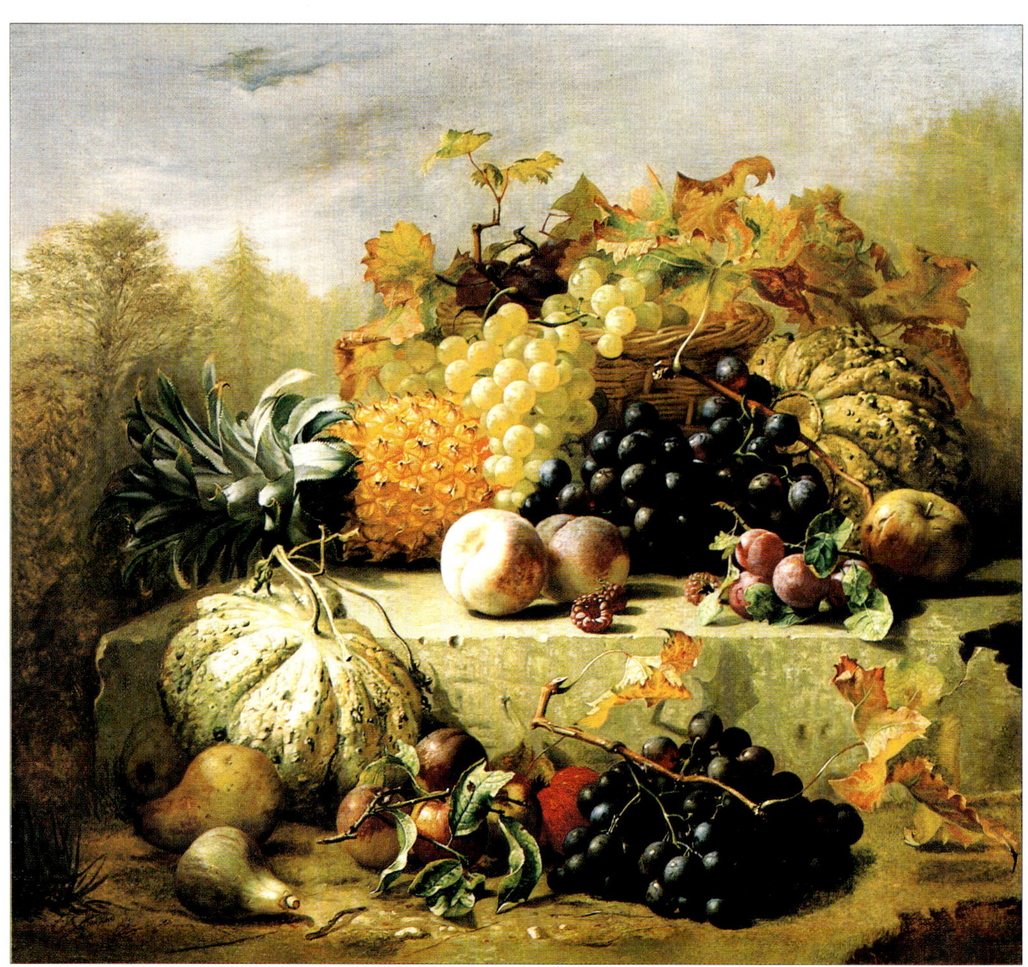

Eloise Harriet Stannard, Still-life of Fruit on a Stone Ledge, oil, 22¾ in x 20 in

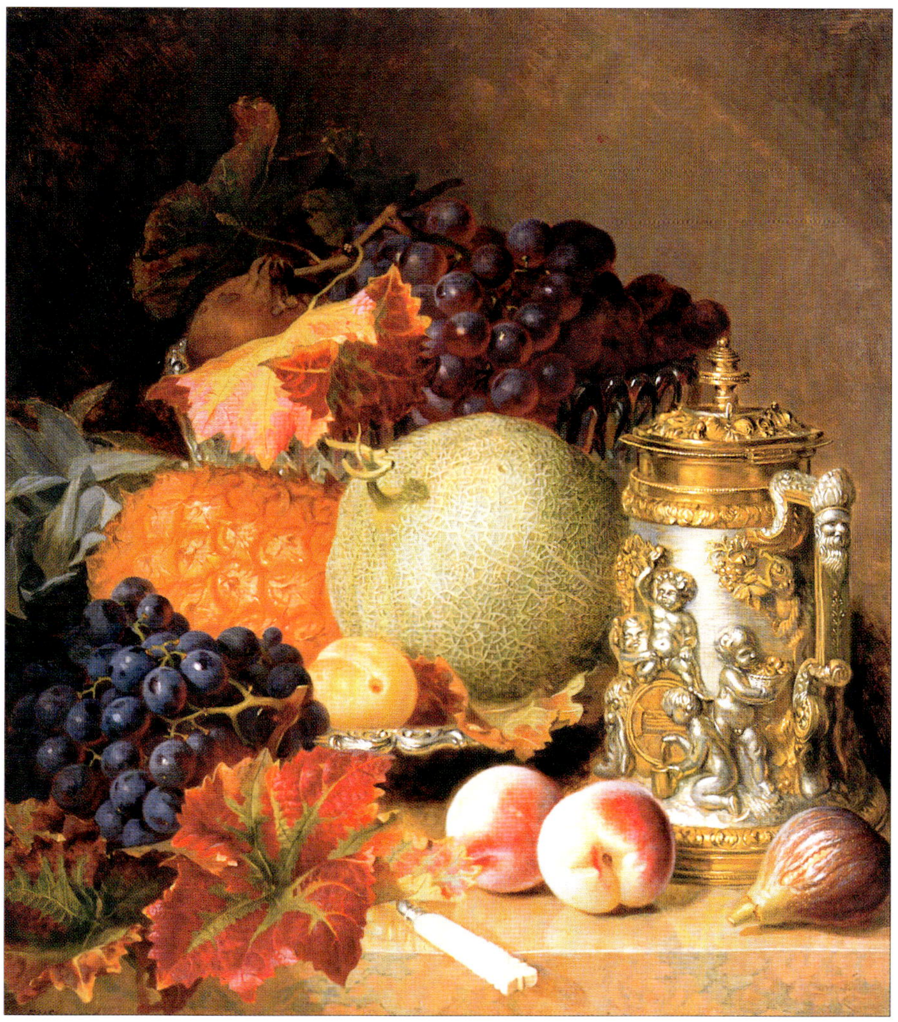

Eloise Harriet Stannard, Still-life of Fruit on a Marble Ledge, oil on canvas. 14 in x 14 in

an effect 'almost equal to oil painting'. Very few examples of watercolour painting are known except for the fruits of an unusual commission for one General Sir Robert Harvey who requested 100 watercolours of the houses, barns, mills, cottages and churches on his various estates. These have been bound into two volumes and, if nothing more, provide a useful historical documentary.

Alfred Stannard exhibited his major paintings in London and Norwich as well as accepting commissions and, unusually for the Norwich painters, cleaning and restoring oil paintings. A *Norwich Mercury* of 1834 reports that he cleaned and relined the city's civic portraits, presumably those not dealt with by John Crome. As he grew older, he devoted more and more time to teaching; predictably the artistic members of his own family were pupils but his star was Henry Bright, who became an exceptionally successful artist, in many respects outshining his teacher.

To be fair, though, even if he lacked his more glamorous brother's genius, Alfred Stannard had a great deal of talent and, until age diminished his powers, produced some excellent, at times quite original, landscape paintings. As well as in his seascapes, these landscapes show an excellent handling of colour; his trees in particular show a very accomplished and attractive treatment of greens. A good Alfred Stannard will currently fetch £50,000 or more.

The Alfred Stannards were a family of painters. In 1827 Alfred married Martha Sparkes, an amateur painter who had once aspired to an exhibit with the Norwich Society of Artists. Two of their 14 children (several died in infancy) became well-known artists; the eldest son, **Alfred George Stannard** (1828-1885) was a competent draughtsman who studied under his father and later, in some ways, outshone him. At an early age he was exhibiting at the British Institution and at the Royal Academy works that were generally more romantic than his father's although at the same time more varied. He travelled more extensively, too, and a visit to Wales in his early twenties brought forth some original material. Later in his life he also visited Switzerland and for a time lived in London, all of which must have broadened his outlook. His painting has breadth too, and at times quite a daring use of impasto, dashing brushwork and lively colour. Some of his marine paintings are reminiscent of his uncle Joseph and of a quality the latter would commend (see p.60). Personally I am drawn to his pastoral paintings with sheep and other farm animals in peaceful, perhaps rather idyllic, rural settings. All his paintings are enhanced by clever use of light and shade, always a life-giving attribute. He married another artist, daughter of the Norwich painter, David Hodgson. Anne Stannard's still-life and bird paintings were by no means in the same class as those of her aunt by marriage and her sister-in-law.

Alfred Stannard's daughter, **Eloise Harriet Stannard** (1829-1915) was without doubt a most brilliant painter who is known to have exhibited 30 works at the Royal Academy, 29 at the British Institution and many in Norwich as well as selling privately. E.H., as she is often referred to, never had to resort to teaching for her paintings were in such demand. Her health was not good but she surmounted physical difficulties and continued painting until the end of a long life. Few flower and still-life painters in Britain have ever been able to emulate her (see frontispiece, pp.60 and 61).

Although E.H.'s work owes something to the Dutch, she was more of a personality artist than her aunt Emily although, technically, the two were comparable. E.H. always painted from life and liked to work outside because of the added contrasts of light, shade and colour and the luminosity that could be achieved by painting in a pure light. She was a master of the art of underpainting which gave her some unique tones to play with and added a transparency and reflective quality where it suited her fruit, flowers and the various gold or pewter accessories. Texture was important to her and the bloom on the grapes, the rough velvet of the peaches and the rocky pumpkins were remarkably realistic. Her work inspires the sensation of touch and smell as well as sight, as all such paintings should – and rarely do!

Having said in an interview that she only painted from nature, the questioner asked her what she did in the winter time? Eloise replied, 'Oh, I put the gold in my paintings.' This, of course, quite baffled the interviewer until she explained that the still-life additions to her flowers and fruit, for instance the borrowed Coronation plate, 'the salt, the rose water dish and even a ewer and tankard', not only added contrast and effect but had no dependency on the seasons.

So much of E.H.'s work was sold to collecting families during her lifetime that all too little can be seen in public collections. This makes it difficult to find illustrations although, at the time of writing, Geoffrey Allen of Mandell's Gallery has acquired a magnificent example. The colours have retained their wonderful richness and luminosity and the realism of the texture is almost unbelievable – mouthwatering in the case of the fruit!

Chapter 5

JOHN SELL COTMAN

Until comparatively recently, writers on the Norwich School have tended principally to focus on John Crome and John Sell Cotman, the two acknowledged heads of their own artistic dynasties. **John Sell Cotman** (1782-1842) is by far the most exciting painter of the School and much has been written about him. There are followers of both Crome and Cotman who have subsequently, in one artistic arena or another, achieved the standard of their mentors, but whose talents and accomplishments have only recently been fully appreciated. In their own time those artists tended rather to be like ships that pass in the night and little was known or questioned about their lives or personalities outside their artistic involvements. These are the people we are still finding out about, the people who are still providing meat for researchers and historians to get their teeth into.

Cotman's life is so fully documented that, other than expressing personal comments and opinions or piecing together odd bits of the jigsaw that had been misplaced, we tend to have a feeling of repetition. Yet in any study of the Norwich School, Cotman would be the last person to overlook. His extraordinary versatility and the enormity of his output has provided ample opportunity for discussion and analysis of his work as a whole or in particular facets and, unusually, the voluminous correspondence, which to a large extent has been preserved, gives an important insight into his character and personality. John Sell Cotman was, despite his erratic temperament, a warm and outgoing individual who obviously derived great satisfaction and fulfilment from keeping in constant touch with his family, friends and patrons and found great release in 'talking' to them on paper. In particular the correspondence with his lifelong patron cum guide, counsellor and friend, Dawson Turner, Yarmouth banker, collector and architectural researcher and writer, has been almost wholly preserved and is something of a biographical study in itself. Dawson Turner was Cotman's lifeline, not simply financially but as a rock to lean on and a fount of good advice; he not only helped Mrs Cotman to invest the life insurance of £1,000 after her husband's death but provided a pension for her and later for her unmarried daughter, Ann.

Difficult as he may have been, John Sell Cotman appears a most attractive personality, the sort of man it would be very easy to fall in love with but almost impossible to live with. His devoted wife and his eldest son, Miles Edmund, while making endless sacrifices, supported him loyally through traumas, misfortunes and ill health. His correspondence confirms that he maintained a close and loving relationship with his family wherever they were.

Art was John Sell Cotman's life blood. Not long before his death he wrote in a letter to Dawson Turner: 'I was born apparently with a love of my Art, as I have never known the time when I was not fond of drawing, and I have often heard my dear mother say I drew "tips" [ships] long before I could speak!!'

John Sell Cotman was born in May 1782 in the Norwich parish of St. Mary, Coslany. His father was a draper, haberdasher, silk merchant and dealer in foreign lace. John Sell attended Norwich Grammar School where his early talent was recognised although there was no art

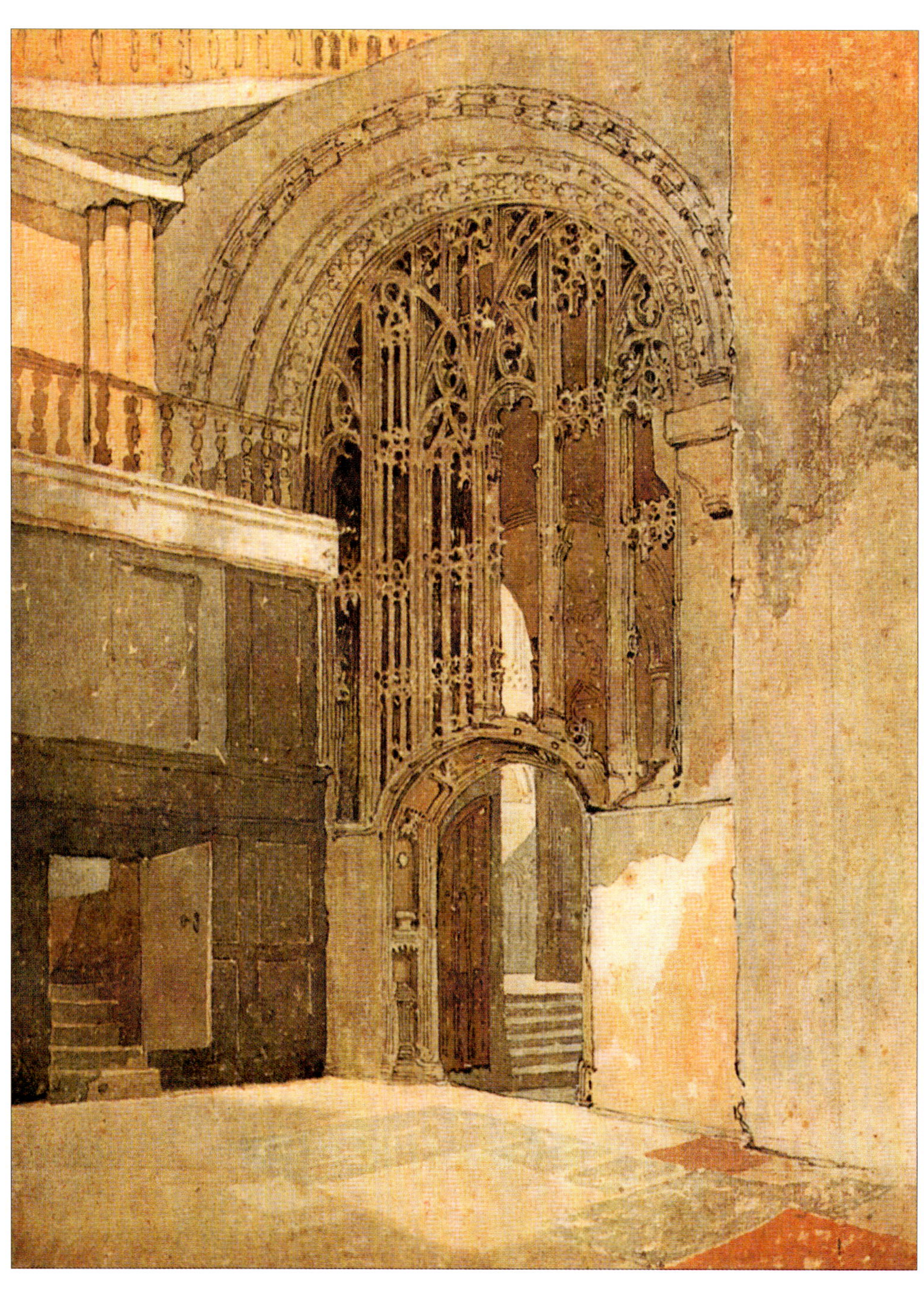

John Sell Cotman, Norwich Cathedral, pencil and watercolour, 14 in x 10½ in

taught at that time. All Sundays, holidays and any spare time he had was spent wandering about the city and the surrounding countryside, pad and pencils in hand, drawing, drawing and drawing. His Headmaster, Dr Forster, in his private life took a great interest in the arts and, in 1805, was elected Vice-President of the Norwich Society of Artists. The one artistic anecdote from John Sell's schooldays, however, concerns Dr Forster's almost paranoid hatred of cats. One

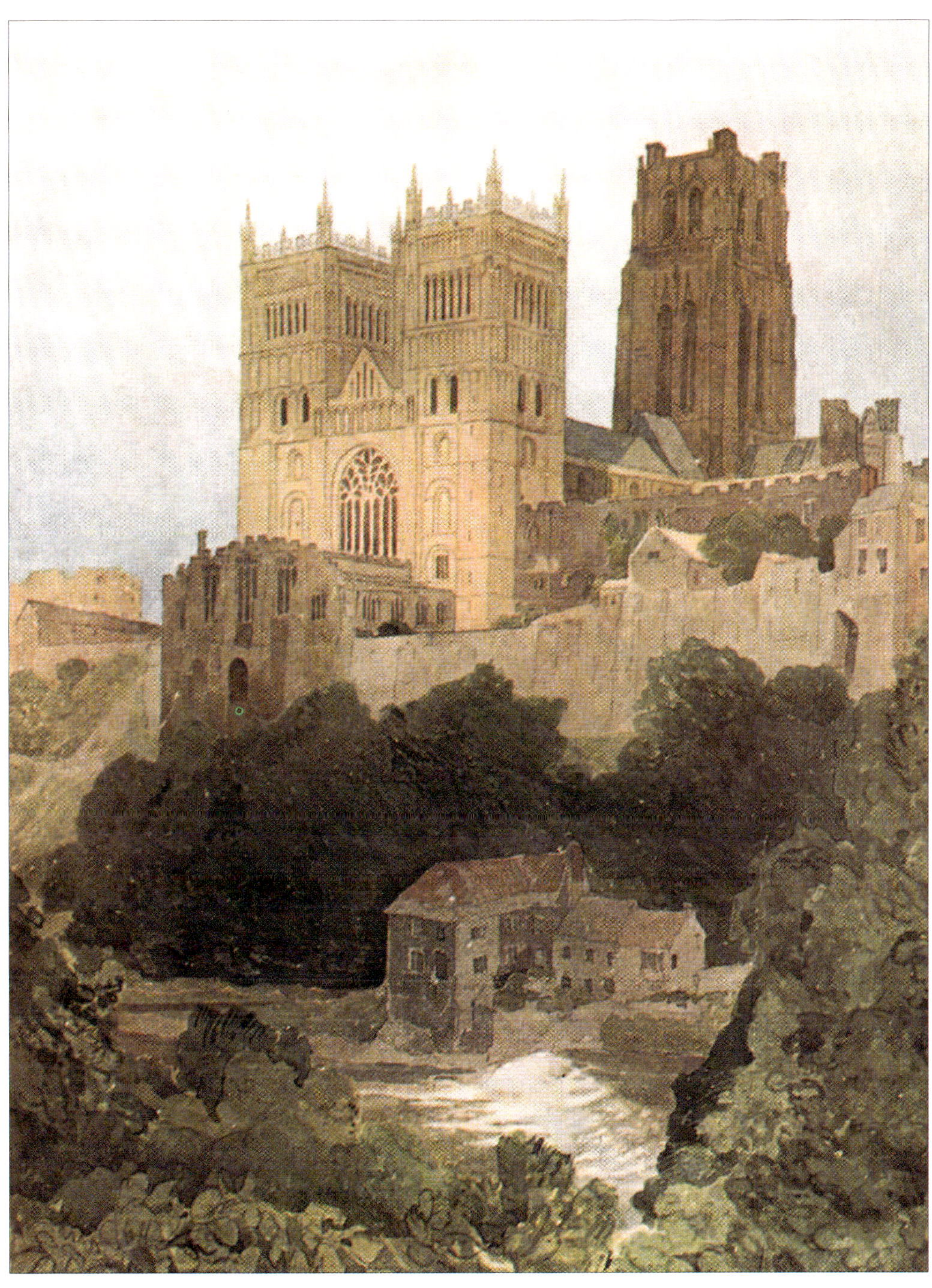

John Sell Cotman, Durham Cathedral, watercolour, 17¼ in x 13 in

morning, on entering his classroom, Dr Forster found a large and realistic cut-out on his desk and faced the staring eyes of a big black cat. The joke rather backfired when he held up the silhouette before the class and said quietly: 'I know the only boy who could have done this' – the first indication that a good artist cannot remain anonymous.

Money was too tight in the Cotman household to give John Sell a conventional art training

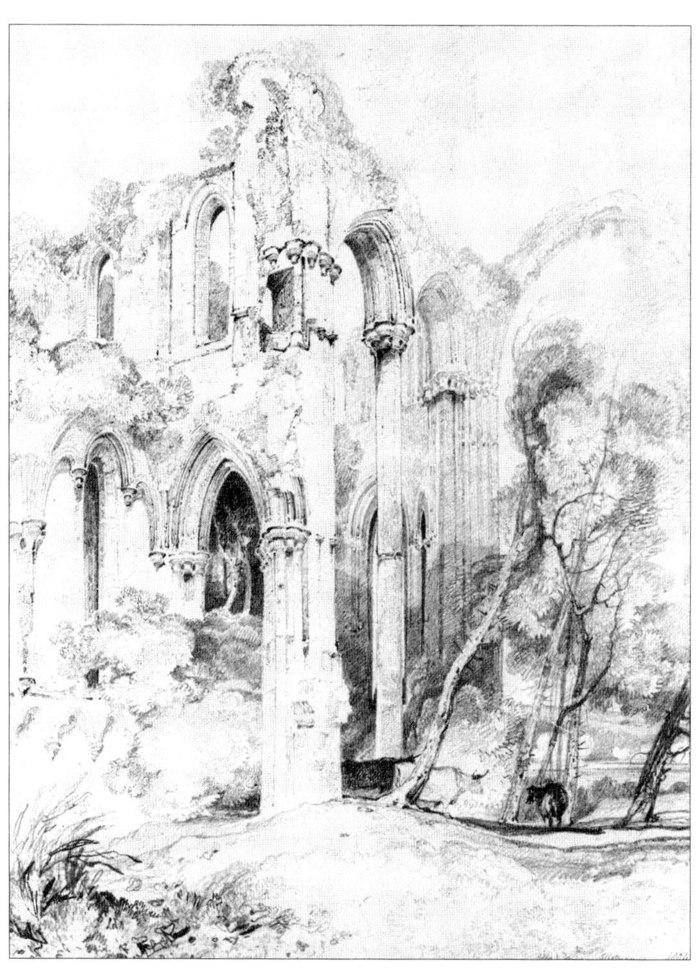

John Sell Cotman, Fountains Abbey, Yorkshire, pencil, 1804, 12¼ in x 10½ in

but, *c.*1798, he was allowed to go to London and work for it. He joined the staff of Ackermann in the Strand where he could learn a certain amount in the drawing academy while working in an artistic environment, colouring aquatints, screen painting and providing decoration for mounts, etc., as required. This work was insufficiently creative to interest John Sell for long and he was not receiving the sort of tuition he craved; following a difference with Ackermann, he left and joined the famous (or notorious) Dr Monro who specialised in mental illness and included George III among his patients. Dr Monro liked to consider himself 'tutor' to young artists who, at the same time, worked for him by copying the works of other, well established, artists which, while teaching them a great deal, added substantially to Monro's personal collection. The small payment and supper after an evening's work was no doubt acceptable. Perhaps the greatest benefit to Cotman of his time with Dr Monro was the valuable contact he made with other artists through the connection. Both Turner and Girtin had been working under Dr Monro, Girtin drawing and Turner tinting and colouring, and they still visited him during Cotman's time there. Joseph Farington, Louis Francia, Paul Sandby Munn and others also became Cotman's friends through the Monro association.

In 1799, a number of these young artists formed a group called the Brothers, led by Thomas Girtin, who met at each other's houses to draw and have serious discussions on matters artistic. Cotman joined this brotherhood, later known as the Drawing Society, and became leader of the group himself early in the 19th century. Undoubtedly the contact with such a wide range of other, older, artists broadened the youthful Cotman's vision and gave him valuable experience which would have been lost to him had he stayed in Norwich. His drawing and work in monochrome progressed rapidly, as did some colour work, and soon he was being mentioned in the same breath as Girtin and Turner. He first exhibited at the Royal Academy in 1800 (six works) and, to the delight of the Norwich press, was awarded the Silver Palette by the Society for the Encouragement

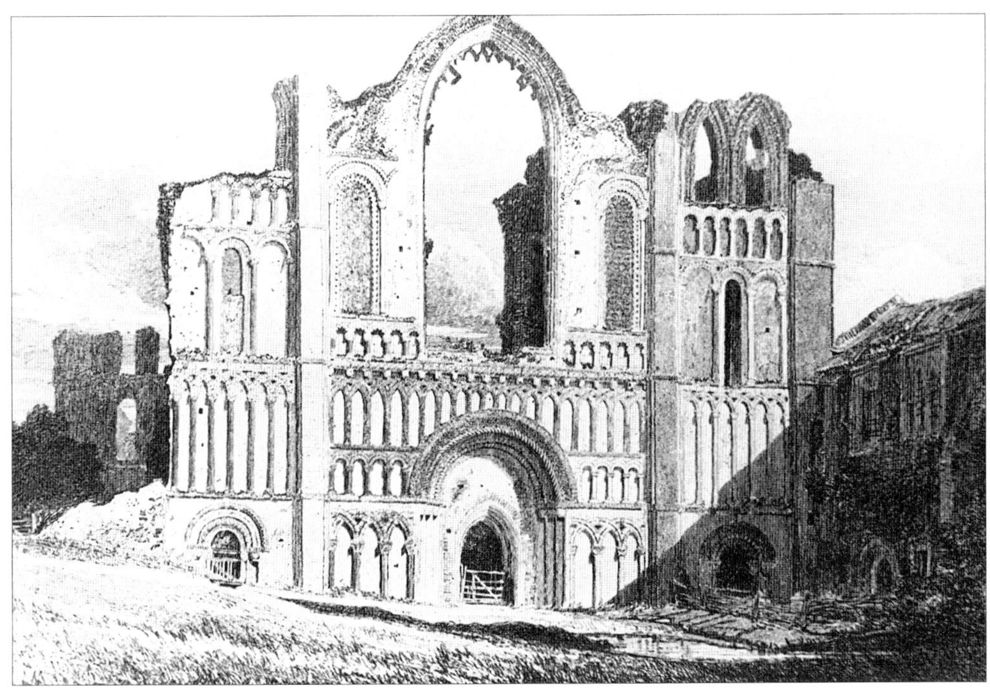

John Sell Cotman, Castle Acre Priory, etching, c.1805, 11⅞ in x 17 in

of the Arts, Manufacturers and Commerce. In the meantime Cotman was supporting himself by supplying drawings to the printsellers and, as his work became more widely known, to private individuals. Some of these people commissioned subjects in other parts of the country which gave him the added opportunity of broadening his own personal range of subjects to go into the store of sketches. All this activity was adding to his experience and expertise and there is no doubt that Cotman made the most of these early years in London and the useful contact with artists he admired. Although always of mercurial temperament, there is nothing to suggest that the extreme depressive phases he endured later had started unduly to manifest themselves.

In 1800 Cotman made a first trip to Wales with Paul Sandby Munn, an experience they repeated in 1802. That first excursion through Wales was an invaluable part of both young artists' development. Cotman sketched and drew extensively and produced some 'finished' watercolours in which his own highly individual style showed itself over and above any London influences; added to this, the very subject matter was an inspiration. The beautiful, majestic scenery, the misty blues and greys of the landscape and the whole unique atmosphere acted like a charm, providing the first indication of the indefinable Cotman magic and his unique ability to reduce a subject to its bare essentials while saying everything there was to say. The Welsh landscape, expressed largely in blues and greys, lent itself perfectly to experiments with the broad wash technique flirted with by Varley and Girtin.

John Sell Cotman, with the confidence of youth and the feeling of being on the threshold of a golden future, returned to Norwich for a while later in 1800. He worked hard using the plentiful subject matter of his native city and its environs to make preparatory sketches and some drawings, returning to London for the winter armed with a large supply of material to work up into finished drawings or monochromes to offer the printsellers or to use for more lucrative purposes if the opportunity arose. He was exhibiting from time to time and attracting some measure of interest, if not as many buyers as he might have wished. Compared to later work, some of these drawings were a little heavy and, perhaps, lacking in subtlety, but his natural skill, fostered by hours of practice, gave them the essential quality of superb draughtsmanship.

The second Welsh tour in 1802 resulted in a further series of drawings, this time displaying a greater delicacy of touch and indicating the rapid progression that Cotman's work was showing. He returned again to Norwich in the late summer intending to spend a few weeks there and to use the time teaching and sketching. He advertised in the *Norwich Mercury* his intention of giving 'Lessons in Drawing to those Ladies or Gentlemen who may think his Sketching from Nature beneficial to their improvement.'

During these exciting early years, as well as the Welsh tours with Paul Sandby Munn, he visited Devon and Somerset and other outer London areas enabling him to add to his portfolio and usually generate enough patronage to cover expenses. During his summer visit to Norwich in 1801, he had experimented with etching, a craft which was to be of great 'bread and butter' value to him in the future although, at the time, it was all part of the youthful urge to try anything and everything that took his fancy. He used the soft ground method of reversing a pencil drawing on thin paper over a copper plate covered with tallow wax; this was traced over using heavier or lighter pressure according to the strength of line required. The wax stuck to the paper exposing the copper to the acid bath to which the plate was subsequently transferred; the richness of the 'burr' was determined by the strength of the copper erosion. This method certainly gave a much softer result than the drypoint technique, much more reminiscent of the original pencil, but the plates were more quickly worn down.

In 1803, again with Paul Sandby Munn, Cotman paid his first visit to Yorkshire where both Turner and Girtin had formerly been captivated by the scenery and each had acquired useful patronage. Cotman and Munn were introduced by a mutual acquaintance to the Cholmeleys of

John Sell Cotman, Trees Near the Greta River, watercolour, c.1806, 12¼ in x 9 in

John Sell Cotman, The Greta Woods, watercolour, 17¼ in x 13¾ in

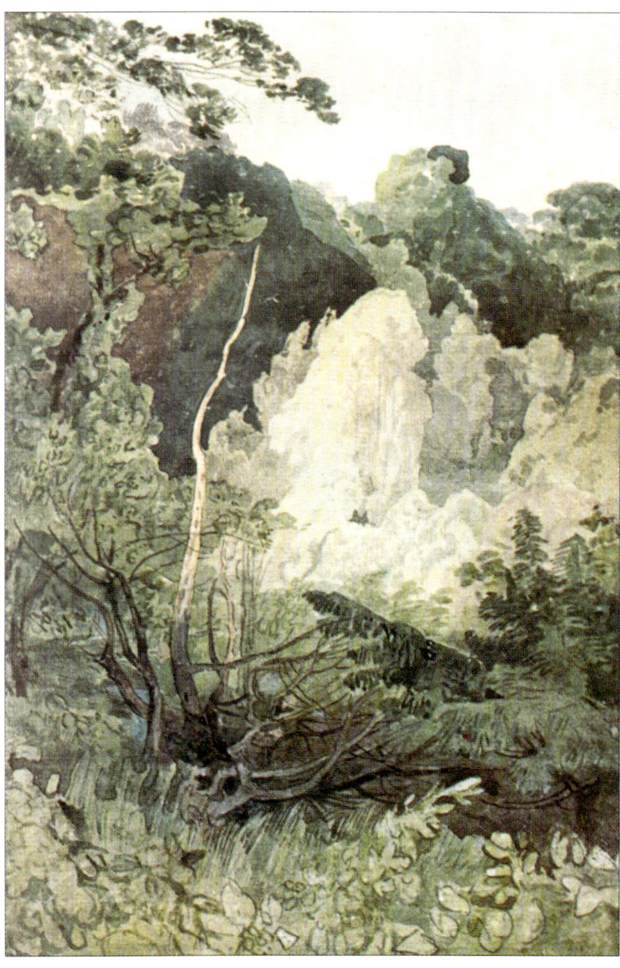

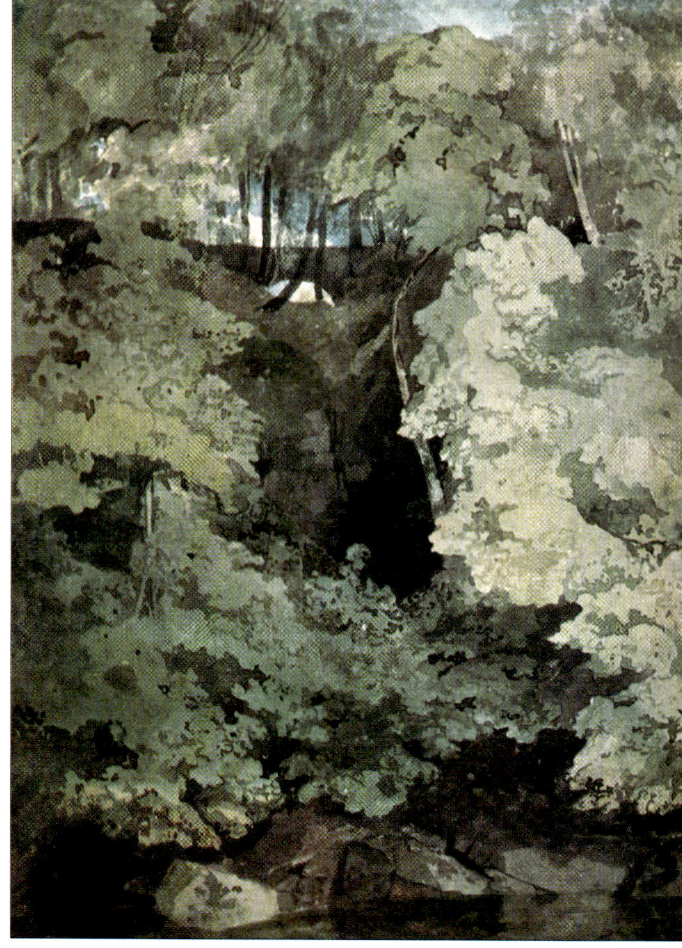

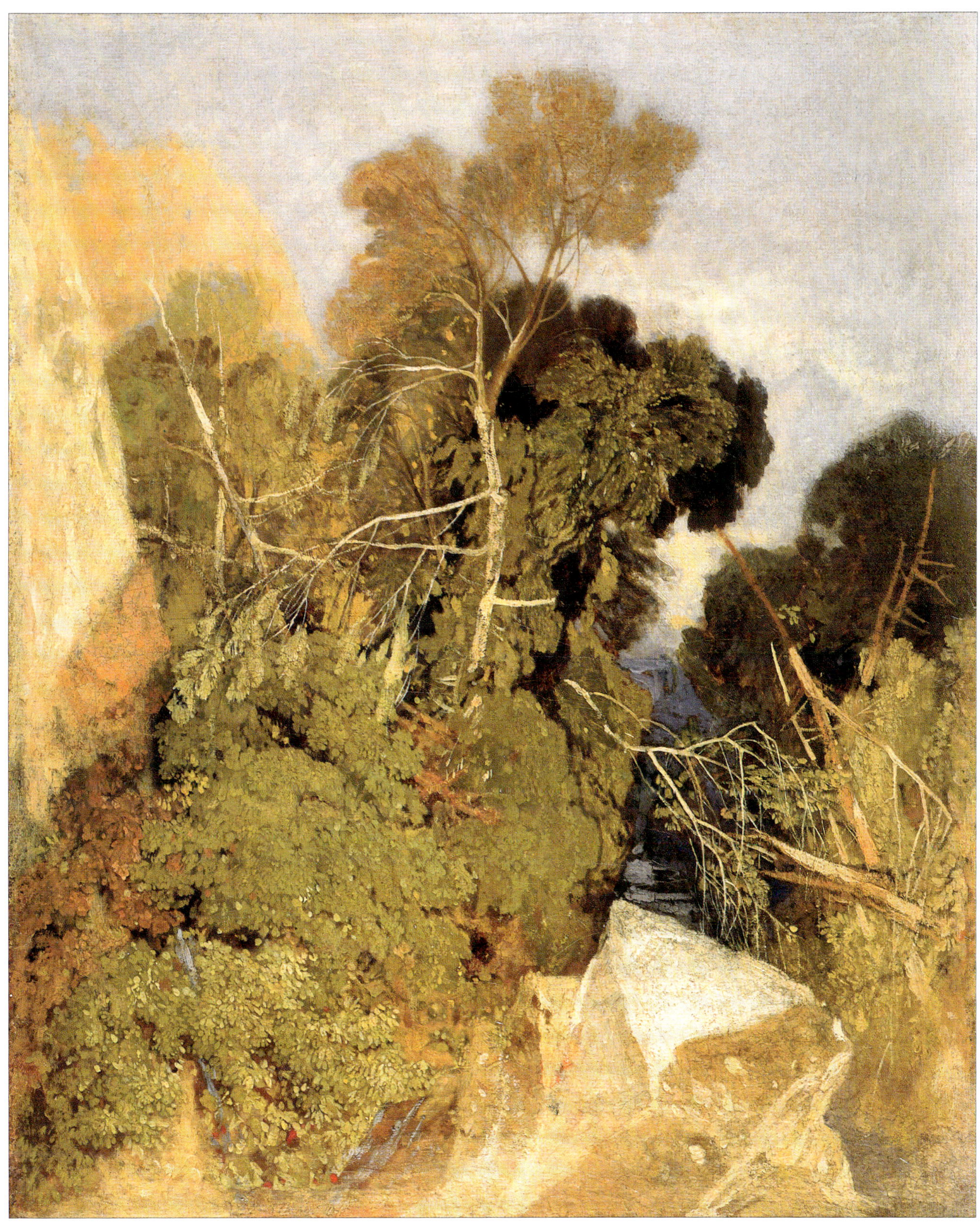

John Sell Cotman, Silver Birches c.1824-8, oil on canvas, 30 in x 24¼ in

Brandsby Hall who made them most welcome and became Cotman's very close friends. He subsequently wrote that at Brandsby Hall he spent some of the happiest hours of his life.

After Munn's return to London early in August of that year, Cotman stayed on in Yorkshire. He made a number of sketching excursions with the family and became informal drawing coach to the Cholmeley daughters. The whole visit and those that followed are meticulously documented in Sidney Kitson's biography of John Sell, sometimes more as a travelogue than a following of artistic development, but the company and the warm friendship of the entire Cholmeley family must have meant a great deal to Cotman who, all his life, craved for and blossomed under warmth and appreciation of his work. He was regarded as something of a phenomenon by the female Cholmeleys who found it quite incredible that one so young could produce such mature and confident draughtsmanship with such accuracy and apparent facility. A booklet published by Leeds City Art Gallery – *Cotmania & Mr. Kitson* – quotes the remaining fragments of a poem written by Harriet Cholmeley in 1803 and entitled 'Cotmania'. It further illustrates the close rapport between Cotman and the family pupils:

> In Brandsby water thou thy brush shall dip
> Peshey shall lecture and thy Tippo skip;
> Upon our Lawns drag out thy three legg'd Chair
> Unfurl umbrellas and make Bullocks stare!
> Once more dear Cotty shall thou lend thine Arm
> When tired and hot to Peshey's 'fairy form',
> Whilst we delighted on your footsteps wait
> Nor think for Dinner we shall be too late.

During late 1803 and the following spring, Cotman worked up many of his Yorkshire subjects which also provided material for the following year's Royal Academy exhibition. It was in 1804, possibly when he was about to set off on another Yorkshire trip, that he first met his life-long patron, Dawson Turner. Details of the meeting are unclear and Turner may have seen the young artist's Academy exhibits and made his own contact for he was ever on the lookout for fine illustrators to use in his architectural writings. Whatever the circumstances, Dawson Turner must have seen examples of the Yorkshire drawings for, in a letter to a friend, he is quoted as saying: 'I have had an eminent artist, Mr. Cotman, at my house lately who has made sketches of all the fine ruins in Yorkshire. They are done in a most masterly manner. . . ' Although their relationship remained on a more formal footing without the warmth and generosity of spirit shown by the Cholmeleys, John Sell regularly corresponded with Dawson Turner from that year, 1804, until the end of his life, a correspondence that has proved invaluable to many students of Cotman's life and work.

Later that year he joined the Cholmeleys at Scarborough where they had been staying and returned with them to Brandsby. Again Cotman spent some months with his friends. Although wealthy Yorkshire landowners, the Cholmeleys appear to have shown no side or snobbery and treated the young artist as an equal both *en famille* and in the company of their aristocratic friends. Cotman, to whom caring and appreciation meant so much, flourished both personally and artistically in this congenial environment, and his good looks, natural charm of manner and exceptional talent enabled him to hold his own and find acceptance in any company. He worked very hard, making the most of the wealth of material, going out almost daily with Mrs Cholmeley and giving tuition to her daughters. A further measure of the family's regard for him is shown in that they took the trouble to accompany him to York to wish him God speed when he left them in November.

From the standpoint of posterity and, indeed, from that of his own vision which took him years ahead of his time, 1805 was the most significant year of Cotman's life – and, at the same time, the most exciting and the most discouraging in terms of his art. I make no apology for quoting eminent art historians on this particular phase, in order to emphasise how many have been captivated, spellbound even, by a magic for which he was so cruelly criticised by many of his contemporaries.

That year in Yorkshire Cotman found himself. Consciously or unconsciously he had been absorbing the best of those artists he most admired – Girtin, Turner, who must have inspired the more imaginative approach, Francia, Varley, Munn. All this time, too, his already formidable technical skill as a draughtsman had been maturing and perfecting, his already keen sense of observation sharpened by teaching. The incredible natural beauty of the subjects introduced to him by his now very dear friends and their affection and esteem added to this new found inspiration. He had experimented a little (as in the Welsh drawings) with the watercolour technique used in what has come to be known as 'the Greta period', but without comparable significance or indication of what was soon to follow.

It appears that Cotman met Mrs Cholmeley in London that spring; she was staying with her brother Sir Henry Englefield, and they invited the artist for a weekend. A further visit to Yorkshire was arranged and, a few months later, he went again to Brandsby. Francis Cholmeley had arranged with his friend, John Brian Sawrey Morritt, Squire of Rokeby Hall and a friend of Sir Walter Scott, to pay a visit accompanied by Cotman; again Cotman was accepted almost as one of the family and, before returning for a further two months at Brandsby, spent several weeks at Rokeby Park where he fell deeply in love with the wonderful trees, rivers and landscape of this enchanting area. 'It was this visit', writes Andrew Moore, 'which resulted in some of the finest and most delicate watercolours in the history of European watercolour painting. His work at this time demonstrates an exquisite control of the medium which is totally his own and at one with his unique vision of the patterns of Nature.' Many years earlier, sadly not early enough, these same gems were described by Laurence Binyon as 'the most perfect examples of pure watercolour ever made in Europe.' And if not Europe, where else?

Cotman's principal biographer, Sidney Kitson, wrote in 1937:

> The year 1805 is perhaps the most important one in the whole story of Cotman's artistic development, for it was then that he entered upon his kingdom and produced work of individual distinction. He had advanced step by step in his self-education as an artist. At first he had imitated the drawings of the early watercolourists, then at Dr Monro's house he had been brought into touch with the new outlook and new methods of Turner and Girtin. Afterwards in working with colleagues at the Drawing Society, he had reached the position of a leader amongst members owing to his livelier imagination and greater technical skill.

Now the others had been completely left behind and, in his new self-confidence and inner development, he 'was beginning to record the lyrical aspect of Nature.'

In his architectural work, the side of Cotman that so attracted Dawson Turner, and his landscapes with buildings, interiors and classical studies, his perfectionist drawing remained always in evidence. But for a draughtsman *par excellence* it is not always easy to translate to a style in which perfect drawing is indicated only by sweeping washes of pure colour. His confident technique produces, through faultless perspective, not only a three dimensional effect but a co-ordination of colour, an almost intuitively subtle use of tonal values, and an awareness of form and shape that involved not only the charm and truth of the composition but the very atmosphere of the subject. One is completely transfixed: therein lies the magic, the skill that can express deep feeling and atmosphere without which even such perfect images would lose their living fire. Let me quote Kitson again, writing of two small studies of the Greta now in the British Museum:

> Both are close studies of trees, seen in the midst of a wood. They are difficult subjects yet Cotman has sifted the haphazard growth and woven his patterns so subtly that the stillness and the fragrance

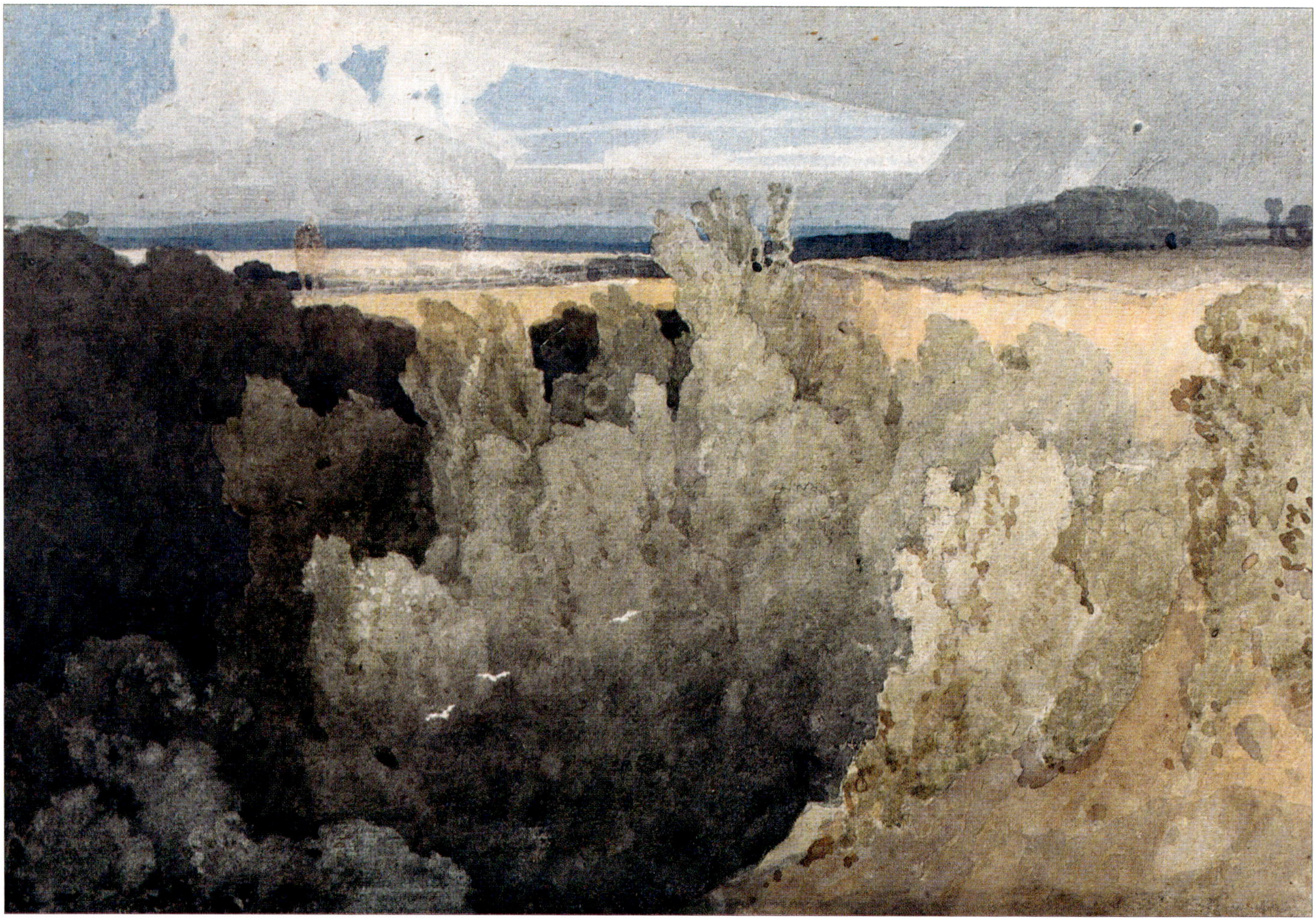

John Sell Cotman,
Brignall Bank on the Greta,
Yorkshire, watercolour and pencil,
8¼ in x 11¼ in

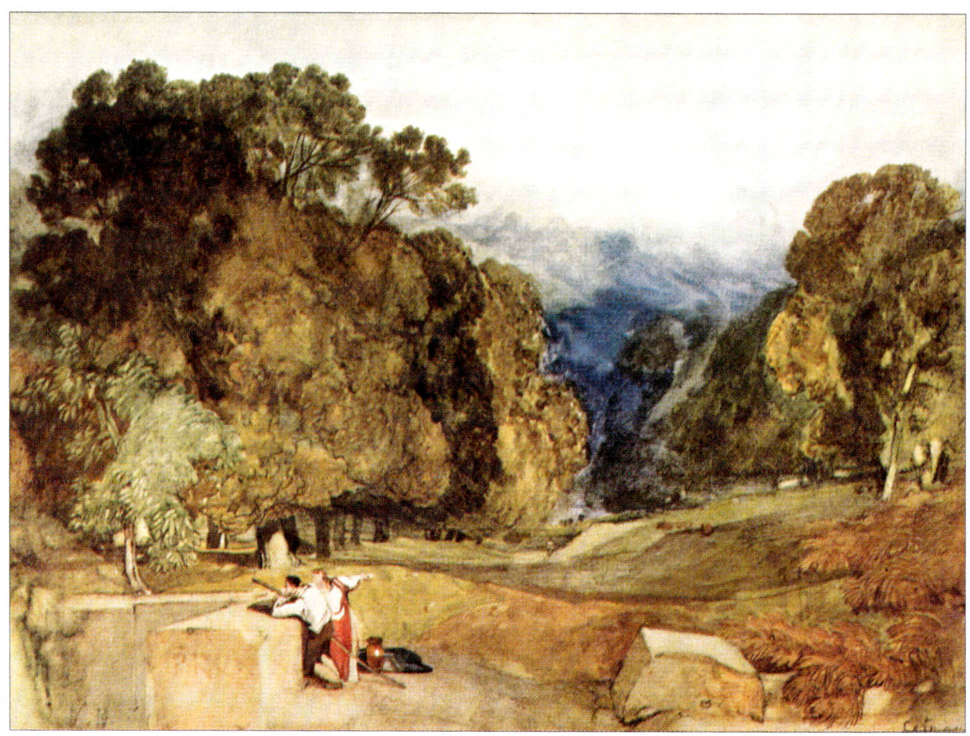

John Sell Cotman,
Park Scene, watercolour,
10 in x 13¾ in

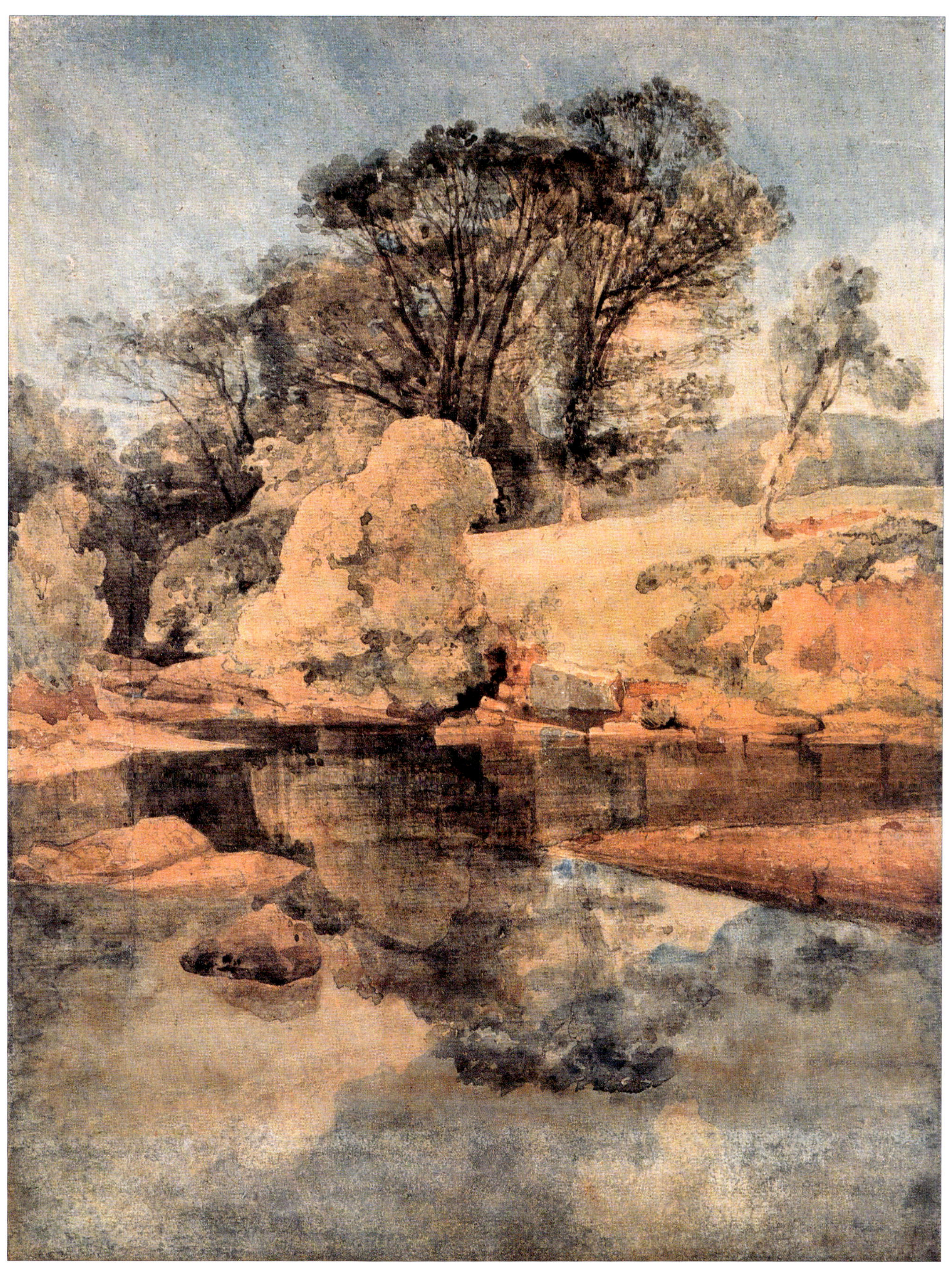

John Sell Cotman, Hell Cauldron (on the Greta) 1806, Pencil and watercolour, 17¼ in x 13 in

> of the scenes can be felt. Another, 'The Scotsman's Stone', is a drawing of the great boulder that lies in the river bed a couple of miles above Greta Bridge. Here the brown water of the moorland trout stream, as it flows quickly past the rock, is rendered with an ease and mastery almost magical. There are other drawings, one with a horizontal band of brown water and great dock leaves; in another a man is creeping up the stream snaring fish. Still another is a study of a part of the bank of the lovely stream . . . it is a scene of unchanging beauty.

'Trees Near the Greta River' (see p.68) and 'The Devil's Elbow, Rokeby Park' are among my own favourites; they are clearly worked directly from nature through the keenest observation of the minutest gradations of tone and colour, through all the combinations of blues and yellows in the trees, bringing out the lyrical quality that so fascinated Kitson and other historians to say nothing of the layman and woman. It is in these magical studies in which the beauty of the scene is always enhanced by the authentic feeling for the atmosphere of the day that the unique mystical genius of John Sell Cotman fully manifests itself. Immaculate as his (then) more conventional drawings may have been, by the Greta he moved on to a different plane.

Adding to Binyon and Kitson, Oppé (1923) refers also to 'The Scotsman's Stone'and the various tree studies as exhibiting:

> . . . one of the most characteristic and perhaps the finest of Cotman's many styles. It is not merely that his colour is at its choicest, especially in the rich tonal depths of the water, that the absence of elaborated drawing leaves the washes clear and clean, with the Japanese delight in transparent tone which Mr. Binyon rightly applauds, least of all that the sober colours adequately represent the modesty and variety of Nature's hues. Over and above all this, his firm drawing builds the masses of colour into a balanced and contrasted pattern and the strength and variety of Nature are thus comprised into an intricate yet convincingly simple structure.

Many years later (1950) Graham Reynolds comments:

> The finest of all Cotman's watercolours are connected with this stay of his at the River Greta, for instance his 'Greta Bridge', now in the British Museum, and 'Drop Gate, Duncombe Park'. These are drawings in which everything inessential is ruthlessly suppressed and yet every nuance of the scene is there. In them Cotman adjoins to his perfectly controlled washes a deep and vivid sense of colour and harmony.

Two years later Leonard Squirrell writes that 'at his finest, Cotman reached a pinnacle of watercolour at which he has not been surpassed since his death a hundred years ago, a perfect combination of truth to nature and personal expression.'*

Such major authorities as Rajnai and Allthorpe-Guyton maintain that Cotman's month in the area resulted in 'one of the finest series of watercolours in the history of European painting'. Of 'The Devil's Elbow, Rokeby Park' (p.75), they write:

> It is without doubt one of [Cotman's] greatest drawings and one of the most original contributions to English art of its time. Such drawings are far more than studies; rather they are the intimate reactions of a highly emotional artist to scenes which stirred and satisfied his aesthetic sense. Here almost for the first time, he had the leisure and the materials which enabled him to sit down on the spot and put down in their completeness the visions which he saw.

Andrew Moore describes the same work as 'one of the finest of the inspired Greta drawings'. Even Sir John Rothenstein, who has written extensively on a range of more modern (by date) artists, wrote in 1965 of Cotman's Greta period: 'Cotman at his best occupies a special place among watercolour painters as master of deceptively simple yet magnificent design; his gravity and reticence make many Turners appear garish and theatrical by comparison.'

An experiment or innovation that really comes off is an exciting experience for any artist and

* *Practice in Watercolour*, Pitman 1950.

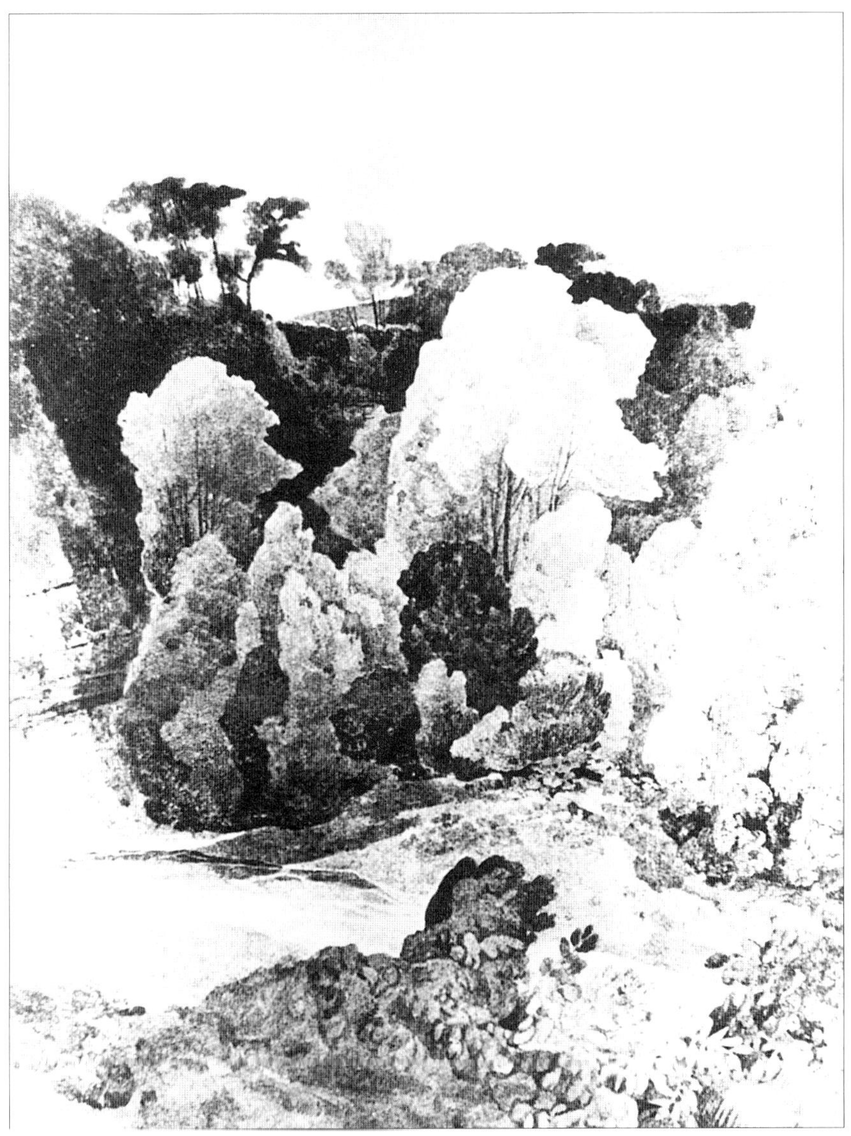

John Sell Cotman, The Devil's Elbow, Rokeby Park, watercolour, c.1806-7, 17¼ in x 13¾ in

Cotman was of an excitable temperament; if only he could have known how art historians of the future were to rate those magical watercolours of the Greta. As it was, contemporary opinion was deflating and disillusioning to say the least, enough to send Cotman into the depths of despair. The general public considered many of these works to be unfinished and not worthy of the artist's talents. His colleagues were intrigued but on the whole noncommittal. John Crome was undoubtedly impressed but only Robert Leman, a more enterprising painter himself, really appreciated the quality that was there. The critics completely failed to understand and proved to be no further enlightened when, many years later in 1824, Cotman, working then in oil, reintroduced the Greta technique into the poetic 'Trees at Kimberley' and related works. The *Norwich Mercury* wrote:

> His watercolour drawings display a brilliance, clearness and accuracy scarcely to be surpassed. His pencil sketches are also superb. But we confess we cannot understand the principle upon which 'Trees at Kimberley – clearing up after a Storm at Mid-day' is painted. Acknowledging as we are most happy to do the power of Mr. Cotman's intellect, we are satisfied that he has some particular aim in adopting a manner so removed from the common course, and we regret to find that it is in this instance as unintelligible to the virtuosi as to the public. We were wholly unable to catch the effect.

If Cotman had hoped that the years might have brought an advancement in understanding, he was again to be disappointed.

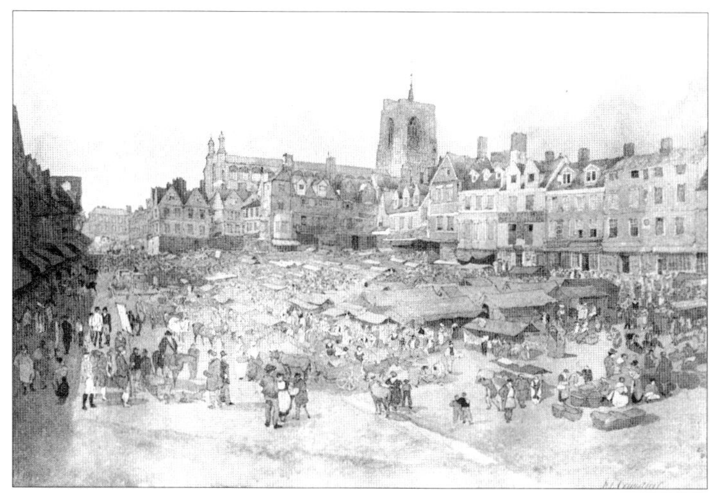

John Sell Cotman, Norwich Market Place, watercolour, c.1807, 14 in x 22 in

Even Dawson Turner showed no comprehension of the Greta watercolours although he continued to commission and buy more and more of the traditional, more architectural, drawings. Of Cotman in relation to these he wrote: 'His joy came from his free abandonment to the atmosphere of his surroundings and the knowledge of his complete ability to put on paper what he saw and felt', totally oblivious to the fact that his words applied in much greater measure to the Greta experience. Not surprisingly a crumb of comfort came from Mr. Cholmeley ('I am grieved and surprised at your want of success far more than I can express') who tried to explain kindly that others can fail to see or understand what an artist is trying to say and that it is a mistake to get too excited about anything, few events in life come up to expectations. He concluded kindly: 'Whether prosperous or unlucky signifies nothing in my regard for you. Be virtuous, be steady, and nothing can influence the friendship and affection of yr. friends here

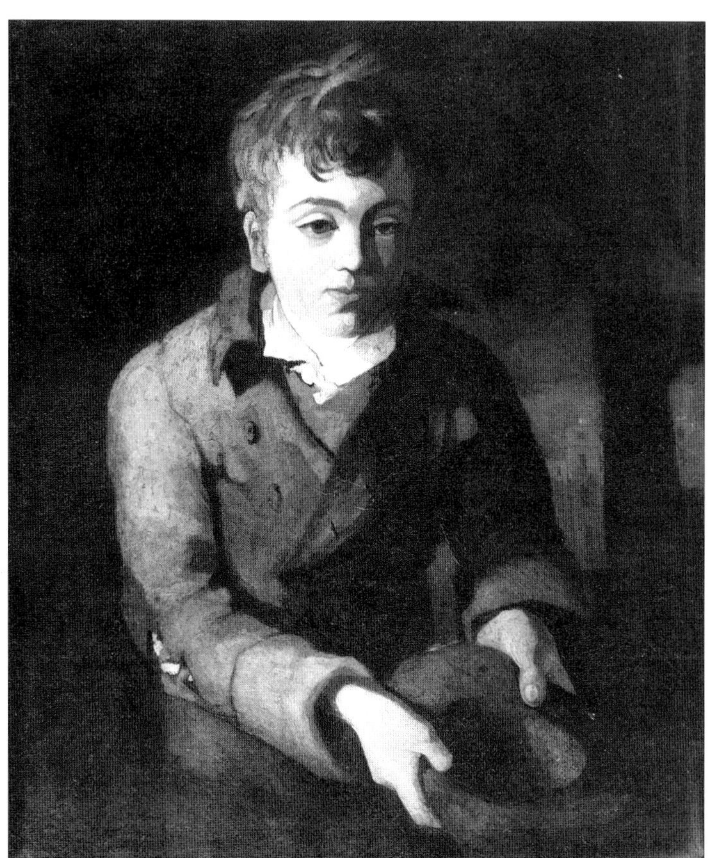

John Sell Cotman, The Beggar Boy, oil on millboard, 1808, 28½ in x 24¼ in

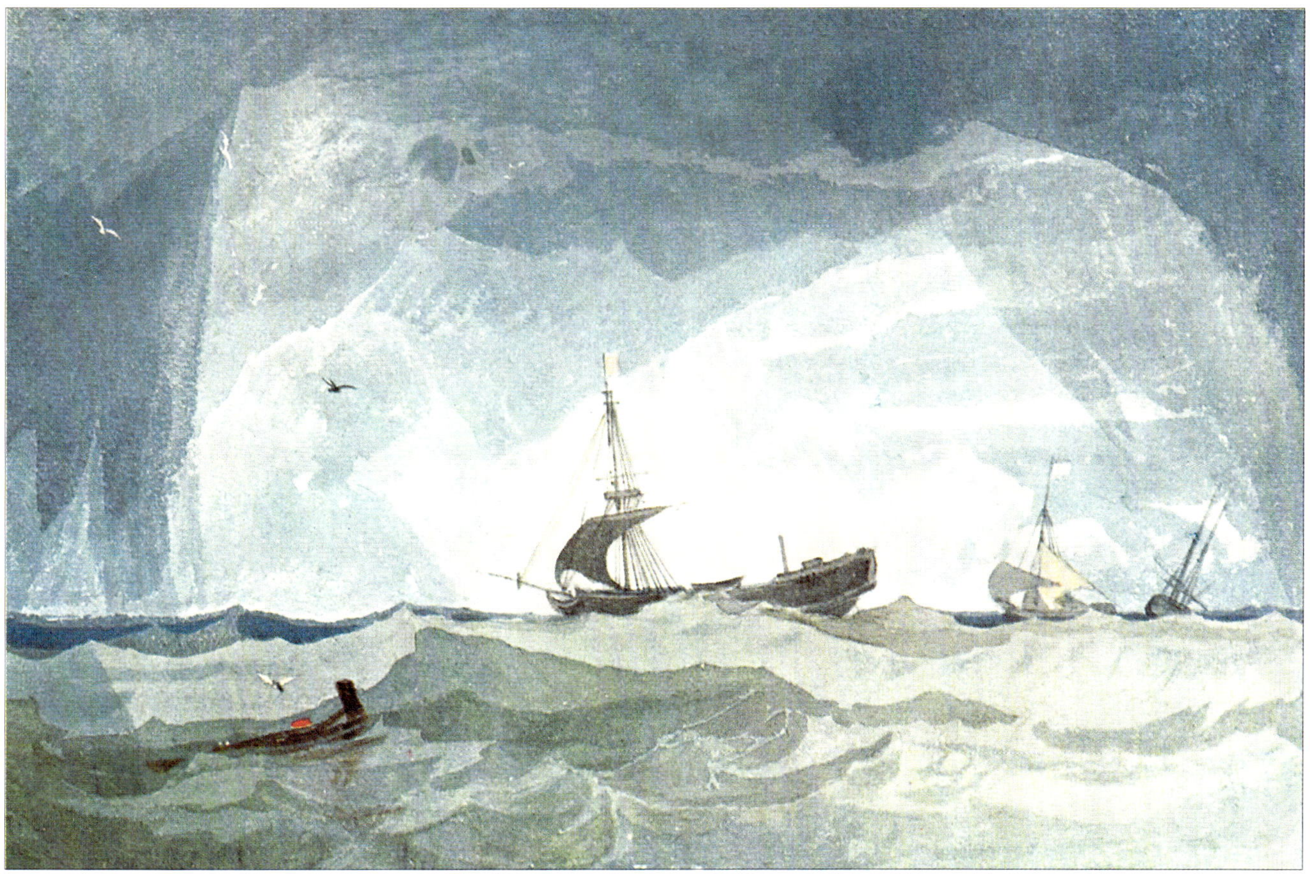

John Sell Cotman, Dismasted Brig, watercolour, 12¼ in x 8 in

towards you. God bless you, dear Cotty, and "forget me not".'

Cholmeley was not in good health and it must have been a terrible blow to Cotman when he died less than three years after the final Yorkshire visit. Mrs Cholmeley, who never got over the death of her husband, died two years later leaving Cotman a small legacy, but nothing could compensate him for the loss of his dearest friends and most loyal supporters. Francis Cholmeley wrote after his mother's death, 'Her friendship for you extended beyond the grave and she left you a bequest of £100. Let me hear from you now and do not let me quite lose sight of you, though the prospect of our meeting grows less every day.'

Cotman pulled himself up after his attack of deep depression following the 'failure' of his finest work; he even reacted by producing some very traditional paintings of extra detailed trees to show that he could paint for the critics *if* he so wished. He had left London for Norwich in 1807 to pursue his teaching as possibly a more stable way of making a living; he also advertised himself as a portrait painter. Undoubtedly John Sell in his way had a certain skill with figures and faces but some of his subjects chosen for appeal rather than commercial portraiture have more character. 'The Beggar Boy' in Norwich Castle Museum is a delight. During this Norwich period he produced a number of oil paintings evincing strong colour and good drawing but, although few survive, they are believed to lack the quality not only of the Greta watercolours but any of his pure drawing. Obviously he had set himself a full programme trying to work himself out of the post-Yorkshire low. To advertise his teaching he put on an exhibition of 'upwards of Five Hundred Drawings'; Kitson describes the collection, some to be used as drawing copies as well as for exhibition: '. . . these early drawings have some of the quality and vision which characterized his work during the Greta period' and adds: 'There is, however, a difference; in these drawing copies Cotman was no longer recording his emotions in the presence of Nature for his own delight and satisfaction, but, instead, he was evolving patterns from his old sketches in his painting room with the definite purpose of endeavouring to initiate others into a kingdom which must ever remain exclusively his own.'

Cotman also contributed substantially to the Norwich Society exhibitions at this time; he was elected a Member in 1808 (submitting 67 works) and became Vice-President in 1810. Yet another innovation was his circulating library of drawings, a method of 'teaching' favoured by Ackermann; he advertised:

> J.S. COTMAN
> has opened to the Public on the plan of a Circulating Library a Collection of SIX HUNDRED DRAWINGS, consisting of Landscapes, Compositions or Design, and Figures, Coloured Sketches from Nature, sketches in Claro Obscuro, and his original Pencil sketches from the Saxon, Norman and Gothic architecture, chiefly from Yorkshire, Essex and Norfolk.
> Quarterly subscription Ticket – One Guinea
> J.S. Cotman will attend the delivery to the subscribers, that he may facilitate their copying them by his instructions.

In 1809 Cotman married Ann Miles, sister of Mrs John Thirtle; family life, in spite of increasing his teaching practice and his circulating library, in the house and lifestyle he favoured proved expensive and he was persuaded to accept an offer from Dawson Turner and move temporarily to Yarmouth in 1811. Never could it be said that Cotman shirked hard work and the total output of his life in all media must have been phenomenal.

Times were becoming harder and patrons fewer for all the Norwich artists. Norwich itself was beginning to lose some of its prestige as a centre for the arts causing a diminution of pupils. Also, Cotman was fighting the long established teaching practice of John Crome. Thinking that he might gain through printed work, he put much time and effort into perfecting his etching technique. Using some of the best of those delightfully spontaneous early drawings, he produced for the experience and his own pleasure some attractive soft ground works. This inspired him (*c.*1810) to advertise a forthcoming collection of etchings in the hope of attracting subscribers. Many of the 26 plates for 'Miscellaneous Etchings' were Yorkshire subjects and he put much care and effort into their preparation, this confirmed by the fact that the whole collection was assembled between September 1810 and July 1811. The subscription list, of some 240 names, was encouraging and included Dawson Turner, the younger Cholmeleys and a number of their friends, Dr Monro, Lord Palmerston, the Marquis and Marchioness of Stafford and some of his artist colleagues – Crome, Thirtle, Ladbroke, Freeman and others.

In the light of his new found interest, Francis Cholmeley lent Cotman some copies of Piranesi etchings which proved a great source of inspiration to him. He tried to buy a set for himself but it proved too costly; however Dawson Turner bought a set which was there for both of them to study and admire. These examples had given Cotman a tremendous feeling for classical subjects and for treating suitable architectural subjects in the classical manner. Cotman embarked on another tour of Norfolk in search of good material for a second set of etchings of his own, visiting Walsingham and other centres of architectural interest including many of Norfolk's wonderful heritage of churches. These drawings and etchings of Norfolk antiquities occupied him intermittently until they were eventually published in 1818 as 'A Series of Etchings Illustrating the Architectural Antiquities of Norfolk'. A very special presentation copy to Dawson Turner is now in the British Museum.

The etching period in Norwich and Yarmouth roughly dates from 1810 to 1820. As well as those already mentioned, Cotman embarked on another series of about a hundred which was to be called 'Specimens of Norman and Gothic Architecture in the County of Norfolk' but, although many single plates were published and some used as source material for drawing copies, the project in its entirety was not completed. The drawings themselves provide valuable records for many of the subjects no longer exist. 'Engravings of the Most Remarkable of the Sepulchral Brasses in Norfolk' was published in 1819.

There is so much to admire in Cotman's etched work – deservedly well-known British subjects

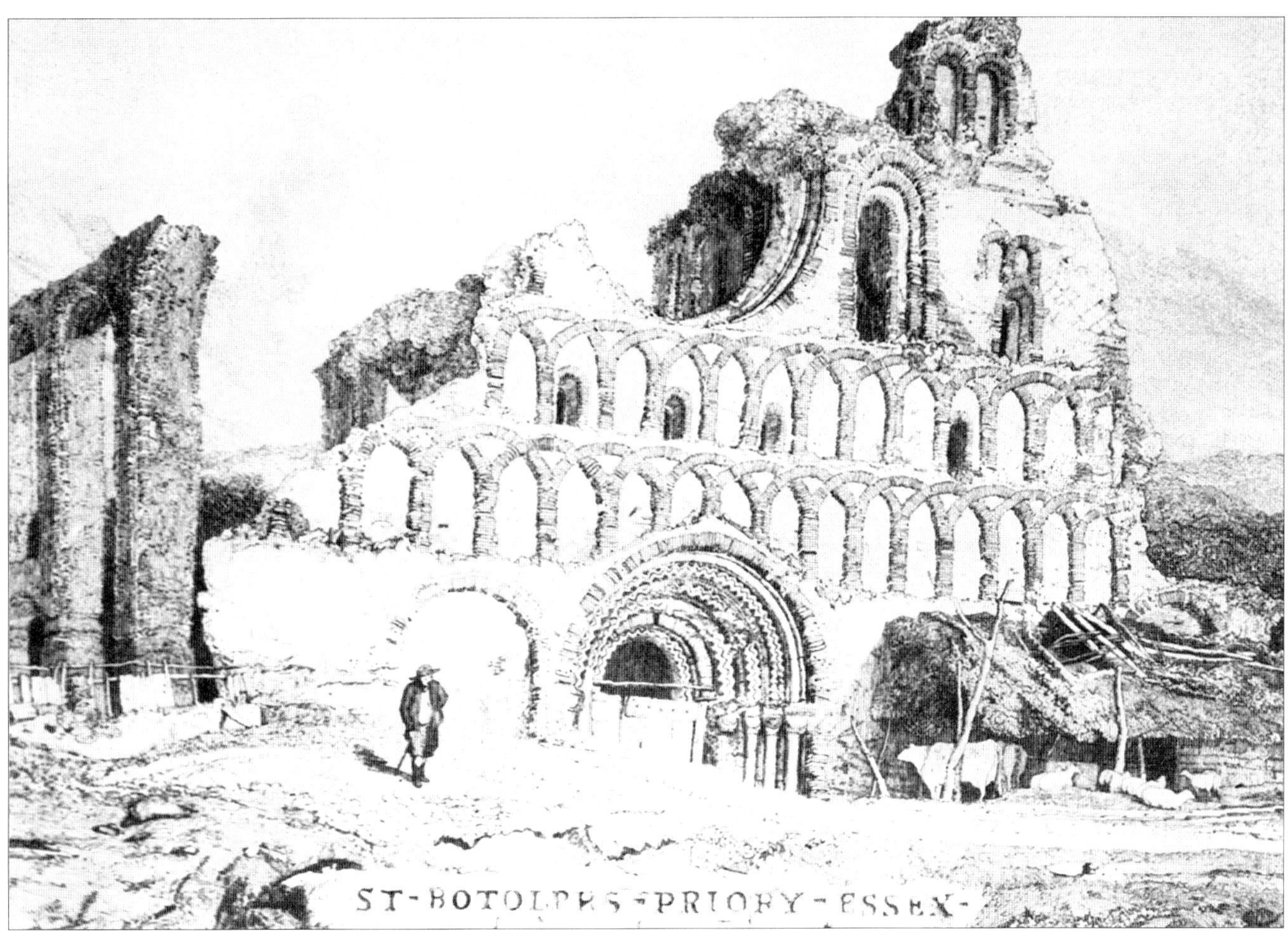

John Sell Cotman, St. Botolph's Priory, Essex, etching, 1804-5, 10⅛ in x 14½ in

are the extraordinarily complex 'Croyland Abbey, Lincolnshire' (published 1811) and 'St. Botolph's Priory, Essex', also 1811, both of which clearly indicate the Piranesi touch. Many of the Norwich subjects are also outstanding and the 'Doorway Leading to the Refectory of Rievaulx Abbey, Yorkshire', has all the gentle quality of the original drawing the Cholmeleys had admired so much. Dawson Turner, while not enamoured of Cotman's more forward looking watercolours, viewed this etching phase in a totally different light. Not only was he full of admiration but saw how he could make capital out of it himself and, at the same time, offer Cotman regular work and security. Consequently he invited Cotman and his family to move to Yarmouth; he would pay the artist a salary of £200 to tutor his wife and daughters and employ him personally as illustrator of his many literary projects. Cotman prevaricated for a while, but the steady income was a great draw, especially as a second child was on the way, and he eventually consented provided a suitable and congenial house could be found. After a slight delay caused by Cotman's ill health, they moved in April 1912, thereafter spending 12 years at their home in Southtown which still stands and bears the commemoration plate.

Kitson refers to this move as 'the descent to Yarmouth', almost as though Cotman was degrading himself by deserting the cultural climate of London and Norwich for a plebeian, unaesthetic, environment, almost an admission of defeat. Kitson also tends to overstate the 'drudgery' of this new life, working hard for Dawson Turner and teaching his family, inferring that what he was doing meant compromising his talent by neglecting the other facets of his art, watercolour, oil or whatever he fancied. Judging by Cotman's own correspondence during this time and the fact that he stayed in one place for 12 years, he enjoyed most of what he was doing and became completely involved in his architectural work.

Daily he repaired to the Bank House to his pupils but he certainly did not spend all his time teaching. He travelled all over Norfolk in search of the subject matter Dawson Turner was

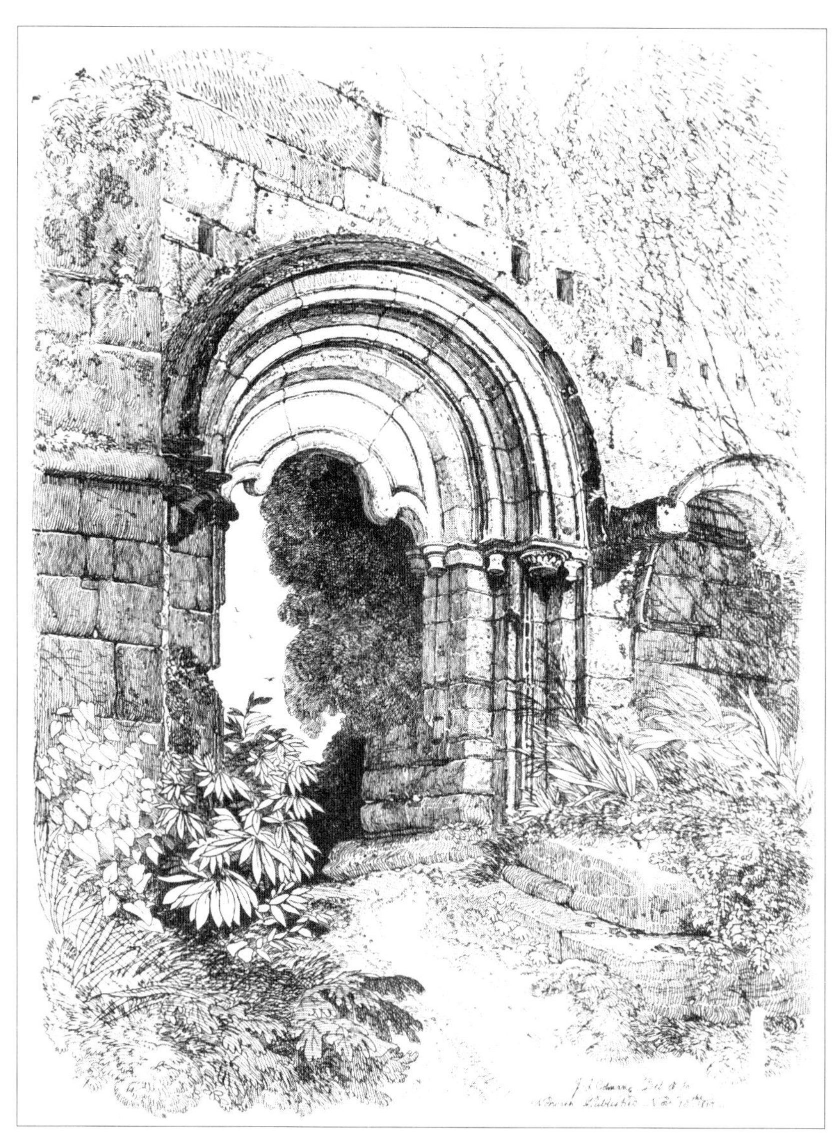

John Sell Cotman, Doorway Leading to the Refectory of Rievaulx Abbey, Yorkshire, etching published 1810, 11⅞ in x 8⅞ in

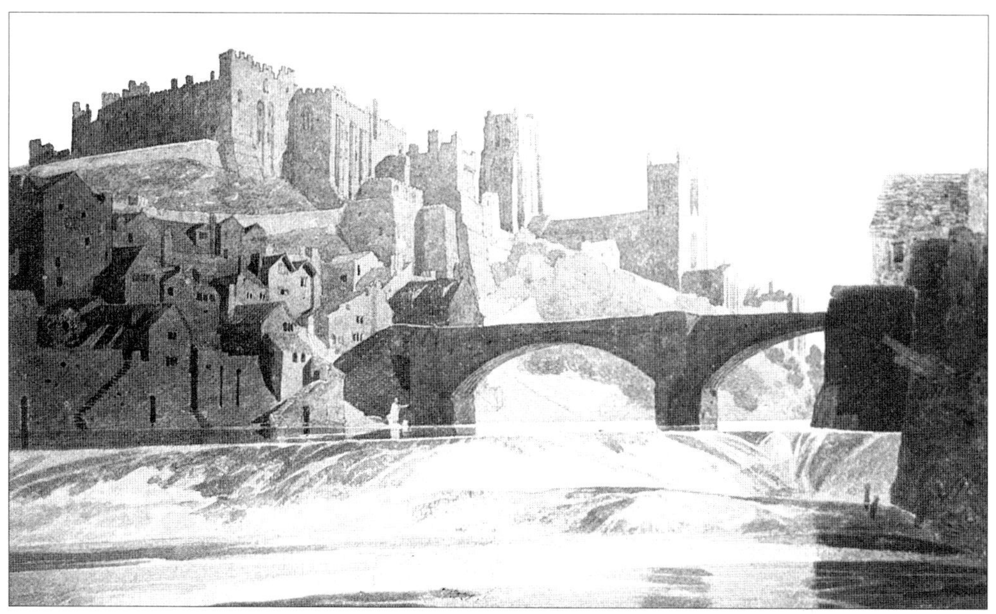

John Sell Cotman, Durham Cathedral, watercolour, c.1809-10, 12½ in x 21 in

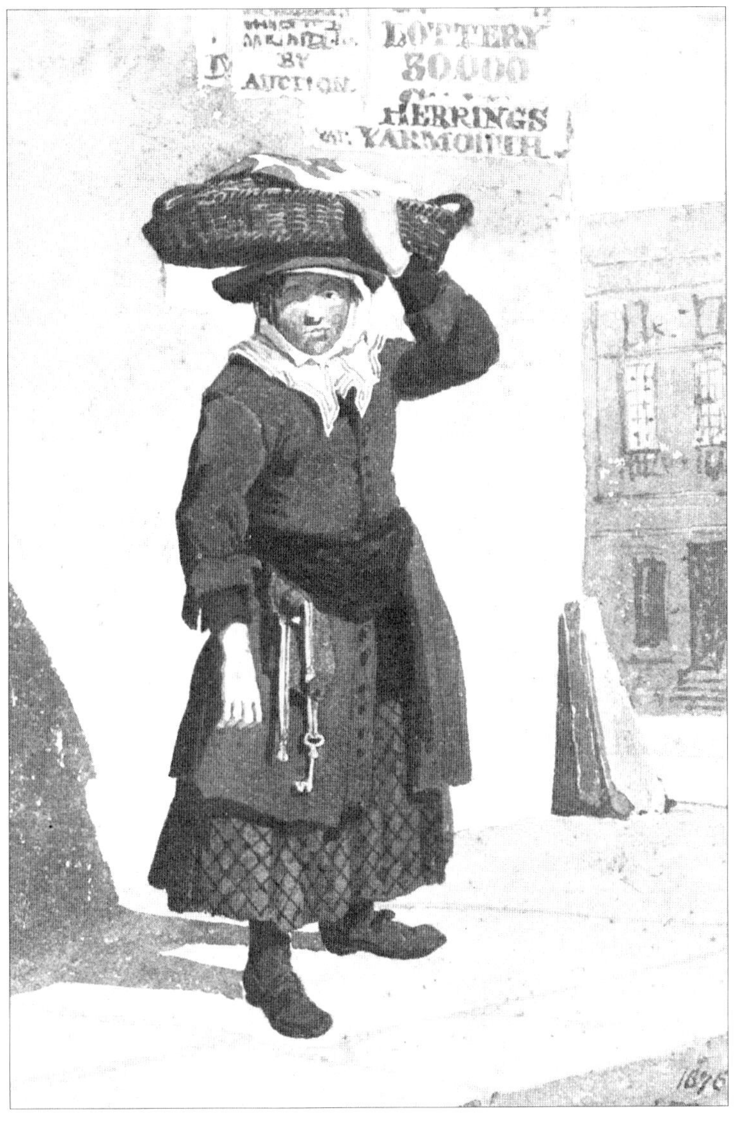

John Sell Cotman,
The Fishwife, watercolour

Watercolour drawing from the Yarmouth period

looking for, and often combined teaching and sketching by taking Mrs Turner and any or all of her daughters with him. Mrs Turner herself was a talented lady, an able portraitist and a competent draughtswoman. She also understood her tutor, and her unobtrusive kindness to him was certainly instrumental in keeping life on an even keel. She was a clever etcher, too, which enabled her to involve herself with the major work in progress and to understand the rigours of that exacting craft. Kitson mentions that, in addition to other work, Cotman was turning out at least one etched plate a fortnight for Dawson Turner. But this was what Cotman himself had become deeply involved with at this time and, bearing in mind his capacity for hard work and pleasure in the result, I doubt if he regarded it as 'drudgery', especially as there was a certain amount of help with the hack work. He had ample freedom in the quest for subjects, although Dawson Turner encouraged him to visit every church in Norfolk, and the different venues and their subjects must have given his pupils an added interest in their own work. While all this was going on Cotman seems to have found time to indulge in some work of his own; his early love of 'tips' never left him and anything to do with the sea and ships was a potentially appealing subject. There are many recorded drawings and paintings of Yarmouth beach and offshore shipping, if not worked up at the time certainly derived from sketches made during his Yarmouth period. The family were not left out either – there is a charming drawing of his plump little daughter, Ann, with a toy boat.

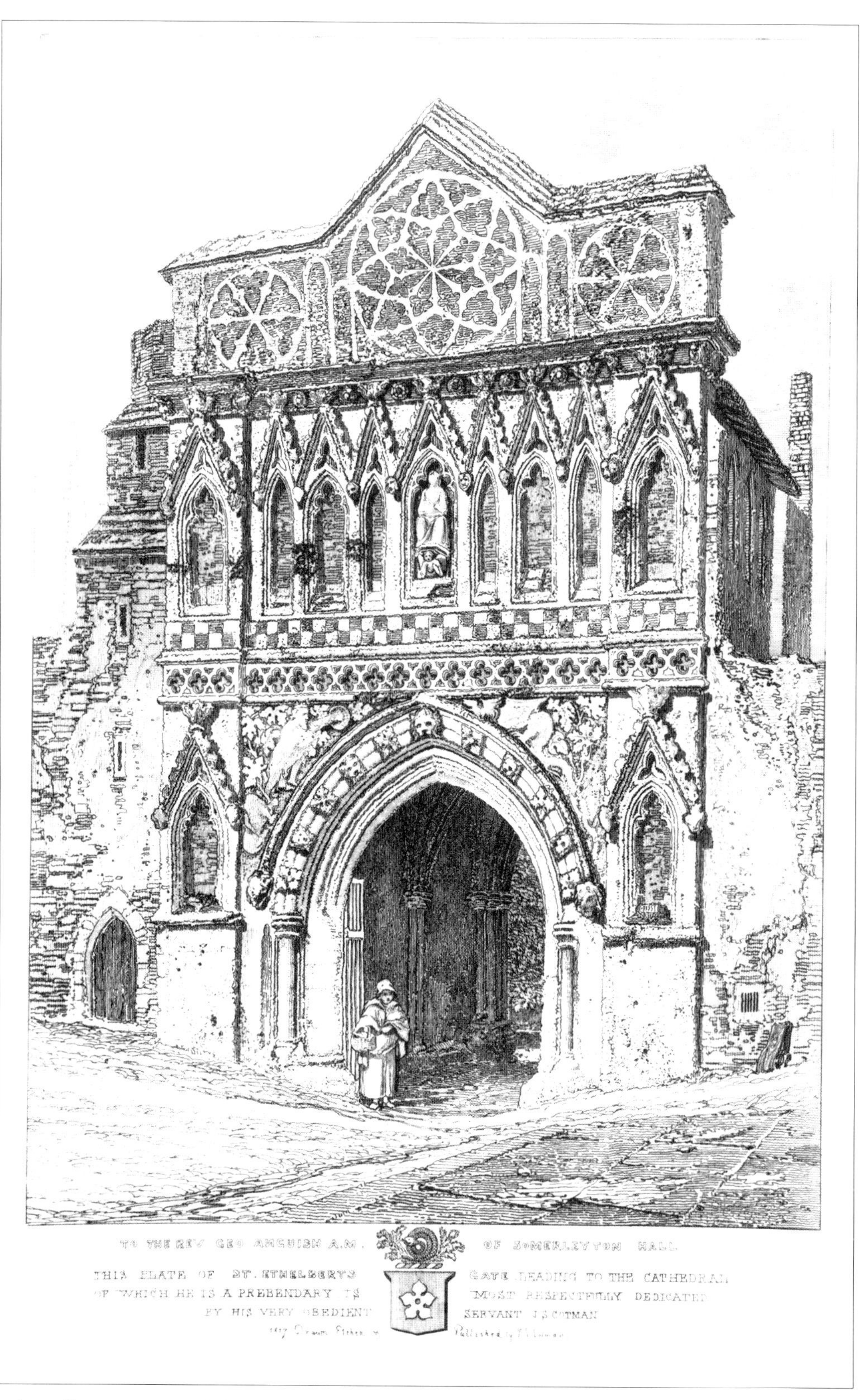

John Sell Cotman, St. Ethelbert's Gate, Norwich, etching published 1817, 14⅝ in x 9½ in

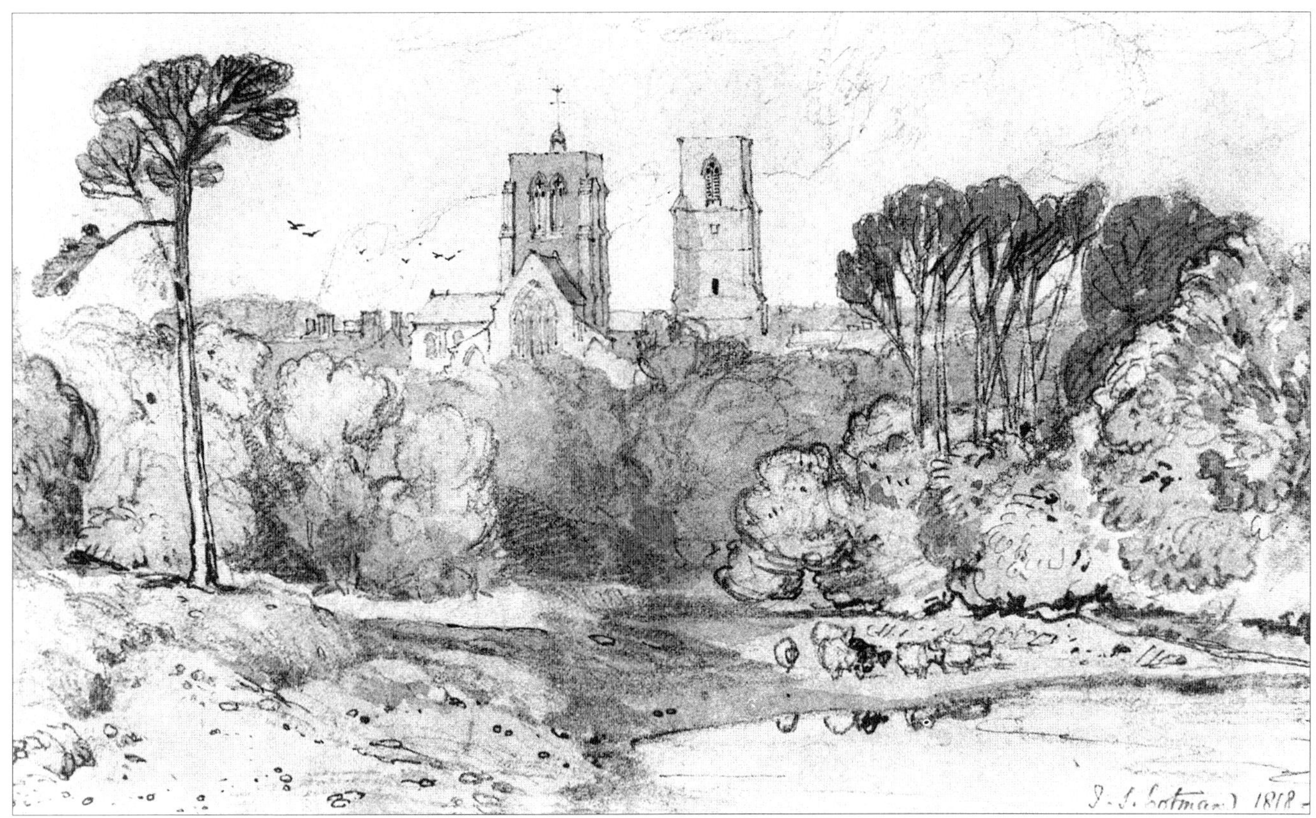

John Sell Cotman, East Dereham, Norfolk, pencil and brown wash, 1818, 5½ in x 9 in

With the security of a steady income, family life itself must have been more agreeable for all concerned. After Ann, John Joseph was born in 1814, Francis Walter in 1816 and Alfred Henry in 1819. Eventually on Dawson Turner's advice Cotman bought his house, any feeling of doubt about Yarmouth or his patron seeming to have vanished. Many, many years later, in 1841, Dawson Turner wrote enthusiastically of Cotman and his work, all he had done for him [Dawson Turner] and the great benefit his daughters had derived from Cotman's teaching. Cotman acknowledged his words with gratitude referring to his sincere respect always for Dawson Turner's advice and judgement and remembered 'the very, oh very many, recollections of happy hours spent in your valuable society'. To a friend he added, 'I loved my employer – his family, and all his doings'. Not the words of a man being domineered or subjected to unwanted discipline.

The highlights of the years based in Yarmouth were the three Normandy visits which resulted in some of the most stupendous drawings of all time. Dawson Turner had decided to produce a book(s) on the antiquities of Normandy, the text to be his own, the illustrations by John Sell Cotman. Accounts of these tours have been documented many times,* most of the information being derived from Cotman's letters to Dawson Turner and to his wife giving accounts of places he visited, the countryside he travelled and the sometimes rather unpleasant inns in which he stayed. Dawson Turner used his share of the correspondence to complete *A Tour of Normandy* (1820) which is well worth looking out for.

Setting off first in 1817, Cotman spent a few days in London *en route,* visiting another old friend and sometime patron, Sir Henry Englefield, who added 'an unlimited order for drawings from Amiens, Abbeville and Beauvais'. Arriving at Dieppe a few days later Cotman was completely fascinated by the charm of the countryside, a fascination which continued through Montivilliers, Le Havre, Lillebonne, Rouen, Granville and Avranches, back to Le Havre via Caen, Harfleur and many charming villages and small towns on the way. The lodging houses in no way lived up to the scenery but during the five and a half weeks of wandering Cotman made many, many sketches ready to be used when he returned. While most were worked up into etchings for Dawson Turner, many more were turned into pictures for himself, sometimes years later, including the

* Kitson; also Andrew Moore's Catalogue of the Bi-centenary Exhibition in Norwich Castle in 1982.

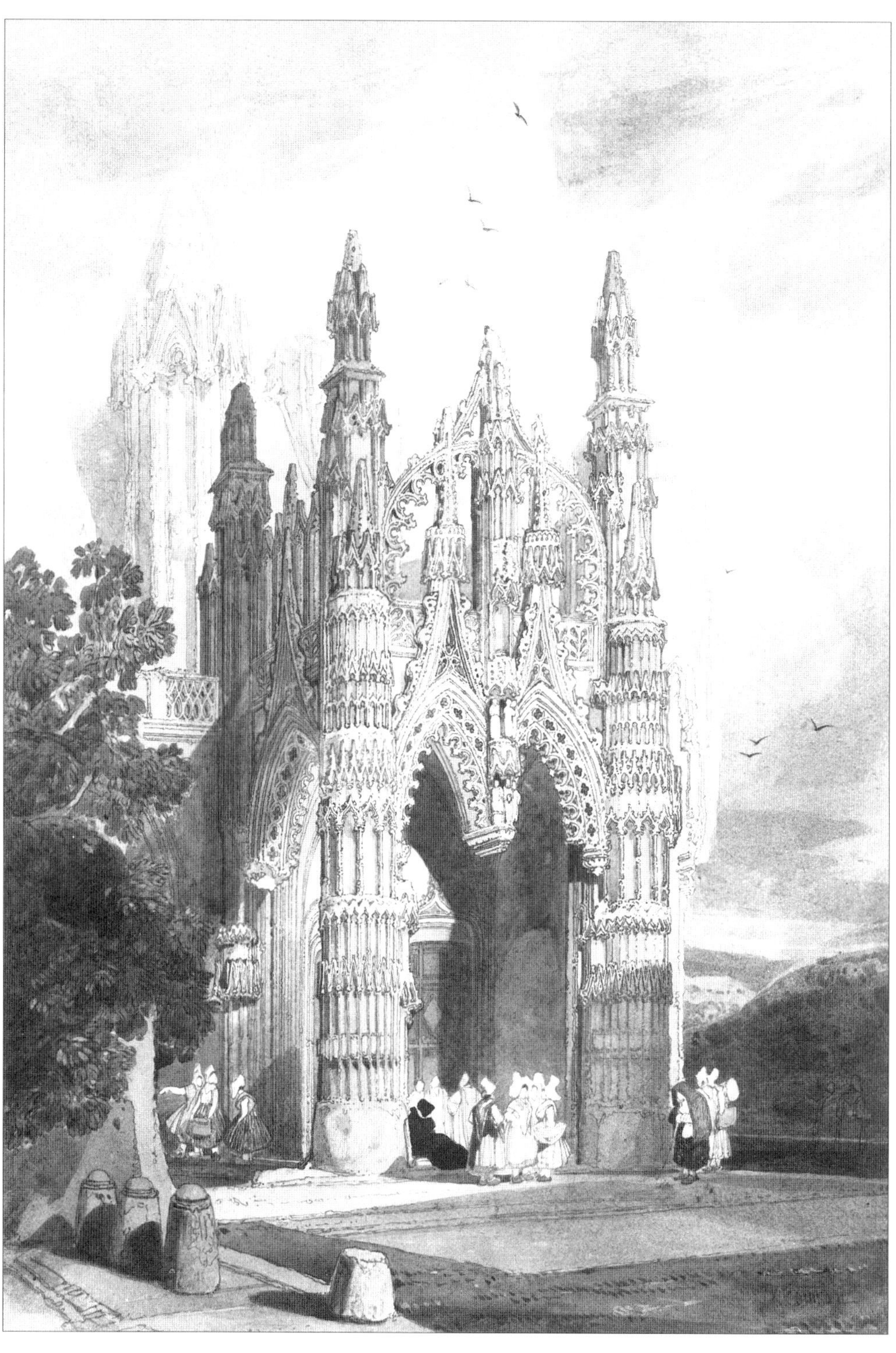

John Sell Cotman, South Porch of the Church of Louviers, watercolour, c.1825-26, 18¼ in x 12⅞ in

monumental 'South Porch of the Church of Louviers' and 'The Abbatial House of the Abbey of St. Ouen at Rouen', which show Cotman's pure drawing at its unsurpassable best.

Initially Cotman had been rather reluctant to embark, a year later, on a further Normandy tour, largely owing to the unfortunate accommodation. However, he relented on hearing that, although likely to be in France for almost twice as long, he would be joining Mrs Turner and her daughters who were already enjoying a continental holiday. Obviously there would be more attention paid to creature comforts than for a mere man with a sketch book travelling on his own.

This time they visited many of the places Cotman had been to on his first trip and added the

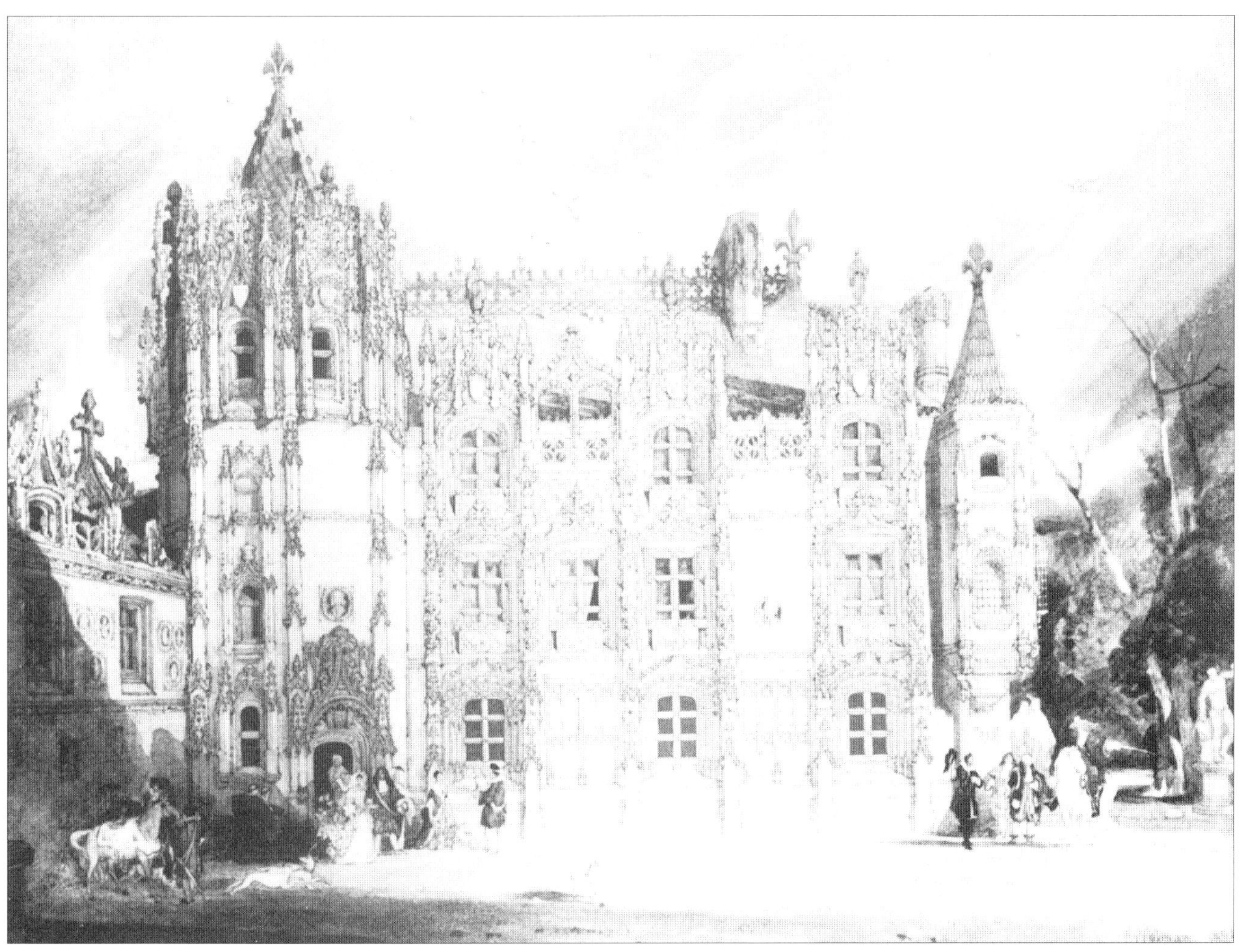

John Sell Cotman,
The Abbatial House of the Abbey of St. Ouen at Rouen,
pencil, ink and watercolour, 1825, 16¼ in x 22½ in

district east of Rouen including Valognes and Cherbourg. Dawson Turner himself joined them for a few days at Caen and Falaise. Undoubtedly the Turner ladies found Cotman a great help even if his own sketching activity was slowed down a little; it seems that he did rather more intensive work after they had left. The Turners had introduced him to friends in France so the whole tour was more congenial than the first and, over the two trips, he practically fulfilled Dawson Turner's requirements of some 400 sketches to be spread over six volumes of 'Architectural Antiquities of Normandy' for which he, Dawson Turner, would provide the letterpress.

Cotman himself was keen to go yet once more to Normandy. As well as planning a collection of views of the cathedrals, he had an urge to make more landscape sketches, a tour of the Normandy landscape as opposed to architecture, which he could use himself for other purposes at a later date. He was so enraptured by the countryside that he felt the need for memories of his own as well as slavishly following the whims of Dawson Turner. To quote Derek Clifford:

> The pursuit of architectural material to feed Dawson Turner for use in his researches led him to Normandy in 1817, in 1818 and again in 1820. These resulted in the publication (in 1822) of 'Architectural Antiquities of Normandy', in which Cotman's plates illustrated his patron's text. At first Cotman's natural leanings towards antiquarianism threw him whole-heartedly into the work, but as eventually Dawson Turner's hobby changed from discovering the origins of Gothic architecture to collecting autograph letters, Cotman rebelled against the need to make factual drawings and began to allow himself to see again as an artist and not as a *camera lucida*. Though artistic merit was not required of these drawings, they never fell below a high level of competence and often have a more positive quality, although in many of them the mechanical means leaves a certain unsympathetic starkness. Now and again throughout his Normandy tours, and particularly the last, the artistic vision swamps the antiquarian and some superlative drawings result. Some of these were designed for a book on 'Picturesque Normandy' which, like so many of Cotman's projects, died for want of encouragement.

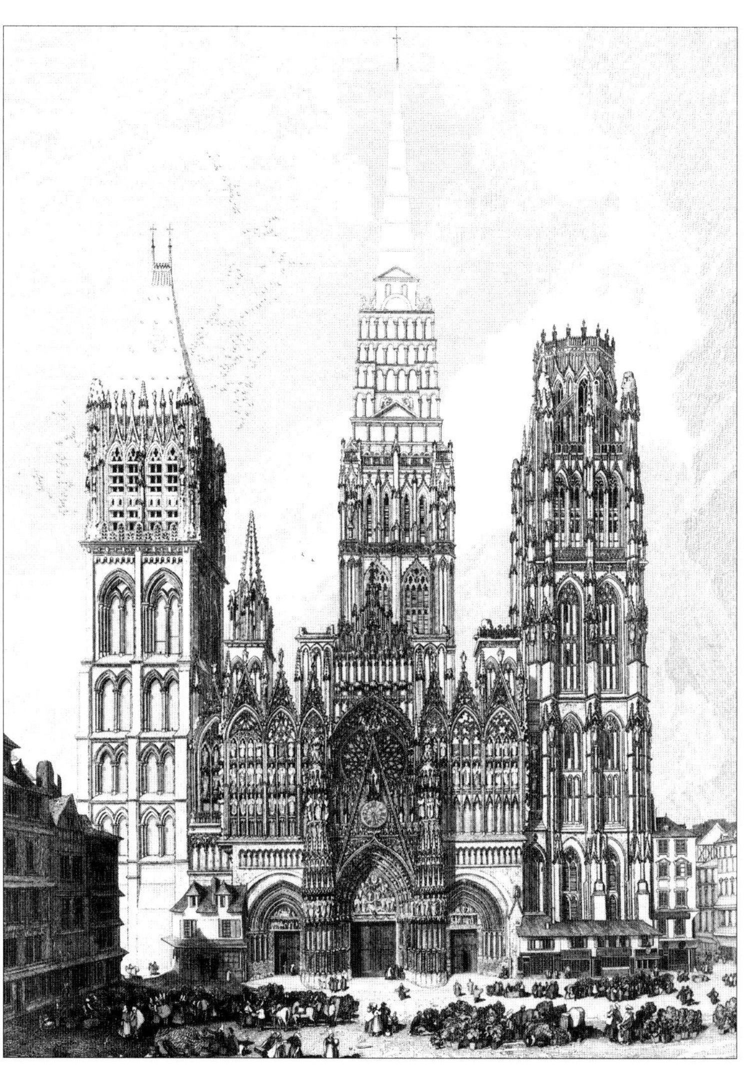

John Sell Cotman, Cathedral Church of Nôtre Dame at Rouen, west front, etching published 1821, 21¼ in x 15⅞ in

Unfortunately Cotman's last Normandy tour was cut short by an injury to his leg, perhaps partly the result of the miles and miles of walking he had undertaken. He was laid up while in Caen, rather worrying the friends he had made there by leaving before they regarded him as fit. His general health had not been at its best even before the accident.

Once back in Yarmouth, Cotman worked almost every waking hour at the mammoth undertaking before him. In the end 'Architectural Antiquities of Normandy', reduced to two volumes, was published in 1822. The choice of subjects was Dawson Turner's with suggestions from the publishers, not always those Cotman himself would have selected, but he still had the sketches and, of course, the promise they held for him. The whole thing is an undoubted achievement although historians are agreed that both its value and its attraction lie in Cotman's superb illustrations; Dawson Turner's contribution is pretty shallow and no doubt, in the end, the thought of filling six volumes proved too ambitious for him.

Certainly the project enhanced Cotman's reputation, especially among his fellow artists in Norwich. During his time away from the city, the secession had taken place but he had played no part in it. Now things were coming together again and exhibitions, as John Sell noted, were getting back to normal. In 1821 Cotman exhibited two of his Normandy etchings which brought forth an enthusiastic response from the *Norwich Mercury*: 'Mr. J.S. Cotman has two magnificent etchings of buildings from his book on Normandy. This gentleman's talent has been so highly appreciated by the world of art, that no commendation we can bestow would add a grain to his celebrity. This work is highly honourable to himself, his county and his nation.'

Undoubtedly these kind words and the general approval and appreciation with which the

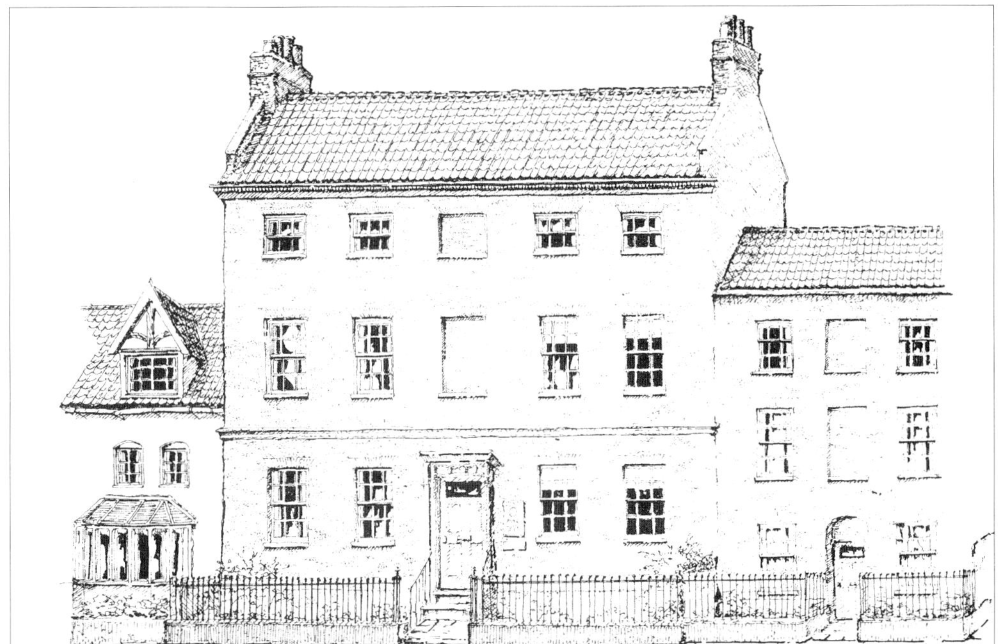

Pauline Sutcliffe, 1986, contemporary impression of Cotman's house at St. Martin's Palace Plain, Norwich.

Normandy volumes were received were gratifying to Cotman but he paid the price for his hard and intensive work. There had been one or two periods of characteristic depression during the years of preparation but physically the effects had also taken their toll. On a brief visit to London he collapsed and was unwell for some little time suffering from a liver infection.

As we have seen, by this time Dawson Turner's enthusiasm for antiquarianism was beginning to wane. Cotman, after such intensity of focus on one particular enterprise, was beginning to feel in limbo, and that Yarmouth had rather worn itself out for him. The death of Crome meant that more teaching opportunities should be forthcoming and, above all, he felt the need to return to his native city.

The return to Norwich in 1824 heralded a new decade in John Sell Cotman's life, a time when he produced a wide diversity of drawing and painting, a time when bouts of black despair alternated with periods of excitement and *joie de vivre,* of ill health and well being, of highs and lows in almost every facet of his life and work. As he grew older his uncertain temperament became more so and fluctuations in fortune and health over this time only added to the effects. The financial insecurity which, despite payment in hard work and intense effort to some extent of his own choosing, had been alleviated during the Yarmouth years started again to rear its head and cause much anxiety. The family had returned to the large and imposing Georgian house in St. Martin's Palace Plain, which at one point Cotman planned to turn into a veritable art centre, and the expense of maintaining such a house was more than the Cotmans could reasonably expect to afford. While conceding that times were hard with crippling post-war taxation, and that Cotman's true worth, with the possible exception of his architectural drawings, was not fully recognised during his lifetime, as Oppé rightly points out, Cotman was doing no less well than most of his artist contemporaries; they were just more frugal and chose a more manageable life style. He was something of a magpie, too, and prints or books that attracted him had to be his if the money was in his pocket. If the sun was shining, there was no thought of the rainy day!

Early in 1824 Cotman advertised in the *Norwich Mercury*:

> School for Drawing and Painting in Watercolour, St. Martin-at-Palace,
> J.S. COTMAN
> intends immediately after the Christmas vacation to open in Norwich a SCHOOL FOR DRAWING proposedly to embrace every instruction necessary to give the Professional Student and Amateur Artist!

To quote Kitson, he planned to create 'a school of art where the nobility and gentry of Norfolk and the citizens of Norwich might foregather to receive his instructions in the elegant arts of drawing and design.' He fitted the house with reproduction antiques and bric-à-brac and hung etchings and drawings all round to create what he felt was the right atmosphere.

Together with his family, he embarked on making drawing copies once more, and sorted out a suitable selection from his Norfolk architectural studies and some of the Normandy drawings. About 200 other Normandy drawings, together with some of those for the 'Monumental Brasses' and other etchings, were entered in a one day sale to help pay for the removal from Yarmouth and for 'suitable' furnishings for the house and teaching accessories. Unfortunately the sale was not very rewarding; the buyers were mainly dealers who tended, as dealers will, to 'share out' the spoils at the lowest possible prices. Kitson gives us an interesting sequel to this unfortunate sale. Some 70 years later many of the Normandy drawings were found in a locked drawer and, it being at the lowest point of the First World War, the finder handed them over to the Red Cross. After the Armistice in 1918 they were yet again sold at Christie's but for prices many, many times higher than in the original sale. The distinguished buyers included the Tate Gallery, Manchester City Art Gallery, the Whitwell Institute and many private collectors.

As well as his teaching, between the bouts of ill health or depression Cotman was producing some exciting work of his own. He was also taking a much more active part in the Norwich Society, showing a large quantity of works in almost every exhibition except during the pause in 1826/7 when the new accommodation was awaited. In 1823 his 19 exhibits included examples of the Normandy drawings with monochrome wash which had, and still have, a very personal and arresting attraction. The local press almost purred:

> It is a sincere gratification to us to see MR. COTMAN'S works once more gracing the room. He is a man of uncommon powers, both intellectual and practical, and when he strikes out a style of his own the very licence he uses is an indication of talent which sets him above the level of common faculties. His design is always magnificent, and the practised eye of the artist discovers this, the capital property of his mind, at a glance . . . there is, whether in his pencil or watercolour drawings, an elegance and taste pervading the whole, which is as delightful as it is true . . . the period drawings might safely challenge exhibition with those of any artist in Britain.

Fulsome praise indeed from the *Norwich Mercury*. Yet, in 1824, the paper's critic virtually denied his kind words by, as in 1806/7, criticising some of Cotman's finest work which was beyond his understanding.

Cotman was made a Vice-President of the Society in 1831 and 1832, President in 1833, and played a very active part in important initial loan exhibitions in 1828 and 1829. He became involved with the introduction of artists' conversaziones of 1830-32, when artists tried to encourage a wider appreciation of their work by exhibiting, discussing their work and organising lectures and demonstrations. It has to be remembered that during the years of intensive sketching and etching Cotman hardly touched colour and in the second year of showing again with the Norwich Society (1824) among his 52 exhibits the reaction began to show. For almost the first time since the earlier Norwich period, oil paintings were included of varying quality. A number of the Yarmouth sketches were painted up using both oil and watercolour with some success including the famous 'Dismasted Brig,' (see p.77), perhaps the best known marine watercolour of all. Familiar oils included 'Dutch Boats off Yarmouth', rather reminiscent of Cuyp, 'After the Storm' and 'View from Yarmouth Bridge Looking Towards Breydon just after Sunset' which was highly praised by the *Norfolk Chronicle*. For a time he tried translating the Greta technique into oil with, regrettably, the same reaction from the local press which was otherwise treating him kindly at this time. Yet, by present day criteria, these are some of the most beautiful of his oils. The maligned 'Trees at Kimberley', so very much misunderstood in its day, is very much in the Greta tradition while 'Silver Birches', also 1824, is magical. Andrew Moore points out that 'the lyrical quality reaches its climax in this composition', Kitson describes it as 'one of the most distinguished of all Cotman's paintings' and Binyon sees it as 'one of Cotman's finest and most fortunate works'. Sadly suffering the ravages of time and poor restoration, 'The Silent Stream, Normandy', is still pure lyric poetry. As his colour became more brilliant, the effect frequently suffered although 'The Mishap', another well-known piece, is an attractive 'transitional' example – the atmosphere of the Greta is still there but the muted colours are just beginning to give way to bolder, though still subtle, golds, greens and warmer tones. From there his oils entered a very blue and gold phase, the brilliance of the colouring sometimes approaching the garish.

His watercolours of the early part of this Norwich period also became too gaudy for many people's taste. Some of the continental subjects, so indescribably beautiful in monochrome or muted shades, were almost killed by intense blue skies and added vivid colour. The *Norfolk Chronicle* found them 'too gaudy and we regret the absence of that sweet grey tone which is so charming in nature.' Other watercolours including, again, some of the Yarmouth subjects, happily were more moderate and Cotman was made an Associate of the Old Watercolour Society in 1824, an election made with the influence of Dawson Taylor's daughter, Lady Palgrave.

1826/7 was a bad year for Cotman; he became so mentally and physically ill that his family and Dawson Turner almost feared for his reason. Partly this was down to his natural temperament but overwork undoubtedly played a part; not only had he pushed himself to the limit during the Yarmouth years but there seemed so many things to do, so many old skills to be resurrected, that he worked himself almost to extinction during all the time he was not teaching. Then there was the feeling of being unable to keep up with expenses. Pupils were not so abundant as he had hoped and expected, any more than sales. As well as the effect of the economic depression following the Napoleonic Wars, Cotman suffered to some extent by the diversity in his work and the fact that, given that in much of it he was years ahead of his time, too many people lacked understanding and appreciation of his unusually advanced talent and its achievement. Drawing, too, was becoming less highly regarded as the fashionable accomplishment for young ladies; the visual arts had had a long run in Norwich but music was beginning to take over.

About this time Cotman sought the advice of Dawson Turner who pointed out the obvious, that he was trying to maintain a house and a lifestyle far beyond his means. He suggested a return to Yarmouth but Cotman felt there would be even fewer opportunities there and it was for that reason he had returned to life and work in Norwich. Dawson Turner replied:

> Different as is your situation from what your talents ought to command, or what your former prospects may have led you to expect, there really does not appear to me to be anything in it to justify the dreadfully gloomy view you have taken. You have raised yourself a phantom, which your tender regard towards your family and apprehension for the consequences prevent you from examining close; but, my friend, the only way to combat our evils is to look them in the face, and he who has once done that has already gained half the battle.
>
> There is much cause for regret in your circumstances, but never for despondency. The times are wretchedly bad; they are unfortunate to everything but particularly the luxuries of life, with which retrenchment naturally first begins. But they will rally again, as we have often known them do before, and with your sense and experience the lesson now forced upon you will not be lost. In your own drawings, too, I cannot doubt but you will find resource. You have lived long enough to learn that your present style will not succeed, and you have talent enough to adopt any other. The public is a body that cannot be forced. Some extraordinary geniuses may have succeeded in guiding it but they are few, and the great part of those who have made the experiment have failed. Such among us who have to live by it must be content to follow its taste.
>
> What seems to me in your case particularly important is to do nothing hastily or rashly. You have done very wisely in giving notice to quit your house: before you fix up another, wherever it may be, see carefully what you can appropriate to this purpose. Above all do not fear that by altering your residence or mode of life, you will sink in the estimation of the world; in my opinion you will rise.

The long letter and the well intentioned advice shows Dawson Turner's ongoing concern for Cotman and his family, but John Sell must have winced a little at Dawson Turner's reference to 'an able draughtsman, a competent drawing master and a bad man of business driven to despair by his temperament and circumstances.' To some extent he took Dawson Turner's advice to pander to popular taste even if it went against the grain; he also started house hunting in Norwich but, predictably, could find nothing he fancied any more than he fancied moving back to Yarmouth. Further despairing letters to his counsellor prompted Dawson Turner to write to Cotman's father, even suggesting that John Sell might lodge with him temporarily while the rest of the family returned to the Yarmouth house. Understandably John Sell was not minded to heed connivance behind his back; an almost desperate letter to Dawson Turner gives some inkling of his state of mind: '. . . the sun has set for ever on my career and all is darkness before me. Embarrassments are rising about the sale of my South-town house and my wanting to quit this house is not accepted. My pupils diminish to such a degree that it is impossible for me to live in any, save a workhouse or prison.' He was torturing himself, too, about the effect all this was having on Miles Edmund: 'The prospects of Edmund, my fellow labourer, are dead, Sir, he has set steadily to work from 9 o'clock till 6, totally against my wishes, I have seen the effects on his tired face. Sir, I have destroyed my child, my friend, my companion.'

As on previous occasions, however, from this pit of despair something triggered a burst of creative energy, a new mood of hope took over, his health rallied and the family must have heaved sighs of enormous relief. Maybe Cotman suddenly decided to prove himself without the advice which, though requested, did not appeal to him. Whatever it was, by 1830 he was on the crest of a wave and producing some of his best work in all media and in a variety of styles. In 1831 he acquired a new and affluent patron, Francis Gibson, a banker from Saffron Walden. Gibson was an unusually perceptive man even, to Cotman's immense satisfaction, buying some of the Greta watercolours. Cotman was also developing a new technique of mixed media painting using with his watercolour a sort of flour paste which gave opportunity for greater richness and depth and a wider tonal range than with the watercolour alone. It was an adventurous medium, capable of producing such a variety of results, not always intentional, that it gave Cotman a whole new focus. Ink, gum arabic, chalk, wiping out, scraping, anything for effect – but with some quite stunning results. 'Storm on Yarmouth Beach' is one of the most dramatic examples, as is 'St. Benet's Abbey', but it was an adaptable technique that lent itself to all manner of subjects and effects. Apart from the innovations, his drawings and watercolours seemed to be finding favour once more and even pupils seemed on the increase. Miles Edmund was helping in the teaching practice, producing drawing copies and generally making himself useful, not least in providing a steadying influence during his father's moods which, though now shorter and of less severity, never went completely away.

With the renewal of energy and stability John Sell took a more active interest in city activities, attending Shakespeare readings and various lectures and entertainments. In 1828 he went with both his sons on a sailing holiday, all three of them finding and sketching new subjects everywhere they went. It must have been a time of great benefit and rehabilitation to them all and, the following year, Joseph Geldart joined Cotman's class becoming a wonderful friend to all the family, particularly John Joseph in his later years.

Cotman was not alone in his instability which recurred briefly late in 1829, partly alleviated by an influx of pupils and involvement with the conversaziones. Even the long suffering Miles Edmund was inclined to depression, although his ability to keep it under control made him appear the staple of the family along with his mother and sister Ann, although she referred to herself as 'a strange girl whom it would take a conjuror to make out'. John Joseph was mentally unbalanced to the extent of being for a time put into care, Francis Walter was retarded almost to the point of being unemployable, and Alfred became totally insane and was confined to an asylum shortly before his father's death which may well have been hastened by this event. Whatever his faults, John Sell Cotman loved all his family dearly. His concern shines through most of his letters and is an accepted fact of history, although his own black periods must have affected his, no doubt impulsive, temper more than he realised. John Joseph Cotman wrote of his father, 'Intense labour and want of sufficient success tended much to depress his spirits and render his temper harsh, the effects of which, on our own, was much felt.' Miles Edmund had learned to cope, to understand that it was not his father's intention to hurt them, but the ultra-sensitive John Joseph was obviously more affected.

In the early 1830s, while the more buoyant mood still held, the professional artists of Norwich staged an exhibition of old and modern masters about which John Sell Cotman, as a committee member, became very excited and worked night and day to make a triumph. The conversaziones were drawn into the whole venture and its success was most gratifying for him. 'It was the most brilliant thing ever witnessed for Norwich and NOT one thing went amiss. It was as far beyond my expectations as possible, and I was one of the most sanguine upon the subject of any. I saw to a great extent what it might be, but could not have calculated on its entire success.'

During a London visit that same year he made many sketches of 'subjects to be worked up for London exhibitions'. A year later he sailed to London again but with Miles Edmund; they used the boat as a lodging and sketched during the day, London subjects followed by shipping on the Medway. This visit must have brought the two even closer than before – it was the first year in which the annual advertisement appeared as J.S. COTMAN & SON. Kitson comments: 'At this period connection between the output of father and son is so intimate and so complex that in some instances it has puzzled collectors and dealers ever since'.

After those few years of varied and productive work with only a few hiccups, John Sell was once more dropping into his despairing mood when, in 1833, the post of Professor of Drawing at King's College School, London, became vacant. Cotman had been hankering for London for some time and had spent some stimulating breaks there with Dawson Turner's daughter, Lady Palgrave. It was her influence together with that of her father that put Cotman in the running and he immediately summoned new energy and started collecting a good portfolio and testimonials. He had in his time become acquainted with some very eminent artists who proved most helpful and there was a glowing reference from the Mayor of Norwich, Samuel Bignold, whose family had been taught by Cotman and who was a loyal admirer. Cotman became so determined and so enthusiastic about his preparation that his family and Dawson Turner must have been trembling with anxiety lest he be disappointed.

Eventually his appointment was confirmed and, as might be assumed, John Sell Cotman was in his most exuberant form. He sent celebratory gifts home to his family in Norwich; for the moment it seemed that everything was going his way: London, where he most wanted to be and a prestigious position with a steady income. He wrote to his wife in Norwich: 'This is what I have always loved and tried to realise. Much as I have loved London, I have never trod its gold paved streets feeling so much a man of business and so much to belong to it as now.'

Congratulations abounded from all sides, not least the Norwich press, always ready to bask in the reflected glory of one of the sons of the city. It was decided that the family should stay in Norwich until John Sell had established himself. Initially he took John Joseph with him as assistant leaving Miles Edmund in charge of the Norwich practice although the roles were subsequently reversed when John Joseph proved too unreliable. Kitson reminds us of the thought Cotman always had for his fellow artists; even at this exciting time, he expressed concern for the misfortunes of the Cromes and suggested to Dawson Turner that a little help for old Mrs Crome might be appreciated.

Once in London, Cotman began to enjoy himself. Not only was he finding new stimulation in teaching 50 pupils but also in the association with other good artists and by the general ambience of the London art world. Soon his pupils increased to 200, but on his Easter visit to Norwich, in spite of the excitement and his own enthusiasm for the new London life, he realised that Miles Edmund's teaching income was not enough to keep up with expenses in Norwich. John Sell's own earnings were sufficient for himself and John Joseph in London but there was the problem of temptation in the form of bookshops and printsellers all around him. He approached Dawson Turner for a loan which was, rightly, refused on the grounds that his magpie instincts had, over the years, provided him with a saleable collection of prints, books, antiques and miscellanea as well as his own work. Cotman was immediately filled with remorse, writing to Dawson Turner in a spirit of atonement to 'my loved and valued friend of many a long year'. He duly, if regretfully, arranged for a sale of his surplus assets and realised enough money to help him over the present hump and keep him from sinking into another slough of despond. The very fact of the sale still hurt, particularly as his own works made poor prices and mainly sold to his artist colleagues, more perceptive, no doubt, than the average citizen of Norwich. In spite of the London compensations, he became depressed at the thought of losing his Norwich home and possessions and the fact that his King's College salary was not more in keeping with the family's needs.

Always unpredictable in his mood swings, it took the burning of the Houses of Parliament in 1834 to lift him out of himself. Along with J.M.W. Turner and other painters, he was soon on the scene making the most of an exciting new subject. Very soon after this, again thanks to contacts of Lady Palgrave and Dawson Turner, a house in London large enough for his family and without being too expensive became available to him so that, early in 1835, the family was once more united under one roof. His gratitude to the Turners and his joy at having a home and family again knew no bounds and life once more became a relatively equable affair.

Miles Edmund became his father's (unpaid) assistant while Mrs Cotman, daughter Ann, and even to some extent Alfred, all worked hard on drawing copies. John Sell was particularly pleased with Ann's drawing but the joy of making his position a family concern with an atmosphere (as he wrote to John Joseph in Norwich) 'all full of life and fun' made for a steadier time for them all. The volume of students grew and grew and Cotman genuinely tried to gain and keep 'their love and respect'. He must have had a way with his students, for controlling such large classes cannot have been easy; certainly he needed the help with drawing copies which eventually, for they were all numbered, reached 4,139. He wrote to John Joseph at one point: 'Edmund, Ann & Alfred and I are all drawing mad; Ann and Alfred working for the college pupils with great effect [in] every way. They have done crack subjects and they take wonderfully. Little do they ken by Whom they are done, when given under my name.' Cotman had no compunction about appending his name to those he felt worthy of him!

Although his health was never robust, Cotman appears to have been reasonably stable at least during the early college years. It would be fair to say that worries about the mental state of some of his sons perhaps diminished his own tendency to be temperamental. By 1835 he was showing signs of physical failing, according to correspondence between Lady Palgrave and her father – their concern for the Cotmans was always evident and it is hard to imagine how differently Cotman's life might have developed without the association. He had not included his copper plates in the Norwich auction but decided to part with them late in 1835. They sold to a publisher called Bohn who published them three years later, 238 etchings in two volumes entitled 'Specimens of Architectural Remains in various Counties of England, but especially in Norfolk, etched by John Sell Cotman with Architectural Observations by Thomas Rickman Esq.' This would no doubt have boosted Cotman's ego somewhat especially at a time of some relief, his son Francis having found work of sorts in a Manchester warehouse.

Two things superseded health problems for Cotman, his passion for collecting and his capacity for innovation and fulfilment from a new direction in his work. In spite of the Norwich clear-

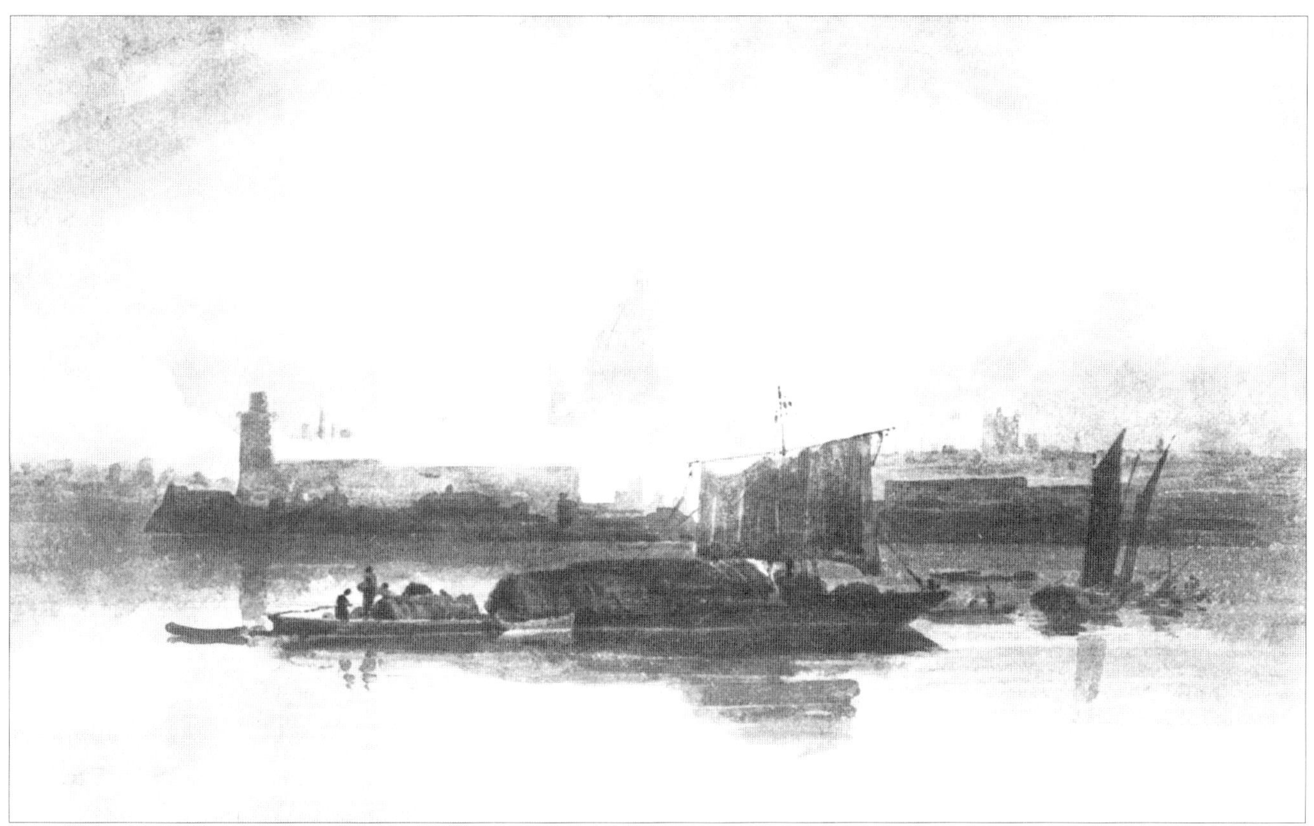

John Sell Cotman, London River, watercolour, c.1831

out, he soon began to accumulate more and more collectables, haunting the salerooms where he thought there might be exciting bargains on offer. Even as early as 1836 he wrote that he had 'added most wonderfully to my library, very, very fine and most rare volumes, and most useful to me – and also very cheap'. Other letters mention treasures he had found at the sale of John Constable's books and prints – 'more' of the Sebastion Bourdon landscapes, a volume of 244 prints by Teniers for which he determinedly bid against Bohn, and so on. He justified this spending as reference material for himself and his students and to equip his classroom with 'Cast, Models, Drawings and Prints on all subjects to raise the character of my department,' but the posthumous sale at Christie's after his death also included a goodly collection of 'German, French and English books, curious antiquarian works and books of prints.'

Cotman continued with his personal work as well as teaching and, using his mixed media technique to its fullest capacity, sought out some novel subjects on which to exercise his imagination and creativity. By 1839 he had started to exhibit in Norwich once more, perhaps inspired by a generous tribute from the Mayor of Norwich. He was invited to the opening of a new factory, to a pageant by the children and to the celebratory dinner in the evening chaired by the Mayor, Sam Bignold.

'It is not generally known but it ought to be', announced Mr. Bignold in his speech, 'that a highly talented artist, holding a distinguished situation in King's College, has come from London for the express purpose of perpetuating by a graphic record, the procession of the day. I give you the health of Mr. Cotman.' (Cheers.)

Cotman was intensely gratified and expressed his pleasure in the best way he knew, thanking the Lord Mayor and promising to make a drawing of the procession in all its parts 'and present it to the Norwich Yarn Company as an heir-loom, a thing they may not have in the factory'. He asked for volunteers to subscribe to any publisher willing to give a 'representation of the drawings in a series of etchings, the profits of which are to go to the children of the factory forming the procession.' This, predictably, raised great cheering and, although the project never actually materialised, the suggestion certainly raised Cotman's prestige in the city.

John Sell Cotman always had the interests of his family at heart and, although it would have

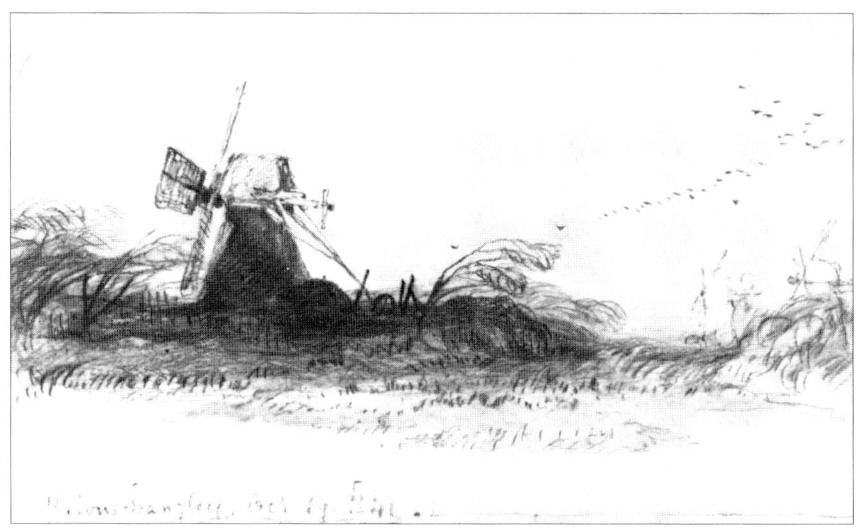

John Sell Cotman, four examples of the last drawings

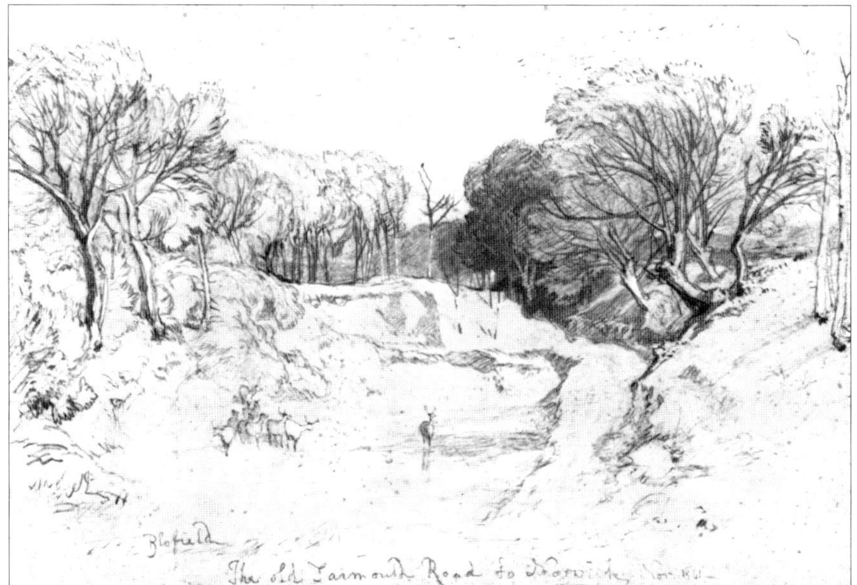

meant losing his invaluable help, when he heard that the City of London School had a vacancy for a Drawing Master, he pulled all the strings he possibly could to collect testimonials for Miles Edmund and helped him accumulate a good portfolio of drawings. In the face of 600 applicants, Miles Edmund was unsuccessful, but his father's efforts had been unstinting. It was not long after this, however, that King's College created an official post of Assistant Drawing Master, giving Miles Edmund recognition in his own right and also a salary. As an interesting side issue it is noteworthy that Dante Gabriel Rossetti became Cotman's pupil in 1837 – Rossetti's father was Professor of Italian at King's College. It is too much of a digression to study here the influence of Cotman on Rossetti but, despite the latter's subsequent allegiance to the Pre-Raphaelites, it is undoubtedly there.

Miles Edmund himself battled against ill health during this time, no doubt aggravated by coping with his father's moods. In his turn, John Sell worried about both Miles and John Joseph for the latter was also causing concern. His parents tried to persuade him to join the rest of the family in London but John Joseph was determined to try to be independent and stand on his own. Perhaps it was Alfred who was the major problem; although both parents did their best to cope with him at home, eventually they had to admit defeat when he became uncontrollably violent. Can there ever have been a more classic example of a family each suffering on behalf of the others and thereby increasing their personal anxiety and consequent health problems?

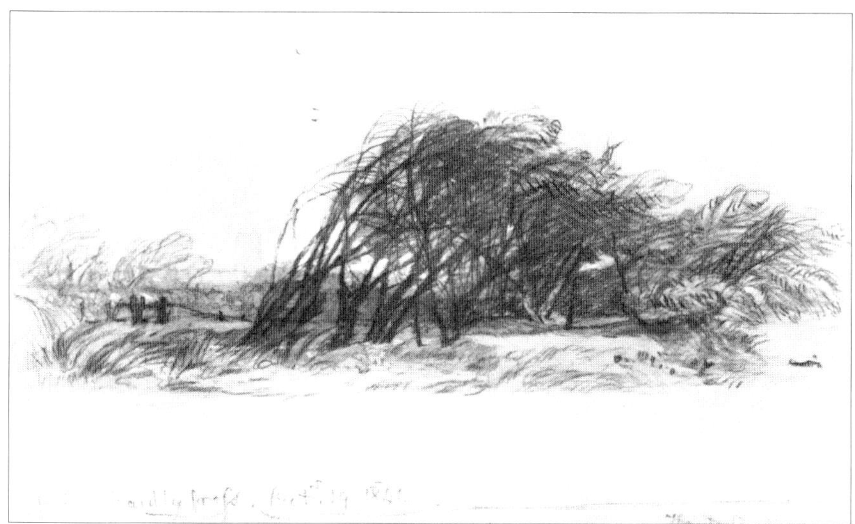

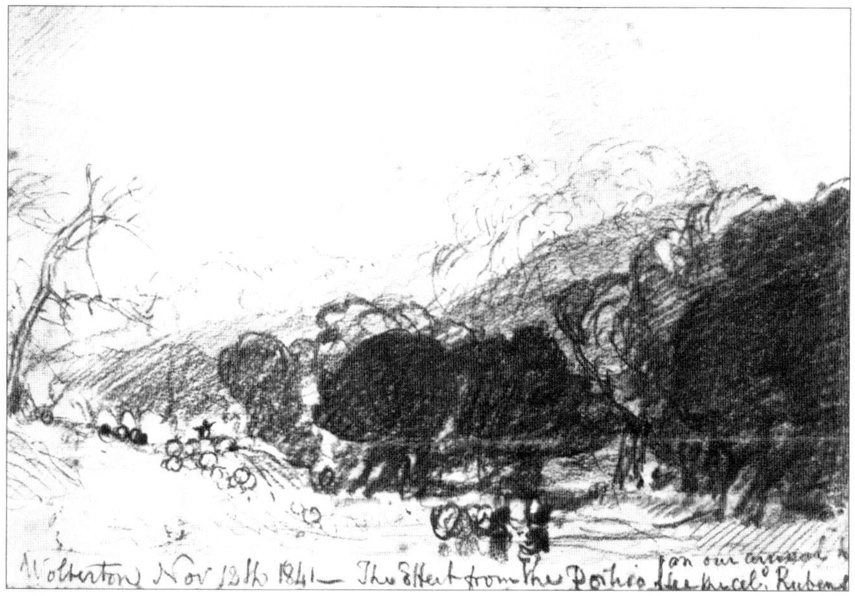

Around 1840 Cotman's health seems to have been enjoying a reasonable phase and he was painting hard. He started another session of oil painting with some interesting results, notably the charming 'Boys Fishing', of which Kitson and others make special mention. Cotman must have been enormously prolific in this latest phase for after his death, Kitson in his biography states that over 50 oil sketches were sold, also 32 oil paintings, yet all the previous work in the medium went in the Norwich sale of 1834. Mixed media paintings, among them some of the cream of their kind, and some excellent drawings were the fruits of this prolific period, 'an outstanding period' as Kitson describes it. Aided by Miles, he continued to make drawing copies for the ever increasing volume of pupils, which had more than doubled. But as Cotman wrote to Dawson Turner: 'Who would not work for such pupils as I have, I love them all and I believe they respect me.'

In 1841 Cotman made a sentimental journey back to Norfolk feeling a desperate urge once more to spend some time in East Anglia. As it turned out, his promised two weeks stretched to two months while he journeyed all over Norfolk drawing as if his life depended on it. Those who have studied Cotman's work agree that these drawings, spontaneous studies of nature just as he saw her, are some of the most inspired of all time. Andrew Moore has written: 'The evidence of his many surviving drawings in black and white chalks,* often dated and inscribed, reveal the joy with which Cotman sketched the scene of his native county' and 'the drawings represent the

* Many of these drawings in black and white chalk on grey paper are now in the British Museum.

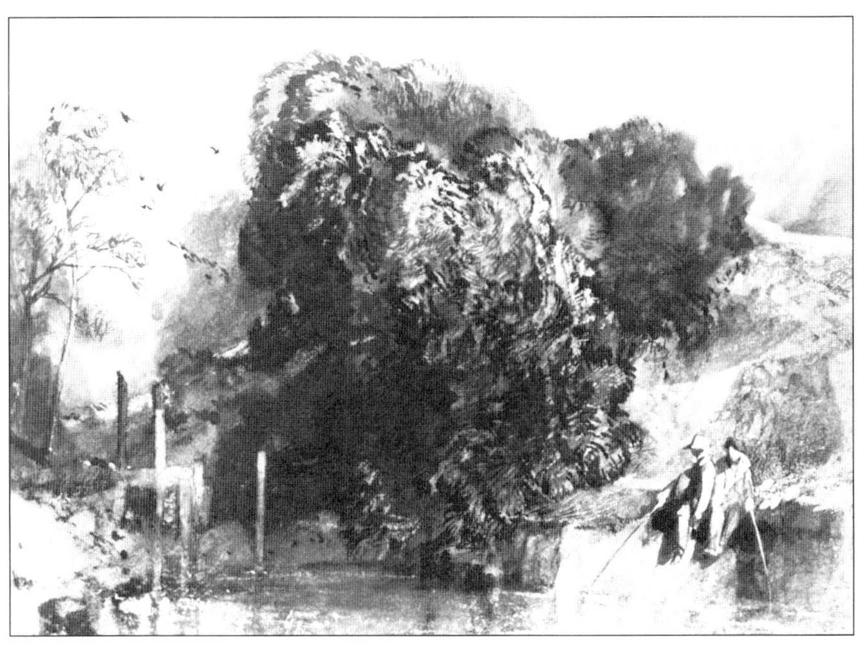

John Sell Cotman, Boys Fishing, oil, 1839, 13¼ in x 17 in

consummation of Cotman's late career'. Rajnai speaks of the 'burst of creative energy' on that last visit to Norfolk when he 'eschewed colour and proved himself the great colourist he was by achieving everything colour can offer through the wonderfully sensitive modulation of monochrome'. Mallalieu calls these inspired drawings 'Cotman at his best'.

Kitson describes 'many of the drawings in black and white chalk on grey paper' as 'some of the most powerful direct-from-nature studies of all time. They cast aside all artifice and draw the natural world as he saw it – trees, country churches, houses, rivers – all from Norfolk.' Derek Clifford adds: 'They are extraordinarily powerful and evocative fragments and show that Cotman had renewed yet again his vision in the presence of nature and was at the beginning of another phase of development'. Was something telling him that he was seeing the beloved county for the last time and for that reason seeing with a purity and perfection of vision that even he had never before experienced?

Cotman stayed with John Joseph, working from his lodgings and spending time with his father and old friends including ten days in Yarmouth with Dawson Turner. This seems to have been a time of great happiness and fulfilment for him and we have all gained from the legacy of those magic weeks. Late in November he returned to London, to further family worries, especially with Alfred, and concern for Miles Edmund's health. He actually started to work up some of the Norfolk drawings into oil paintings including what Kitson calls his unfinished masterpiece, 'From the Garden Front of my Father's House at Thorpe-next-Norwich', an unusually large piece. As 1842 wore on Cotman's health began to fail; Joseph Geldart's brother Robert visited in June and reported that, although Cotman had showed off some of the sepia Normandy drawings, it was plain that 'old Cotman' was seriously ill. In July Ann wrote to John Joseph in Norwich that their father's condition was so grave that he seemed to have lost the will to live. Two days later, John Sell Cotman died.

It is comforting to know that after a somewhat traumatic life, Mrs Cotman was provided for. Cotman had left her everything including a modest life policy and Dawson Turner not only paid her a life pension but continued it for Ann until her death in 1862. Cotman's 'remaining works' were auctioned at Christie's except for those last drawings held back by Miles Edmund along with some of the Normandy sepias and a few Greta drawings. Still there were three van loads and the sale lasted for two days; sadly after the death of Miles Edmund, the improvident and impecunious John Joseph sold the rest of both his father's and his brother's work. Fortunately many were bought by the farsighted James Reeve, Curator of Norwich Museum, whose collection at the time included 600 of Cotman's works. Later he sold over half to the British Museum; most of the remainder eventually reached the collection of the late Russell Colman and thereby to the Norwich Castle Museum permanent collection.

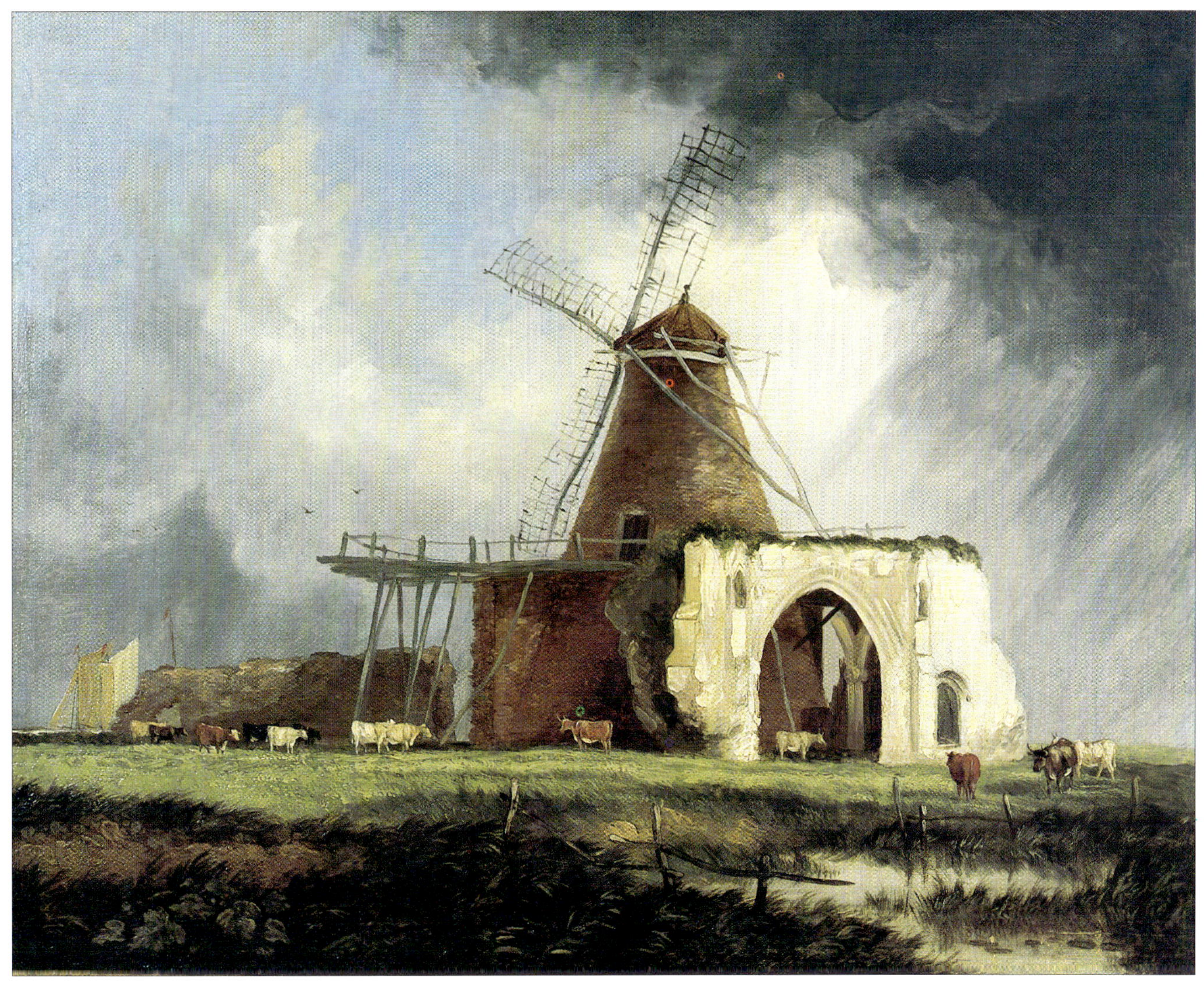

Chapter 6

THE YOUNGER COTMANS

Miles Edmund Cotman, St. Benet's Abbey by the Bure, Norfolk, oil, 16 in x 20 in

It is incumbent on those of us writing about the Norwich School with the benefit of hindsight to give suitable recognition to some of the School's most gifted artists who, in their own time and beyond, were overshadowed by a brilliant father. Ironically it was a cause of much frustration and despair for John Sell Cotman that his most inspired work was neither accepted nor understood in his lifetime, although his reputation became such that his sons seemed almost accessories. Most art historians have written at great length about John Sell and why not? There is ample documentation to work on, he left voluminous correspondence and his output was phenomenal. The diaries and letters of friends and patrons provide yet further information while each succeeding biographer has managed somehow to dig out additional detail. While admittedly there is considerably less material available in respect of his sons, frequently they are unfairly dismissed in just a few lines, almost as shadows of their father.

The elder son **Miles Edmund Cotman** (1810-1858), born at Southtown during the Yarmouth period, certainly followed in his father's footsteps to some extent but much less slavishly than is sometimes implied. Miles and his brother, John Joseph, were totally different in character, and Miles is given much less credit than he deserves for preserving, as far as possible, a semblance of equilibrium. Intensely loyal, self-sacrificing and tolerant, one has to suppose that, temperamentally, he was largely his mother's son; although he suffered from a degree of depression for most of his life, he was sufficiently strong willed to keep it under control and to handle the frenetic moods of his father and brother. Artistically he was extremely talented and first exhibited with the Norwich Society at the age of 13, receiving his first laudatory press review at 15. No doubt such early talent would have been encouraged by his father and for a number of years their work was so similar that attribution was, and in some cases still is, extremely difficult. This difficulty has been compounded by the fact that quite frequently they worked on the same painting; John Sell himself referred to their 'joint efforts'. Furthermore, personal recognition for Miles came later than it should because of constant references to his father's influence. When he became his father's assistant as teacher and producer of drawing copies, his quiet, gentle and supportive nature must have rendered him almost indispensable; coping with John Sell's all-embracing enthusiasms on the one hand and periods of black despair on the other can never have been easy. For 18 years as his father's right hand he was invaluable as a steadying influence as well as practical assistant. John Sell was inclined to take advantage of his son to an extent no outsider would have put up with. For instance, if John Sell was sunk in one of his moods when the time came for him to contribute to the Watercolour Society's exhibition, in order to maintain continuity of his membership, Miles would paint a watercolour for him to which John Sell had no inhibitions appending his name.

Miles Edmund gradually developed his own style; maybe he decided that a definite break was necessary if he was to become noticed as an individual. He was a diligent worker, too, and in spite of his teaching and other duties had exhibited 60 works with the Norwich Society before 1833. He used both oil and watercolour and it goes without saying that he was an immaculate draughtsman; his own talent, heredity, and constant practice making drawing copies ensured that. In all his work this exemplary drawing is quite evident, his style is 'tighter' than his father's and his subjects more consciously drawn – a point respecting his watercolours that was criticised by his father. This, I feel, was being unnecessarily hard, for simply to criticise a style, if the work is of highest quality within that style, is overstepping the mark. Miles was a traditionalist rather than an innovator, having a very observant eye for detail, but he was not only technically correct – from time to time he produced some quite exceptional pieces. My personal preference is for his watercolours and one of my special favourites is 'Interior of a Barn' in Norwich Castle Museum. Colour was a strong point with Miles Edmund; not only was he a master of subtle tonal blending but he had a particular skill with warm siennas, Indian and Venetian reds, which are difficult colours to handle without overheating. Sometimes there are combinations with soft cool greens and warm greys which give the occasional superrealism a totally new and rather exciting dimension. In some of the earlier works, John Sell has just added the skies; the question is, did Miles Edmund want a freer, more imaginative sky above a very detailed drawing or did John Sell want his son to make a drawing which necessitated a level of detail too pernickety for the mood of the moment?

Of Miles' oils, Harold Day writes:

> His work in oils is quite different to that of his father, being more clearly drawn and containing an abundance of detail combined with a good delineation of subject. Miles Edmund often achieves a splendid breadth especially in his skies. Perhaps in certain of his pictures the paint probably appears a little devoid of medium but in others it is just as beautiful, having a very luminous quality. 'Boats on the Medway' in Norwich Castle Museum is a splendid example of his use of siennas and umbers. His study of ship details, rigging and sails and their relationship to weather conditions seems to leave little to be desired.

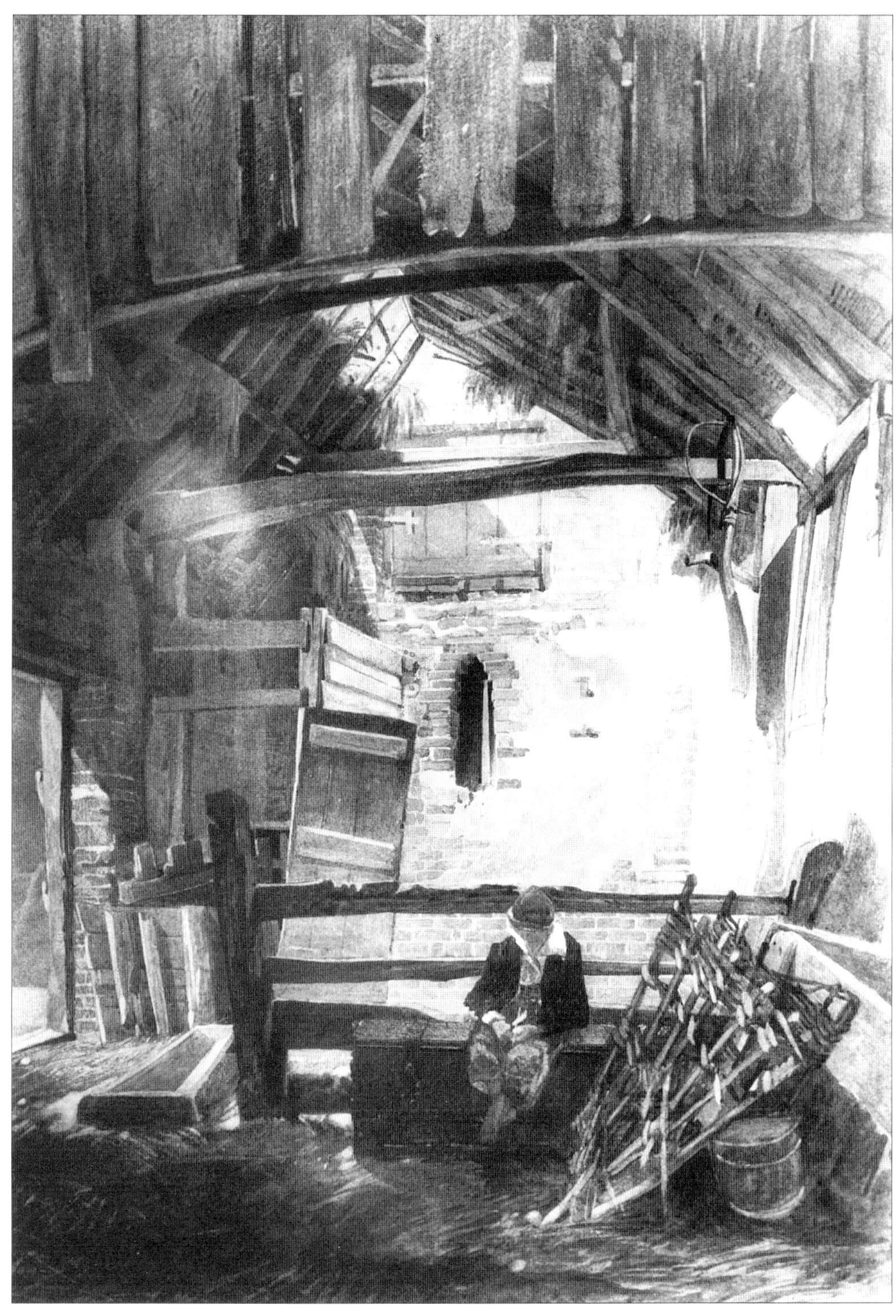

Miles Edmund Cotman, Interior of a Barn, watercolour, 15¼ in x 10⅝ in

This luminous quality is particularly evident in his seascapes where the essential breadth of the sea and sky gives point to the finer details of the vessels and their crews. To me some of his seascapes are more reminiscent of Alfred Stannard than of any work of his father's. An exceptionally large oil in Norwich Castle, 'Wooded Landscape' (47¾ in. x 30 in), is not only impressive for its size but also for its confident handling and shows Miles Edmund Cotman as a much more powerful painter than his reputation in some quarters implies.

While still in Norwich, the industrious Miles attracted several useful patrons; a friend of his

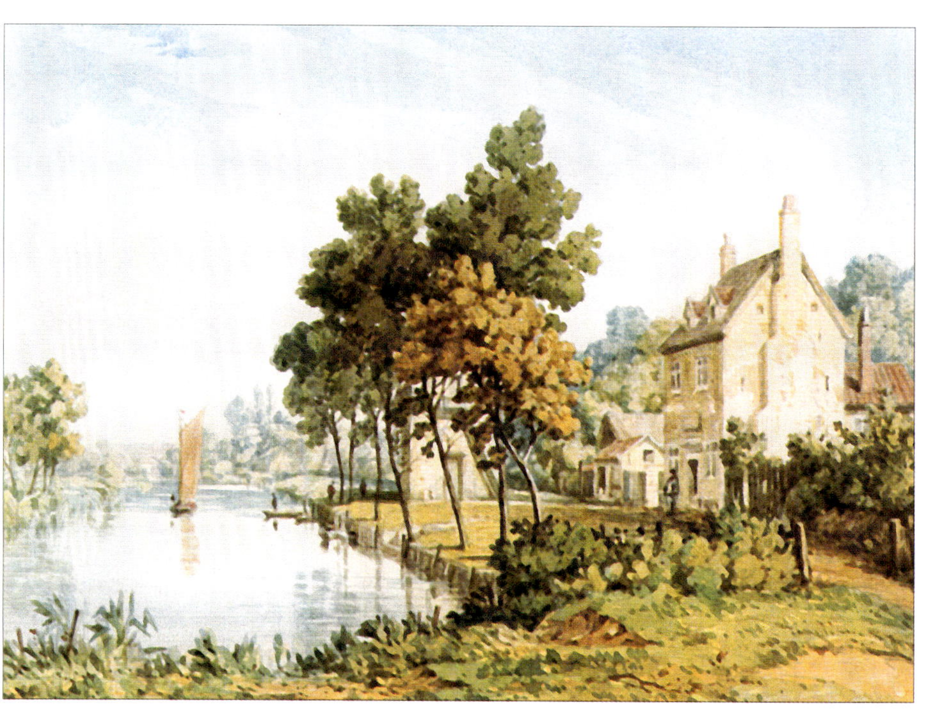

John Joseph Cotman, Bramerton Woods End, watercolour 14½ in x20 in

father, the Rev. James Bulwer, bought a number of his watercolours and no doubt recommended him to other collectors. Despite the comments of the contemporary press (and subsequent writers) about paternal influence, Miles Edmund did attract buyers in his own right and probably built up a more substantial following than is generally realised.

In 1833, when John Sell was appointed Drawing Master at King's College School, London, he took John Joseph with him as assistant leaving the more reliable and responsible Miles Edmund to take charge of the teaching practice in Norwich. Miles welcomed the opportunity to work on his own initiative and wrote jokingly to his brother that he particularly enjoyed teaching the ladies! However, this happy state of affairs was not to last. The volatile John Joseph was not suited to the disciplined regime in London and, after less than a year, the patient long-suffering Miles was uprooted from Norwich to help his father in London and cope with his wild enthusiasms and almost manic depressions. The change met with obvious approval and in 1836 Miles was officially appointed Assistant Drawing Master. During this time he continued exhibiting in both London and Norwich, and his own work in watercolour developed significantly; father and son again worked jointly on certain paintings. One definitely identified as a joint effort was initially bought by the Empress Catherine of Russia and is now in the Fitzwilliam Museum, Cambridge.

In the 1840s Miles also tried his hand at etching; the quality of his drawing virtually assured successful results but time was the enemy of such comparatively slow, painstaking work. A set entitled 'Eleven Original Etchings' was published by Charles Muskett in 1846, followed later by a set of 12. The prospect of marriage was also raised during this period, but was firmly vetoed by Cotman senior on economic grounds. Some years later, however, the marriage took place and the couple produced three children.

When John Sell Cotman returned to Norwich for the last time hoping to refresh himself roaming and drawing the Norfolk countryside, he admitted that Miles was 'really ill' although not to the same extent as he was himself. The fact that the strain of coping with his father's uncertain temperament while working hard himself was the reason for Miles' indifferent health had probably never occurred to John Sell. The gallant Miles soldiered on all the same and, after his father's death in 1842 and a suitable probationary period, was appointed to the professorship himself. He seems to have been well respected by his pupils who no doubt appreciated his patience, sensitivity and even temperament.

It is worth noting here that the loyal Miles, as a tribute to his father after the latter's death, published a set of commemorative lithographs illustrating 12 faithful copies of John Sell's last drawings.

By 1852 the strain of living, teaching and painting in London was becoming too much and,

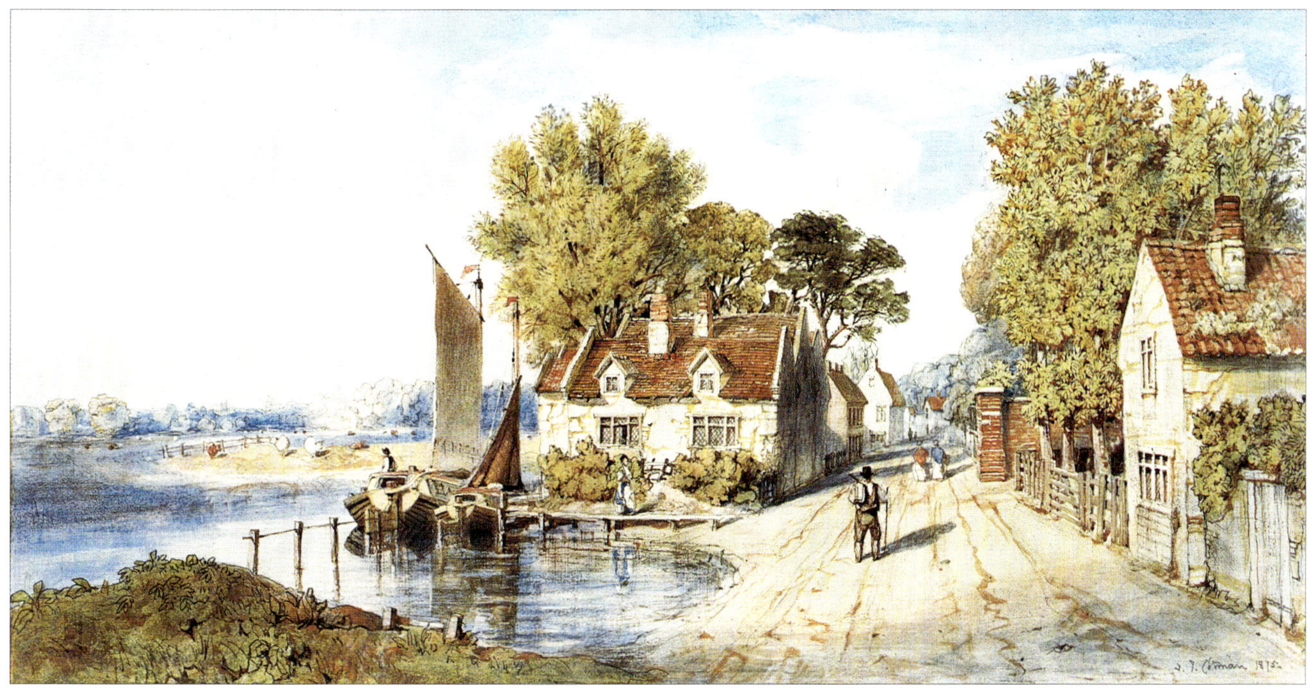

John Joseph Cotman, Thorpe Watering, watercolour, 16½ in x 32½ in

wisely, Miles Edmund decided to return to the relative peace of Norfolk. Since his father died he had continued to help support his mother out of his own resources until her death at their home in Hunter Street, Brunswick Square. Back in Norfolk, he joined John Joseph Cotman at Thorpe and, for a time, took on some teaching at North Walsham. During this time and later when he had given up teaching and the brothers had moved, in 1855, to Great Plumstead, Miles Edmund spent many hours sketching in the country and immersing himself in his painting. Too much of his erratic, temperamental brother was not what he needed. On one of these sketching trips he fell, broke his ankle and was admitted to the Norfolk and Norwich Hospital. To what extent this unfortunate accident contributed to his general decline in health will probably never be known but he died in that same hospital in 1858 with his talent undiminished. With a less stressful life, he might well have continued to develop, given time and space just to be himself.

The second Cotman son, **John Joseph Cotman** (1814-1878), who inherited his father's good looks and much of his progressive talent, was, compared to his brother, an eccentric individualist. He developed his tremendous inherited talent into a dashing, vibrant style, but the fits of depression also inherited from his father were aggravated in John Joseph, sometimes to the point of mental instability.

Like his brother, John Joseph was born during the Yarmouth period but was only ten years old when the family moved to St. Martin's Palace Plain, Norwich, where he continued his schooling – not that he concentrated particularly on his lessons which he avoided if possible, and truancy was by no means unusual. After school it was decided that he should join his uncle Edmund's haberdashery business but the venture was short lived. According to John Joseph, he felt 'degraded' and just wanted to spend his time sketching with his good friend Joseph Geldart, who almost throughout their lives was a staunch support to the vulnerable John Joseph. The latter admired Geldart's drawing from the start. 'At this time', John Joseph wrote in his journal, 'I met a new friend whom I admired and strove to imitate'. John Sell could hardly raise objections to anyone wanting to spend their lives drawing and, recognising his son's talent as well as his temperament, gave him every encouragement.

When John Sell was appointed to his post at King's College School, he obviously thought that by giving John Joseph the opportunity to assist him he was offering his son the chance of steady employment while following his natural talent; John Joseph was a born draughtsman and could have been invaluable to his father. However, the necessary patience and self discipline were beyond him, as was the effort of time keeping which meant that he was just as likely to be in

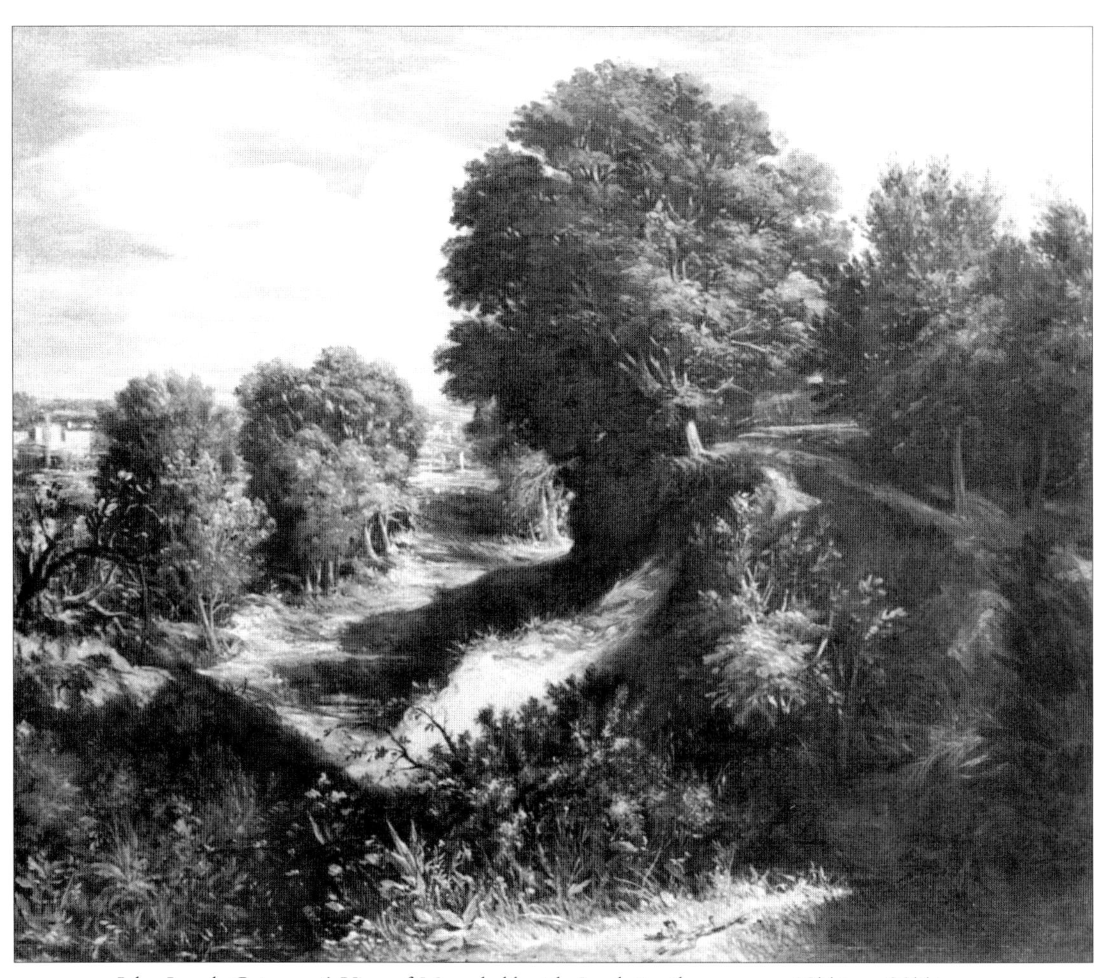

John Joseph Cotman, A View of Mousehold with Sandpit, oil on canvas, 19¼ in x 23¼ in

This tranquil scene surely typifies the peace John Joseph Cotman's disturbed mind must have yearned for.

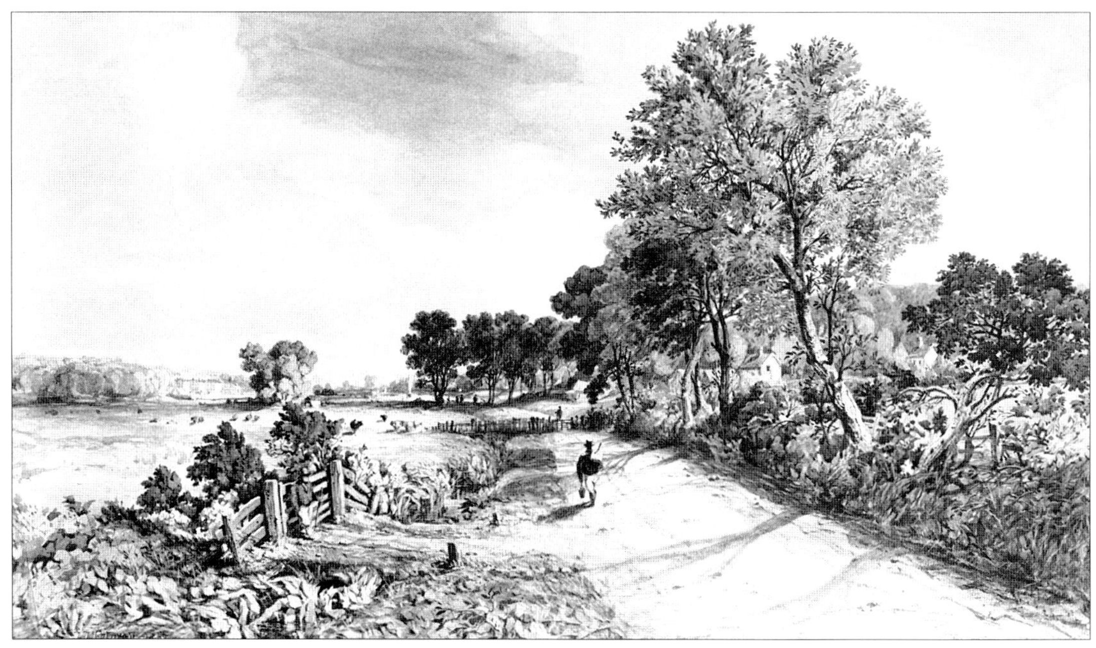

John Joseph Cotman, Whitlingham Lane, Horstead, watercolour, 15 in x 24¾ in

bed or out on his own devices when he was needed. In less than a year he returned to Norwich and took over the teaching practice there while the rest of the family moved to London with the more reliable Miles becoming his father's assistant. Although for a short time, while John Joseph was determined to turn over a new leaf, the practice grew and flourished, before long it started gradually to become less successful. Pupils dwindled and John Joseph became increasingly depressed and self critical; eventually, in 1837, he reached such a pitch of instability that his parents put him in the care of a private asylum for treatment. He made a partial recovery, enough to restart teaching the following year, but pupils were wary of his reputation and strange manner. He managed to keep going with some school work and a few private pupils but was depressed and dissatisfied with himself and his life. John Sell tried hard to persuade him to leave Norwich and join the family in London – there exists a letter in which he almost begs him to do just that – but the stubborn John Joseph refused to admit total defeat and battled on.

John Joseph always recognised his temperamental failings and tried hard to come to terms with them; he kept a journal in which he attempted in his own way to analyse himself and find some answers but the depression only increased when he felt himself to be a failure. His family tried to be solicitous and supportive but he longed to be able to cope independently. He spent most of his adult life in and out of debt and suffering bouts of heavy drinking when despair became too deep to handle unaided. Regardless of past experience, he applied several times for steady teaching posts but, in spite of excellent references from friends and fellow artists and the obvious talent shown in his drawings, he was always passed over. In 1841 he decided to try married life and announced his engagement to Helen Cooper, daughter of a Norwich silversmith. As in the case of his brother, John Sell firmly vetoed it, as much in consideration for the lady as for the obvious economic factor, so the engagement was broken triggering further depression. It was in 1847 after his father's death that John Joseph and Helen married and bore six children.

By 1858, perhaps not coincidentally the year of Miles Edmund's death, the patient Helen could take no more and, along with her children, left John Joseph in a state of despair and isolation. The severe depression increased and with it the heavy drinking during which he pawned or sold more and more of his father's and brother's paintings and anything else saleable he could lay hands on. His sister Ann left him some money but soon it was frittered away. His faithful friend

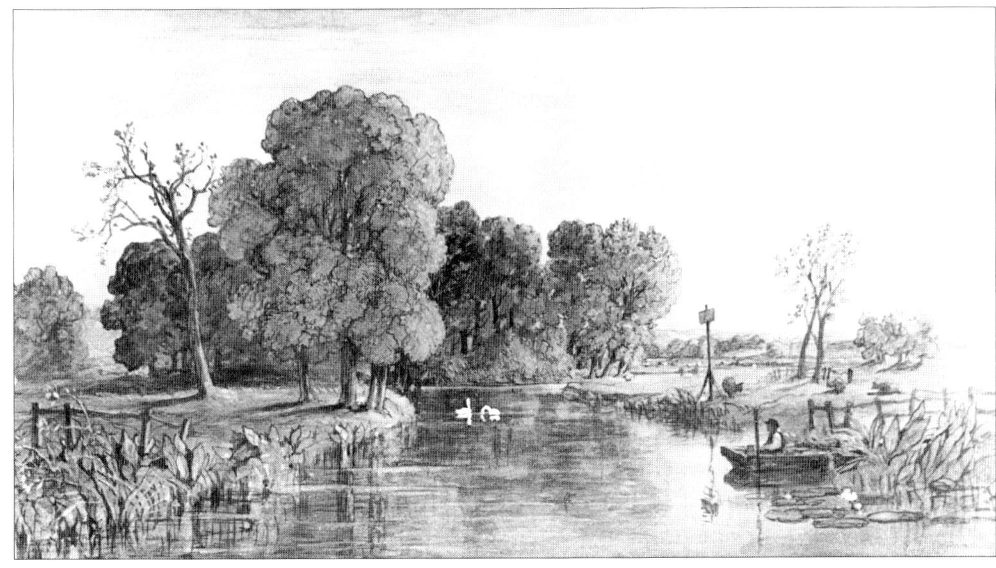

John Joseph Cotman, A View on the River Wensum, near Norwich, watercolour, 1875, 13½ in x 29 in

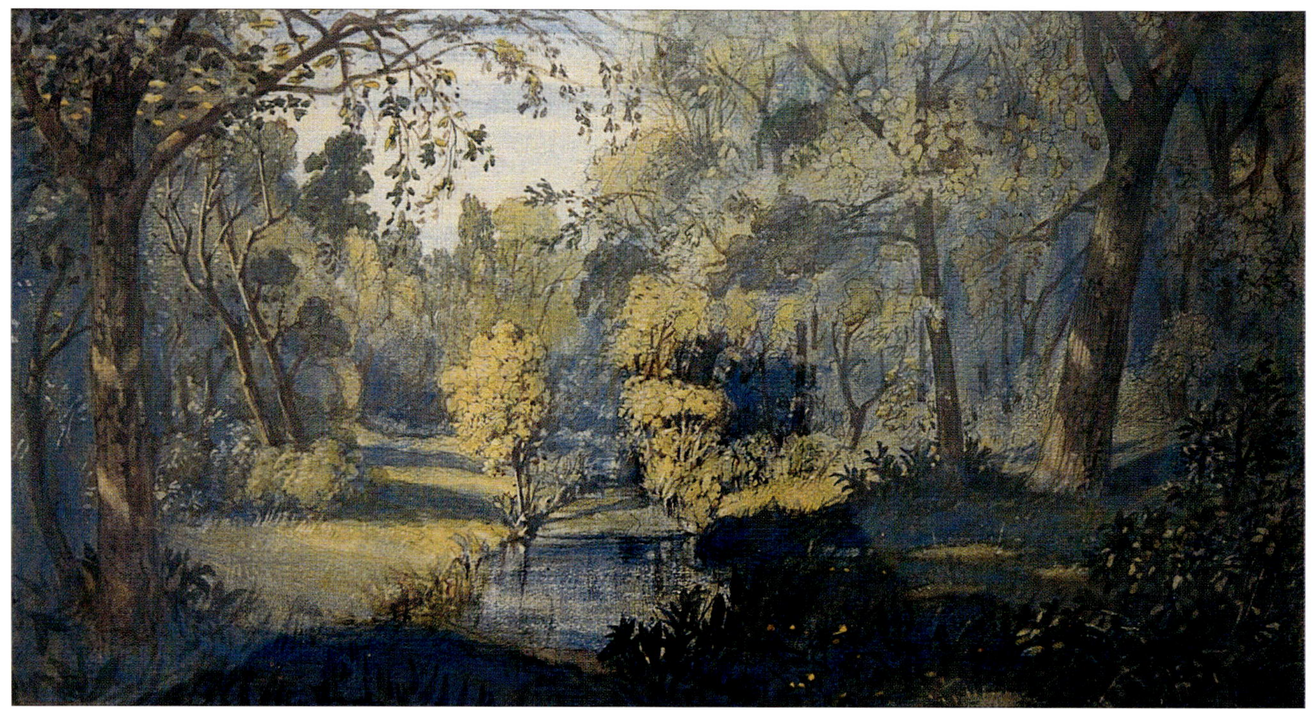

John Joseph Cotman, Wroxham Carr, watercolour, approx. 20 in x 30 in

John Joseph Cotman, View at Carrow Bridge, watercolour, 14¼ in x 6 in

Joseph Geldart helped him out on several occasions and probably provided a lifeline in more ways than one. Like many of his temperament, John Joseph undoubtedly had an attractive side and his close friends seemed to stay with him through thick and thin.

Another valuable ally was James Reeve, Curator of the Norwich Museum, who was kindness itself to John Joseph and would also be able to appreciate the very real quality of his work. John Joseph's last letter to Reeve expresses a genuine and sincere appreciation which must have meant a great deal to Reeve; when the ill-fated artist died of cancer of the tongue in the Norfolk and

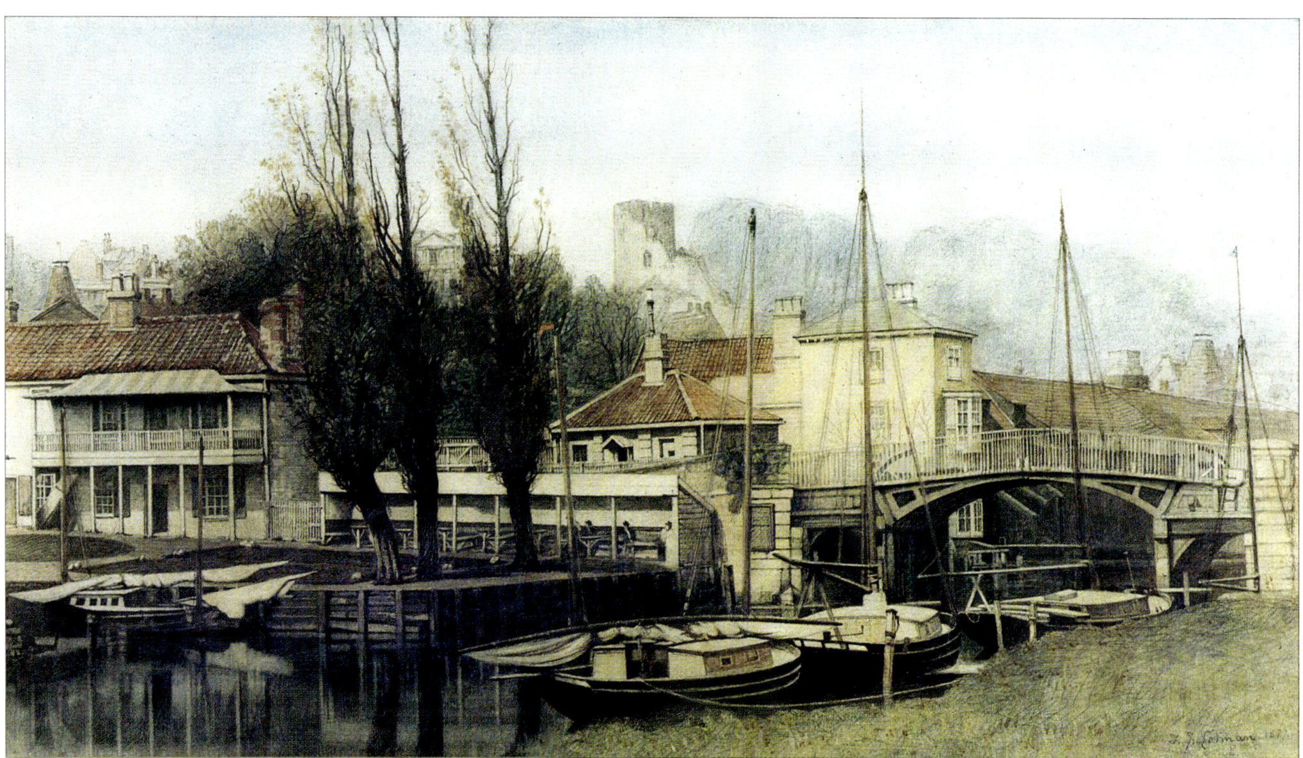

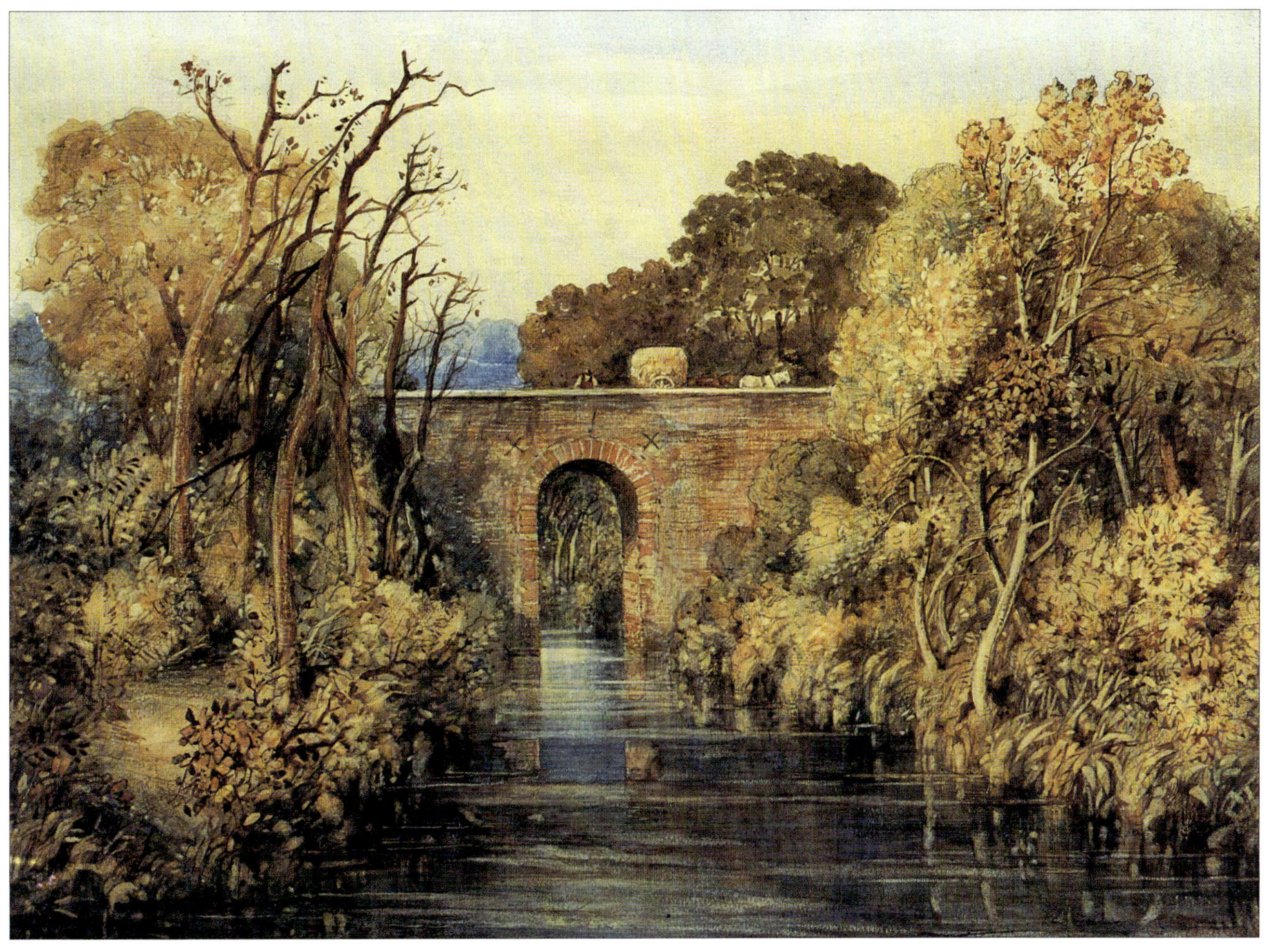

John Joseph Cotman, Little Switzerland, Horstead, watercolour, 1878, 14½ in x 20 in

Norwich Hospital he was completely destitute but Reeve quietly paid the funeral expenses.

In the better times, though few and far between, John Joseph managed a little teaching or sold a few paintings. He was a familiar figure in Norwich, a total eccentric in the eyes of the citizens with his rather odd manners and bizarre style of dress. For such a genius, it seems tragic that he should have been remembered at best as a crank, at worst a madman.

For John Joseph *was* a genius – of that there is little doubt, and his father not only recognised it but tried hard to encourage him with more praise than was ever meted out to the self-effacing Miles. John Sell insisted that, when he first went to London, he could not draw nearly as well as his young son and later impressed on him 'You have a good eye for colour, one of the VERY BEST points in the game – GOOD TASTE.' John Joseph worked in both oil and watercolour but it is his watercolours that shine, making one wonder why he exhibited so little during his lifetime when there was so much worthwhile material. Presumably the necessity for meeting dates and times or working to deadlines was too much for him.

Large horizontal works, usually about 20 in x 30 in, seemed to appeal to him most and gave space for his broad vision. The earlier works certainly prove his father's point about good colour, while his composition is excellent and the drawing faultless. He had a passionate love of the Norfolk countryside. The life and vitality he managed to weave into some paintings of lovely corners of his native county gives one the feeling of actually being there enjoying with him the peace and tranquillity that he failed to find in life. The longing for this peace he portrayed so eloquently gives these paintings a passion that is felt rather than observed; subjects that could be banal are transformed into vibrant, almost three-dimensional, living landscapes. It is hard to explain this combination of vibrancy and tranquillity and the impact, not simply visual, they make on the senses, but it is even harder to explain John Joseph Cotman.

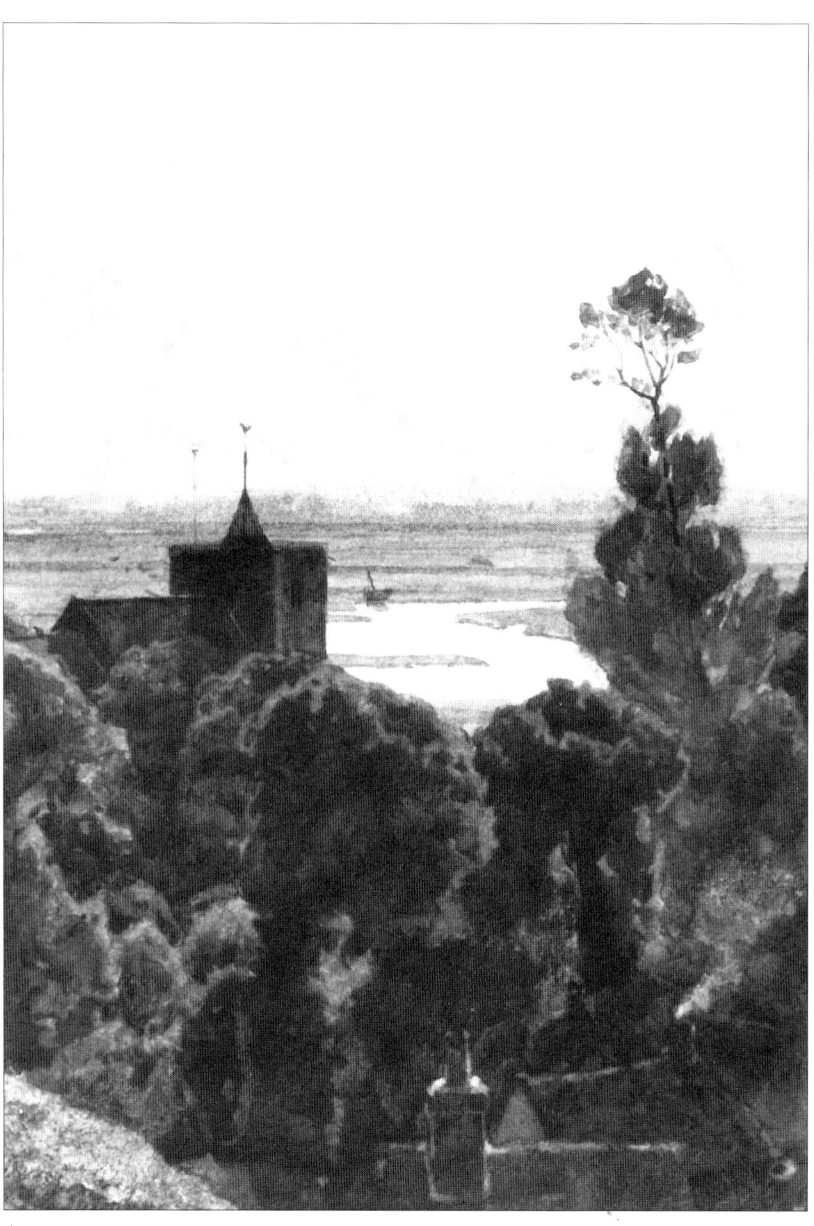

Frederick George Cotman, Landscape with a Church Tower

(Ipswich Borough Council Museums and Galleries)

Later in life his colour changed, not all of the time but increasingly as an expression of mood. The draughtsmanship remained impeccable, likewise the composition, but the colour became, sometimes, completely wild. Fiery, dramatic colours attacked an otherwise pastoral composition with an intensity that no doubt reflected the mental state of the time. Somehow his sense of tonal values stayed with him, so that however much one feels an initial shock at the sheer madness of this riotous, wondrous colour, it does not grate but harmonises within itself. John Joseph went through his father's blue and gold phase using it even more dramatically, but the richness and jewel-like quality has its own appeal. This extraordinary handling of colour for its own sake probably indicates the only means he could find to satisfy the crying need for colour, joy and drama in his sad and squalid life.

Brief mention should be made of John Sell Cotman's nephew, **Frederick George Cotman** (1850-1920), son of his youngest brother Henry Edmund to whom John Joseph was briefly apprenticed. Frederick George was an extremely talented, very versatile painter who, having been born in Ipswich and never living in Norfolk, tends by virtue of the Norfolk name to be overlooked by the writers on Suffolk painters and given cursory attention by writers on the Norwich School. Although at best he could only be termed a fringe member of the Norwich School, his background is such that in discussion of the younger Cotmans he should not be ignored.

Born in the parish of St. Clement's, Ipswich, in 1866/7 he became a private pupil of William Thomson Griffiths, the Head of Ipswich School of Art. He also assisted his tutor with lessons in the school and at some of the smaller, junior schools in the area. His first experience of exhibiting was in Norwich in 1867 which exhibit earned him a medal.

In 1868 he joined the Royal Academy Schools where he proved his skill as a draughtsman and talent as a painter by winning four silver medals and one gold. The gold was for an historical painting. 'The Death of Eucles', which came to roost in Ipswich Town Hall. He exhibited at the Royal Academy from 1871 for most of the rest of his life. Two of his well-known teachers, Frederic Leighton (1830-1896) and Henry Tanworth Wells (1828-1903) employed him to work on their own paintings, notably Leighton's famous 'The Daphnephoria'. During the holidays he assisted the Colchester still-life painter, the great Edward Ladell.

Frederick George Cotman, working in both oil and watercolour, painted landscape and domestic genre subjects as well as portraits, in which field he initially established himself as a London society painter; one of his most impressive conversation pieces portrays the Marchioness of Westminster, Lady Theodora Guest, and Mr Guest playing dummy whist. Two of the genre

Frederick George Cotman,
The Dame School,
oil on canvas,
14¼ in x 19¾ in

(Ipswich Borough Council Museums and Galleries)

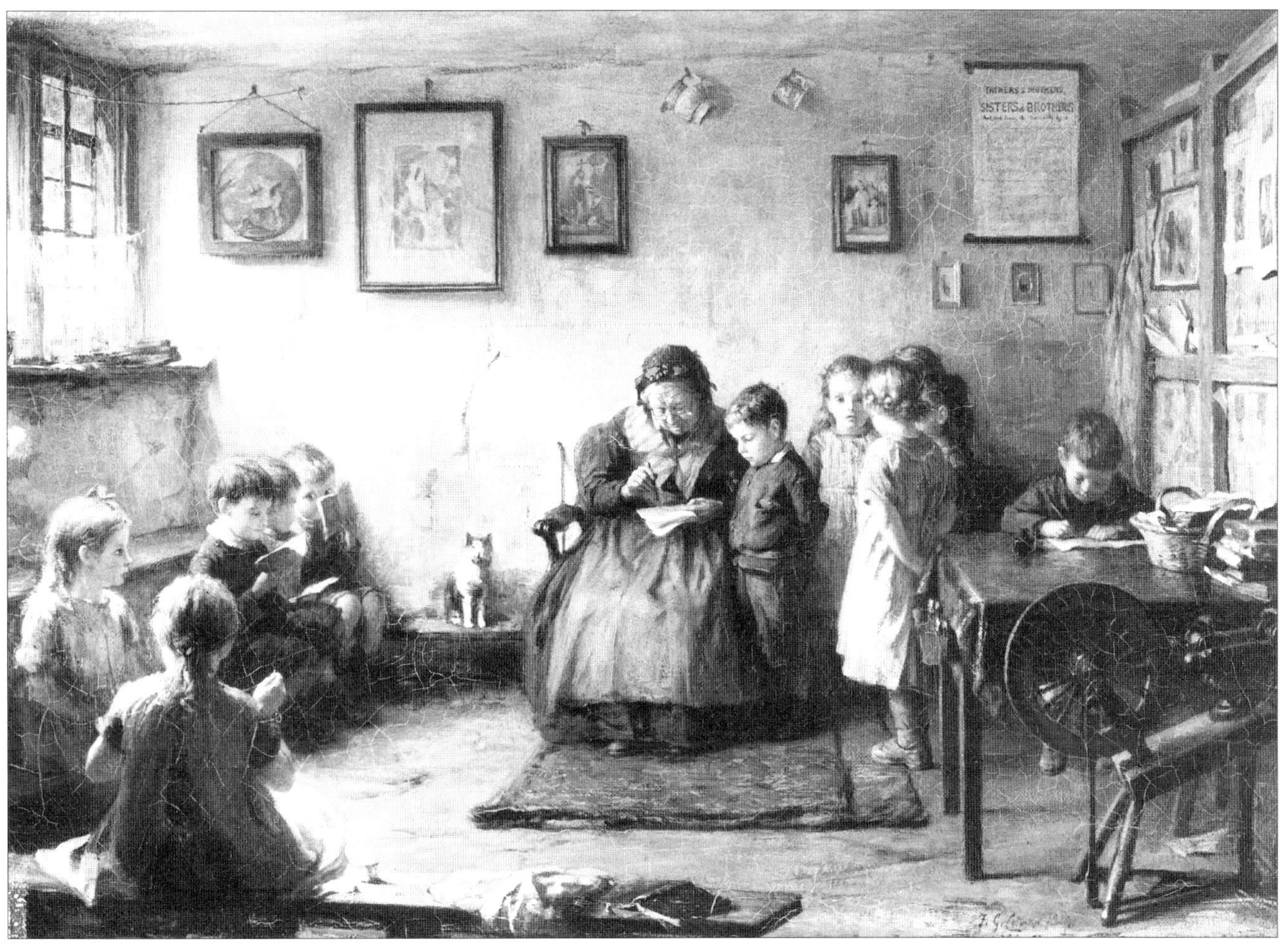

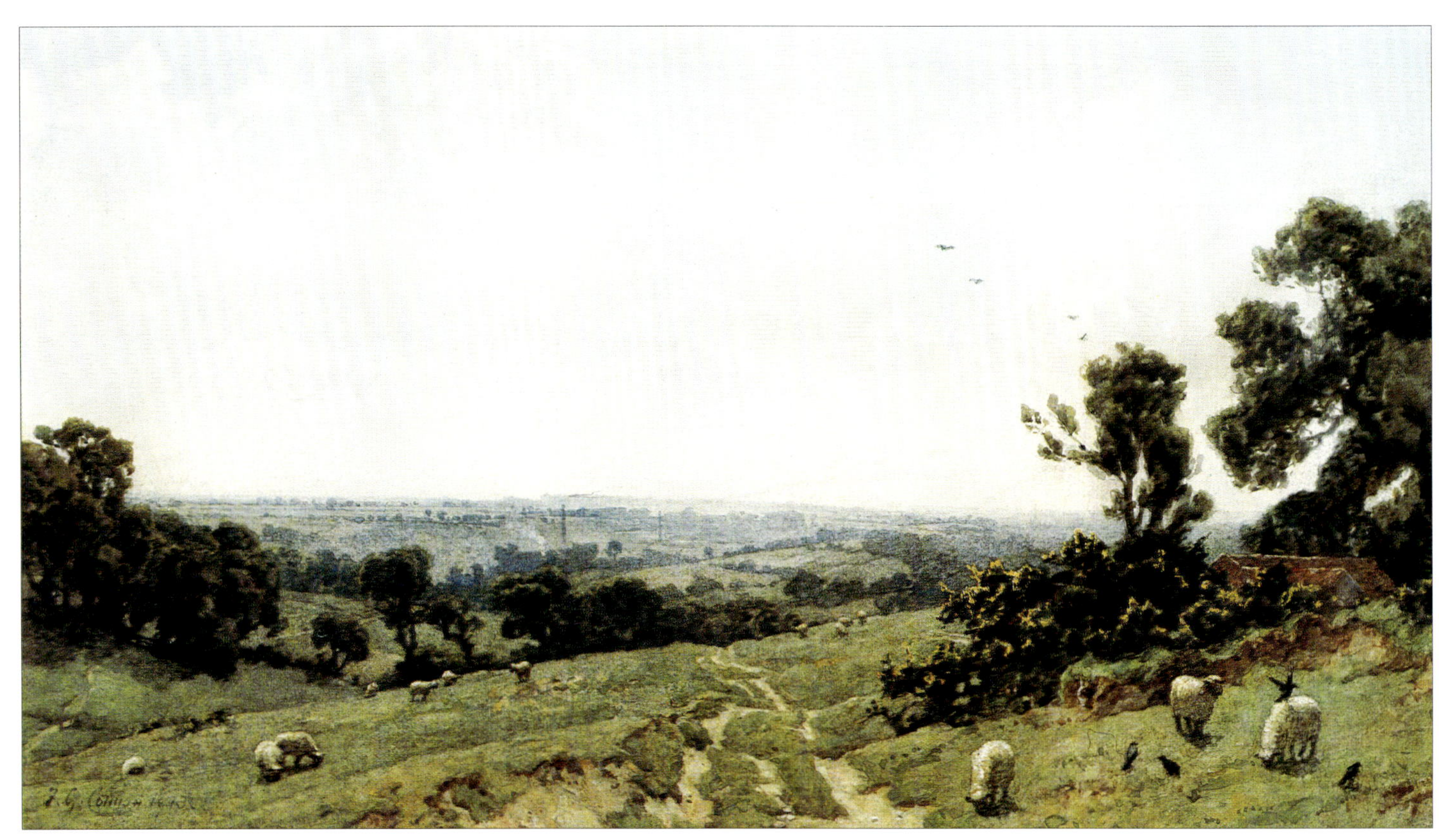

Frederick George Cotman, Upper Orwell Valley, watercolour, 10¼ in x 26 in

pictures are in the permanent collection of the Liverpool Walker Art Gallery including his best known, 'One of the Family'. 'The Dame School' in the Ipswich Museums collection is a charming study of the dame in her typically Victorian room surrounded by her small charges – to say nothing of the cat. His landscapes cover a broad spectrum; although in a slightly more modern idiom, his rural scenes are more reminiscent of Crome and Vincent than his uncle, although a street scene I have seen has something of the family flavour and showed a mastery of architecture. A very original semi-landscape of old Lowestoft, now in a private collection, shows him in a completely different, more romantic, light.

Although he spent much of his life in London, Frederick George was a founder member of the Ipswich Art Club, remaining a life member. In about 1901 he left London for Hemingford Grey, finally moving to Felixstowe for the rest of his life. He shared a Norwich exhibition with Sir Alfred Munnings in 1905, keeping at least a link with the family's home city.

The fact that he was made a Member of the R.I. in 1882 and of the R.O.I. in 1883 indicates the standing of this underrated artist and his work. He was well represented in an exhibition of paintings from the Cotman Family Collection in Norwich Castle in 1983 – Norma Watt has described him as 'a man of more than ordinary strength of personality'. In their various ways, this perhaps describes all of the painting Cotmans.

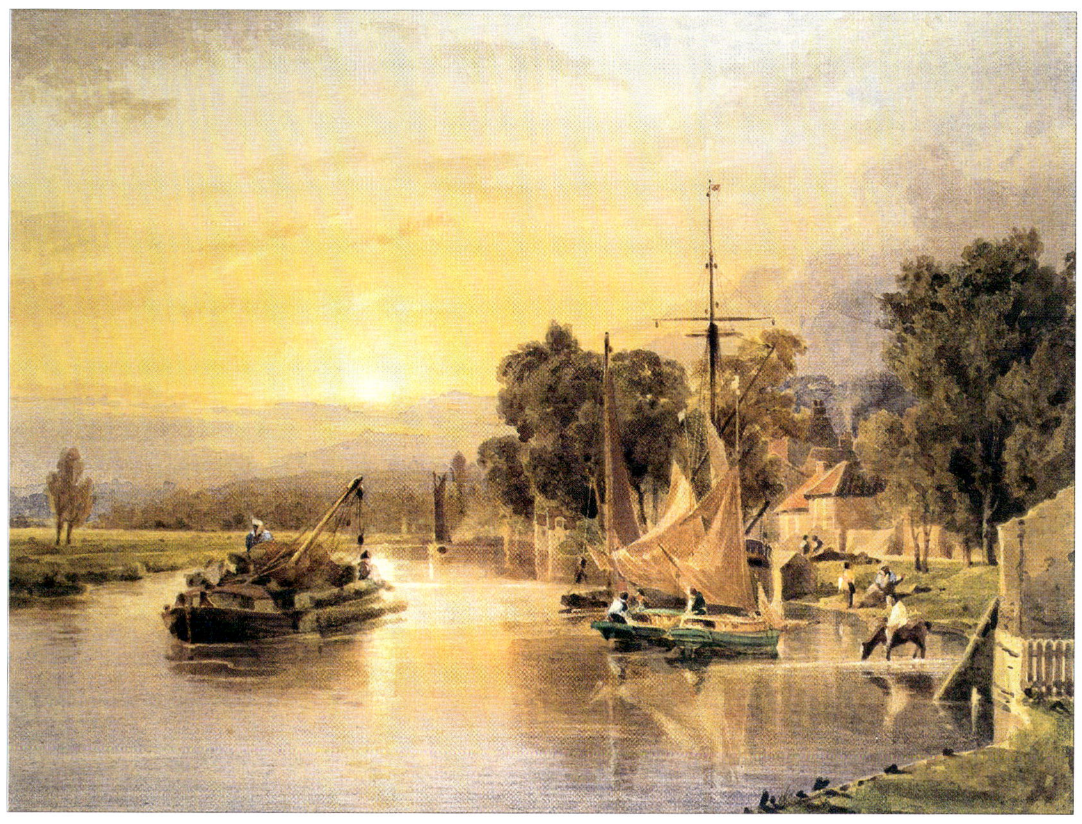

John Thirtle, *Thorpe Staithe*, watercolour, 10 in x 13½ in

Chapter 7

JOHN THIRTLE

'There is no more shadowy and elusive figure among the artists of the Norwich School than John Thirtle.' So wrote Marjorie Allthorpe-Guyton in her Catalogue of Thirtle's drawings in the Norwich Castle Museum. As she says, little is known of his life and what is known is rarely documented, yet, as a watercolourist, he was second only to John Sell Cotman and possibly John Middleton as the most talented exponent of that elusive medium. The young Henry Ladbroke, whose vision extended well beyond his time, wrote: 'As a man of genius, Cotman was much Crome's superior and, as a colourist, Thirtle far surpassed them both.'

It would seem that Thirtle's life was singularly uneventful and, apart from his London apprenticeship as a picture framer, he probably seldom left Norfolk. **John Thirtle** (1777-1839) was born in Norwich, the son of a shoemaker who had his own business in Elephant Yard. John was apparently born in a nearby house in Magdalen Street; whether Thirtle senior was carrying out his business there at the time and later moved to Elephant Yard or whether that property was for business only is unclear, although the family did own two properties in the City. The senior Thirtle, followed much later by his son, was a churchwarden at St. Saviour's and is thought to have been a God-fearing, conscientious man of good works.

It was in or around the year 1799 that young John Thirtle was sent to London to learn the picture framing business with the attendant crafts of gilding and carving. He returned to Norwich in 1800, so it is quite possible that some of his time in London was spent with John Sell Cotman who had moved there from Norwich in 1798. At that time one established picture framer in Norwich was the well known Benjamin Jagger. Marjorie Allthorpe-Guyton quotes from a rather strange letter of 'advice' to the young Thirtle:

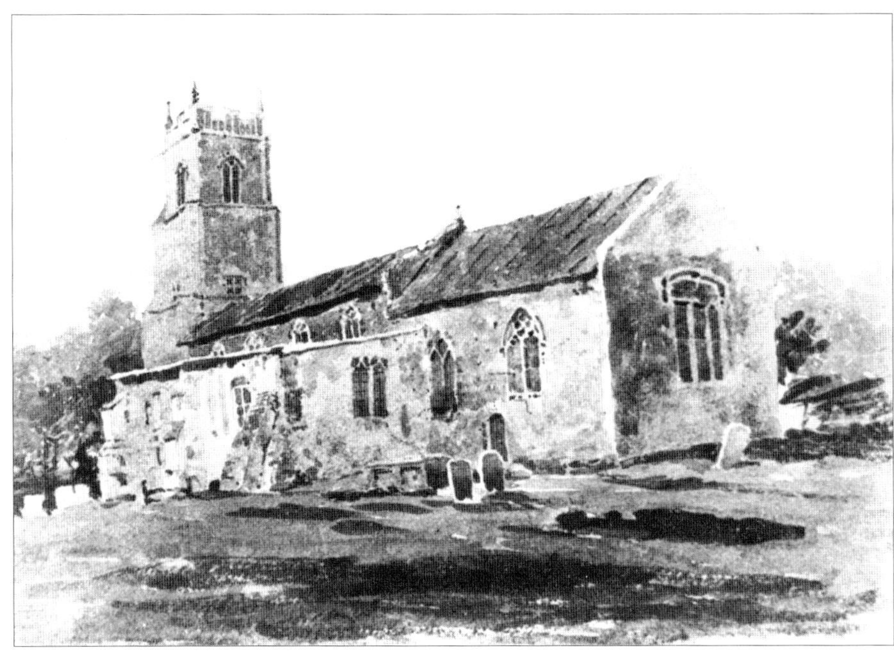

John Thirtle,
St. Mary's Church,
Wroxham, Norfolk,
watercolour and pencil,
c.1814

> . . . am glad to hear you are at Mr. Attwood's – take care to continue there for 2-3 months and part of these as carver – 'tho you will, if in Gilding Shop, see their Methods of Working and thereby practice on Evenings – that alone will not be sufficient, you must Enquire about the shops and where the best work is done – you sh'd also see the Methods of the City, for there they work quick, cheap and skewy. This method you must also learn – don't forget the putty. Work – your time is at best very short. As to the Cannons, Stannards and Cross and such like Gentry you'll have nothing to do with, neither with their Methods or connections – they will all come to the Dgs. I never knew one of these people succeed – they are not for journeymen.

Suffice to say, Thirtle's enduring craftsmanship owes little to this advice!

Presumably in his spare time John Thirtle was working away at his drawing and painting in addition to learning his trade, for his work is catalogued in the Norwich Society of Artists' exhibition as soon after his return as 1805 and 1806. He describes himself in this catalogue as 'Miniature Painter and Drawing Master', so by then he had gained sufficient confidence and experience to pass on his skills to others.

On his return to Norwich, Thirtle opened a shop for prints on the same premises as his picture framing business and teaching practice. Undoubtedly he was a fine craftsman as the number of his surviving frames in Norwich bear witness. His busy life and his achievements seem to suggest that lack of information about this life meant that there was little of it outside his work. There is almost no mention of him in the voluminous correspondence left by John Sell Cotman although the latter was his brother-in-law,* and there is no suggestion that the two were other than friends. Thirtle framed for the Cotmans and displayed for sale John Sell's remarkable collections of etchings.

Thirtle appears to have been one of the founder members of the Norwich Society of Artists and he was made Vice-President in 1812, the same year as his marriage to Elizabeth Miles. Both Elizabeth and her sister Ann were amateur painters and had exhibited with the Norwich Society of Artists where they may well have met their future husbands. While the Cotmans had a family of five, the Thirtles had no children.

By 1814 John Thirtle had become President of the Society but, as we know, along with Robert Ladbroke and his Vice-President, James Sillett, he helped to form the breakaway society, the Norfolk and Norwich Society of Artists. Although the schism had been caused by a difference between the original founders, Crome and Ladbroke, the fact that the breakaway group was joined by such senior officers of the original Society indicates that the difference must have caused some strong feeling. In the three exhibitions mounted by the new Society, Thirtle showed 15 in the first year, six in the second, and none at all in the third. It is illuminating to note that the *Norwich Mercury* commented: 'We lament exceedingly that Mr Thirtle should not have found time for a single drawing. His occupation is doubly to be regretted because he stands highest and

* Thirtle married Elizabeth Miles, sister of Ann Cotman, John Sell Cotman's wife.

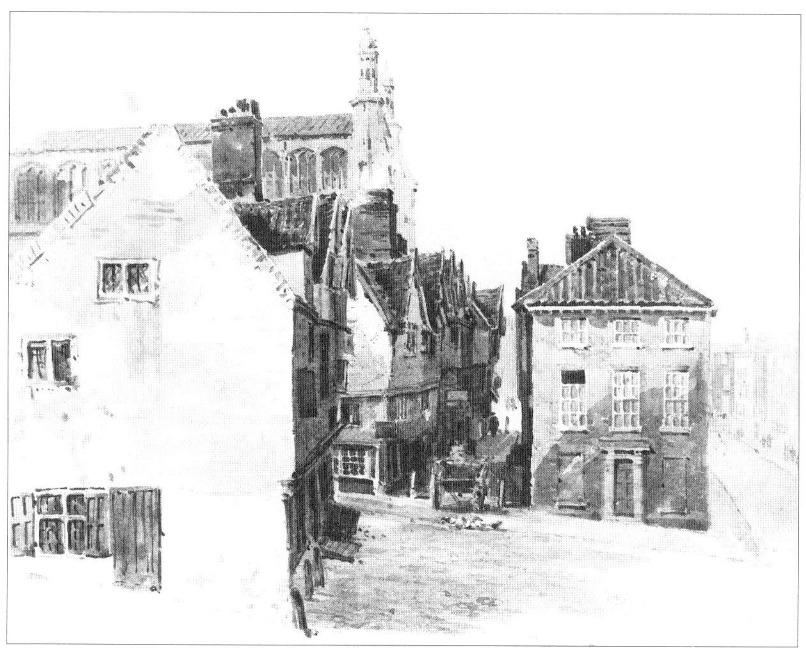

John Thirtle,
Haymarket, Norwich,
watercolour, 10¼ in x 13¼ in

alone in the peculiar and beautiful department of watercolour in which he has evinced such decided excellence.'

As well as his picture framing commitments and certain health problems, Thirtle had been helping John Sell Cotman with his drawings for 'Excursions through Norfolk' which was later published in two substantial volumes. It has been suggested that diplomacy was a consideration as he was framing for both factions.

Despite the competition in Norwich of Jeremiah Freeman and his son William, framers, restorers and gallery owners remembered in the City to this day, Thirtle seems to have established a good business. Considering the number of prolific artists working in and around Norwich at the time, perhaps it is not surprising.* Thirtle is known to have framed for, among others, Clover, Stark and Vincent and in part for Cotman, Crome, Dixon, Leman and fellow painters. Paintings exist by all these artists with frames bearing the Thirtle label. His business was further boosted by a fairly substantial legacy from his father.

Thirtle's draughtsmanship was impeccable combining a rare freedom with accuracy and truth; his teaching of drawing was conducted largely between 1807 and 1817. His best known pupils

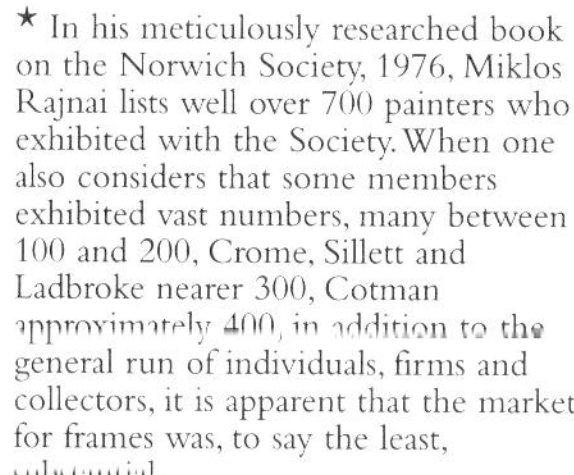

* In his meticulously researched book on the Norwich Society, 1976, Miklos Rajnai lists well over 700 painters who exhibited with the Society. When one also considers that some members exhibited vast numbers, many between 100 and 200, Crome, Sillett and Ladbroke nearer 300, Cotman approximately 400, in addition to the general run of individuals, firms and collectors, it is apparent that the market for frames was, to say the least, substantial.

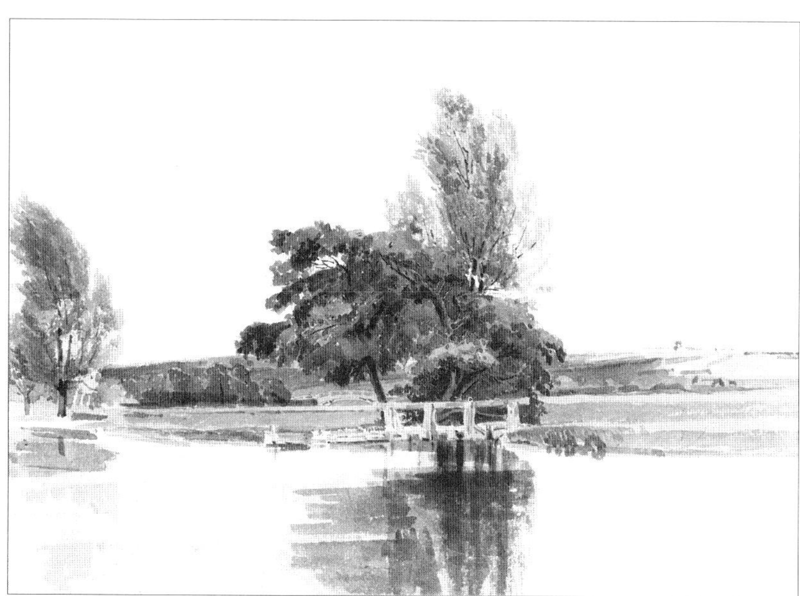

John Thirtle,
Riverside Scene near Norwich,
watercolour, 8 in x 11½ in

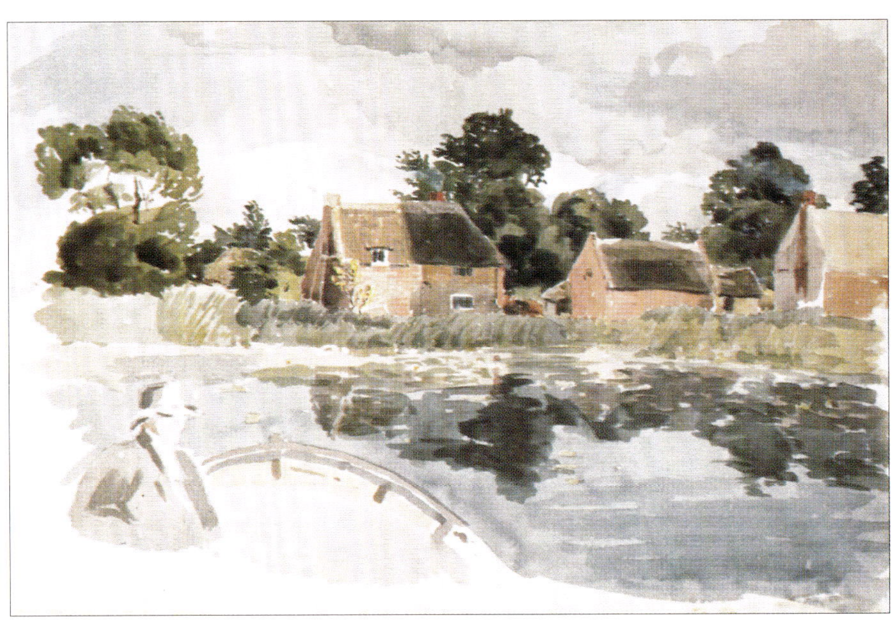

John Thirtle, Hoveton Little Broad, watercolour, c.1813, 8⅞ in x 12⅞ in

A charming 'wet' watercolour showing certain work of Thirtle's to be well ahead of his time.

were Henry Ladbroke, son of Robert, and Mary Blofeld, daughter of a well-known Hoveton family with a strong interest in the arts. Henry Ladbroke, who obviously had a great respect for John Thirtle and his work, stated: 'He was the most liberal man in imparting the knowledge of his art to any whom he took a liking for.' Although Thirtle had originally advertised himself as a miniature painter, no true miniatures have survived and it seems likely that he was applying the term simply to small portraits. Many of these were copies of a fairly average standard and variable quality. The best examples are undoubtedly the portraits of his wife and other sitters he knew personally, indicating that he responded best to 'live' models. Fortunately he abandoned portraiture for landscape fairly early in his career and here he found his true *métier*. Without a shadow of doubt he is one of the finest watercolourists of the Norwich School. His work in the main is fresh and spontaneous and, in many instances, well ahead of his time.

Adding to the comments of the young Ladbroke and the *Norwich Mercury* critic, Richard Mackenzie Bacon, the paper's editor, wrote in 1817: 'Mr Thirtle's drawings in watercolour are certainly without rivals in either place. They have a warmth, a richness and a brilliancy that is very captivating.' More recently, Martin Hardie commented succinctly: '. . . in the field of watercolour alone, Thirtle may well be considered a greater artist than Crome, the rarity of his known work is the reason for his comparative neglect.'

The other reason, of course, is the condition of so many of the survivors. Thirtle's study of chromatics led him to mix a particularly attractive warm grey which he used extensively. Unfortunately exposure to light drained the colour of the blue, the fugitive indigo, leaving the whole work with an overheated appearance. This is little less than a tragedy, for the unscathed works show a very beautiful sense of colour and colour co-ordination and a skilful treatment of light and tonal values. Such values are emphasised in his monochrome work, often in an attractive warm sienna, where the ravages of fading are less apparent.

One of the secrets of Thirtle's success and a practice that he consistently recommended to others was his insistence on working directly from his subject whatever the weather; even in a thunderstorm he would be outside, being particularly attracted by stormy skies and rainbows. As he was consumptive, this cannot have helped his health and probably even hastened his death, but it certainly gave his painting the sparkling spontaneity only achieved by working directly from nature. Scarcely any landscapes outside Norfolk are known and those may well be copies or based on other work he admired, for Thirtle rarely left his native county. Such familiarity with his subjects as well as working from life may well have added to the feeling of total confidence and directness so characteristic of his watercolours. Certain of his subjects were painted many times (namely St. Benet's Abbey or the Cow Tower), albeit in different seasons and weather, and the comparisons make interesting studies.

Various influences have been tentatively pinned on Thirtle but, apart from the inevitable rub

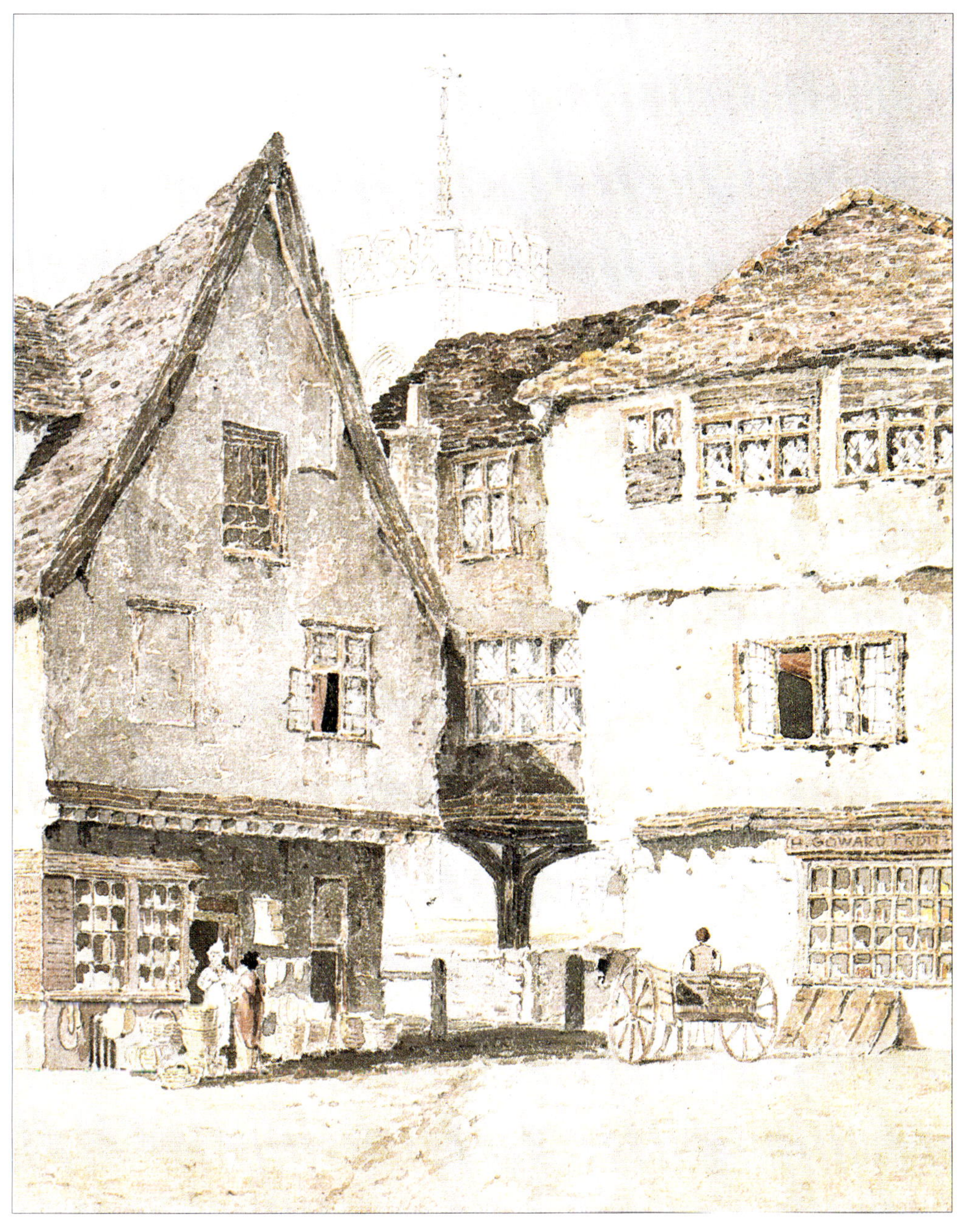

John Thirtle, Tombland Alley, watercolour, 9½ in x 7 in

off between a number of artists working and exhibiting in close proximity, I feel that Thirtle was very much his own man. Maybe there is a certain influence from Cotman in the freer watercolours, perhaps some affinity with Crome in his monochrome studies of which, in Norwich Castle, a classic example is 'Triforium, Norwich Cathedral', *c.*1809. This is a particularly lovely piece showing both his skill as a draughtsman and as a master of tone, a close companion to 'Tombland Alley'. Several authorities cite Girtin as a source of inspiration and De Wint has also been considered as an influence but, somehow, although there are certain individual works that suggest a reason for this, I feel the affinity is probably unconscious. Intuitively one senses a very independent spirit, answerable to no-one.

I am in total agreement with Derek Clifford writing in the Old Watercolour Society's journal in 1966 when he states that Thirtle 'is generally most rewarding in his less carefully finished work.' Here Clifford is obviously comparing the more detailed, 'tighter' later works with those in an almost modern idiom, painted with a complete understanding of medium and its potentialities: beautifully controlled washes and, where the colours are preserved, a faultless

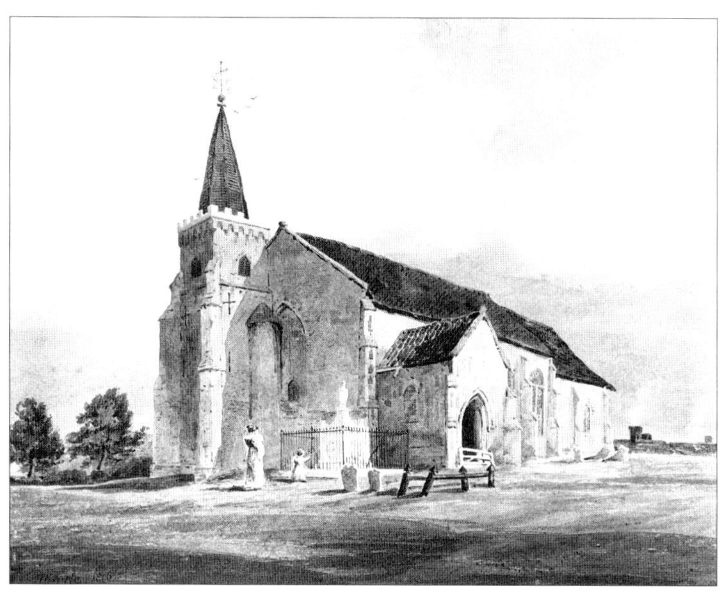

John Thirtle, St. Edmunds Church, Costessey, Norfolk, watercolour, 1816, 12¾ in x 16 in

recognition of tonal values; an inimitable feeling for light and shade and the importance of their subtle use for maximum effect. Some of Thirtle's water scenes have a magic all of their own, particularly evident in his many renderings of the river at Thorpe. The 'Riverside Scene near Norwich', using Cotman's broad wash technique in tones of green and grey has highlights that almost sparkle. Thirtle has perfectly mastered the art of giving water its wonderful reflective quality and of conveying all its mystery, serenity and depth.

Again, where the colours are well preserved, Thirtle's muted green-grey palette or warm, low toned buffs and browns, have a subtle charm and, in a way, give added interest to the occasional use of strong, even striking, colour. An excellent example of this occurs in 'Hoveton Little Broad' which I find enchanting. I particularly admire, too, his use of stronger greens along with an amazing range of lower tones giving richness and depth to woodland subjects. Whether it be water, trees or skies in whatever weather, Thirtle was evidently totally in tune with nature; this quality, added to his skill as a draughtsman of buildings and more solid features, has given us some of the most masterly and atmospheric watercolours of all time. It is just so sad that his predilection for the fugitive indigo has virtually ruined so much work which could so greatly have enhanced his reputation. Derek Clifford offers a crumb of comfort: 'An unfaded Thirtle is a lovely thing and, even when disaster has overtaken it, strong construction and a sense of poetry usually remain.'

Thirtle had another quality, rare in an artist, in that he was a good businessman. It has been said that his success was partly due to his ability to diversify according to demand, although I find it hard to credit an artist with Thirtle's undoubted sensitivity to be painting solely with commercial success in mind. There is no doubt that his framing business was lucrative and successful, and in earlier years teaching was embarked on as an additional source of income. For these reasons he may have felt he could indulge himself where painting was concerned, not least because his work was, in any event, popular and saleable. He did, however, in his later work appear to pander to the prevailing taste for the more detailed, rather sentimental prelude to the Victorian romantics. Needless to say, while personally preferring the more spontaneous work, the competence of the later style is unquestionable and certainly among the best of its kind. Nothing could take away Thirtle's instinctive feeling for the atmosphere of his subjects.

Thirtle died of consumption at the age of 63. As a measure of his success, he left his wife £2,000, a very substantial sum at that time. Mrs Thirtle outlived her husband by many years, reaching the extraordinary age for the 19th century of 95 years.

Thirtle produced his own 'Manuscript Treatise on Watercolour' which, thankfully, is preserved in Norwich Castle Museum. It provides an interesting and illuminating study consisting of 76 handwritten pages, illustrated here and there with his own sketches, and throws considerable light on his approach to his painting. It is quite difficult to decipher, being written up and down the page as well as in horizontal lines, in accordance with the economical fashion of the time

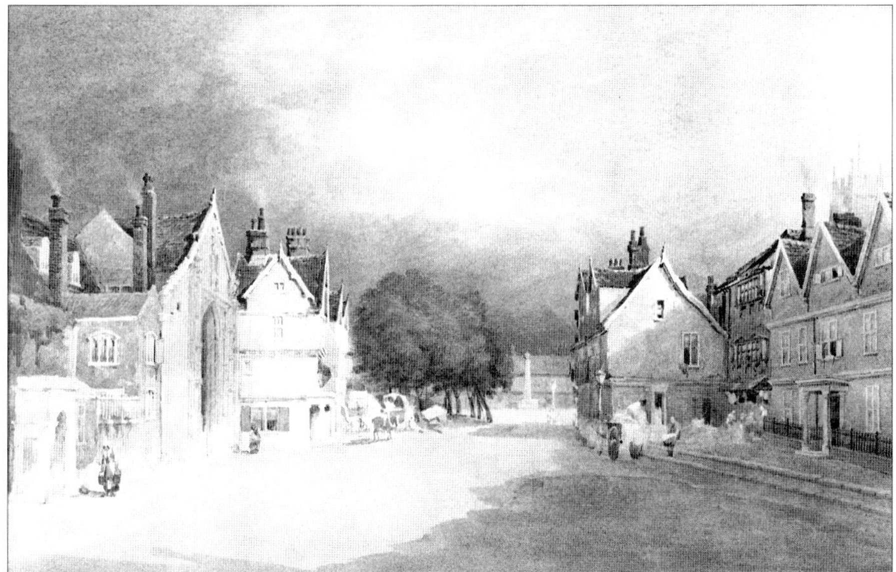

John Thirtle, Tombland, Norwich, watercolour, 14 in x 21¾ in

and for some years after. It is, however, reproduced verbatim in Marjorie Allthorpe-Guyton's Catalogue and, even today, the aspiring watercolourist can learn from it – I take the liberty of quoting some short sections that are particularly appealing:

> The things to be attended to in Drawg. are a Correct outline a proper distinction of Lights & Shadows, a harmony of Coloring. & the Giving of Objects their proper size & degree of distinctness According to their different distances. It is not sufficient that the parts of a Drawg. be correctly shewn & highly finished, it is necessary that they should produce a good effect when they are Combined together as forming a whole – there should be such a harmony of Colourg. as make the whole appear lighted up by the same Rays – & to be seen through the same Medium. the lights should be so distributed & subordinate to each other that they may not distract the Eye nor Draw the attention from the Principal light by which it ought always to be first caught, & the size & distinctness of objects should always be such, & may Enable any one to determine at Once, the nearest parts from those that are most distant.
>
> Remember, that when by the exercise of yr own Judgement, or the Observation of others, you discover any Errors in yr work, sett about correcting them, lest in exposing them to the Public, you Expose yr Defects also. admit not any self Excuse by persuading yourself that you shall retrieve yr Character & that by some succeeding work you shall make amends for your negligence, for if yr work does not perish as soon as it is out of yr Hands, like the sound of Music but remains a standing Monument of your Ignorance. If you excuse yrself by saying that you have not time for the study Necessary to form a good painter, having to Struggle against Necessity, you yrself are only to blame; for the study of what is Excellent is good both for Mind and Body.
>
> . . . both Cattle & the human figure you must begin with the bones & know how many parts of the figure present the bones & skins only to our view. the skull collerbones Elbows knees shinns all the way down to the ankle the rest is muscle & tendon & sinews – of a Cow find how many bones appear rude & bare discover in yourself you will then know what you see & what you draw & will give a proper meaning to your forms Assertain by measurements in proportional parts, what are the proportions of the Human & the same of the Animal learn where the greatest Projections come & where the greatest hollows half yr work is done – follow the animal walking & learn the motion of the muscles in the shoulder one does for both as the Rigging of one mast in a ship does for the other two or nearly so observe then the Muscles of the neck Erect & stooping . . . the hind Quarter will come next for the body remains nearly the same at all Times if you attempt the whole together you will find it like the Bundle of sticks not to be conqured but piece meal you may subdue it.

The fact that Thirtle is recommending such careful study of something that, if added to a landscape at all, is frequently no more than a suggested shape, indicates how very seriously he took every detail of his work and how much care and thought must have gone into even the most deceptively simple of his drawings.

Thirtle's 'Manuscript' has pages and pages on colour and colour mixing which include some truly helpful advice . . . but if only he had understood indigo!

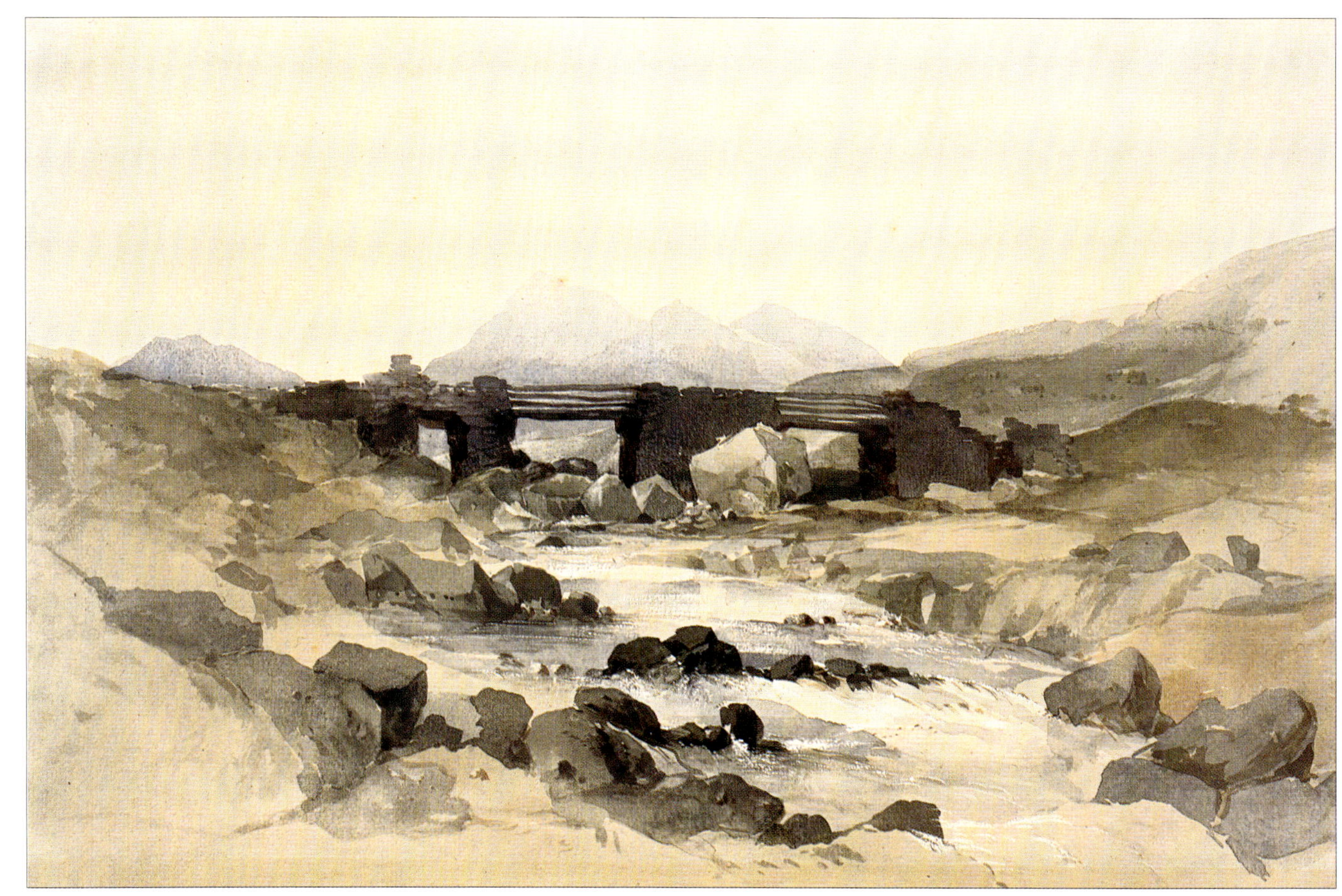

Robert Leman,
Mountain Scene, Snowdon from Capel Curig, watercolour, 12¾in x 19¾in

Chapter 8

LEMAN AND LOUND

The impressive quartet, Lound, Leman, Bright and Middleton, along with the Cotmans and John Thirtle, constituted the cream of the Norwich watercolourists. The magic of Middleton and of Cotman's Greta period in no way put to shame the two talented amateurs, Robert Leman and Thomas Lound. It must be said that although they were classed as amateurs throughout their artistic lives (Leman started, with Lound and David Hodgson, a sketching group known as the Norwich Amateur Club), the term did not carry the present day stigma of what Denis Thomas* has called 'well meaning incompetence'. Reviewing the opening exhibition of the Norfolk and Norwich Art Union formed in the late 1830s, the *Norwich Mercury* commented: 'No one can fail to entertain, who looks carefully into this exhibition, that the amateurs tread closely on the heels of the professional.'

Robert Leman (1799-1863), deserves much greater recognition and appreciation than has, until comparatively recently, been vouchsafed to him. He was born in Suffolk of well-to-do parents who moved to Norwich in his early years. He came of a long line of Suffolk dignitaries and clergymen and married Elizabeth Castleton, the daughter of the Rev. Sir Charles Castleton. One of his earlier forebears was Sir John Leman, a Sheriff of London in 1606, who founded the famous Sir John Leman School in Beccles. It will be observed that he came of more academic stock than most of the Norwich painters; his creative talent may have been inherited from his Aunt Philippa who, unusually for a woman of her time, was a competent practising sculptress.

Robert Leman first exhibited with the Norwich Society in 1819 but exhibiting was

* *Watercolours and Drawings Magazine*, Autumn 1986.

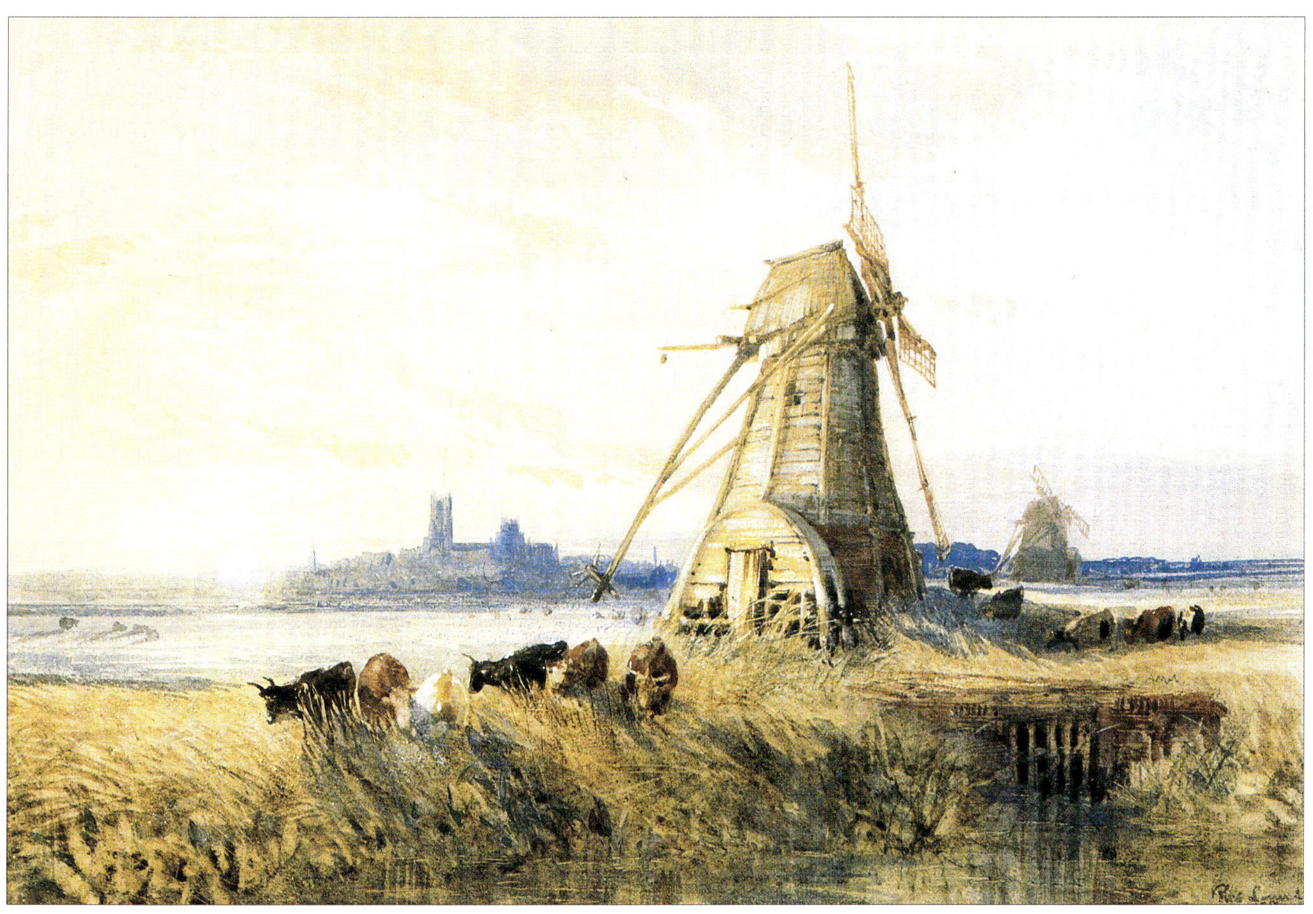

Thomas Lound,
A Distant View of Ely with Windmills at Sunset,
watercolour, 1836,
13 in x 19½ in

intermittent in the early years, presumably owing to pressure of work. As Manager of the Norwich Union Fire Insurance Company, he was a prominent figure in Norwich and served on a variety of educational committees and councils. Harold Day refers to a man of firm decision and integrity which certainly reflects in his face as portrayed in a very fine charcoal drawing by Joseph Geldart and an oil painting now hanging in a private collection. Judging by these likenesses, he was by far the most handsome of the Norwich artists – followed by John Sell Cotman.

It seems quite extraordinary that so many writers on the Norwich School have virtually ignored one of its finest artists. Robert Leman was a natural draughtsman; he became a pupil of John Sell Cotman, no doubt with a view to steering his own talent and love for sketching and drawing in the right direction. Obviously Cotman was a source of inspiration to him for, as an avid collector, he acquired 60 Cotman etchings, two folios of sketches numbering around 150, a selection of Cotman's animal and figure drawings and eight watercolours. The respect, interestingly, was mutual for Cotman is known to have expressed his admiration for Leman's work, especially in the sphere of pencil drawing.

Architectural drawings were for many years Leman's strongest point but the exquisitely drawn and shaded trees and surrounding landscape were always a worthy enhancement. Frequently these drawings have a very classical expression derived, presumably, from the classical element in some of Cotman's work, particularly the latter's etchings when he was seeking to emulate Piranesi.

Andrew Moore describes Leman's works in charcoal, chalk and stump as 'still wonderfully detailed and accurate and with a delicacy all of their own', while Derek Clifford comments: 'There is little that is amateurish about much of Leman's work which would rank large in any company. His pencil drawings are of an even level of professional brilliance, their fault lies in their faultlessness.' One might agree with that if they were of an unfeeling, hard correctness but this is not so – Leman's drawings are both sensitive and sympathetic and create an aura of sheer enjoyment in their creation. One of the advantages of the amateur status – often the best work is done for love rather than money!

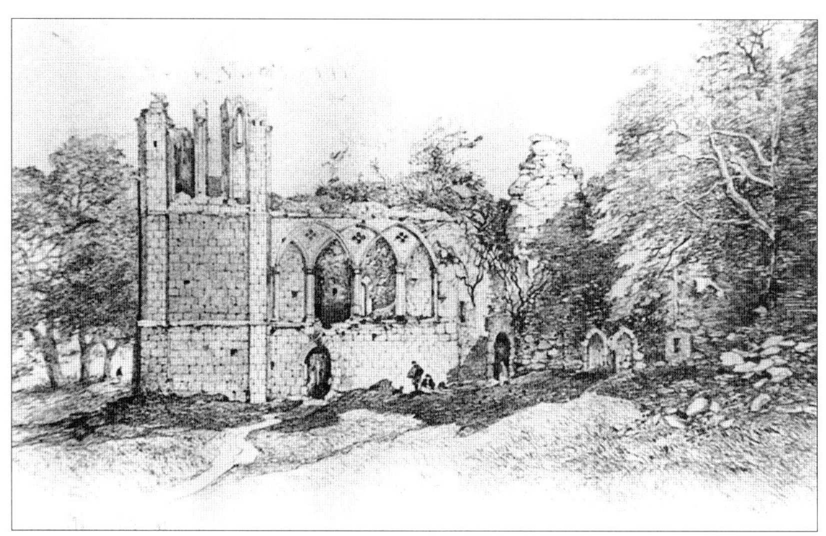

Robert Leman, Easby Abbey, Yorkshire, pencil on cream paper, 13 in x 20½ in

Leman's watercolour technique was based largely on his faculty for good drawing; he used pencil with his colour to excellent effect thereby achieving the best of both worlds. Denis Thomas writes: 'Leman's drawings are handsome, intelligent and disciplined – a description that applies equally to his watercolours, with their serene washes, restricted range of tones, deft simplification of detail, and pale cerulean light.' His pure watercolours certainly illustrate those 'serene washes' and the degree of simplification contrasts markedly with those based on detailed pencil drawing. In the field of watercolour he may have taken something from Cotman, even a rub off from his three particular friends – Lound, Bright and Middleton – but in the main he developed a very personal approach. He visited Wales with Lound in 1851, as well as Scotland and Derbyshire, and his treatment of the rocky scenery, rivers and hills is particularly impressive. He also, later in life, retraced Cotman's footsteps to the Greta region, perhaps as a sentimental journey.

It is interesting to compare the two conceptions of this particular area of Yorkshire. Cotman's is in a more modern idiom in spite of being 40 years earlier and the sheer inspiration of this period of his work would be impossible to emulate. Not that Leman tried – his own Greta watercolours, as well as the pencil drawings, are more detailed, more explicitly drawn than Cotman's. The wild beauty of the area comes across in both artists' work and, inevitably, in the watercolour drawings there is an affinity of colour. Maybe deliberately Leman's are more academic, more formal, and the detail is stated rather than implied. They have an impressive

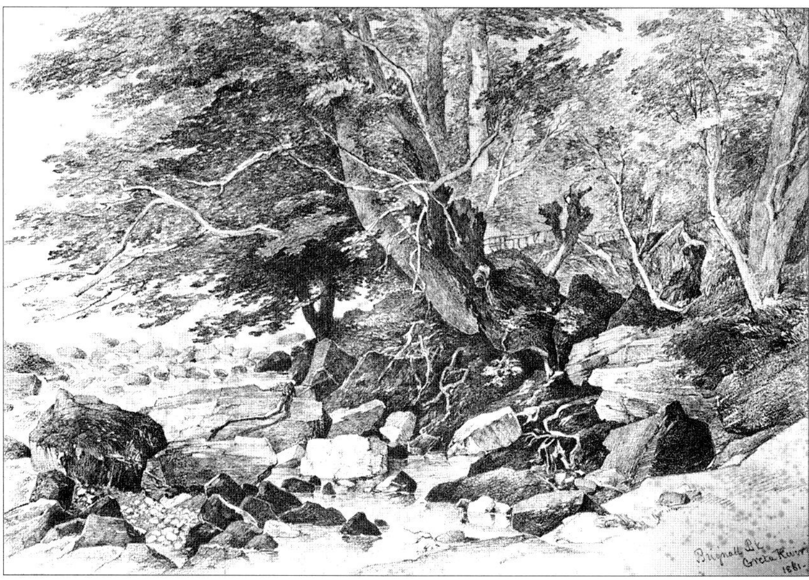

Robert Leman, Brignall Bank, River Greta, pencil, 1861, 14¾ in x 21½ in

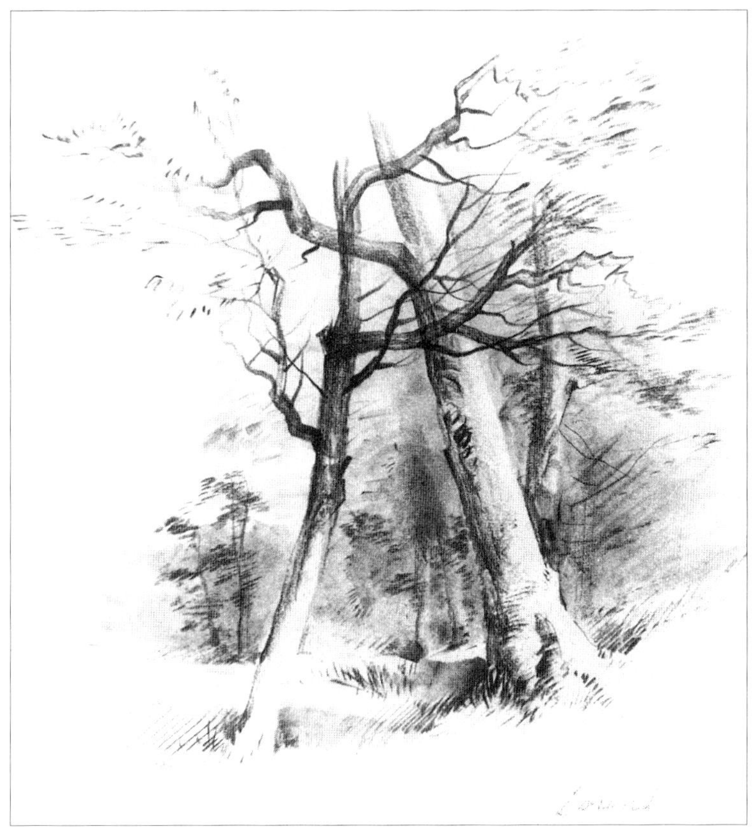

Thomas Lound, Study of Trees, black chalk, 13 in x 20½ in

beauty of their own all the same if less spontaneity than some of the distinctive Welsh studies. 'Snowdon from Capel Curig', for instance, is described by Clifford as 'one of the finest watercolours of the School' (see p.116). Perhaps Cotman had made the Greta all his own.

In his important business position, Robert Leman was obviously not beset with financial problems. His home on Newmarket Road was in the most exclusive area of Norwich and he was clearly in a position to indulge his passion for collecting. After his death, Spelmans of Norwich sold, together with other effects, over 200 of his collection of works by John Sell Cotman, together with others by Miles Edmund Cotman, John Crome, Joseph Stannard, his friends Lound, Bright and Middleton, and a number of other works by respected artists outside the Norwich School. In addition there were about 1,500 drawings and watercolours of his own as well as a selection of copies of Cotman's drawings, no doubt part of his early training. Considering that Leman appears not to have exhibited outside Norwich and, during his business life, to have been fairly sporadic about exhibiting at all, there could be no more conclusive proof that he spent all the time he could sketching, drawing and painting for the sheer pleasure it gave him and is giving now to posterity.

Leman's close friend **Thomas Lound** (1802-1861) was a prolific artist in all media, particularly watercolour. He was undoubtedly talented and extremely diligent but lacked the consummate skill of his fellow amateur and certainly, although the best of Lound is very good indeed, his consistent quality.

Lound was born into a family of brewers and retained the business interest all his life. Very little is known of his young life except that an interest in the visual arts was patently something that was always with him. As well as his own artistic endeavours and personal regular exhibiting with the Norwich Society, Royal Academy and British Institution, together with Leman he helped form the Norfolk and Norwich Art Union, was appointed President of the Art Union committee and, again with Leman, served on the committee of the Norwich School of Design. Lound had many friends among his fellow artists and is said to have been an outgoing and popular character. With David Hodgson he helped to revive the Artists' Conversaziones which had petered out since their early introduction by John Sell Cotman and John Berney Crome. These proved very

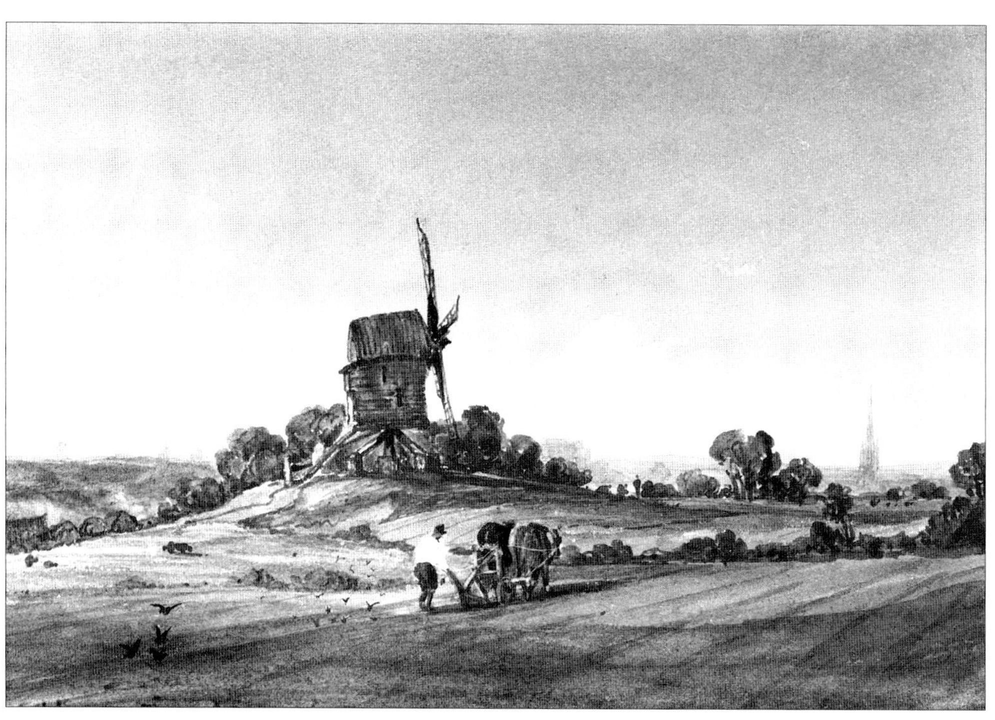

Thomas Lound,
View of Norwich, watercolour,
5¾ in x 9 in

successful by encouraging the interchange of views on each other's work, when drawings, prints and watercolours were laid out on tables for ease of viewing and discussion.

Lound, who was a friend of the family, had drawing lessons with John Sell Cotman and helped himself in the early years by copying the works not only of Cotman, but Crome, Dixon and others. Oddly enough the little influence he took from Cotman shows more in his oils than watercolours. His oils are a mixture of broad treatment and fine brush work but, while undoubtedly competent, lack the assurance of his watercolours. Like most of the Norwich artists, Lound was a fine draughtsman; his charcoal and chalk drawings are reminders of Joseph Stannard and sometimes Henry Bright. Some of his monochrome studies are delightful, always a good test of an artist's ability, and he also dabbled in etching. About 20 etchings are recorded, principally drypoint.

Lound's watercolours vary as much in style as quality; sometimes he used a broad wash technique to excellent effect with just the right focus on a particular point he wanted to emphasise. At other times careful coloured drawings show a completely contrasting approach, and there were others that fell at varying stages between the two. Lound was very susceptible to the influence of other artists around him; John Thirtle and David Cox are frequently recognisable, also Crome, Bright and Stannard. Somehow, in a totally indefinable way, Lound managed to turn this combination of influences into something quite personal to him even when, as frequently they were, his subjects were those first used by others. Out of all this the best of Lound can hold its own anywhere as part of our great watercolour tradition.

The most interesting of all his work and certainly the most personal and, in a way, revealing, are the many, many tiny watercolour sketches he kept either as records of larger, finished versions, material to be worked up at a later date or quick copies of another artist's work he had admired. These little treasures are so spontaneous, so full of vitality and charm, that many people find them much more attractive than his exhibition work. They certainly cast a different light on Lound himself by revealing a sensitivity and a feeling for atmosphere that tends to get lost in the more painstaking work. His granddaughter, Florence Thirkettle, bequeathed to Norwich Castle an album of 83 of these little gems. With the exception of some fruits of sketching trips to Wales and Yorkshire quite late in his career, most of Lound's subjects are local to Norwich.

Like his friend Robert Leman, Lound was spared the struggle for survival of so many of his near contemporary artists. Not only did he sail his own yacht, *Kathleen*, and indulge in photography, but he was a compulsive collector; coincidentally both his daughters married

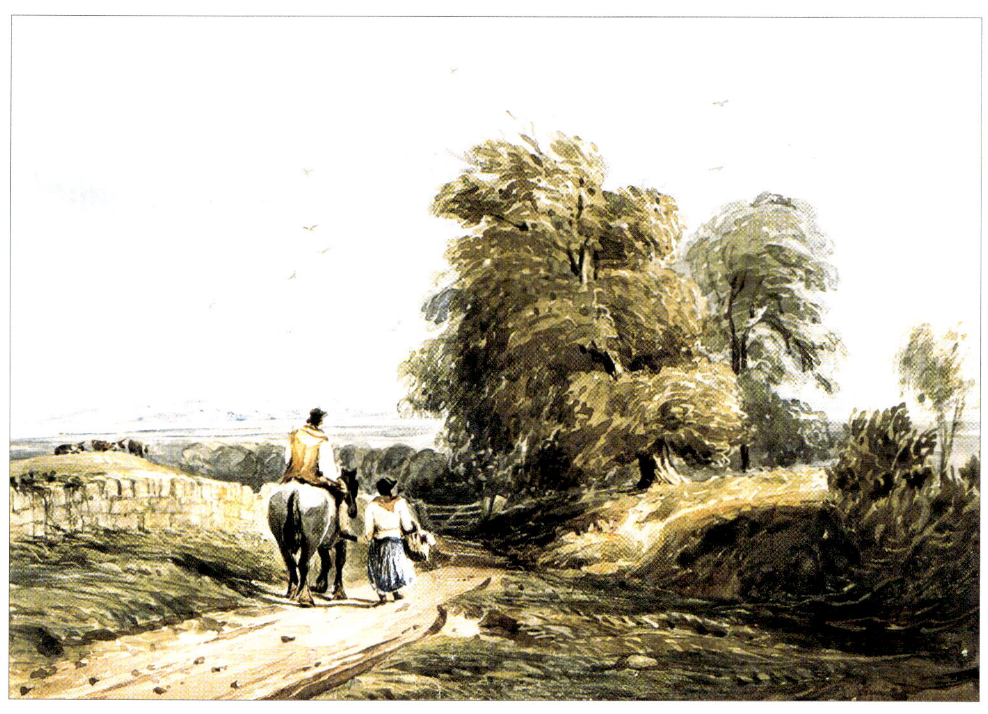

Thomas Lound,
Going to Market, watercolour,
1839, 7½ in x 10½ in

collectors so the whole family must have been surrounded by art. On his death Lound's collection is known to have comprised, along with a substantial miscellany, 75 Thirtles, 24 Stannards, 22 Lemans, 22 Brights, several Cotmans, both John Sell and Miles Edmund, examples of Crome, David Cox and Prout, over 500 of his own drawings and a considerable number of paintings. In addition, he had an extensive library of art books.

Lound may have had money, talent and possessions, a good business and absorbing hobbies, but his health was not good. This was undoubtedly aggravated by the sad deaths of his wife and son in the same year, 1859. Two years later he died of an apoplectic fit in the King Street home where he had spent most of his life.

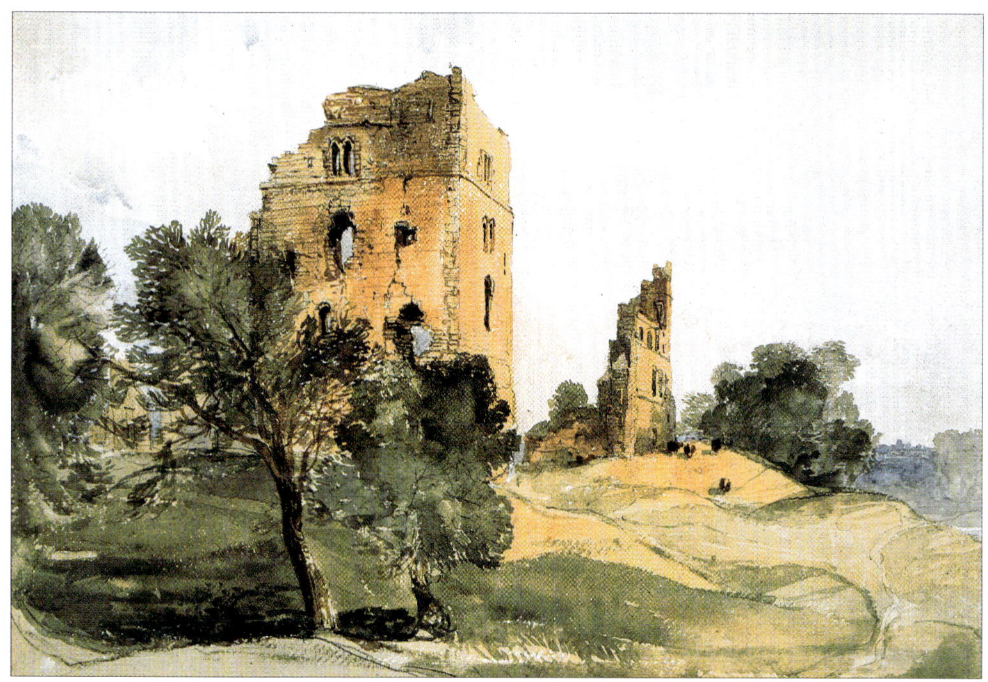

Thomas Lound,
Castle Acre, watercolour,
13 in x 20 in

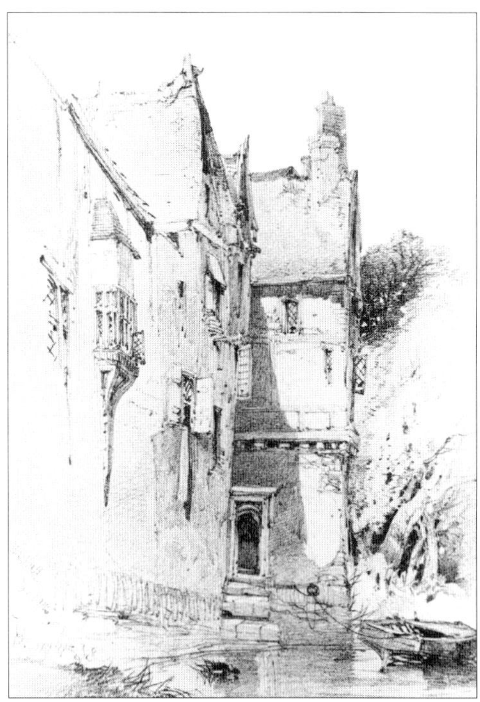

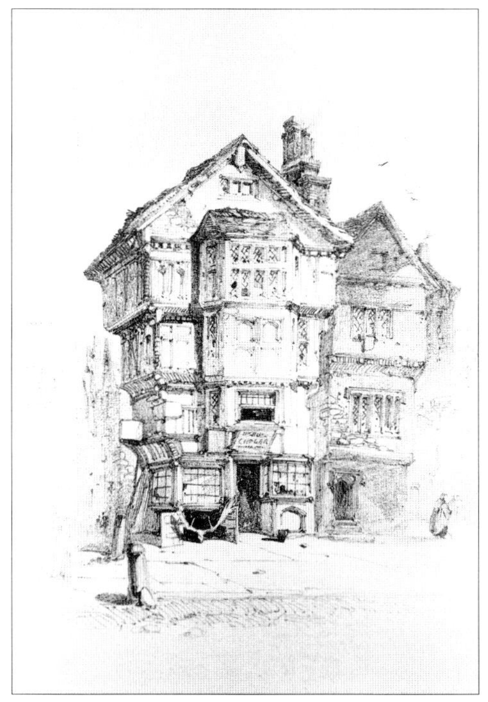

Henry Bright,
Parham Old Hall, Suffolk,
pencil and bodycolour, 1838

Henry Bright,
Old House, Norwich,
pencil and bodycolour

Chapter 9

HENRY BRIGHT AND JOHN MIDDLETON

Henry Bright (1810-1873) was one of a handful of Norwich School painters born in the neighbouring county of Suffolk. His birthplace was the small and unspectacular town of Saxmundham where his father, Jerome Bright, was a highly respected and apparently prosperous clockmaker.* Although several died at an early age, Susan and Jerome Bright had nine children whose dates are recorded on the family vault in the Congregational Church at Rendham where the family worshipped. Henry was the youngest child.

Not a great deal is known of his childhood but he appears to have been brought up in comfortable circumstances. He attended school in Saxmundham, 'Mr Farrow's School for Young Gentlemen', which at the time was run by one Owen Haxell, known to the 'young gentlemen' as 'Custards'. Whether it was a parental decision or his own, on leaving school Henry was apprenticed to a chemist in Woodbridge and, later, to another in Norwich. Henry Bright had always enjoyed drawing and the fact that the Norwich chemist, Paul Squire, had an interest in the local art scene and was a keen collector no doubt provided inspiration for his young apprentice. He met John Berney Crome and John Sell Cotman from whom he took some lessons in his spare time; any further time available was spent sketching, meeting such kindred souls as Thomas Lound and Robert Leman, and participating as far as possible in local artistic activity. Kitson maintains that Paul Squire was himself an amateur artist but this is not corroborated elsewhere.

In spite of the artistic distractions, Henry Bright qualified as a chemist and worked for a time as a dispenser in the Norfolk and Norwich Hospital. His heart was not in his work, however, and his parents must have decided that his artistic talents deserved encouraging and transferred his indentures to Alfred Stannard. With his other artistic contacts and advisers and more time to spend

* Jerome Bright (1770-1846) is included in Bailey's *Watchmakers and Clockmakers of the World.*

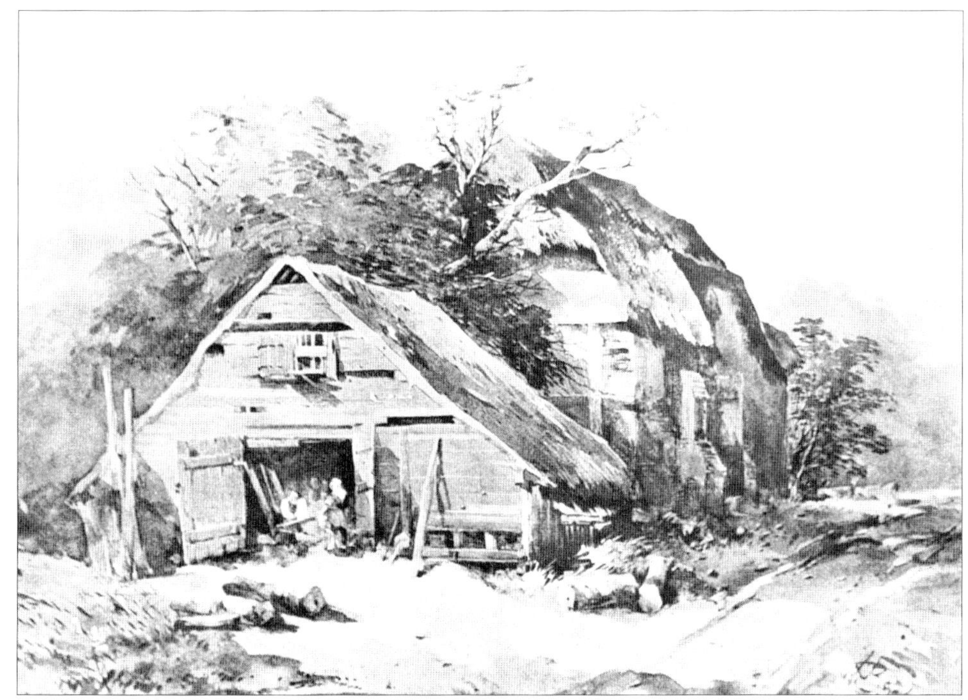

Henry Bright,
A Barn, watercolour, 1847

studying the arts, Henry Bright undoubtedly felt more at home than when dispensing medicines.

In 1833 he returned to Saxmundham to marry Eliza Brightly after which the couple lived for a time with Bright's family. In order to broaden his horizons and to find more outlets for Henry's work, the young Brights moved to London in 1836, to 12 Spring Terrace, Paddington, where they lived for ten years and where, sadly, Eliza died at only 31 years of age. Henry Bright then moved to Grove Cottage, Ealing, presumably to escape the memories and steep himself in his work.

From the time of his arrival in London, Bright was exhibiting as widely as possible, sometimes in the company of other Norwich artists seeking the experience and prestige of exhibiting in the capital. Stark, Priest, Henry Ladbroke and Miles Edmund Cotman all showed at the Society of British Artists and the British Institution. In 1839 Bright, who at the time was preoccupied with watercolour, was made a Member of the New Society of Painters in Watercolour. His second exhibit at the Royal Academy in 1844, 'Entrance to an Old Prussian Town', was purchased by Queen Victoria.

Henry Bright made the fullest possible use of his time in London, painting for exhibition purposes, fulfilling the commissions that frequently came his way, and building up a prestigious teaching practice. He tended to exploit any useful social contacts he established, not being in any way shy in coming forward. During research for the catalogue of his work published by the Norfolk Museums Service in 1986, a list was found in Glyde's *Ipswich Painters* headed 'A List of a few of the distinguished pupils Mr Henry Bright had the honour to instruct in Painting and Watercolour during 20 years of the Practice in London.'

The 'few' extends to 102 names which include mainly titled, noble or aristocratic ladies and gentlemen, such as Her Imperial Highness the Grand Duchess Marie of Russia, the Most Noble the Marquis of Grandby, Don Peddrorenna of the Spanish Embassy and M. Jules Dubois of Paris. The Norwich artist, John Middleton, is also listed. Inevitably some of Bright's distinguished and wealthy pupils also became useful patrons, no doubt part of the Bright technique. In the Catalogue of the Liverpool Academy exhibition of 1836 Bright, who never suffered from false modesty, styled himself 'Draughtsman in Crayon to her Royal Highness the Langravine of Hesse Homberg'. During the teaching period he is reputed to have been making some £2,000 a year which, over a century and a half ago, was the sort of exceptional income that most artists could only dream of.

Bright published several instructional manuals for the use of his pupils and others and

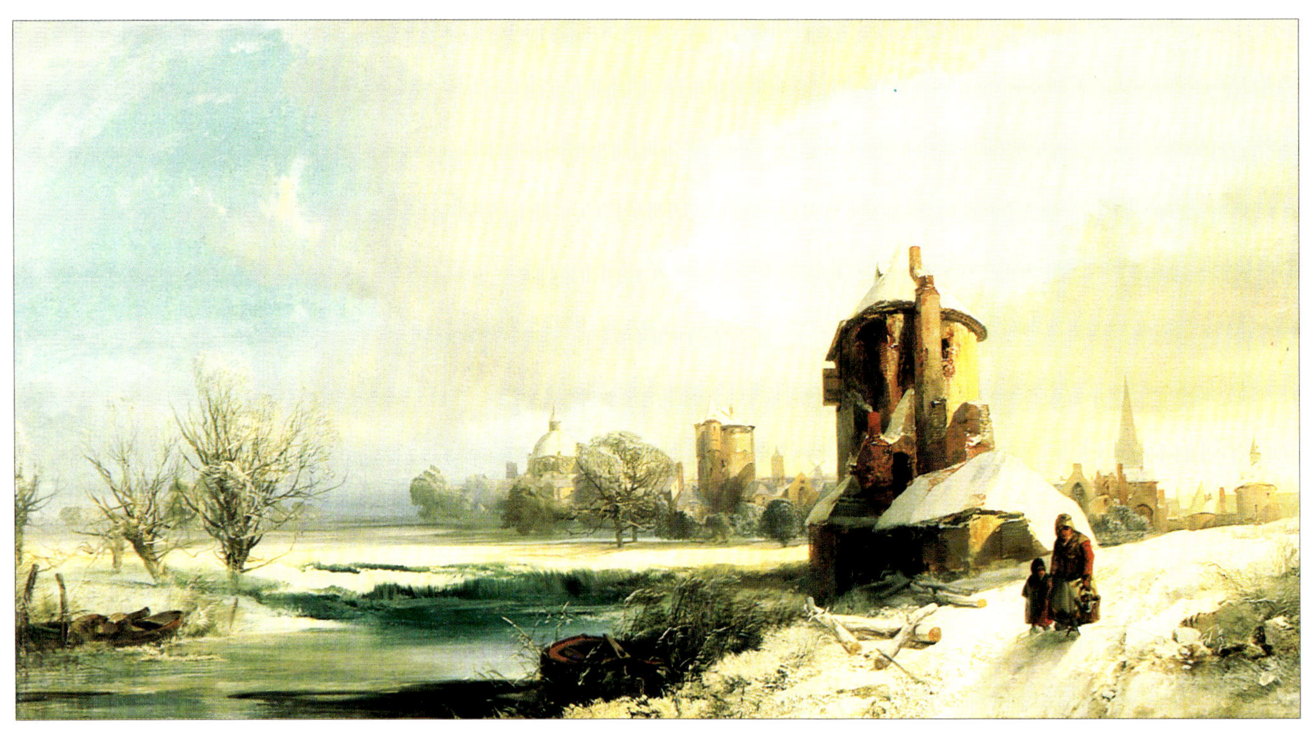

Henry Bright,
Winter Scene, Haarlem,
oil, 1841, 23½ in x 44 in

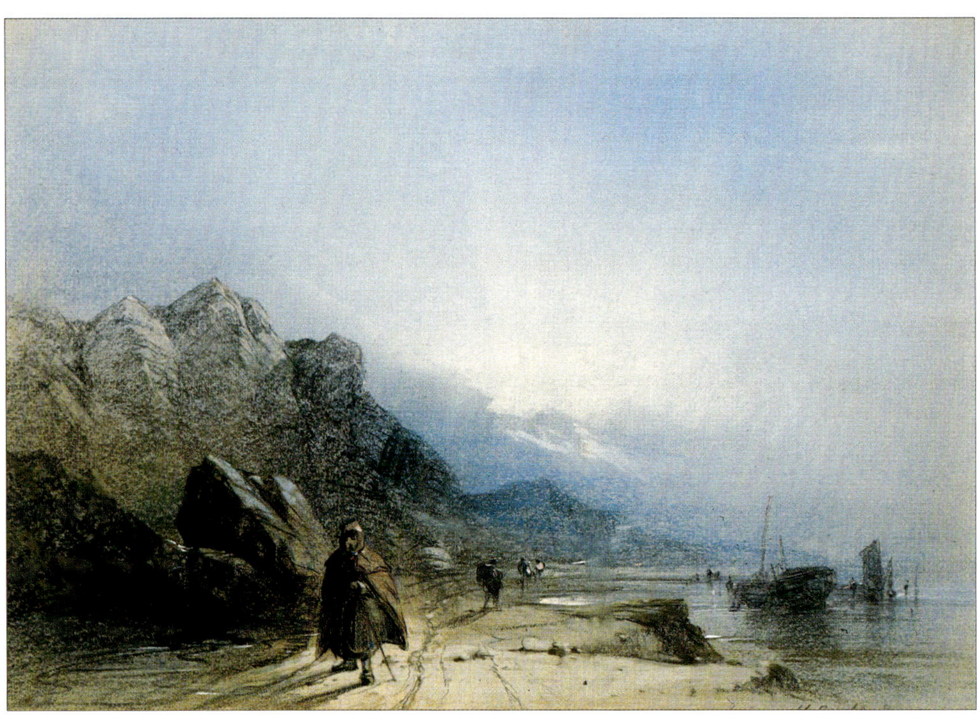

Henry Bright,
A Fresh Morning in the Highlands,
oil on canvas,
23½ in x 42½ in

contributed to various art journals. His *Rudimental Drawing Book for Beginners in Landscape* was published in six numbers by Ackermann in 1843, followed by *Bright's Drawing Book on Landscape* in eight numbers and *Advanced Drawing Book for the Pencilling Tints* in six numbers. Unfortunately the file copies of the *Drawing Books* which were held by Rowney's were destroyed in a Second World War bombing raid. Bright's published work also included a number of chromolithographs.

Bright also became involved with Alfred Stannard in the production of a particular brand of crayon which he used himself to great effect as well as benefiting financially. As if all these activities were not enough for one person, he travelled during the 1840s to Holland, Germany

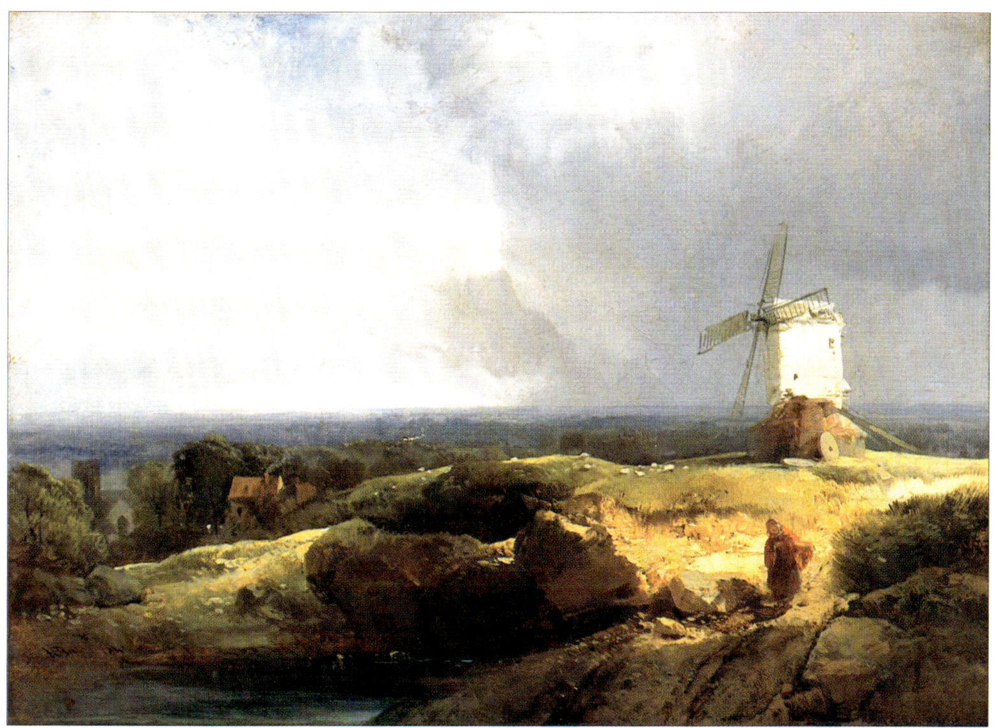

Henry Bright, *Landscape with Windmill*, oil on canvas, 15¼ in x 21 in

and France as well as going on a number of sketching holidays to Scotland, Wales, Devon and Cornwall. He still maintained his connections with Norwich, exhibiting there as well as in London and other major cities.

Pressure of work had evidently taken its toll for in 1858, on account of ill health, Bright returned to Saxmundham with his two daughters, stating that never again did he want to live in London. Two years later he moved to Norwich where he had so many friends and where, from then on, he exhibited more frequently than in London, although he often visited the capital and exhibited in the most important exhibitions. He was also involved in artistic activity in Ipswich, no doubt because a number of his influential patrons came from the Ipswich and Bury St. Edmunds area. He became one of the Vice-Presidents of the Suffolk Association of Fine Art based in Ipswich and moved to the town in 1868 where he continued painting for exhibitions and executing commissions until his death at the home of his niece in 1873. He is reputed to have said not long before his death that he had enough commissions to last him ten or 20 years.

It is fair to say that Henry Bright was the most versatile, the most energetic, the most innovative and certainly the wealthiest of the Norwich artists. Bright was also one of the most talented, a talent which some critics have felt was too slick and impersonal; but that it was quite brilliant no one can deny. He was a superb draughtsman, the essential common denominator, and was master of whatever medium or mixed media he chose to use, always in complete control and supremely confident. His success can be attributed to his strong personality as well as his inborn talent.

Opinions of Bright's work are as diverse as the work itself and it is both interesting and illuminating to quote from various authorities. Personally, much as I admire his *pure* watercolours with their sensitive tones and beautifully controlled washes, my preference is for his (often early) drawings. Meticulous in pencil, chalk or pastel, to me his pencil drawings have the greatest charm, often on tinted paper with subtle suggestions of body colour or chalk. These little masterpieces, particularly the architectural subjects and studies of trees, are so delicate and sensitive that it seems impossible to identify their creator with that of the sometimes quite awful, later large oils and pastels with their violent colouring. Perhaps Bright was more of a mood painter than he is given credit for – if so, it explains many things that continue to puzzle art historians.

Perhaps it seems churlish to make too much of the unfortunate monsters which seem totally out of character. In his pure watercolours and early oils developed in the 1840s, Bright shows a

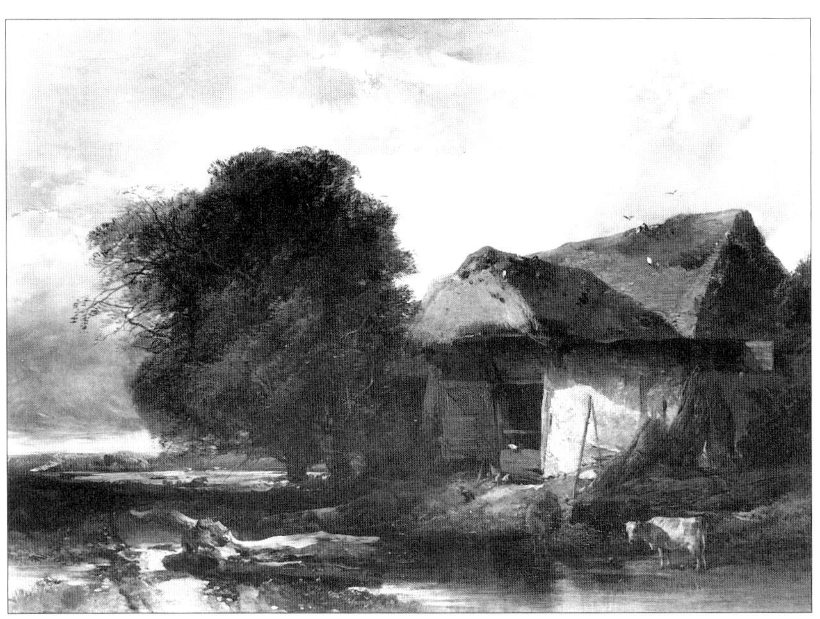

Henry Bright, Old Barn, Suffolk, oil on canvas, 1847, 15 in x 21 in

muted and very beautiful sense of colour and his use of light can be magical. He also had a strong sense of atmosphere and weather, giving his work a haunting, rather romantic appeal especially where there are lowering, stormy skies over a landscape enlivened with skilful and significant touches of light. In quieter vein is the painting 'Rocks and Trees' with soft, subtle, luminous greens. Marjorie Allthorpe-Guyton sums up Bright's work when she writes of '. . . an able craftsman with a facility in pencil, oil and watercolour whose sure touch often redeems the mannerisms of his formulae.'

Perhaps only John Sell Cotman among the Norwich painters invited such a diversity of opinion, good, bad and indifferent, as Henry Bright. I find it extremely sad that so many critics, both in Bright's own time and since, have homed in, maybe because they shout so loudly, on those large, brash canvases and have torn their creator to shreds. Compared with his faultless academic drawings, his more delicate watercolours and, indeed, some pastels, the offending mammoths were few in number and should be ignored or treated as an experiment that did not come off.

Harold Day does just that and, while I am frequently at odds with Day, here we see eye to eye:

> Painting and drawing seemed to Henry Bright second nature. His fluency and delicacy of touch are almost unrivalled. He had a great flair for crystallising a subject and accenting salient points in such a way that the viewer is carried into the picture, the eye compulsively following the beautiful flowing lines. It is perhaps as a draughtsman that Bright shows his mastery, though he had the most sensitive feeling for colour which, on occasion, gives rise to great atmosphere in his works. The distant rain cloud or glancing sun rays are depicted with an ease which makes their effect convincing. The use of a palette knife in the sky gives a crisp touch to the impasto cloud – sometimes the cloud by means of the knife is splintered, to give a delicious spattering of light. Added to this masterful handling, Bright sometimes introduces his 'electric' blue pigment.

Later Day adds: 'It is difficult to find a Henry Bright painting or drawing without great merit; he is perhaps the most consistent East Anglian artist. Even in his very late period one can only say they lack the strong light we associate with his earlier works.'

Rajnai is a harsher critic: 'The ease of deft execution conceals the meagre content of many of his paintings in which nature is often used as a stage for bombastic effects.'

Hemingway, after discussing Crome, Cotman and the Stannards, adds: '. . . otherwise the most talented of the later artists were Henry Bright and John Middleton.' Oddly he makes no mention of Bright's professional draughtsmanship but continues: 'Some aspects of Bright's work reflect the influence of the Stannards, and of Leman and Lound with whom he remained close friends.'

While I do not feel Bright owes a great deal to other influences, with the possible exception of Alfred Stannard and, to a small extent, John Sell Cotman, Hemingway (and he is not alone) identifies a single painting, 'Beach Scene', with its 'fresh, spontaneous technique', with the oils of

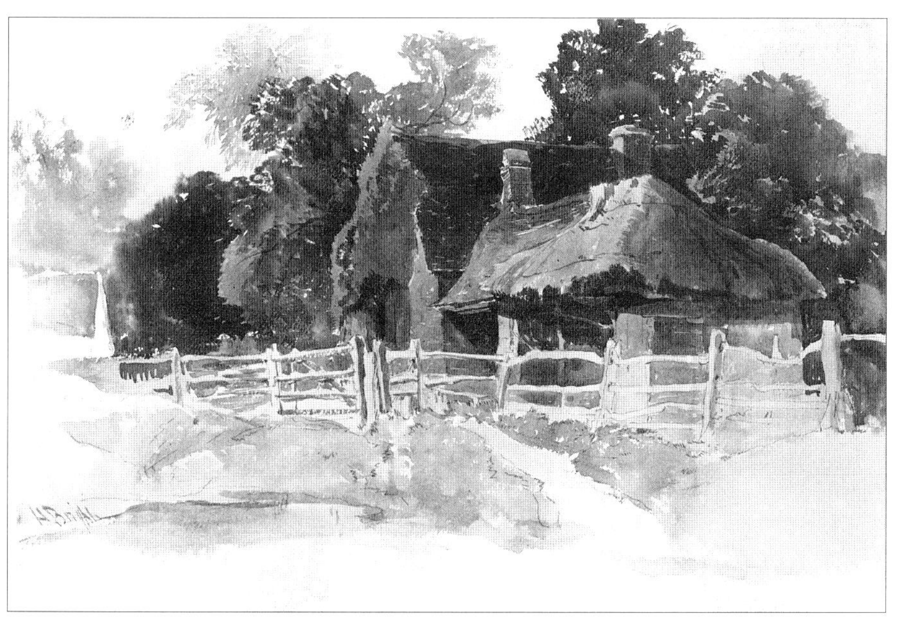

Bonington, but a single work must surely spell coincidence. The writer goes on: '. . . but many of his works have an unpleasantly theatrical quality which is alien to the modern taste. A comparison with treatments of the theme by earlier artists show how Bright was moving from the Romantic naturalism of the early Norwich School towards the sentimental mood and superficial mannerisms of so much Victorian Landscape painting.' At the same time, he concedes that Bright enjoyed an extremely successful career.

Henry Bright,
Old Sheds, Thorpe Road, Norwich, watercolour,
11¾ in x 18 in

Personally I find it hard to think of Bright as a sentimentalist but, as I have said, this diversity of opinion is both interesting and edifying.

One expects and invariably receives a balanced view from Derek Clifford: 'At this time [1830s] another star of more than average brilliance appeared in the person of Henry Bright.' The same age as Miles Edmund Cotman and four years older than John Joseph, he is, writes Clifford:

> . . . more definitely of the new age than either of them. Bright was an original artist. He was a draughtsman of superlative competence and a technical innovator without equal. Although a prolific worker, his pure watercolours are comparatively rare and not always easy to recognise as they usually predate his distinctive, later manners. Bright developed his typical style from the basis

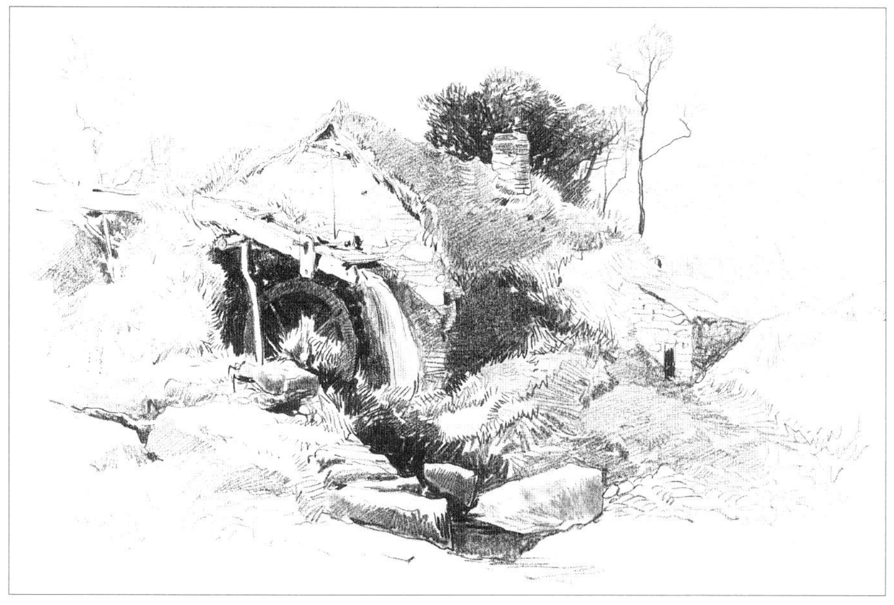

Henry Bright,
Watermill,
pencil and stump on grey paper,
10½ in x 14½ in

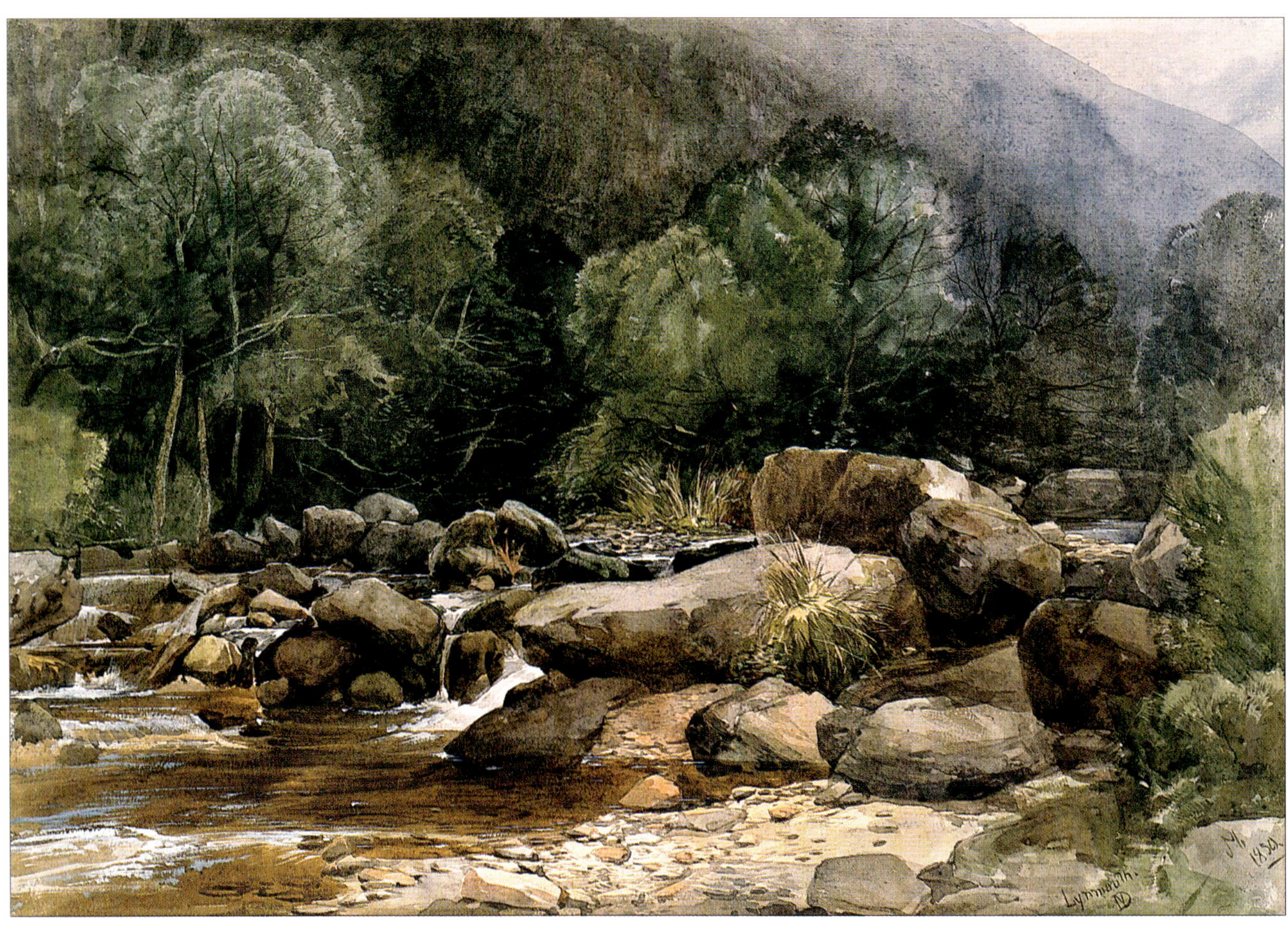

John Middleton, Lynmouth, North Devon, watercolour, signed with monogram, inscribed and dated 1850, 13 in x 19 in

of the reinforced black chalk and the brilliant dark toned paste drawings which John Sell Cotman was doing in the mid thirties, and came so to mix his media that one regards a Bright drawing as a unique hybrid in which watercolour, body colour, gummed shadows, charcoal and pastel are indiscriminately used. The result of this *mélange* is almost invariably brilliant, almost dazzling, but at his worst his pictures are over glossed, overcoloured, Victorian photographic postcards.

To the modern eye Bright's work done before manipulative effeciency over-whelmed his taste is the more attractive, but his fully developed personal style has admirers; and although admiration is not often extended to his large exhibition pieces, the same could be said of almost any mid-19th century watercolourist.

Writing in 1966 in the journal of the Old Watercolour Society, Clifford brings forward some later thoughts:

> One of the best known, most prolific and most successful of the Norwich men was Henry Bright. Bright was technically of a superlative level of competence . . . which was a pity because we would sometimes welcome more feeling and less exuberant skill. Much of his slickest and most regrettable work was done in pastel though even these are fine things. His watercolours are a good deal more rare. They vary a lot in style and, were it not that they are often signed, we should be hard put to it to associate his various manners. At his best, and in watercolour he was usually at his best, there is a directness of vision and a freshness of hand which is uncommonly pleasing. Sometimes, indeed, he reaches even greater heights as in the 'Tonbridge Barns' picture of 1847 where the fine drawing and the flashing, clear, clean washes combine to make drawings that are marvellously brilliant.
>
> Although rightly he has many admirers, I think that the impact of his work lessens on familiarity; it lacks a quality which I am inclined to call innocence, but which may really be sincerity.

It is an acknowledged fact that contemporaries are one's sternest critics. Writing in 1844, Thackeray stated: 'Mr Bright's landscape drawings are exceedingly clever but there is too much of the drawing master in the handling, too much dash, skurry, sharp cleverness of execution.' If

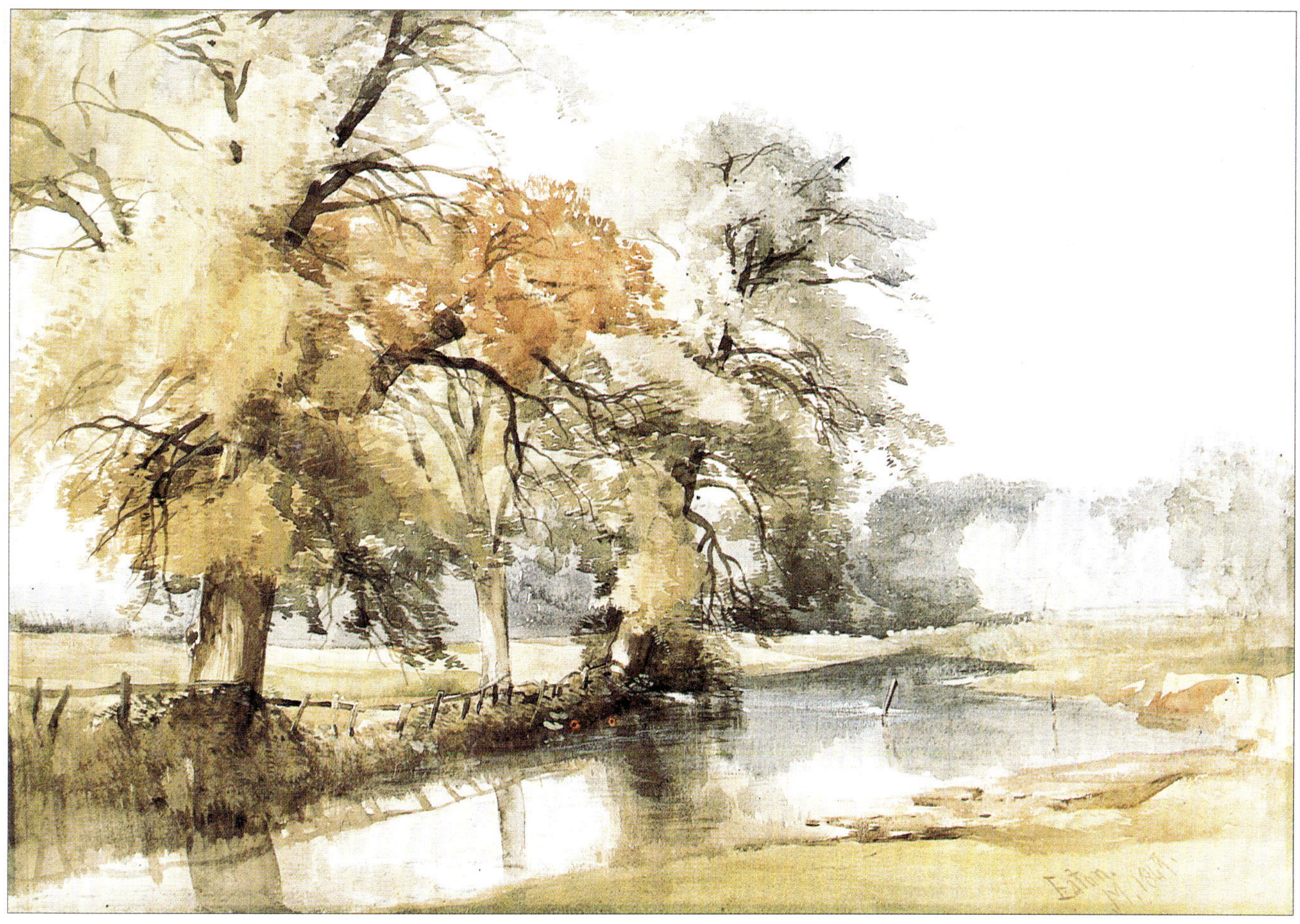

John Middleton,
The Tree-lined River at Eaton, Norwich, watercolour, 1847
12½ in x 18½ in

It is hard to believe that this superb watercolour is a product of the mid-19th century, and not a contemporary piece

financial success is any criterion, however, Bright undoubtedly had the last laugh. It is significant, too, that as well as admiring pupils and many others becoming patrons, his work was purchased by such artistic and knowledgeable luminaries as Clarkson Stanfield and J.M.W. Turner. His own friends were undoubtedly supportive; Thomas Lound added a number of Brights to his extensive collection, and the quantity catalogued in Mrs Middleton's sale suggests that she and her talented son took pleasure in his work.

One other interesting characteristic of Bright was his willingness to collaborate with other artists, a practice many lesser painters have considered *infra dig.* The earliest known example was his collaboration with Sir Francis Grant on 'The Melton Hunt', purchased from the Royal Academy by the Duke of Wellington. He is also known to have painted a castle wall as a background to one of Sir Edward Landseer's dogs and to have collaborated with Herring, Baxter, Earl, Frith, Creswick and other less familiar names. Particularly appealing is 'Dog and Rabbit' in Sheffield Art Gallery, shared with Thomas Earl.

Although even the most eminent historians appear to have little information about the man himself or his life outside the world of art, his fellow artists, pupils and patrons appear to have found him a congenial friend and colleague. Maybe he had little or no life outside this magic world, maybe he lived, especially after the death of his young wife, to paint, teach and enjoy the company of like-minded friends.

As far as I am concerned, the supreme tragedy for the Norwich School was the death of **John Middleton** (1827-1856) at the age of only 29. Without a shadow of doubt, he was the most naturally gifted of the watercolourists, a brilliant exponent of that most elusive medium. Some authorities claim that he peaked so early that, even a few years before his death, his work was losing its fire and life; rather I think any failure totally to live up to early promise was the effect of the consumption taking toll of his energy and ageing him before his time.

Although Middleton continued to work while he could, even to work well by most standards and to draw as long as he could hold a pencil, he must have been indescribably frustrated at the physical limitations that were overtaking him. Also, like John Thirtle, he produced his best work *in situ,* a luxury denied him as illness advanced.

Middleton was born into a reasonably well-to-do family, educated at Norwich Grammar School and studied art under John Berney Crome. His father, who also died at an early age leaving the young John with business responsibilities from 1848, was a business successor of Daniel Coppin, father of Emily (Mrs Joseph) Stannard. He was also interested in the natural world and in particular made a study and collection of ferns. John's mother was a competent botanical painter who exhibited with the Norwich Society in the late 1820s. Undoubtedly these parental interests influenced those of the son and further encouraged John Middleton's love for and appreciation of the natural scene.

As a painter he blossomed early and before he was even 20 was receiving laudatory notices in the local press. Even after his father's death, he was able to spend reasonable time drawing and painting so that, thankfully considering his short life, there is a significant legacy. He exhibited regularly in Norwich and London where his work was consistently well received; in spite of his short career, 14 paintings were shown in the Royal Academy and 15 in the British Institute.

As well as the teaching received from John Berney Crome, Middleton was for a time a pupil of Henry Bright although it could truthfully be said that Bright himself was, to a degree, influenced by the younger man. In spite of the difference in their ages, the two became good friends and the fruits of a painting holiday spent together in Tonbridge, Kent, show some remarkable similarities. Although with watercolour Bright was at his best, as a purist there is no doubt which of two talented exponents had the edge.

Middleton painted in oils as well as in watercolour and also produced some 50 to 60 very competent etchings; any minor influence from John Berney Crome is only apparent in his oils. The etchings were, in the main, issued in small sets such as that published under the title 'Nine Etchings by John Middleton', *c.*1852. He experimented with both soft ground and copperplate, using his own subjects but carefully and skilfully adapting them to the more unrelenting

John Middleton, A Stream in June, oil on canvas, 22¾ in x 17¾ in

John Middleton, Alby, Norfolk, watercolour, 1847

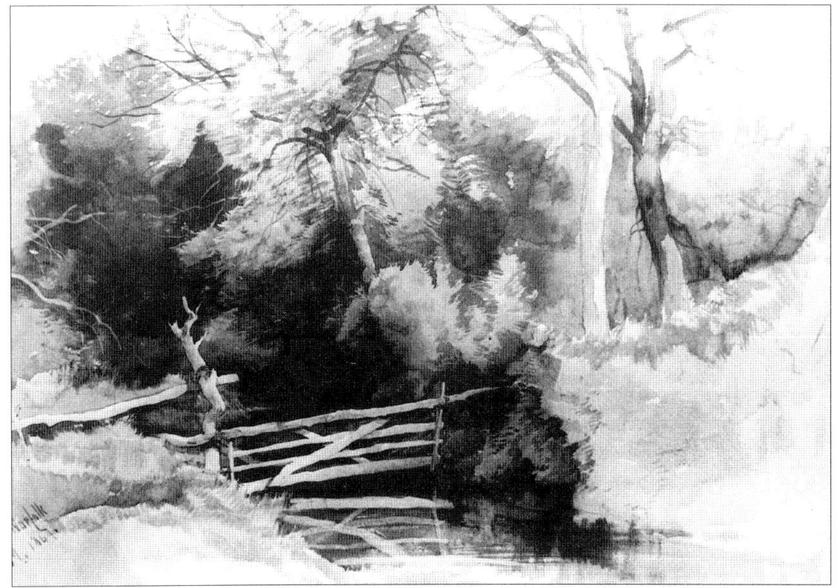

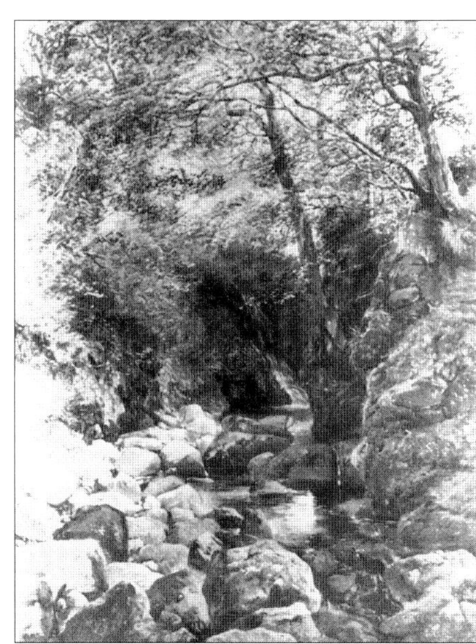

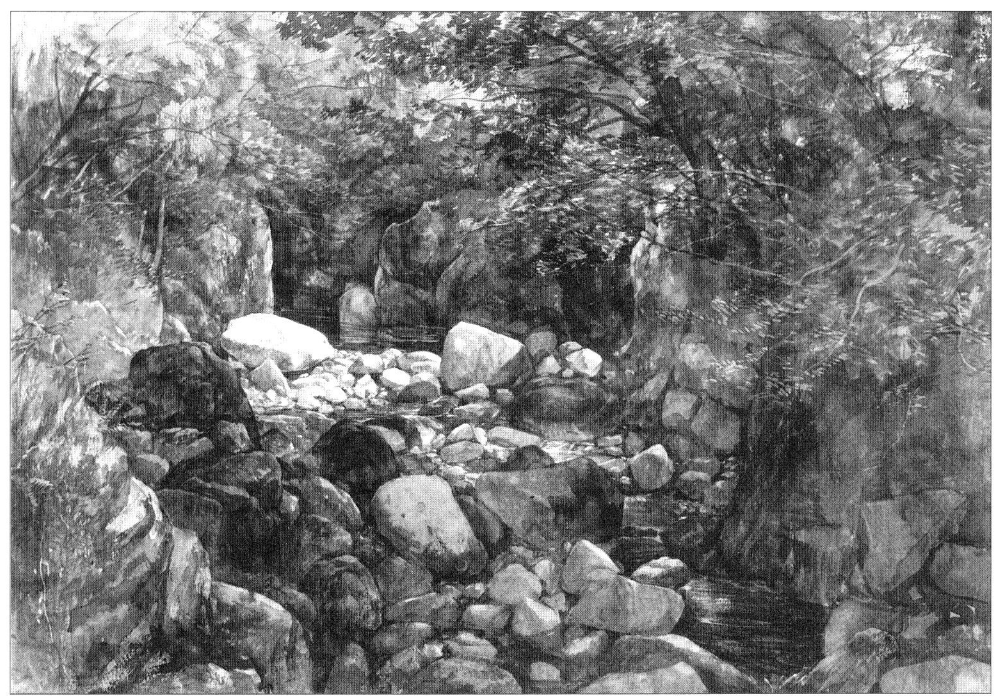

John Middleton,
Sunshine and Shade, Ivy Bridge,
watercolour,
12¾ in x 19 in

medium. Because little is written of his oils, these are not to be disparaged; were it not for the outstanding quality of his watercolours they might have been quite highly acclaimed. Often his choice of subject was similar to those of his watercolours; his palette included his favourite greens as well as some rich, warm tones, and the same immediacy of execution gave them more than a hint of the spontaneous vitality so characteristic of his work in the more fluid medium. It is in some of his later oils that decline begins to show and an uncharacteristic darkness creeps in. There is in Norwich Castle Museum a very large oil of Gunton Park which, although dated 1849, has a haunting, almost disturbing, element. Much more research needs to be done on John Middleton's life and work.

In 1847/8 Middleton lived for a while in Kensington, London, this being the period during which he spent most time with Henry Bright as a pupil and on the trip to Kent. It was a time when he was maturing very quickly, more than holding his own with professional co-exhibitors in the Royal Academy and the British Institute. Not only did he uphold the great Norwich tradition but enhanced it. Given, at the most, ten productive years, it seems, as I suggested in the case of Joseph Stannard, that he was inspired and stimulated by a sense of urgency that heightened his powers of observation and perception. In turn this added to his skill in the handling of his medium and the understanding of its potentialities. One is reminded of the war poets, those young soldiers who, in the face of death, gave us some of the most unforgettable poetry – Rupert Brooke, Julian Grenfell and Wilfred Owen all died in battle. Middleton's watercolours have a self-expression readily allied to that of, say, Rupert Brooke and Siegfried Sassoon; Sassoon survived the war, of course, but his war poems have the emotive intensity of one who has diced with death.

Comparatively little has been documented of Middleton's life but, in such a short life occupied with business commitments and a painting passion, perhaps there can be little else to say. Apart from the Tonbridge trips with Henry Bright during his time in London and a later visit to Scotland, Middleton rarely left the Norwich area. No doubt his poor health discouraged travel, while Norfolk abounded with his favourite subjects.

John Middleton had inherited and added to his parents' involvement with growing things and he was devoted to the natural landscape. Many of his subjects are studies of leafy lanes and glades, even of little clearings with massed trees and foliage, enchanting corners enclosed with the warm intimacy of lush summer greenery. His handling of every conceivable tone of green and gold and their seasonal variations is phenomenal and his exquisite use of light and shade enhances this mastery of tonal values. Sunlight plays an important part in these leafy compositions, peeping

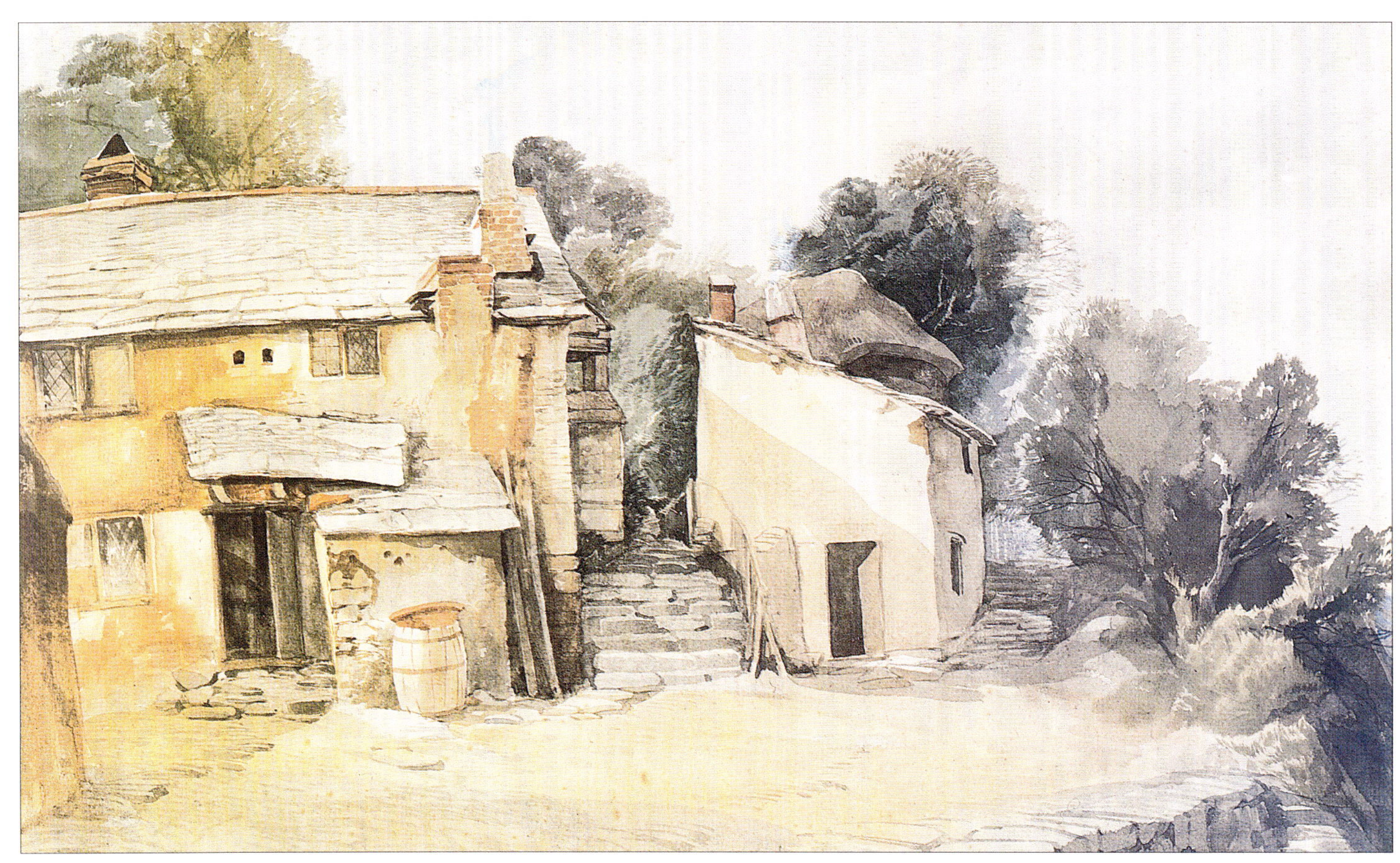

John Middleton, Clovelley, watercolour, approx. 12 in x 20 in

through the trees, exploding in brilliant shafts or just enveloping the scene in a warm haze. John Middleton had, it seems, a passion for summer's warmth and sensual abundance, and his love of the sun may well have been intensified by contrast with the consumptive chills. Rarely, does one see a watercolourist of such purity, an attribute enhanced by his skill in making the white of his paper work for him to give transparency and sparkle.

Perhaps the most striking thing about Middleton's watercolour work is its modernity. It is hard to believe that he was working in the mid-19th century when one looks at the broad, clean washes, the bold, distinguished brushwork, the confidence, the assurance and, above all, the wonderful freedom. The only comparisons within the Norwich School are Cotman's Greta paintings, evincing the same tonal purity and broad, controlled washes, and perhaps the best of Leman. In no other facet of Cotman's work does his feeling for natural colour and tone, light and shade, come through as convincingly yet, 40 years earlier they were just not understood.

However hard one tries to describe Middleton's work, words seem to fail and, sadly, outside the Norwich area there are all too few on public display for people to experience the emotions they engender. The inherent serenity, the intensity, the sensitivity, the feeling embodied, arouses empathetic emotions that very few artists' work is empowered to do. In spite of his formidable talent there is no shred of slickness in Middleton's work, the sincerity is unmistakable. Maybe herein lies the distinction between Middleton and Bright, an elusive quality but all important.

'Alby, Norfolk', in Norwich Castle is a watercolour embodying all I have said about John Middleton's work and talent. I cannot resist quoting Derek Clifford on the same painting:

> In Middleton's picture we are more directly involved with the emotion of the scene, the receding backwater, the sunlight and the shadow, the reflections on the still surface; we can hear the water voles moving under the bank, and the insects humming about the hot foliage, and somewhere behind us in the meadow cattle are pulling noisily at lush grass. It is easy to forget that we are looking at a picture, because it has caught us up so completely in its world of summer sunshine.

A little later Clifford adds: 'The directness with which Middleton captured these arcadian days

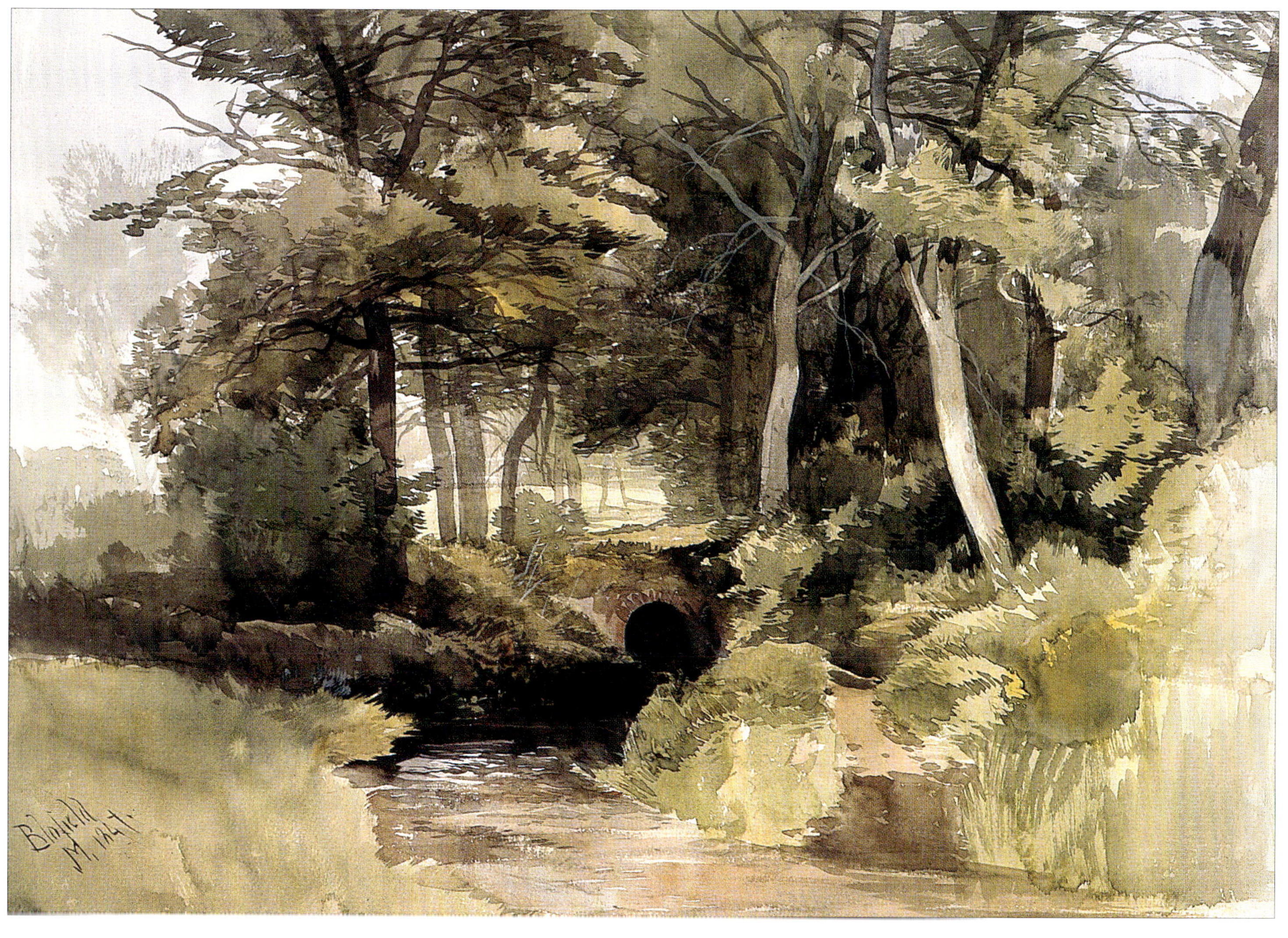

John Middleton,
Blofield 1847, watercolour, inscribed with title, monogram and date 1847,
13 in x 19 in

gives to these pictures something of the lyrical quality of Cotman's "Greta Worlds" drawings.' I make my point with the assurance to readers that only *after* writing the preceding paragraphs did I refresh my memory of Clifford on Middleton. The effect of the latter's genius is strangely emotive even on those whose critical faculties are sharpened by years of looking at pictures.

As always, writers and critics have sought for influences but often, I feel, this business of influence is somewhat overdone. Bright, Leman, Lound and Middleton were all close friends and it would be hard to say who actually influenced any or all of the others. Leman and Lound were both more visionary painters than most of their predecessors but Middleton had a much more advanced approach than either. He undoubtedly learnt from Bright in the sphere of technique but Bright also took something from him, as two painters working together in the same environment with the same subjects can hardly fail to do. It seems natural that any group of artists of similar outlook, working in the same medium, should gain something from each other – it was ever thus and rightly so, but direct influence is something else. Middleton may have been influenced by the Greta watercolours or have been inspired by the innovative technique but, in the main, I feel he was very much his own man blessed with an intuition that was all his own, possibly an intuition that made him, like W.H. Davies, '. . . look thy last on all things lovely . . .' In terms of influence, rightly or wrongly, I would say the responsibility rests with his mother.

In November 1856 the *Norwich Mercury*'s obituarist, more sensitive than his paper's critics of Cotman's day, wrote that Middleton rendered '. . . quiet corners of the countryside with an intensity of vision and intuition and sensitivity of line, wash or brush stroke charged with a freshness of vision now probably to be the more closely studied and the more valued.'

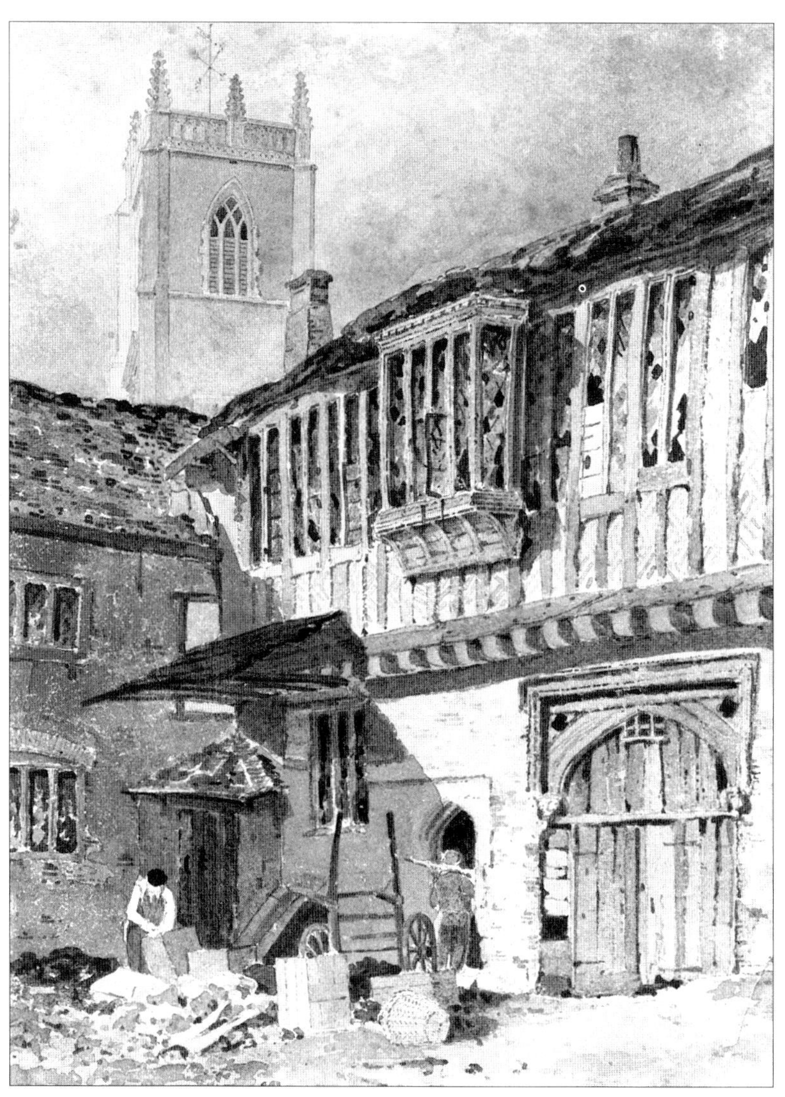

Henry Ninham, St. Andrew's, Norwich, watercolour, 7 in x 5¼ in

Chapter 10

MORE FAMILY AFFAIRS

Reputed to be of Huguenot descent, **John Ninham** (1754-1817), was by trade a Heraldic Painter and Engraver running his business from Chapel Field, Norwich. He specialised particularly in painting panels for the coaches of nobility and aristocracy sent to him by various coach builders. He was also a professional copperplate engraver and printer, his subjects including some of his own drawings and etchings; the best known were his 'Views of the Gates of Norwich' published in 1861 from the original ink and wash drawings of 1792/3, now in the Fitch collection.

John Ninham was one of the original members of the Norwich Society having an interest in and an appetite for a more academic type of painting than coachwork. Although mainly known for his drawing and engraving, he did some oil painting of no particular merit; Norwich Castle Museum has a beach scene which has a certain charm but lacks real technical quality. Little is known of his personal life. He is said to have had minimal formal education but a great thirst for knowledge which he shared with his son, Henry.

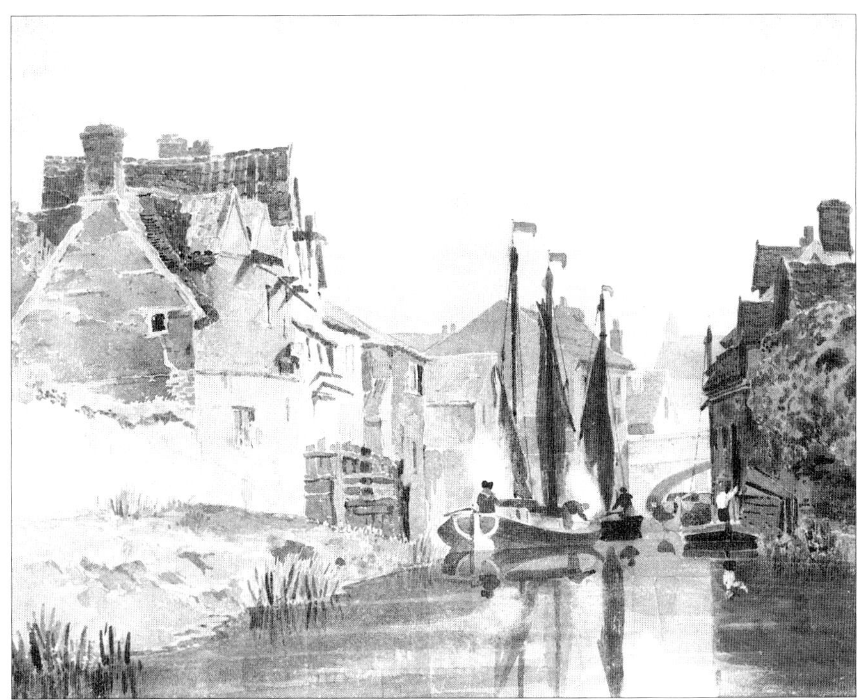

Henry Ninham,
St. James Fyebridge and Whitefriars, Norwich,
watercolour, c.1830s,
9½ in x 11¼ in

Henry Ninham (1793-1874), one of the eight children left when his mother died in 1817, inherited his father's aptitude for drawing but displayed a greater natural talent. He took over the family business of heraldic painting and engraving on his father's death and, no doubt through the Norwich Society, with whom he started exhibiting in 1816, was in great demand with the etchers in their midst. He printed, among others, the plates of the Rev. E.T. Daniell, possibly the only one of the Norwich artists whose reputation rests almost solely on his etchings.

Henry Ninham was an enterprising individual; he extended copperplate engraving to a teaching practice where he taught etching and perspective drawing for which he was eminently qualified. He liked to experiment with techniques of etching, varying drypoint with softground for some unusual effects; Alfred Priest was one of his more noteworthy pupils. One unfortunate occurrence arose out of a commission from Dawson Turner to print plates of some of Crome's etchings to be published posthumously. Certain of these plates had been altered at some time and the shadow of suspicion fell on Ninham who spent 20 years, with ultimate success, trying to clear his name. The whole affair must have been a great trial to one who was patently an honest man.

Although Ninham is not well known outside Norfolk and Norwich, he has left the city a valuable legacy by his faithful topographical renderings of its ancient buildings, many of which no longer exist. His printed works include eight original etchings of 'Picturesque Antiquities of Norwich', 1842, a number of views of the ancient city gates, 'Remnants of Antiquity in Norwich', and 15 miscellaneous views of Norwich and Norfolk. He was a fine architectural and topographical draughtsman with a good grasp of perspective and feeling for accuracy; this he extended into watercolour, concentrating largely on the same type of subject. As his own experience grew, he broadened the teaching practice to include 'every Department of Drawing and Painting'. Although he did produce a few oils, his work in watercolour was eminently superior and much more suited to his chosen subjects. John Sell Cotman himself referred to Ninham as 'a very clever painter' and the topographical studies, which included some interesting, lesser known buildings and also some unusual river scenes bordered by fascinating old houses and decrepit buildings, certainly explain why they found a ready market. His colour work I find pleasing; his delicate tones, beautiful soft and gentle greens, greys and browns, are carefully chosen and blended to enhance, rather than distract by over colouring, the quality of his draughtsmanship. His drawing of Sir Benjamin Wrench's Court in Norwich Castle Museum is obviously of great importance as a Norwich Society

David Hodgson,
St. Peter's, Norwich,
oil on panel,
19½ in x 18¼ in

archive. According to Derek Clifford his 'most notable achievement' was a full faced peacock 'the size of a shilling'. Was this some sort of a challenge – the subject, whatever its size, seems singularly uncharacteristic of Ninham?

Ninham deserves to be more widely known but his subject matter and his lifelong ties with Norwich have naturally limited his reputation. He is said to have been a genial little man, kind and friendly to everyone, who died at 81 years of age in Chapel Field Road where he was born, a Norwich man and a man of Norwich through and through.

Charles Hodgson (*c.*1770-1856), was a schoolmaster who turned to drawing and painting making it something of a subsidiary career. Initially he taught as English Assistant at North Walsham Grammar School and married a North Walsham girl, Nancy Chiswell. Later, c.1798, he moved to Norwich becoming Mathematics Master at Norwich Grammar School in addition to opening his own boarding Academy in St. Andrews 'for the admission of young Ladies and young Gentlemen'. The course of the young peoples' studies was advertised as 'an enquiry into the constitution of the English Language, Writing and Arithmetic.' Charles' father had died when he was only 14 years old and he was put in the care of a Mr Simon Browne, also a schoolmaster, who obviously gave his foster son a good education.

In Norwich he made friends with both Crome and Ladbroke who would undoubtedly have encouraged him in what was perhaps initially a hobby, drawing and painting. He joined them in the formation of the Norwich Society with whom he exhibited as well as occasionally showing in London with the British Institution and the Royal Academy. He had an undoubted talent and had he been able to devote more time and concentration to his art he would certainly have built up a greater reputation. His main interest was plainly in architectural draughtsmanship, usually in pencil, watercolour or both, and although little of his work appears to have survived, a number of watercolours of churches, cathedrals and other buildings are listed in old Norwich Society catalogues.

In 1806 with his young son, David, he took a sketching holiday in Wales which gave him a variation in exhibition subjects. The rocky Welsh scenery would lend itself to his good drawing and feeling for perspective while his low key palette of delicate and cool colouring would suit the natural landscape. Some Swiss scenes are also recorded indicating that at some time he visited Switzerland, and it would have been interesting to see what he made of the stronger colour contrasts and comparative brightness.

Charles Hodgson has the reputation of having been quiet and well liked among his pupils and fellow artists. He became President of the Norwich Society in 1813 and stayed with Crome during the secession, continuing to exhibit until 1825 when he was appointed Architectural Draughtsman to the Duke of Sussex. Although these appointments were often somewhat honorary, obviously they indicate a reasonably high level of ability for the artist to gain such recognition. It is difficult for today's art historians to make any really valid assessment when so few works have survived.

Later in life Hodgson moved to London and from there to Liverpool where he seems to have had relatives; there he died in 1856.

David Hodgson (1798-1864), son of Charles, was actively encouraged by his father to make a career in art, possibly regretting that he had, himself, come to it at a time of life when he was already committed to an alternative career. David inherited some of his father's academic talents all the same and during his life had various literary works published including some poetry. Further evidence of a poetic interest is shown in the catalogue of the Norwich Society's exhibition of 1819 which lists (by David Hodgson)

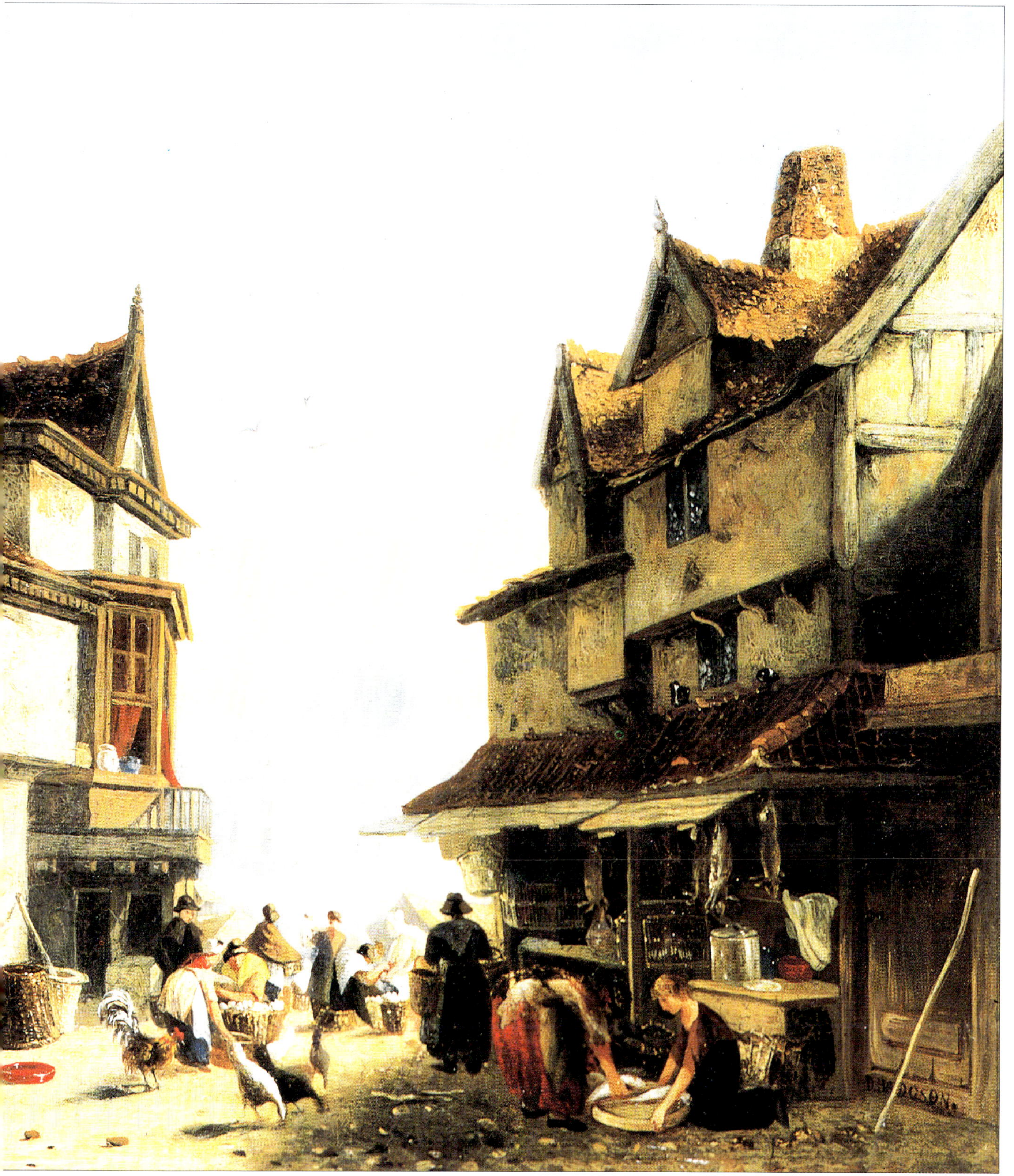

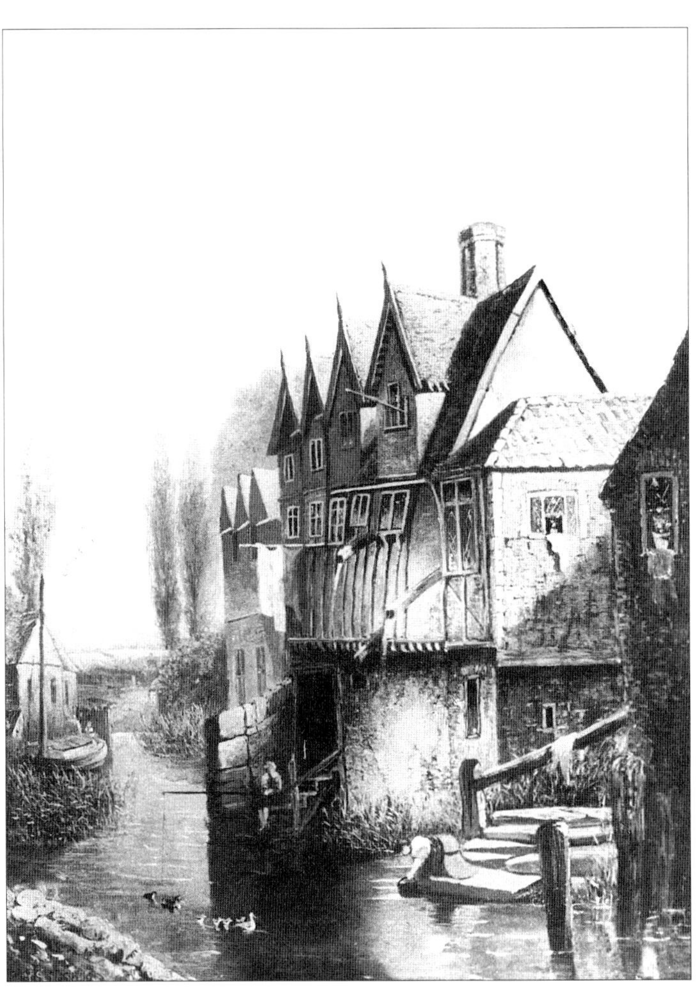

David Hodgson,
Old Houses by the River Wensum, Norwich,
oil on canvas,
23½ in x 17½ in

Design from Scott's The Lay of the Last Minstrel' with the accompanying quotation of Canto 11. Of his very early life, little is known except that he attended Norwich Grammar School where he was taught art by John Crome and mathematics by his father. He first exhibited with the Norwich Society in 1813, the year his father was made President, and became Secretary in 1822. His time in this position covered a very difficult period and, along with John Berney Crome, he made great efforts to introduce new members and patrons, writing many persuasive letters and generally publicising the Society and its contribution to the cultural and artistic life of the city of Norwich.

In 1818 he advertised himself as a drawing master stating that he was offering 'A Course and comprehensive series of Lessons in Perspective'. This was certainly his strong point; his sense of perspective was virtually faultless, a very necessary adjunct to the drawing and painting of architectural subjects. He was clever, too, with interiors where correct perspectives are, if anything, more important and certainly more difficult to achieve. He was consistently praised in the 1820s by the local press which ever was and still is enthusiastic about faithful renderings of its city.

David Hodgson worked in oil as well as in watercolour, pencil and etching. His etching was undoubtedly influenced by John Sell Cotman with its slightly classical flavour and his printed work included a series published in 1843 known as 'Antiquarian Remains principally confined to Norwich and Norfolk', 20 etchings based on earlier sketches. In Norwich Castle Museum there are two albums of sketches and watercolours, possibly intended for later working into oils but of a quality superior to most of the oil paintings he produced. These comprise, as well as the buildings, interiors and townscapes for which he displayed his most individual talent, landscapes and tree studies, the landscapes, one feels, having taken a certain influence from James Stark. These latter are, however, in the minority and within his own sphere he remained faithful to his personal style which changed little over the years.

Although more oils than watercolours have survived, some of these are unfortunate. Basically

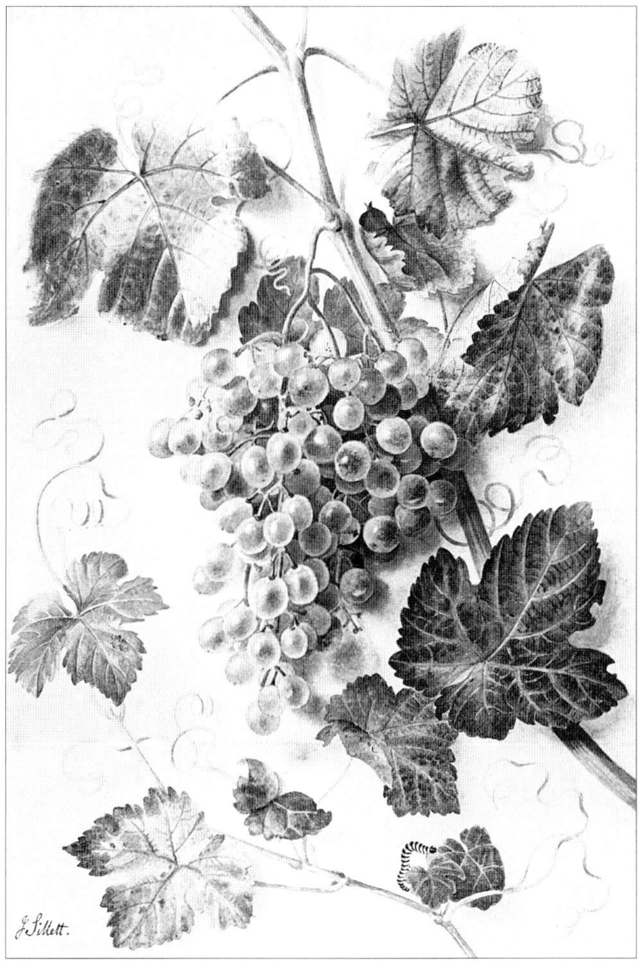

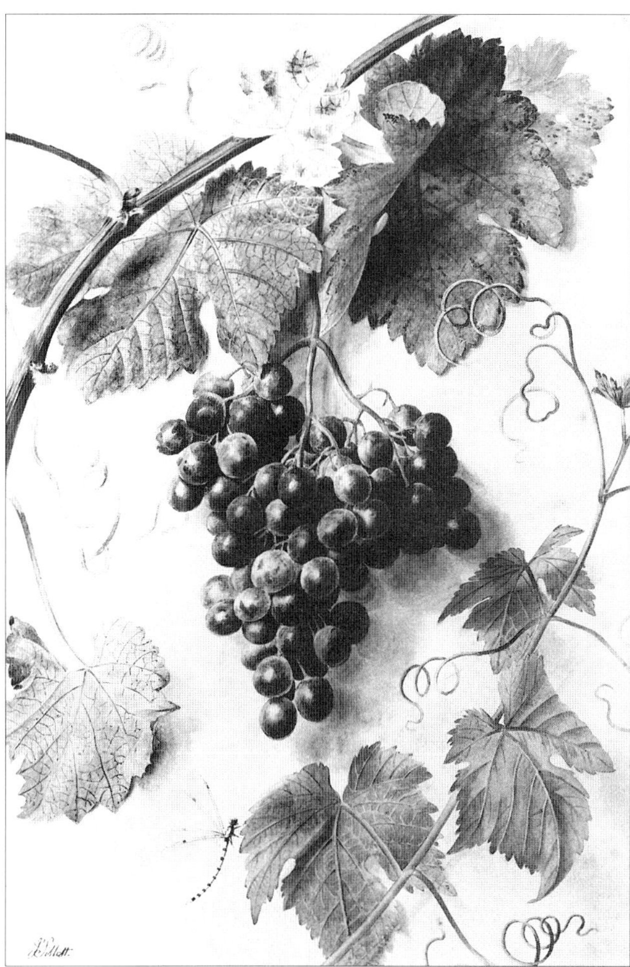

James Sillett, White Grapes, watercolour, 19½ in x 13¼ in

James Sillett, Black Grapes, watercolour, 19½ in x 13¼ in

Hodgson's exemplary draughtsmanship is there; in fact, considering the heavier medium, his detail and accuracy are quite extraordinary. He was, however, heavy on the paint, in some cases to excess, and his feeling for colour in oil is much less sensitive than in his more delicate watercolours. Having said that, a few works stand out as being quite remarkable. Time spent in Ely in 1858 resulted in several drawings and paintings of the cathedral and his large rendering of the Octagon Chapel is an almost incredible achievement. By this time his colour had mellowed somewhat and improved and here in the drawing, despite the heavy medium, he has excelled himself. The symmetry of the arches, the overall perspective and balance, and the wealth of intricate detail add up to little less than a masterpiece.

Until 1856, when he moved to Greyfriars, David Hodgson lived and worked in his studio in Tombland making, it must be said, an excellent living. He was an extremely diligent worker and dedicated teacher. After the death of his father, in whose work he had also assisted, he was appointed Art Master at Norwich Grammar School. He exhibited regularly in Norwich both with the Norwich Society and other venues including the newly formed East of England Art Union and, not surprisingly, his work sold extremely well locally and even further afield. Outside Norwich he exhibited at the Royal Academy, the British Institution and the Suffolk Street Galleries in London, as well as in Manchester, Liverpool, Newcastle and Birmingham. He was patronised by some important collectors, particularly at the British Institution where he showed regularly from 1822 to 1864, the year of his death.

In 1825, the same year as his father's allied appointment, he was made Painter of Domestic Architecture to the Duke of Sussex. In 1823 he had married Frances Stone; they had a son and a daughter but there appears to be no record of artistic succession, although the daughter married Alfred George Stannard. Outside the family, however, he remained friend and mentor to many grateful and affectionate pupils.

It would be fair to say that **James Sillett** (1764-1840), was one of the most versatile of the Norwich painters. He was one of that select band of artists who seem able to turn a hand to any subject in any medium with at least a modicum of success. The Silletts were originally a Suffolk family although James was born in Norwich. After leaving school, like Ninham he was apprenticed to a heraldic painter; feeling the need for something more creative, he joined the Royal Academy Schools where he studied from 1781 to 1790. While in London he supported himself by fitting in some scene painting with William Capon, another Norwich man, at Covent Garden and Drury Lane, and doing some copy work for the Polygraphic Society. He first exhibited with the Royal Academy in 1796 and thereafter for 41 years, usually his meticulously painted flower and fruit studies along with the occasional miniature landscape.

In 1801 he married Ann Banyard from East Dereham, Norfolk. They lived for a short while in Norwich where Sillett set up as a drawing master and miniaturist, but moved to King's Lynn in 1804 to be nearer Mrs Sillett's relatives. Again James Sillett set up a teaching practice and also produced some topographical views of the town which were later published in Richard's *History of Lynn*. He obviously maintained his links with Norwich, for in 1806 he joined the Norwich Society as an Honorary Member and exhibited regularly with evident success. He moved back to the city in 1811 and became much more involved with the Society, becoming Vice-President in 1814 and President a year later.

Sillett had made friends with Robert Ladbroke and joined him in the 1816 secession; some said the break with Crome was as much the responsibility of Sillett as Ladbroke but, in view of the various differences between some of the artists at that time, it would be difficult to apportion blame. Suffice to say it all blew over in a few years and Sillett was the first to return to the main Society – not before he had exhibited 90 works with the seceding group.

It can be deduced that Sillett was a prolific artist as well as a versatile one which, considering the

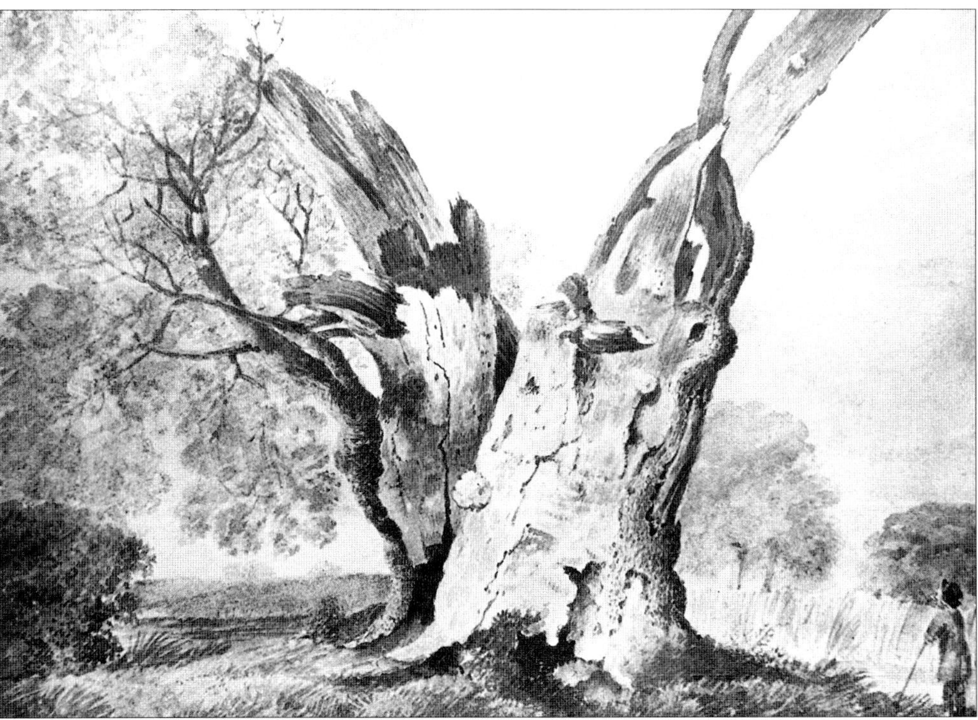

James Sillett,
The Old Oak, Winfarthing,
oil on panel, 1817,
19½ in x 18¾ in

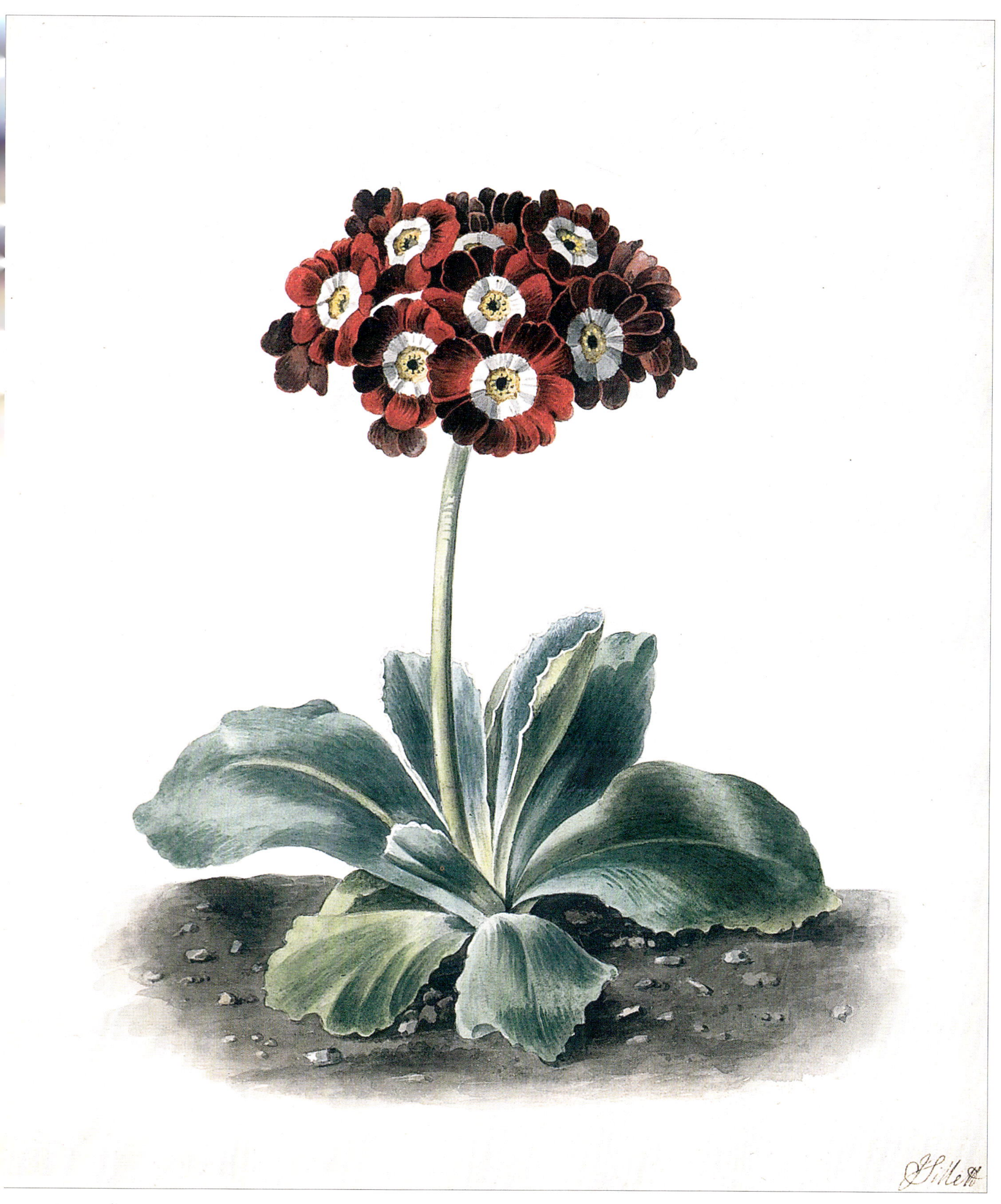

James Sillett, Merry's Pompadour Auricula, watercolour, signed, 11 in x 9 in

detailed nature of most of his work, is in itself remarkable. He was once quoted in the local press as having said: 'There is more beauty in the delineation of flowers from the garden and the human figure than in pig sties and cart sheds'; he seems to have painted everything *but* pig sties and cart sheds so this may have been deliberately directed at what he felt to be the preponderance of earthy rural subject matter chosen by some of the Norwich painters. His own landscapes, sometimes on copper, sometimes on panel, were usually small even when not strictly miniatures. They had an old-fashioned (even for the time), rather classical feel with highly detailed trees and foreground landscape looking into a hazy distance, thinly painted. Even some moonlight scenes and seascapes are recorded, again in a rather Italianate style, and the occasional architectural subject. Additionally, in the latter vein, in 1828 he published 'Views of the Churches, Chapels, and other Public Edifices in the City of Norwich' (59 subjects), possibly intended as a companion to Ladbroke's studies of the Norwich churches. There are also several monochrome topographical studies in Norwich Castle which, although not his best work, are interesting in their own way. More appealing as far as I am concerned are his more detailed little watercolour drawings of such elegant subjects as the Monument in the Church of St. John Maddermarket to Christopher Layer, d.1600, with his wife and six children, Mayor of Norwich and Member of Parliament, and the beautiful Font in the Church of St. Peter Mancroft.*

The cream of Sillett's work lies in his still-life and flower painting although he expressed resentment when classified simply as a still-life painter. Fruit, game birds, decorative birds and flowers were executed in both oil and watercolour. The oils certainly owe something to the early Dutch influence (he visited Holland in 1828), being highly finished, detailed, and combining realism with a certain stylism. Often his flowers in oil have the heavy heads in small containers one associates with the early Bosschaerts and sometimes van der Ast; others have rather more freedom but always they are painted with care for the flowers themselves.

Of all Sillett's wide repertoire, though, his really beautiful botanical work stands highest (see p.141). He has, by some experts, been ranked with the great William Jackson Hooker. His watercolour studies of fruit, particularly grapes which seem to have had a special appeal, come into the same category having the true botanical quality that combines strict accuracy with delicacy and charm (see p.139). There is a Study of Mallow (1802) in the British Museum in which this delicacy is more than usually emphasised. The petals of mallow, in spite of their strong colour, are virtually transparent like those of certain old roses, but to reproduce this semi-transparency in natural colour on white paper is one of the greatest challenges to the skill of the botanical artist. Sillett has admirably achieved the desired result and so enhanced the whole delightful spray. Many botanical works, although accurate and finely painted, can appear slightly hard. Sillett often overcame that by putting the suggestion of a shadow behind his flowers thereby giving them an extra dimension and more decorative effect. Much of his botanical work has been used for book illustration.

'The Old Oak Winfarthing', 1817, is Sillett's most well known work and has become a historical piece. Here again the draughtsmanship is immaculate and the clever shading gives a vivid realism to the great tree. The strange encrustations and indents on the bark and the one-sided foliage are given Sillett's usual closely observed detail and his persistent involvement with the distant landscape is shown by a delicate impression. The figure he has added is typical of those he occasionally introduced, not necessarily to the enhancement of the picture; these people have a primitive quality which seems at odds with the classicism so frequently employed in the same painting.

Sillett lived to draw and paint. Not long before he died he commented that 'existence would no longer be desirable when deprived of the use of my pencil.' He left a daughter, Emma

* The font was restored to its former glory, as Sillett would have known it, in 1926.

(fl.1813-1833), who also painted flowers, birds and other forms of still-life. Little is known of Emma Sillett – maybe a painting daughter was regarded less highly than the sons in that particular era – but one authority describes her as her father's only rival, indicating a painter of some quality. She helped him in his teaching practice, too, which would have entailed a certain level of ability and qualification. She is barely represented in Norwich but, I am told, there is an example of her work in the Fitzwilliam Museum, Cambridge.

Samuel David Colkett (1806-1863) was the son of a Norwich chemist whose shop in St. Stephen's Street was taken over by his wife after his untimely death. Colkett junior seems to have had a somewhat precocious talent having first exhibited with the secession in 1818 at the age of 12 as 'Master S. Colkett'. In 1820 he became a pupil of James Stark and continued to paint in the style of Stark and Crome, in a way bridging the gap between the early Norwich painters and the Victorians. Between 1822 and 1833 he exhibited regularly in Norwich, also at the Royal Academy and the British Institution. Along with several other Norwich artists about the same time, he moved to London in 1828 where he exhibited successfully throughout the period. It seems that it was during this time that he married.

He returned to Norwich in 1836 and set himself up in Prince of Wales Road as a drawing master, also offering a restoration service. He experimented successfully in this field and introduced some new and effective methods of restoration. He also did a certain amount of picture dealing, apparently not being inclined to put all his eggs in one basket. Colkett was one of those people who, even if successful where they are, feel the need for a change every so often. In 1844 he sold up his collection and moved to Great Yarmouth where he again set himself up as teacher, restorer and dealer in old masters advertising his services to 'the nobility and gentry.'

After a while Yarmouth also palled and he moved with his family to Cambridge in 1854 where he was taken seriously ill a few years later. He died in June 1863, a man of many parts and many friends who appears to have successfully overcome any difficulties caused by a congenital deafness.

Colkett painted primarily in oils. Such watercolours as he produced, if they can generally be judged by the few I have seen, were over fussy, busy little pictures, quite unlike one's general conception of watercolours. His oils were a very different story. Although some may seem mediocre most were highly professional and a really good Colkett is on a par with anything Stark produced in similar style. His colour sense was especially satisfactory, particularly the range of greens so prevalent in country landscapes, and lovely mellow earthy tones. At one stage he was using rather an excess of paint, almost moulding it into shape and perhaps making things unnecessarily hard for himself. His best work was accomplished during the second Norwich period in the late 1830s and certainly most of his rare larger works were painted at this time. Rural Norfolk was obviously his first love and although some critics have accused him of 'prettifying' his pictures, those of us who know Norfolk well can accept that he was painting the natural scene as he saw it.

Colkett had an interesting way of appearing to build up his paintings with the aid of some impasto and an observant eye for nuances of light and shade. Grassy banks in the foregrounds were there to be clambered over into the rest of the picture and the apparently three-dimensional leafy trees could almost be heard rustling as only Norfolk trees seem permanently to do (see p.144). He plainly took to heart Crome's insistence on breadth, handed down via Stark, and his skies in particular give that feeling of space even in a fairly overgrown scene. In spite of a few lesser lights, a good Colkett is very, very good. Perhaps the least significant were

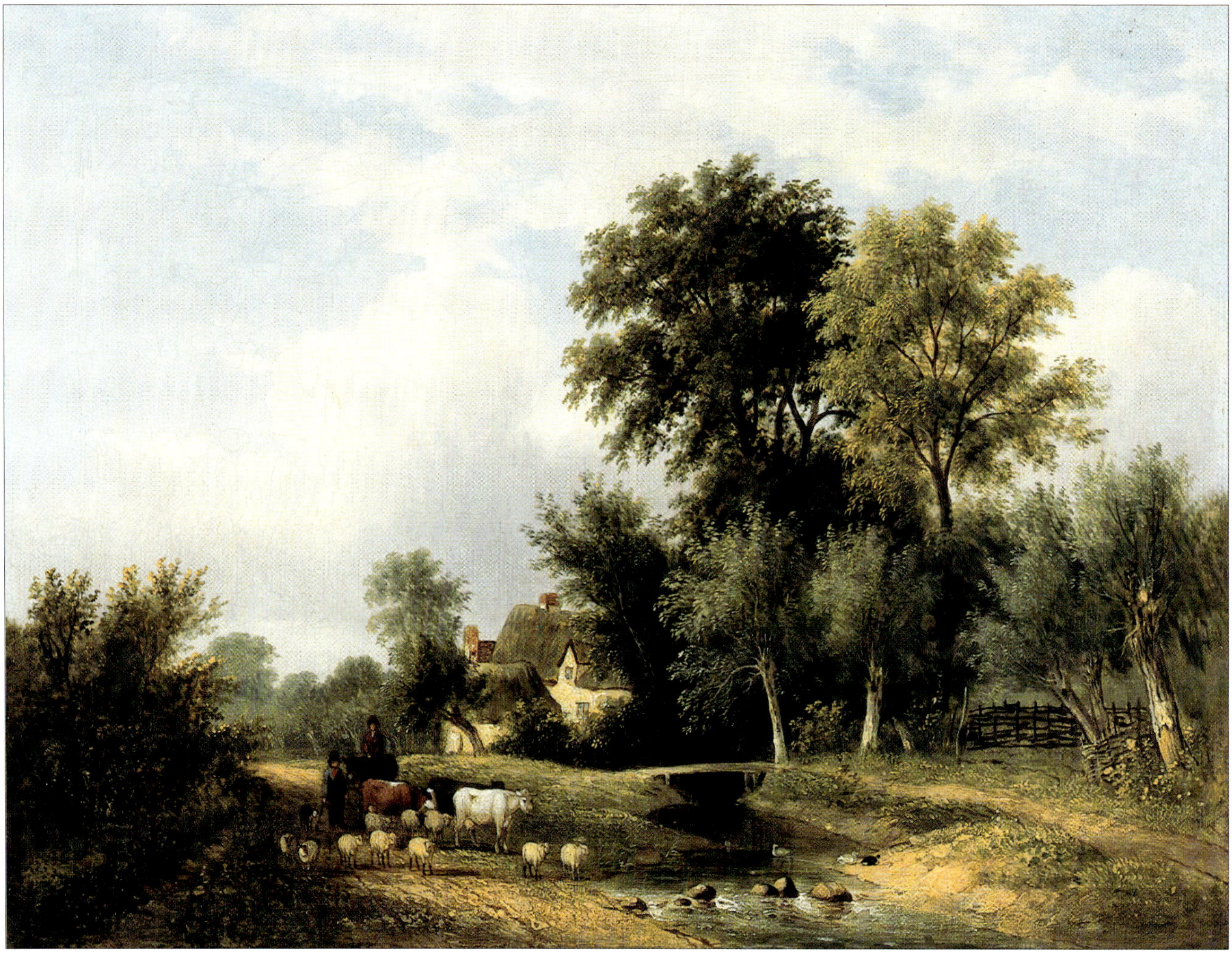

Samuel David Colkett,
By the River Tudd, A Norfolk Wooded Landscape,
oil on panel, 14 in x 18 in

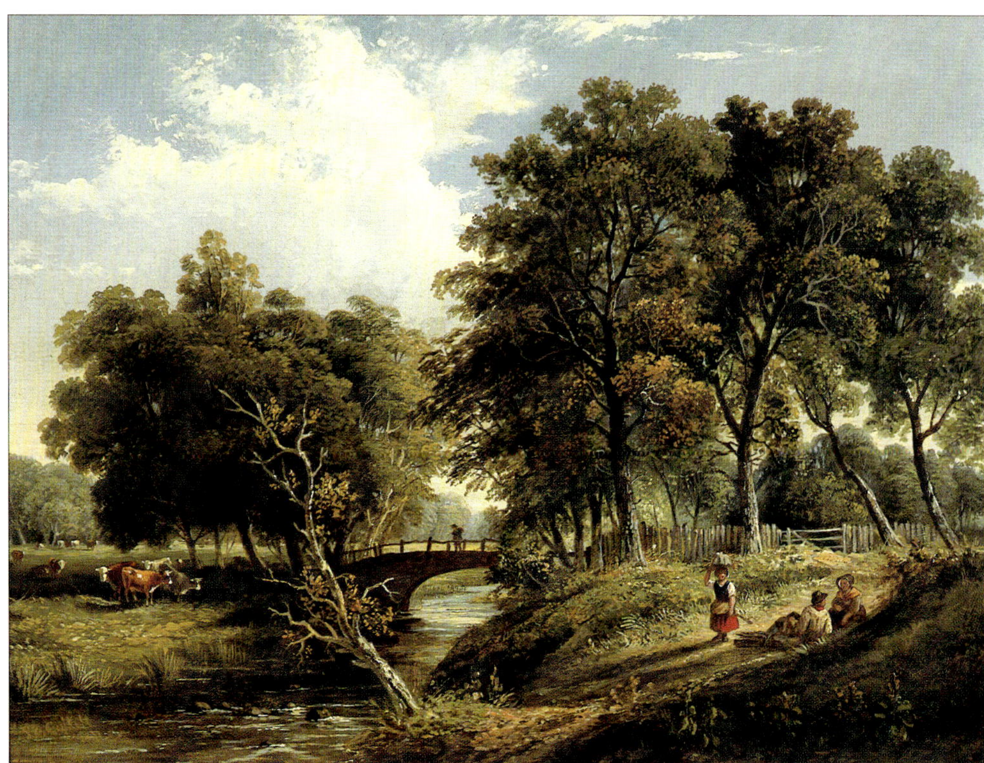

Samuel David Colkett,
Norfolk Pastoral Scene,
oil on canvas, 14 in x 18 in

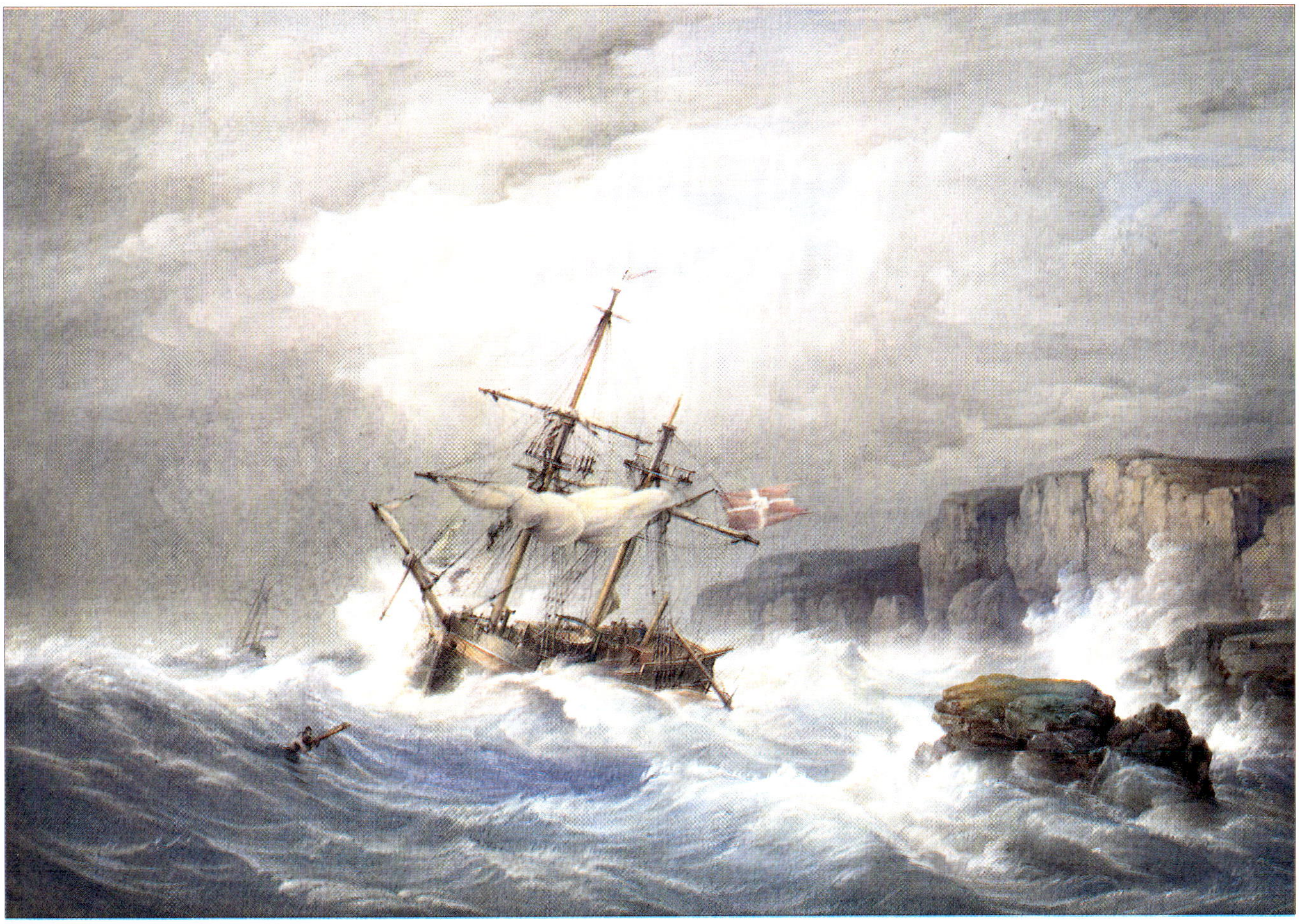

William Joy,
A Ship in Distress off a Rocky Coast, watercolour over pencil, 16 in x 22 in

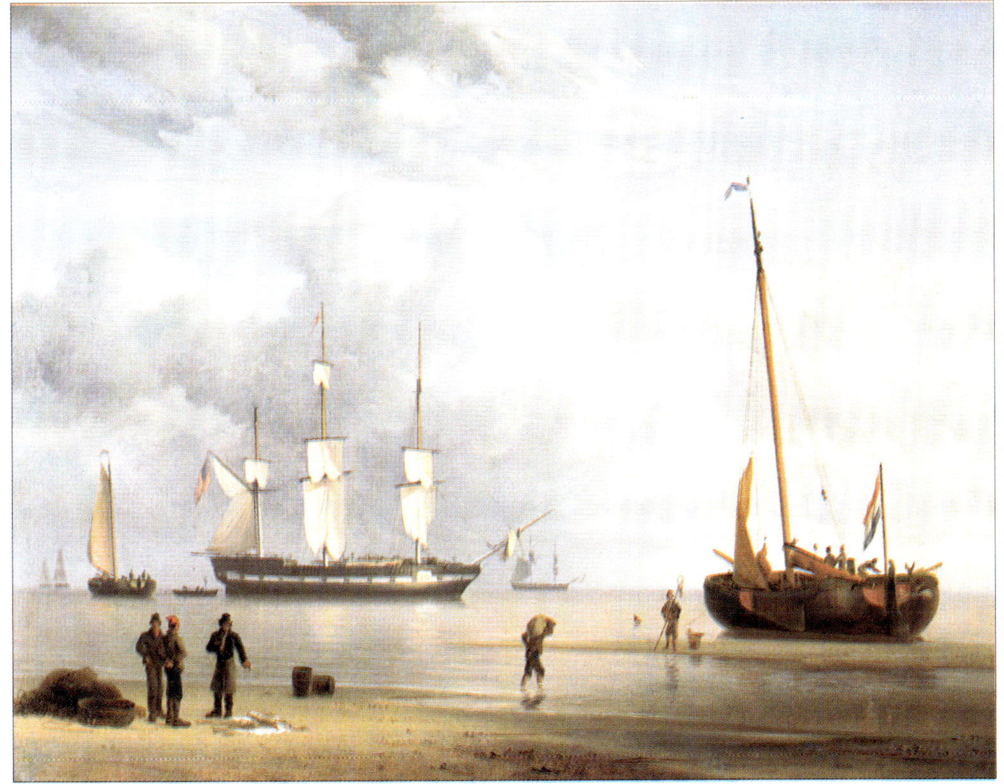

William and John Cantiloe Joy, Beach Scene, Taking Provisions, Man o' War at Anchor, oil on canvas, 15 in x 20 in

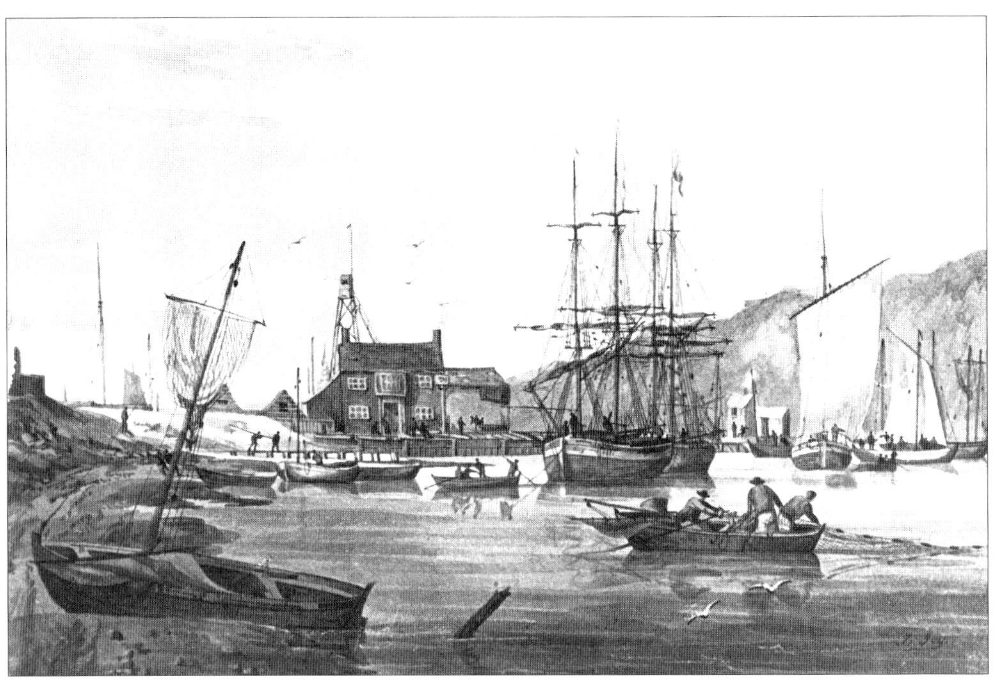

William and John Cantiloe Joy, Off Yarmouth, watercolour, signed, 6½ in x 9½ in

the beach scenes painted during the Yarmouth period which had less to offer his personal style. He has been accused on the other hand of poaching the subjects of Crome and Stark, an unfair accusation bearing in mind the number of times most of the Norwich artists repeated the favourite subjects.

Victoria Susanna Colkett (1840-1926), daughter of Samual David, who perhaps made a more significant name for herself, has little association with Norwich as most of her work was done after her family moved to Cambridge in 1854, and primarily Cambridge subjects, architectural subjects and street scenes are recorded. There are two examples of her work in Norwich Castle and the fact that the Witt Library holds a file for her implies a certain standing. She also exhibited fairly regularly at the British Institution. There is sometimes confusion regarding her identity as some of her work is signed Victoria Hine. In 1874 she married Harry Hine (1845-1941), a well-known and accomplished watercolour painter and a full Member of the Royal Institute of Painters in Watercolour.

Two brothers, **William Joy** (1803-1867) and **John Cantiloe Joy** (1806-1866), were born in Yarmouth, sons of a mail coach guard on the Ipswich-Yarmouth line, who is said to have done a certain amount of painting in his spare time. Whether or not, his two sons displayed a definite flair at a very early age which their father quite naturally encouraged.

There lived in Yarmouth at that time a wealthy eccentric and school friend of Lord Nelson, one Captain Manby, who spent a great deal of money establishing life-saving stations and invented a mortar for firing lifelines to wrecks. He was also Barrack Master at Yarmouth and a patron of the arts with a particular interest in marine paintings of which he was an avid collector. He even did a little amateur sketching himself on his various sea voyages, some of which sketches in years to come William Joy was to work up into paintings. However it came about, the two Joy brothers were brought to Manby's notice as budding artists and he was sufficiently impressed to give them every possible help and encouragement. He organised a studio for them in the Royal Barracks at Yarmouth in 1818 where, for good practice, he allowed them to copy works by Pocock, Powell and Francia from his own collection. When it came to developing their own original sea paintings, for he had instilled into them some of his passion for the sea and ships, he spent a great deal of time teaching them the construction of many seafaring vessels, their individual features and details that distinguished them. One only has to look at some of the paintings to appreciate what a wealth of knowledge he must have imparted to the two privileged young students who certainly responded to his interest and teaching.

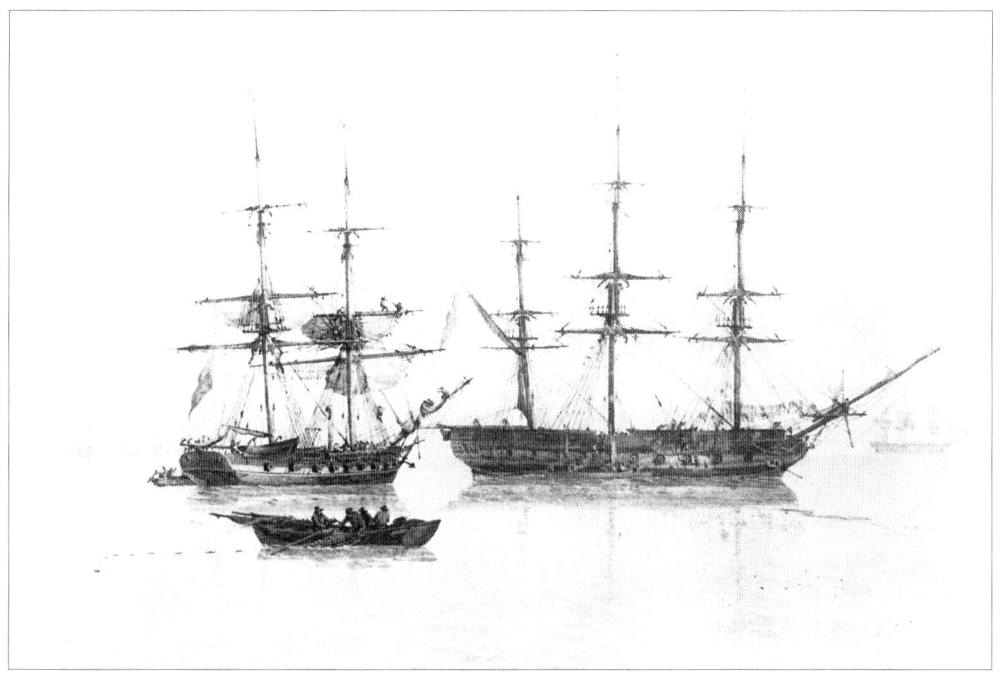

William and John Cantiloe Joy, Evening Calm with Frigates at Anchor off Yarmouth, watercolour, 11¼ in x 17¼ in

William Joy had already exhibited with the Norwich Society in 1814, which may have been the first contact with Captain Manby. After two years in his 'studio', Manby organised an exhibition of the brothers' work in the Barracks in honour of the King's birthday. This event, to which Captain Manby invited many of his influential friends and fellow collectors, including the patron of Crome and Cotman, Dawson Turner, was the beginning of a highly successful career for them both. Soon they found themselves in receipt of some good commissions, frequently worked on by them both, and their painting made rapid strides. They exhibited regularly with the Norwich Society following the Yarmouth showing, receiving some good press reports which also acknowledged their debt to Captain Manby for his help with the practical details so necessary to marine painters. The Captain's concern for his young protégés was such that when he went off on his periodic sea voyages he made a point of asking Dawson Turner to look in on them and give them encouragement.

In 1829 William Joy went to London at Captain Manby's instigation to widen his field of patronage; again Manby was instrumental in finding some useful introductions. John Joy followed a little later and soon they were fully occupied with important commissions and working for exhibitions. At this time, quite naturally and sensibly, Captain Manby decided that they should stand on their own feet. Certainly few young artists are given the extent of help and encouragement, coupled with many useful introductions, that Captain Manby meted out to the Joys. It could be said that paintings of shipwrecks and storms at sea were a way of drawing interest to Manby's institutions and inventions but I feel that, whether or not this was so, a genuine interest was there.

The brothers, who remained very close all their lives, worked in London for some time, then moved temporarily to Portsmouth in 1832 on a Government commission, painting various fishing craft for record purposes. They returned to London for a time before moving to Chichester and, later, back to London for the rest of their lives.

As I have said, the Joys frequently worked together on commissions with entirely satisfactory results but, in their own paintings, their individuality showed and there have never been problems of identification. William Joy worked in both oil and watercolour. It goes without saying after the specialist instruction from Captain Manby that his shipping was correct in every detail, but he invariably painted scenes of rich drama showing monstrous seas with huge waves tossing the craft or almost enveloping it, stormy skies with strange dramatic light, masses of whipped up foam as the waves broke on shipwrecks or other objects, always with a feeling of power in the handling. His colours were generally inclined to be cold, steely greys, even some

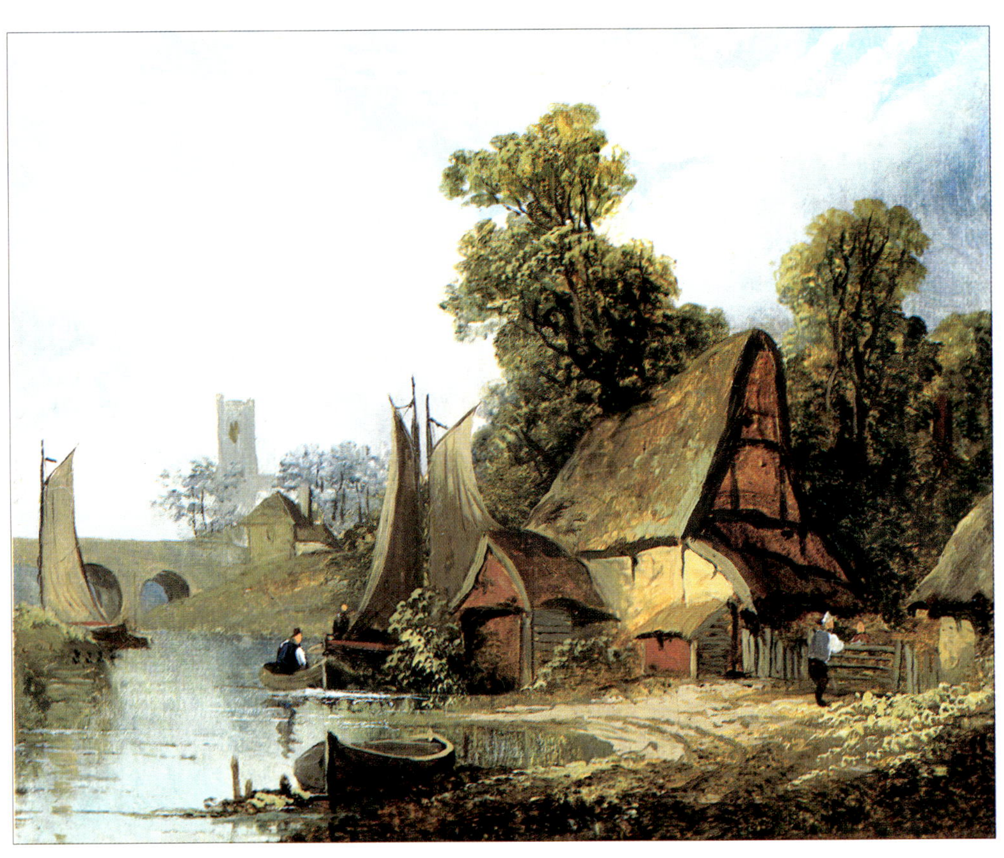

Joseph Paul,
Norfolk River Landscape,
oil on canvas, 8 in x 10 in

use of black, strange sludgy greens interspersed with an almost grassy shade tempered with other shades of grey and indigo. One can understand the appeal of his work to passionate lovers of the sea, in whatever mood, and shipping of all kinds. His work has been compared with that of Brooking and Joseph Stannard but, professional as it is of its kind and much as it may be comparable in factual detail, it lacks Stannard's personal charisma. There exist paintings of the seas for those with that intense, almost obsessive, feeling for all things maritime but Stannard's are paintings of the sea for all who love and admire good painting.

John Cantiloe Joy primarily used pencil and watercolour when working to please himself. He was also a perfectionist in his detail and the drawing and composition of his shipping are immaculate. Unlike his brother, he seemed to prefer calmer waters and less dramatic skies. His colour was warmer with greater variety but softer and less disturbing, and he added life by making more use than his brother of human figures. Perhaps I have overstated the differences; inevitably there were similarities as well and, when they worked together, the very differences were complementary. Both were masters of their subject and did credit to Captain Manby's early teaching and their own observation of the moods of sea and sky. Their work in the main is highly collectable although some of the later works started to become too pictorial; possibly they were seeking to attract a more populist market or possibly they had worked their subject to exhaustion and tried to vary the presentation.

Joseph Paul (1804-1887), has been treated rather as the joker in the pack with some authorities refusing to recognise his connection with the Norwich School. This is overlooking a very valid Norwich connection and the quality of some of his original paintings which are belatedly finding quite an appreciative following.

Robert Paul, Joseph's father, was a portrait painter who had exhibited with the Norwich Society and probably encouraged his son's talent for there seems no record of Joseph having any formal training. He was influenced by Crome and Vincent and, following an early period of quite reasonably competent Norwich scenes, he started painting Norfolk landscapes which, bearing in mind his later reputation as a copyist, have been wrongly attributed to a variety

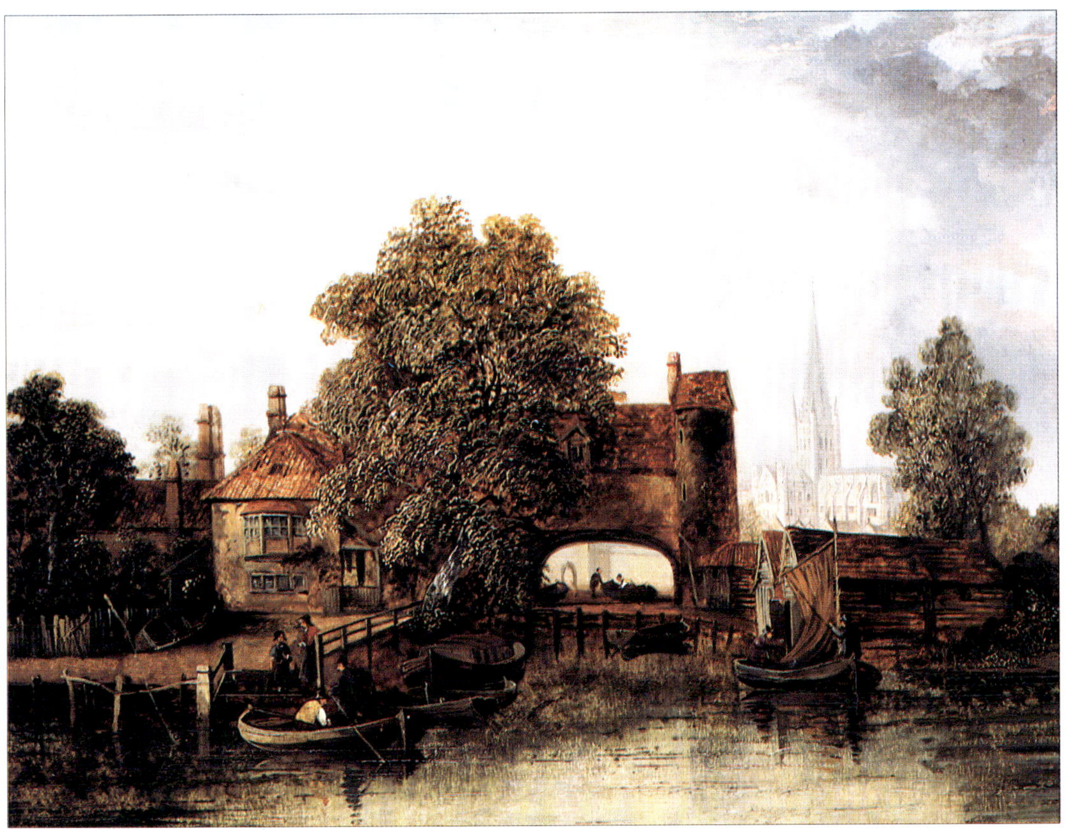

Joseph Paul,
Pull's Ferry, Norwich, with Cathedral, oil on panel, 14 in x 18 in

of other artists. Some of these attributions may have been quite flattering but of little use to the artist himself or later collectors. On the other side of the coin, certain less knowledgeable collectors have found to their cost that they had paid over the odds for something that, to an untrained eye, was not quite what it had seemed.

Joseph Paul was something of a character and also a heavy drinker and, following trouble with the city authorities, lost himself in London about 1830. There he took up copying old masters, Canaletto, Rembrandt and others, presumably still anxious to keep painting but not wishing to be identified by a personal style. This style, however, came through most of his copies and, with the benefit of hindsight, those pastiches were reasonably easily recognised as by Joseph Paul or, at least, not by the original artist. This is not to say they were simply parodies; they were well painted and different enough in the handling to absolve him from accusations of plagiarism.

Nevertheless, his penchant for copying made people suspicious and even when he returned to Norwich and was once more painting 'typical' Norwich School subjects they were wary. Time is sorting out the sheep from the goats and there are some excellent and original Pauls about. These are mainly his own compositions vaguely based on the Norfolk landscape with its familiar windmills, churches, lanes, fields and abundant trees. They have rather more freedom than some of the early Norwich paintings and his colours are warm and attractive. Leave out the copies and there is little that discredits the Norwich School.

Joseph Paul also had some reputation as a singer – of sorts. Maybe the drinking helped! He was married five times but, in spite of a wayward life, he lived for 83 years, a ripe old age for the mid-19th century.

As well as an artist father, Joseph Paul had an artist son, John, an extremely capable equestrian painter. Here it must be admitted that there is little that relates to the Norwich School except possibly some of the landscape backgrounds to his horses which certainly have a Norfolk feel about them. Apart from some early views of London, he is known primarily for his horses, and sometimes dogs, which are beautifully drawn and show a good grasp of anatomy and manner. His colours are muted and sensitive and the only similarity with his father's work lies in the simple fact that the creative talent existed.

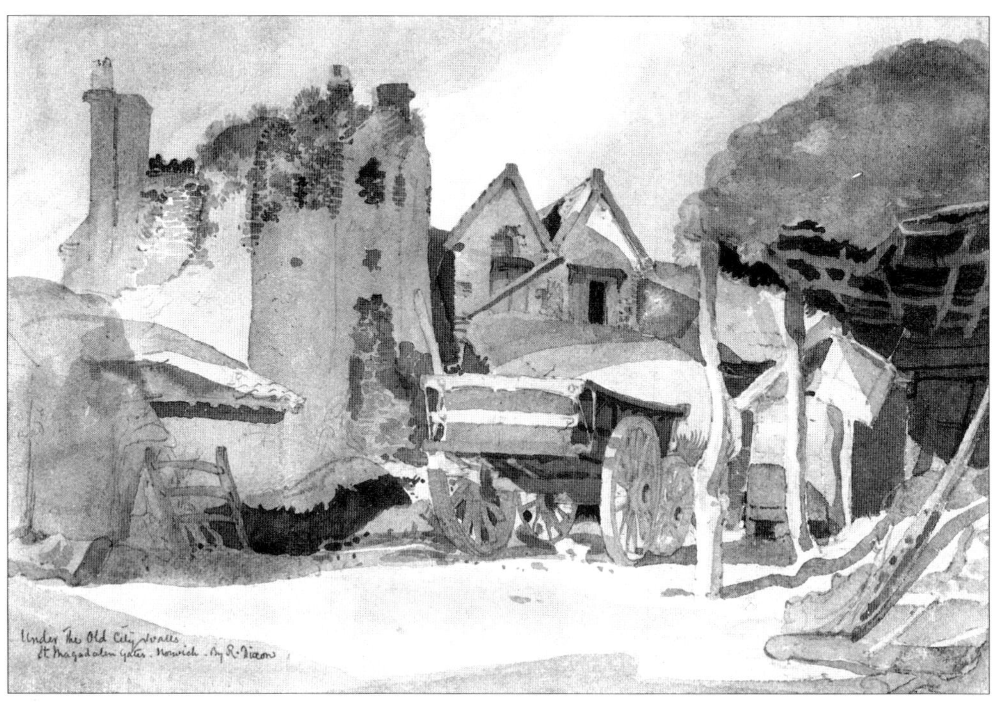

Robert Dixon,
Under the Old City Walls, St. Magdalen Gates, Norwich, watercolour, 8¼ in x 12¼ in

Chapter 11

THE BEST OF THE REST

By referring to the best of the rest, I may have given the impression of 'also ran' but this is wholly unintentional. Some years ago I commented in an earlier book that writings on the Norwich School invariably appeared rather disjointed and mine are no exception. The strange and diverse nature of the subject precludes a straight chronological or otherwise orderly approach, so all writers on the subject have dealt with it in their individual and disorderly way hoping that, like the School itself, it all comes together in the end.

During the early days of the Norwich Society, the name of **Robert Dixon** (1780-1815), was one of the most prominent, along with those of Crome, Ladbroke, Thirtle and Hodgson, constituting the bulwark of the Society prior to Cotman's return to Norwich in 1807. Like so many of the Norwich painters, Dixon's life was all too short; one muses already on the complex corporate identity of the Norwich School but with how much greater depth and diversity would it have developed had such painters as Joseph Stannard, Middleton, Vincent, Daniell and Dixon painted through a 'normal' life span?

Robert Dixon was a talented and versatile artist but little is known of his early life or his family. A Thomas Dixon is recorded as having been a glazier at St. Peter Mancroft church; also one John Dixon, a churchwarden at the same church, was a glass painter, so there could be family connections. Dixon displayed an early talent for he was trained at the Royal Academy Schools and, *c.*1800, became employed as a scene painter at Norwich Theatre Royal. He was also involved in the decoration of the new Ipswich Theatre which opened in 1803. His work was undoubtedly of extremely high quality for not only did the *Norwich Mercury* comment that it was appreciated by 'lovers of the classical and chaste style of decoration', but William Capon, a Norwich man who became one of London's foremost stage designers, invited Dixon to work for him in London. The offer was turned down; Dixon was obviously content with his life and work in Norwich which was consistently well received.

In addition to his work in the theatre Dixon established a private drawing practice, giving

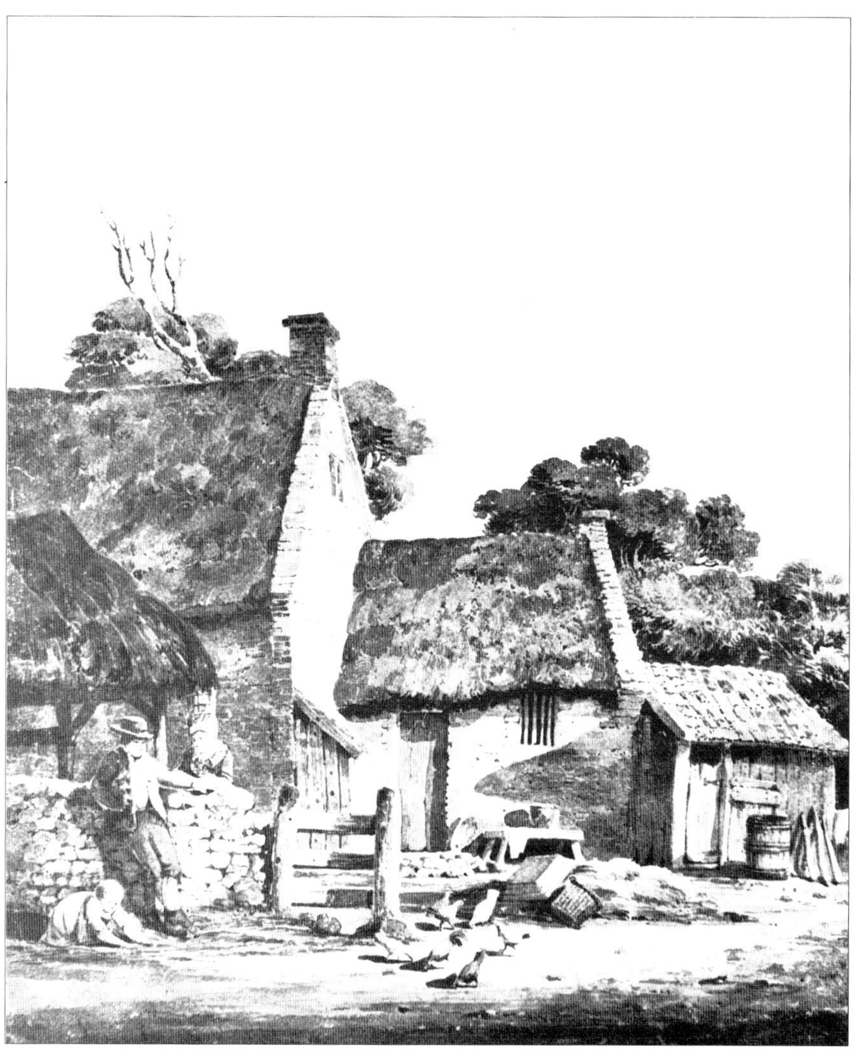

Robert Dixon,
Farmyard Scene,
pencil and watercolour, c.1809

lessons in Norwich, Scole, Harleston and Diss, and advertised his willingness to undertake commissions for interior decoration. From 1805 he exhibited with the Norwich Society, in that first year contributing 16 studies. He was appointed Vice-President to Robert Ladbroke in 1809 although ill health forced his resignation from the Society only three years later. His colleagues' respect for him is indicated by their organisation of an exhibition of his work in Sir Benjamin Wrenche's Court soon after his death in 1815 at the age of 35. This was with a view to helping his widow and six children, the members of the Society themselves adding a generous financial donation.

Dixon's work is interesting and varied. Some of his watercolours are bold and plainly influenced by his scene painter's training and experience; others are quite accomplished works in the more generally accepted watercolour tradition. It is possible both to like and actively dislike Dixon's watercolour work. Discounting the rather heavy, more theatrical pieces, he still used two very different styles of which I find the more 'finished', finely drawn, work the most attractive. I particularly like such examples as 'St. Leonard's Priory, Norwich', 1809, certain of his cottage scenes and the delightful seashore subjects of which Andrew Moore has written: 'His on the spot studies of fishermen on the shore and the effects of sunlight and twilight on the sea and the horizon have an immediacy and perception akin to John Constable's studies.' Like several other Norwich artists, Cromer seemed particularly to attract Dixon as a painting venue, as did Sheringham and the coastal strip between. He seemed to have some unexpected empathy with the seashore that gave him the heightened perception and depth of feeling that characterises these little gems.

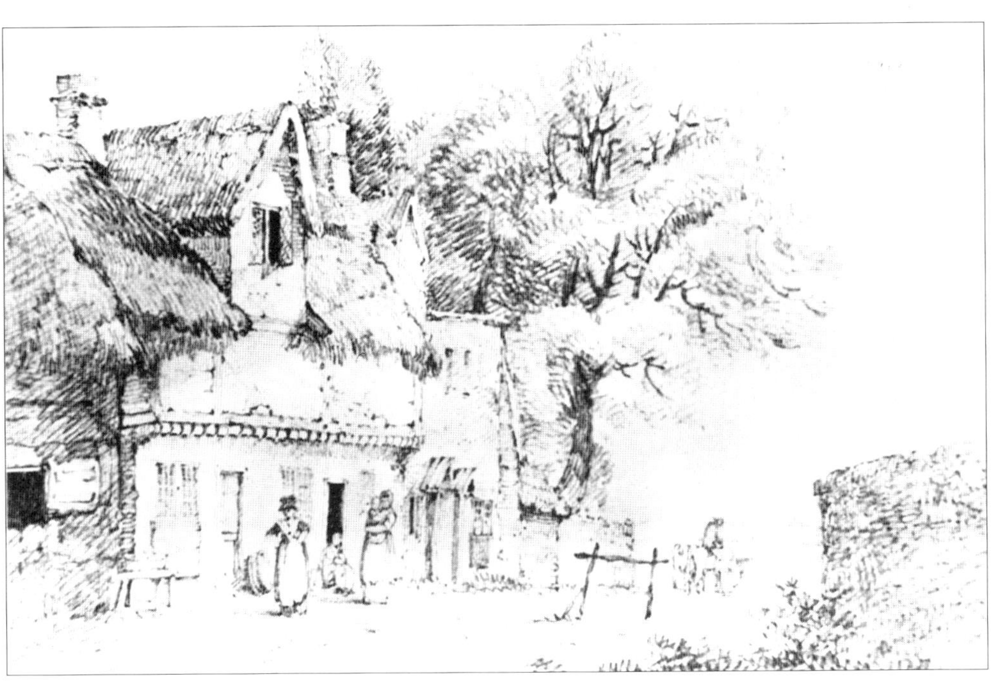

Robert Dixon, View at Heigham, Norwich, 1809, pencil

Sometimes Dixon experimented with a freer wash technique. Perhaps Cotman's influence encouraged this form of expression but if he took the idea from Cotman, the results bore no comparison with Cotman's own work. 'The Cromer Road to Aylsham', also 1809, while illustrating this use of washes in a rather art school manner, simply comes back to the scene painting effect though probably less confident. Such watercolours do no justice to Dixon's very real talent although in some others the washes are comparatively well modulated and the result quite pleasing if in rather an illustrative way.

Dixon also painted some oils but this was not a regular medium. In these oils he shows his predilection for country cottages adding to the rather 18th century feeling, but they are pleasant and competently executed.

Perhaps surprisingly, being diametrically opposite to scene painting, Dixon's pencil drawings are exquisite, quite exceptionally so, and here his natural talent lies. With a simple pencil he manages to create some wonderfully atmospheric effects, his draughtsmanship is impeccable and at the same time gentle but full of vitality. It is his drawing that explains his success as a teacher.

Like most good draughtsmen, Dixon's repertoire extended to etching using the soft ground method of the time which gave something of the same gentle effect of his pencil work. The desire to experiment with etching probably derived from Crome who had recently resurrected the craft. Of Dixon's etchings, although basically done for his own pleasure rather than commercial gain, and often based on his inevitable country cottages, 38 were published in 1811 under the title 'Picturesque Scenery of Norfolk'. Andrew Moore has commented: 'The first 38 plates reveal an assured response to the spontaneous quality of the soft ground medium which belies the relatively unsophisticated manner of the drawing.' But, as I have said, the drawing quality had no need of sophistication; Dixon's personal flair and response to his subjects said all that was necessary.

Dixon's was an enigmatic personality, the more so to today's biographer because so little is known of him; had he lived longer and made more of a name in his own time, as he probably would, earlier writers might have taken more notice. Day refers to him as an intelligent, gentlemanly man of good humour and many friends. He was also quite exceptionally well read signifying that he came from a good family who valued education.

This assumption is based on the fact that many of his drawings and paintings have an accompanying verse or quotation. Certain of these subjects, however, are outside his usual country cottage/Norfolk landscape idiom. For instance 'Cupid Benighted' with a quotation from Girdlestone's *Anacreon* Ode 111, or 'Ralpho interceding for the Fiddler' with a quote from

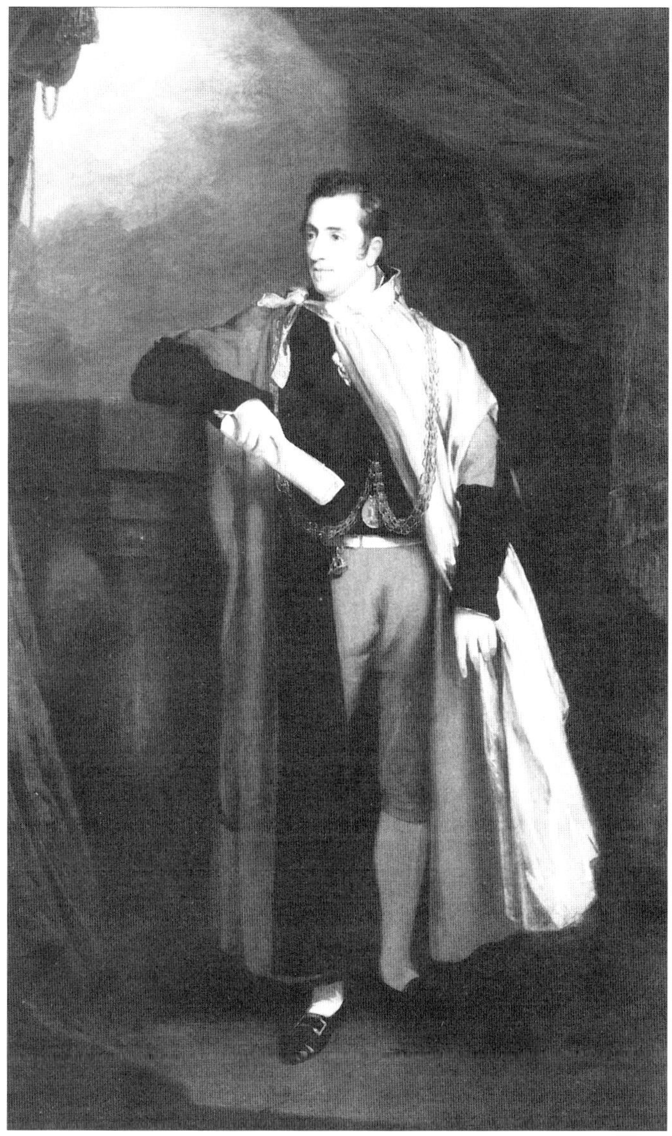

Joseph Clover, Portrait of Thomas Back, Mayor of Norwich, oil on canvas, 1809, 94 in x 58 in

Hudibras, Part 1 Canto 2, suggest that Dixon may have been involved in book illustration along with his other activities. Perhaps this work in itself inspired his own literary explorations for we have one of his 'Drawing from Nature' subjects inscribed:

> The God of day does to his Thetis haste,
> In clouds of Gold, and shining purple dress'd:
> Each labouring husbandman his setting waits,
> And to his course but welcome home retreats. (Mountford)

The premature death of Robert Dixon leaves many unanswered questions. He was still diversifying to an extent too great for us to guess how his talents would eventually have been channelled or whether he would have remained something of an artistic dilettante.

Joseph Clover (1779-1854) was born in Aylsham, Norfolk, a few miles out of Norwich. All we know of his artistic background seems to be that his grandfather, an earlier Joseph Clover, is said to have been the father of veterinary art.

The younger Clover started his career as an engraver but transferred to portrait painting which proved much more rewarding for him. Opie, the famous portraitist, must have had some connection with the broader family for Clover met him when his uncle was being painted; watching the great man work inspired Joseph to turn to painting himself. Opie was so impressed by the young man's talent that he not only encouraged him but also took him on as a pupil for four years from 1807, even, towards the end of the time, allowing him to work on his own paintings.

Clover seems to have divided his time between Norwich and London. He had many friends among the Norwich painters, particularly John Thirtle, and while living in London intermittently between 1816 and 1848 for a time shared lodgings with James Stark. He exhibited portraits with the Norwich Society from 1813 onwards and it was the commissions gained through these exhibitions and a one-man show of his own in 1811 at a venue on Elm Hill that kept up the connection with Norwich and encouraged frequent visits. He travelled extensively, too, both in this country and abroad; as a successful portrait painter he could afford the little indulgences denied to many of his colleagues.

His many, many sitters included such prominent subjects as the Marquis of Stafford, Countess de Grey, General Cookson, Dr Edward Rigby, M.D., F.L.S., F.H.S., the Rev. Pendlebury Houghton and his daughter, the Rev. C. Townley Ward, L.L.D., Thomas Back, Mayor of Norwich over several years, Barnabas Leman, Mayor of Norwich 1813 and 1819, Crisp Brown, Mayor of Norwich 1817, Charles Augustus Tulk, M.P. for Sudbury, Omer Effendi, Private Secretary to the Pacha of Egypt, Lady Buckley and Alderman John Browne of Norwich. Among his colleagues he painted James Stark and George Vincent, each of whom added his own landscape background to his portrait, which were hung in the Sexton Room of the Norwich Assembly Rooms. Other civic portraits hang in St. Andrew's Hall and are very impressive pieces, perhaps the more so as Clover painted in a relatively modern idiom for his time, fairly freely and with generous use of paint. One very imaginative work illustrates Bloomfield's 'The Harvesters' from *The Farmer's Boy* for which Clover used real models in their appropriate setting.

Because of his high reputation as a portrait painter, Clover is less well known than he should be for his landscapes in oil and particularly watercolour. Although he did sometimes exhibit landscapes, they were not part of his commercial life and the fact that they constituted, in the main, pure pleasure, no doubt accounts not only for the variable quality but also for the charm and spontaneity of the best of this work. His watercolours were delightfully 'wet' and painted with a freedom far ahead of his time; how they were received in his own time seems not to be recorded, neither did it matter to him, as it did to John Sell Cotman, if they were, executed as seems likely, simply for pleasure. A number of his oil sketches are in Norwich Castle Museum, like most of his sketched work probably executed for record purposes. There are sketch books in the Castle collection, too, notably a series following the route of a trip to Northumberland, again letting his sketchbook act as camera. Clover was a good draughtsman which always adds to the quality of any sketch work. The best of Clover's seems to date around the 1810-11 period, although there is a good record in watercolour sketches from his tour of Wales in 1828; this includes a quite exceptional view of Kidwelly Castle. He was very clever at making the white of his paper work for him adding to the more modern appearance of his work, and, as with Constable, in his oil sketches a touch of red often added character.

Clover would have made a good landscape painter but he was wise, given that his portraits provided a generous living, to keep this personal work for recreation and enjoyment. It might have identified him more widely with other Norwich School painters but he has a more than compensatory place in the annals of portrait painting. He obviously held the interests of the Norwich Society as of great importance and in its later years, 1828-31, when its fortunes were in decline, contributed substantially to its diminishing funds. He may have helped to prolong its life but, by then, the Society was beyond saving.

His contribution to the City was recognised when he was given the honour of laying the foundation stone of the old Carrow Bridge. It is thought that, following the demise of the Norwich Society, he spent his later years in London.

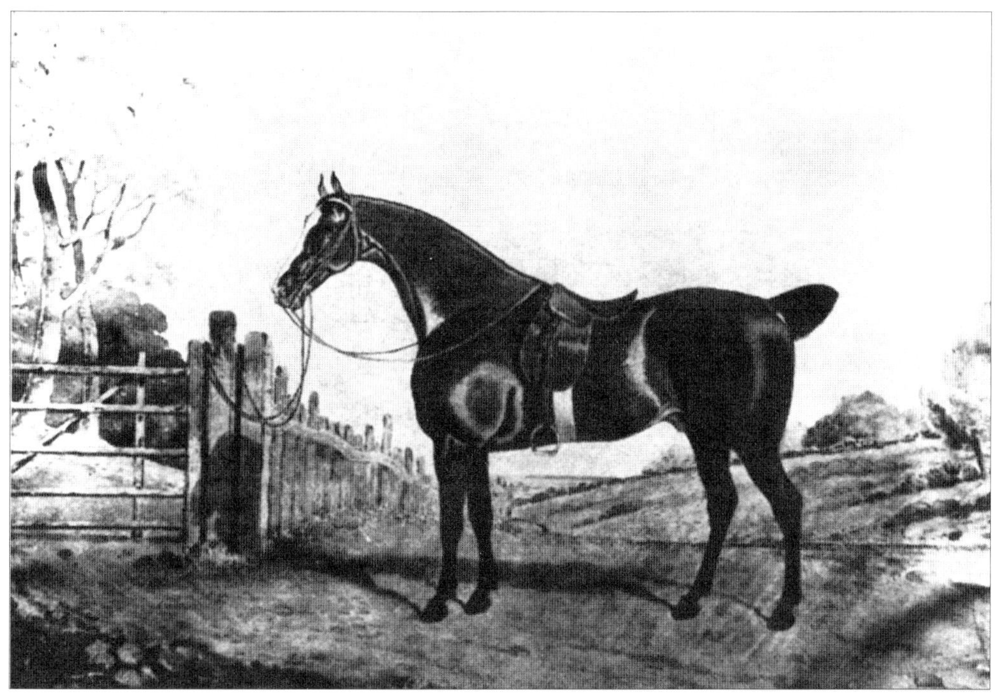

Edwin Cooper,
Bay Hunter in a Landscape

Like Clover, **Edwin Cooper** (1785-1833) diverted from landscape to become a professional painter of animals. Cooper was born in Bury St. Edmunds, Suffolk, where his father, Daniel, was drawing master at a school and a miniaturist in his own right. Presumably his son, who displayed an early talent, studied under his father; he was painting professionally by the age of 21 and accepting commissions, especially for paintings of horses.

Cooper met John Crome quite early in his career and first exhibited four works with the Norwich Society in 1806. By 1810 he was exhibiting both horses and cattle and taking a number of commissions from Norfolk landowners. He had moved, presumably with his family, to Beccles which brought him nearer Norwich and his patrons; he was made an Honorary Member of the Norwich Society. An added attraction of the move would have been the Beccles Race Meetings which had begun very early in the 18th century and continued with only a few intermissions until the early Victorian era. These meetings were supported by the local aristocracy and the landed gentry, all potential patrons. He subsequently styled himself 'Cooper of Beccles' to distinguish himself from the various other Coopers painting around that time, including his younger brother.

Edwin Cooper distributed his favours and exhibited with both the main Society and the secession, although the best of his work was kept for Crome's domain. Altogether over the years he exhibited nearly 100 works, all animals, primarily horses, having landscape backgrounds which were always fresh and convincing with particularly good skies. His figure work, though variable, was usually more than competent, especially when part of a commission, as in the case of 'Sir Jacob Astley's Huntsman, Mr J. Hewitt, Michael Beasley on his Favourite Hunter', and 'Edward Loombe on Sparkle with Hounds', the latter an exceptionally large canvas measuring 41 in x 54½ in.

Cooper had an excellent mastery of anatomy and a strong painting technique but the real secret of his success with the 'horsey' fraternity was a personal love of horses that always shone through. Round about 1824 he spent some time in Newmarket, sharing a studio with Ben Marshall, while executing commissions for race horses. In his hunting scenes, the dogs were contemporary with the horses, but dogs introduced incidentally often had something of an old world, almost 17th century, identity – whether by accident or design. Norwich Castle Museum has an interesting self portrait of the artist himself in hunting garb with his own dog.

Cooper did some work in watercolour which is much gentler and lower toned than his oil painting and, again, appears almost of an earlier era with a quaint charm all of its own. It has been said that he painted portraits of houses but I have seen only one example to bear this out. His drawings in a rather cartoonish vein were excellent, full of movement, life and humour, borne out by a series of prints called 'The Life of the Race Horse', tracing this life from the fun of youthful exuberance to the knacker's yard. These were etched by J. Sendall and published by Ackermann; the original drawings are in the Paul Mellon Collection in the United States.

Although older than some of the Norwich painters, Cooper was still only 47 when he died. The company he kept and the lavish hospitality of his hunting and racing patrons, gave him too much of a taste for the bottle which proved to be his undoing. According to a *Country Life* of 1919: 'Edwin Cooper in his later years seldom got to work on a picture until he had mastered a bottle of port.' As ever, the Norwich Society rallied round and put on an exhibition of over 200 of Cooper's works to raise funds for the widow.

Alfred Priest (1810-1850), was born in Norwich, the son of a chemist who gave him a good education in the hope that he would follow his father into the pharmaceutical profession. Alfred had other ideas and went off to sea, but the life failed to come up to his expectations and he returned to Norwich subsequently to be apprenticed to a surgeon at Downham Market. In this, also, he quickly lost interest, having found a new enthusiasm for art. He studied etching under Henry Ninham and, later, under the specialist etcher and engraver, E.W.Cooke. There are over 50 recorded etchings, not all totally original often being 'after' other artists such as John Sell Cotman. That said, his etched work is extremely competent, often small but very appealing and not as well known as it deserves.

Priest knew the other eminent etcher, the Rev. E.T. Daniell, and also the Cotmans who – especially Miles Edmund – became close friends. After his time with Ninham, Priest became a pupil of James Stark, who taught him oil painting and to some extent influenced his style. He first exhibited at the Royal Academy in 1833; after he married and moved to London in 1835 he exhibited regularly at the Academy, the British Institute and the Suffolk Street Galleries.

Priest was talented to the point of facility and, although there was no great depth of feeling about his oils, they were more than competent and extremely decorative. His brushwork was fluent and he was quite happy when it suited his purpose to borrow the devices of others such as Constable's occasional use of scattered light flecks to give the effect of shimmering sunlight.

Priest's main strength lay in his marine painting, a subject possibly inspired by Cooke's own seascapes. His skill with transparent effects gave all his 'watery' subjects, fords and rivers as well as the ocean, an authenticity sometimes missing in his landscapes, and his style of brushwork lent itself to sea and sky effects. There was a feeling of movement and vigour about these sea paintings; perhaps something of his early yearning for the sea was still waiting to come out. In all his work the use of rather unusual colour was eyecatching and effective – warm greens, ochres and browns even in his seas obviously appealed more than cold greys even when stormy skies were dominating. His later work, probably on account of failing health, started to appear laboured and comparatively dull and did nothing to enhance what had been a growing reputation.

A portrait of Alfred Priest by his friend, Miles Edmund Cotman, indicates a handsome, debonair individual exuding confidence and probably charm of manner. An unexpected characteristic was a fondness for children for whom he wrote fanciful poems. He returned to Norwich in 1848 said to be suffering from tuberculosis not helped by a certain intemperance. Another Norwich painter's life was cut short when he died in the city at only 40 years old.

Well-to-do academics are not the people generally associated with the Norwich School but in the person of **Edward Thomas Daniell** (1804-1842), they are at least represented. Daniell was the son of a baronet, a former Attorney-General of Dominica; he was born in London but, after the death of his father, when he was only two years old, moved with his mother to Norfolk. He

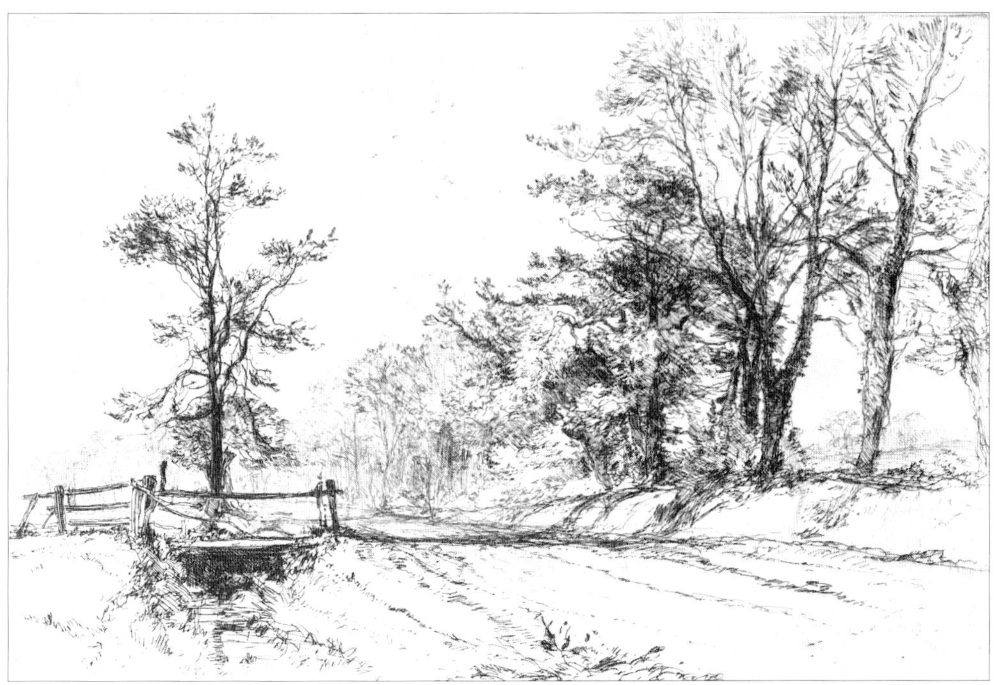

Edward Thomas Daniell, Norfolk Lane, etching

attended Norwich Grammar School where his interest in the arts was no doubt inspired and fostered by his Art Master, John Crome.

Daniell graduated from Balliol, Oxford, in 1828 and having a passion for travel took himself off during 1829-30 on one of his several continental trips, to France, Italy and Switzerland. During his vacations from Balliol he had spent much time with Joseph Stannard in his studio; although Stannard was not a teacher, he made exceptions for his brother and his friend, Edward Daniell. The latter was also a close friend – and patron – of John Linnell from whom he had some further tuition and he was undoubtedly influenced by John Sell Cotman. Daniell had a particular penchant for etching and the drawings made on his early travels were obviously done with future etchings in mind. In 1831 he went with an Oxford friend to Scotland and further developed his etching ability by studying the technique of the Scottish etchers. Unlike Crome and Cotman, he liked to work in drypoint where a rich, dark tone is achieved by drawing directly on to a metal plate with a needle, using considerably increased pressure for the darker passages. The needle, a very hard one of tempered steel, scores a line with a slight 'burr' on each side of it and this burr holds the ink with a softer effect than the normal etched line where the acid eats in vertically. At the same time the line is stronger and darker than the delicate effect of the soft ground.

Daniell's ultimate vocation, he had decided while at Oxford, was the priesthood and he was ordained deacon in 1832. He served his curacy in Norfolk, at the same time continuing with his etching and becoming more accomplished as time went on. He was ordained to the full priesthood in Norwich Cathedral in 1833 and appointed curate to the large parish of St. Mark's, North Audley Street, London. He left his etching plates in Norwich to be printed for him by Henry Ninham. While in London he painted a few small oils under Linnell's guidance and exhibited regularly at the Royal Academy and the British Institute. The subject matter available in London did not appeal as etching material as much as the Norfolk scenery, and in any case Daniell probably had less time at a stretch for the more exacting craft. He made friends with many distinguished London painters, notably Linnell, J.M.W. Turner, Samuel Palmer, who was married to Linnell's daughter, David Roberts, Sir Edwin Landseer and William Mulready. He was instrumental in enabling Linnell to paint the only known painting in oils of J.M.W. Turner who always adamantly refused to have his portrait painted in spite of many requests from other artists for the privilege. Daniell invited Turner and Linnell to dinner in company with other contemporary artists. He seated Linnell directly opposite Turner so giving him the opportunity for direct and concentrated observation of his subject. Linnell disappeared briefly after the meal to make some quick pencil sketches with the likeness clearly in his mind; he later produced the

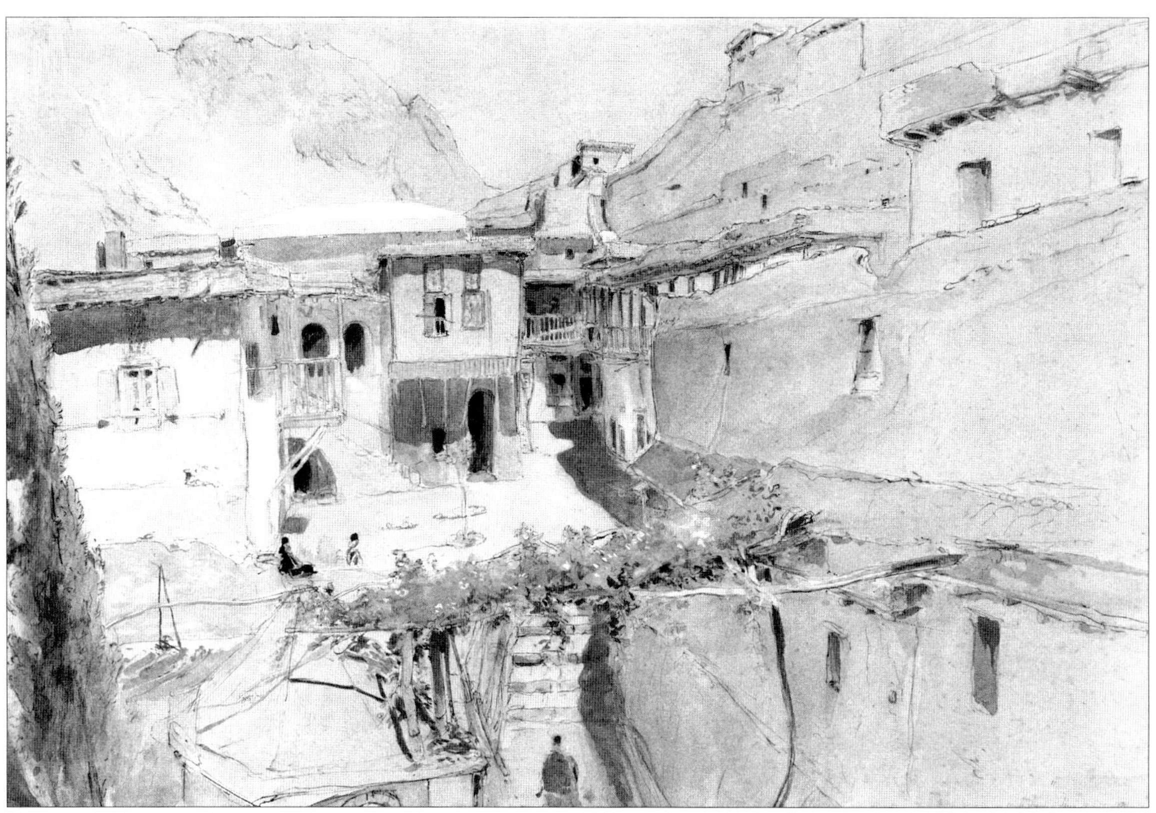

Edward Thomas Daniell, Interior of Convent, Mount Sinai, pencil, watercolour and body colour, 13 in x 19½ in

finished portrait which, in recent years, has been in the National Portrait Gallery. Daniell collected paintings avidly, and when the Palmers were going on honeymoon to Rome he commissioned Samuel to make a copy of one of Raphael's frescoes in the Vatican. As well as his parochial work, Daniell served on the committees of various artistic bodies, always maintaining his strong interest in the arts.

He became particularly excited by Roberts' drawings of Palestine and these and his love of travel gave him the urge to visit the Middle Eastern countries and work there for a time himself. In 1840 he resigned from St. Mark's and went sketching with some enthusiasm in the Aegean and Adriatic regions, Greece, Palestine and Lycia. His journeyings were almost complete when the opportunity arose to join an expedition being made by a survey ship to collect antiquarian remains which had been found at Xanthus – his brief was to go as the party's recording artist, an irresistible suggestion. Sadly, however, Daniell contracted malarial fever from which he failed to recover and he died in Adalia in 1842. Yet another Norwich School life was prematurely cut short and inestimable talent lost. Fate was not kind to the artists of the Norwich School and it is quite remarkable how the School held together in spite of all the odds.

Although he is always dubbed an amateur, Daniell was a highly individual artist with quite a rare talent. He is one of the few artists whose reputation hangs almost solely on his etchings; some historians class him as one of the finest English etchers, and most agree that he is the best in the Norwich School. While I personally find some of Cotman's soft ground etchings more visually attractive, I do appreciate that Daniell's are etchings in the truer sense and technically of a very high order. At the same time, I find it rather sad that more attention has not been paid to his watercolours and drawings which, in some instances, are of an extremely high quality, as Laurence Binyon pointed out as long ago as 1933.

Daniell's style is completely his own; his drawings have a delicacy of outline, at the same time crisp and confident, and are frequently washed in muted but distinctive tones. Very few pure watercolours appear to exist but those that do are impressive in their very simplicity, having a powerful feeling for the atmosphere of the landscape involved. It must, of course, be said that the unique subject matter of much of Daniell's work contributes to its strong individuality and it is the fruit of that last ill-fated Middle Eastern tour that is most interesting and instructive. Perhaps these

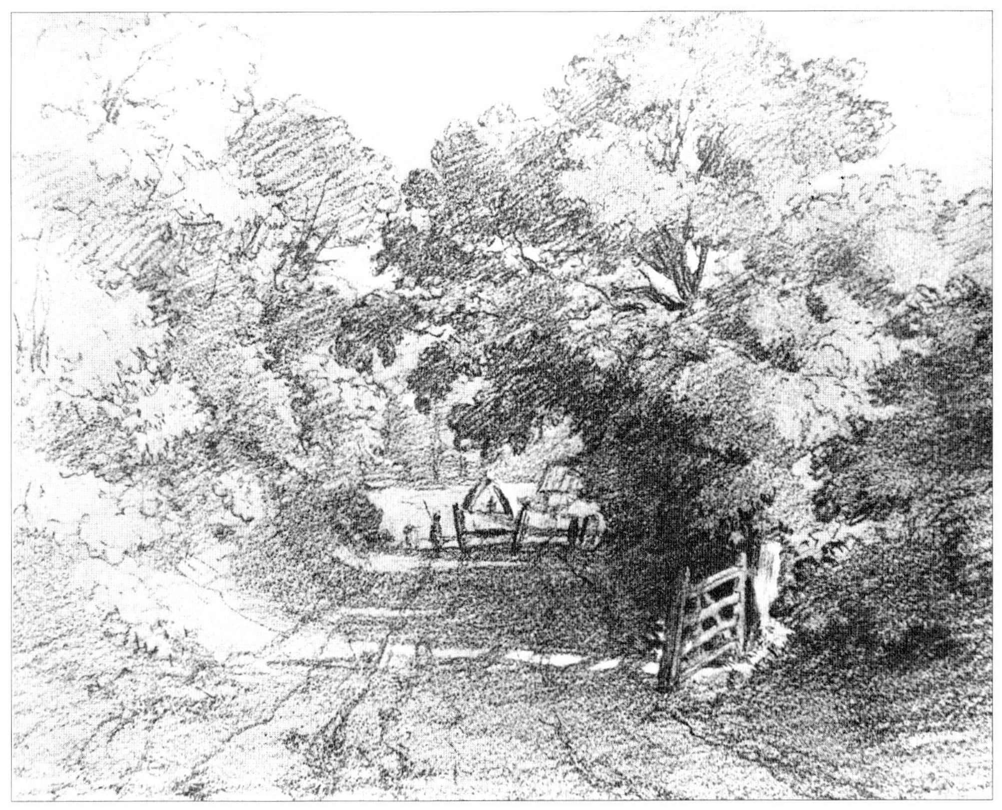

Joseph Geldart,
Lane with Covered Cart,
chalk drawing, late 1830s

drawings are slightly reminiscent of Roberts' own; certainly they are not, in the main, inferior.

There are 120 of the drawings in Norwich Castle, 64 in the British Museum and a few in the Victoria and Albert Museum. Most of them are in ink on a buff coloured paper with very light, tonal rather than coloured washes. They are in Daniell's personal and distinctive style, combining economy and freedom with an illusion of detail created by an ability to express the atmosphere, the inherent ambience of any situation, with few but – oh so – vital strokes. Daniell could create a sense of space, a feeling of heat or cold, of poverty or plenty, with apparent lack of effort indicating a talent or skill, possibly both, that has yet to be fully recognised. There is, additionally, the documentary value of these Middle Eastern depictions of a century and a half ago, the mountains, rivers and vegetation and the mid-19th century views of the Holy Land, of Nazareth and Bethlehem, as well as of more secular situations. I am particularly attracted by 'Interior of Convent, Mount Sinai', a large drawing expressing all that is best about the understated artistry of Edward Thomas Daniell applied to an extraordinarily complex subject.

One hears all too little about the art of **Joseph Geldart** (1808-1882) whose work I find most satisfying. He is almost as well known for his friendship with the Cotman family and in particular his loyalty and support for John Joseph in the darkest days of poverty and depression after the deaths of his father and brother.

John Sell Cotman himself was delighted when Geldart appeared as a potential pupil. Joseph Geldart came of Flemish stock who emigrated to England in the 17th century. His father was a Norwich wine merchant who articled his son to Brightling, a Norwich solicitor. There appears to have been no shortage of money in the family and young Joseph enjoyed travelling, especially on the Continent, to Italy, Switzerland and anywhere else that took his fancy. It was on one of those tours, when he had been doing a great deal of sketching by way of a record, that he decided to seek help with perfecting his drawing, and perhaps even working up the drawings to something more ambitious. He therefore, with an introduction from Brightling, approached John Sell Cotman in about 1829 and showed off his sketches. John Sell was considerably impressed by the quality of Geldart's drawing, as well as by the material content of the work and its possibilities for both of them. On Geldart's first visit to Cotman's studio he showed his master, along with others, a sketch of the Via Mala which Cotman immediately appropriated and, using chalk on grey paper, worked up then and there before the admiring eyes of his new pupil. This superb drawing, now in Norwich Castle Museum, meant a great deal to Geldart and he treasured it for many years.

'It had a double interest for me', he wrote some years later,

> . . . in the fact that, in my first lesson, it was made before me by John Sell Cotman from a very slight and imperfect sketch made by me the year before; and also because the Master was at the time suffering from one of those fits of deep melancholy to which he was periodically subject and which rendered it almost impossible for him to speak or look up. I remember after fifty years as though it were yesterday.

Geldart became a close friend of both the young Cotmans; in fact the two families kept in touch until John Sell's death and Geldart continued, when in Norwich, to befriend John Joseph Cotman. When these two had first met, John Joseph greatly admired Geldart's work and wrote of his 'new friend' whose drawing he 'strove to emulate'. The Cotmans were never slow to give praise where they felt it was due; the fact that the recipient was an amateur or just a beginner made no difference.

Geldart's natural talent blossomed under John Sell Cotman; both were born draughtsmen and found a rare empathy with each other and each other's work. Geldart's drawing, although it improved so much under Cotman's tuition, never lost its individuality which says a great deal for them both. Geldart liked to use charcoal with highlights of white chalk, either on tinted paper or, occasionally, with a light wash. He had a good eye for composition and his feeling for light and shade was exceptional. His drawing was quite free and vigorous but, at the same time, always accurate in detail and perspective, a combination used with a natural flair that many professionals might envy. Enviable, too, was his ability to create drama and effect simply in monochrome. To what extent he attempted portraiture generally I do not know, but there exists in the Cotman family collection a wonderful study, expressing the character and personality one associates with the subject, of Miles Edmund Cotman.

Although he seems rarely to have used colour in his own work, Geldart had such an intense interest in the science of colour that he gave up his legal profession and spent some years in Italy trying to unravel the colour secrets of the Venetian painters and studying the old masters from the colour technician's aspect. Titian particularly interested him and provided him with hours of analytical study. One reads in various sources stories of how Geldart was frequently to be found in the cafés of the Venetian Piazza demonstrating his theories in coloured chalks on the marble topped tables. It has been suggested that this study of colour and colour principles may have inspired the unusual dramatic colour combinations experimented with by his friend John Joseph Cotman. Perhaps these were less wild than is generally assumed and he was trying out Geldart's theories with enthusiasm – and possible exaggeration?

It seems strange that Geldart himself used colour so rarely in the face of such interest and intensive research; possibly he found it just did not work for him, sensibly accepted the fact and went on drawing. Harold Day mentions one or two oils in the Cotman collection that are reminiscent of Ladbroke, rather heavy and laboured. But who needs colour in the face of such draughtsman's skill, far better expressed in simple monochrome?

Geldart's talents were obviously widely ranged. After a legal training and an interest in the visual arts, both practical and theoretical, it is surprising to learn that he eventually became Editor of the *Norfolk News*. Many artists make good writers and vice versa; after all it is just another form of creativity expressed through a different medium and, by the standards of the Norwich School, Geldart lived long enough to try out different lives. For the purposes of this book, however, the artist's life takes pride of place.

Chapter 12

THE FORGOTTEN PEOPLE

There are a few artists not immediately associated in the public mind with the Norwich School who some authorities include and others ignore, but who are too much part of the Norwich scene to pass over entirely.

As well as Joseph Clover, two portrait painters are worthy of mention. **George Clint** (1770-1854) is better known nationally than Clover, having been born and working primarily in London. He visited Norwich frequently all the same, exhibited regularly with the Norwich Society, and let it be known that he hoped to retire there.

Clint started his career as a miniaturist and engraver but soon turned to portraiture, concentrating for a time on theatrical portraits of leading actors and actresses of the day, such characters as W. Farren, Farley and Jones as Lord Ogleby, Canton and Brush in *A Clandestine Marriage,* 1819. He first exhibited with the Royal Academy in 1802 and was made an Associate in 1821. He acquired a number of Norwich patrons and started exhibiting portraits with the Norwich Society in 1823; he was the only one of six portrait exhibitors to become a full member of the Society. The *Norwich Mercury* gave him credit for his 'pre-eminence in the field of portraiture'.

Clint's portraits were more highly finished than Clover's and his ability to catch a likeness and express personality were frequently remarked on. As well as members of the Norfolk aristocracy and some civic dignitaries, his best known Norwich portrait is that of Sir John Harrison Yallop, Sheriff of Norwich 1805, Mayor of Norwich 1815 and 1831, painted in 1815 and now in Norwich Castle Museum. This is a very splendid portrait indeed which commanded fulsome praise in its time. Clint made many friends amongst the Norwich artists and is known to have painted, probably among others, Joseph Stannard and William Henry Crome. We must be grateful to these artists who painted each other for giving a visual identity to those whose works we enjoy.

Horace Beevor Love (1800-1838) was the other regular portrait exhibitor with the Norwich Society; of his colleagues he drew John Sell Cotman and painted A.J. Stark and John Berney Crome. He painted miniatures as well as full portraits and a number of landscapes and other subjects are listed among over 100 Norwich exhibits but, again, he died very young and his work seems not greatly to have influenced Norwich posterity.

James Bulwer (1794-1879) was a close friend of the Cotmans, a frequent sketching companion as well as pupil of John Sell, and patron both of John Sell and Miles Edmund. He was an amateur painter with a decided but slender talent. Bulwer was born in Norwich and graduated from Jesus College, Cambridge, in 1818, the same year as he took Holy Orders. As Derek Clifford comments, he was 'one of those parson antiquarians who seemed to have time for an astonishing amount of extra-clerical activity.'

Bulwer's first curacy was in Ireland after which, for some reason, he spent about two years travelling in Portugal and Madeira. This was followed by a curacy in Bristol and a return to Norfolk in 1840, first as curate of Blickling with Aylsham, then vicar of Hanworth-cum-Stody from 1818 until his death. Always he kept up his antiquarian interests and was fascinated by the old churches of Norfolk which frequently appeared in his watercolour drawings. This was very much a shared interest with John Sell Cotman and no doubt the focus of many of their excursions together around the Norfolk countryside.

Compared to the Cotmans, Bulwer's work is slight and rather pedestrian but perhaps one should not make such comparisons – in their own right Bulwer's watercolours, watercolour drawings rather than watercolours *per se,* are pleasant enough and quite competent. Perhaps the fact that he and Miles Edmund Cotman together illustrated Blomefield's *History of Norfolk* has rather unfairly invited this comparison. A number of Bulwer's watercolours are in Norwich Castle Museum.

More in the accepted Norwich tradition and still undervalued is **Obadiah Short** (1803-1886). Probably during his lifetime his unfortunate background and lack of real stability meant that he carried less influence than many of his contemporaries. Obadiah Short's father was an army officer who was killed in action in 1809; his mother died almost at the same time and he was brought up in Norwich by his grandmother, a lady in reduced circumstances who could not afford a formal education for the boy who had always to make his own way in life and fight his own battles. He started work at only 12 years of age as a weaver and continued in this work until 1829.

In the meantime he had developed an interest in art and was determined to see what he could make of drawing and painting himself. He had been 'adopted' by one Dr Dalrymple, John Crome's physician and also a collector and patron of the arts, who gave him an introduction to the Earl of Leicester. This allowed the budding artist an opportunity of studying a worthwhile collection of first class paintings and other beautiful things. The enterprising Short walked from Norwich to Holkham where the Earl, who obviously took to him, let him stay as long as he liked, studying what and where he liked in the way of artistic treasures.

Short learnt a great deal simply by copying paintings and, through a friend of John Crome, borrowed contemporary work as well as old masters to copy. As he became more proficient he was encouraged by Dr Dalrymple's commissions to draw pathological subjects, an exercise which could only help Short with his drawing and thereby art work generally. This unusual combination of aids to learning may well account for his very individual style of drawing exemplified by sketches in Norwich Castle Museum. This work at its best has much that is extremely pleasing and deserving of more attention.

His oils, too, which he exhibited in Norwich occasionally during his lifetime, although rather heavy are well composed, well drawn and painted, sometimes rather reminiscent of Robert Ladbroke. I feel, however, that this darkish, weighty effect is not down to any influence from Ladbroke but rather to Short's study and copying of old masters and other earlier works. He was not particularly prolific which could be another reason for a lack of deserved recognition.

To make a living at painting in the relatively early stages would have been difficult if not impossible but, in 1834, Short accepted the offer of a designer's post with a Norwich firm, work that was at least compatible with the artistic approach. He stayed with the firm for 50 years, working on his landscapes, mainly in oil, very occasionally in watercolour, in his spare time. He appears to have accepted this life as a fair compromise without asking or expecting anything more. Short actually lived to be 84, a life without great ambition but, equally, without great stress. He was a contented soul and a dedicated lifelong Christian.

Antony Sandys (1806-1883) was of Italian descent but born in Norwich; he exhibited quite extensively in the city although he is regarded as something of a fringe painter of the Norwich School. He is first recorded as working for a dyer, most likely the father of James Stark, whose son would certainly have encouraged his interest in the arts.

He started portrait painting and by 1830 appears to have been considered of exhibition standard as there is a record of a portrait exhibited in the Norfolk and Suffolk Institute that year.

He seems to have exhibited only portraits for nearly 20 years; Harold Day illustrates an elegant self-portrait and portraits of his son and Henry Ninham. He later started to paint still-life and, eventually, landscapes, the subjects of which extended over most of the country including the Lake District, Derbyshire and Scotland. Plainly he enjoyed travel and portrait painters of that time, before the ubiquitous camera, were often better off financially than landscape artists, so not only could he afford to travel at will but he also acquired a good collection of Norwich School paintings, notably those of John Berney Crome.

His landscapes display good draughtsmanship and sense of composition but his colour is not to everyone's taste. He enjoyed dramatic contrasts but his rather strange purple shades tend to mar rather than create effect. This, however, should not detract from his very real ability and when his colour is modified the result is certainly pleasing.

His son **Frederick Sandys** (1829-1904) is even nearer to the fringe of the Norwich School but his work is well represented in Norwich Castle Museum. He was born in Norwich and became a close friend of the Rev. James Bulwer and William Barnes Freeman who both became portrait subjects. He first made his name as an illustrator as well as a portraitist; working predominantly in chalk he provided some very superior illustrations for *The Cornhill, The Argosy, Good Words* and other periodicals.

The quality of his draughtsmanship, learnt in the Royal Academy Schools, and his attention to detail is quite remarkable and he had a particular interest in and feeling for decorative antiquities. His illustration of the painted screen in Hunstanton Church (Norwich Castle Museum) is a most beautiful piece of work and there is a particularly fascinating drawing of an ancient lock belonging to a chest in the Muniment room of the Castle.

Later in London, where he spent much of his life, Sandys became involved with the Pre-Raphaelite movement when some of his portraits acquired the Rossetti touch, and he illustrated the poems of Christina Rossetti and Swinburne. Undoubtedly he had an exceptional talent although his lifestyle is said to have been less than impeccable.

William Barnes Freeman (1813-1897) is perhaps considered a little late for the general conception of the Norwich School period but, as grandson of John Crome's great friend, Jeremiah Freeman, who had introduced him to Crome in his youth, he can claim a certain connection. William Barnes Freeman had also studied under Crome's successor at Norwich, later becoming a pupil of John Sell Cotman.

Freeman exhibited quite widely, at the R.A. and in many Norwich exhibitions, although his work is of uneven quality. In some of his early drawings he has plainly tried to emulate John Sell Cotman but they are rather insipid parodies and his draughtsmanship was inferior to most of the Norwich artists. His landscapes in oil and watercolour are often fussy and over laboured but he was a great deal more successful with seascapes. The very subject encouraged the breadth so often lacking in his landscapes and there was less need for accomplished drawing. Maybe as a subject it had greater appeal for he was certainly able to give his seas and skies more atmosphere and feeling than is expressed in his country scenes.

His father had been Mayor of Norwich which no doubt gave him a higher profile than he might otherwise have achieved.

Daniel Coppin (1771-1822) the father of Mrs Joseph Stannard, was a reasonably good amateur painter and a founder member of the Norwich Society with whom he exhibited from its inception. He was a friend of John Crome and worked with him to promote the Society in its early days. He became President in 1816. Although I have never seen his work, we have it on the good authority of Dickes that he was a competent landscape painter. His wife also painted, mainly still-life, and often copied or partly so, which no doubt gave daughter Emily her initial interest in the subject.

Michael Sharp (fl.1801-1840) was another friend of Crome. He was born in London, the son of a Norwich music master, but came to Norwich as a young child and, for some reason, made almost a second home with the Cromes. John Crome obviously thought a great deal of him and actually called one of his sons, Michael Sharp Crome, after him.

Sharp painted mainly figures and portraits and studied under Beechey as well as Crome. There is in Norwich Castle Museum a portrait by him of Mrs Crome and he painted Crome in 1813. Sharp exhibited regularly with the Society as well as in London, became Vice-President of the Society in 1816 and President a year later. Rumour has it that he painted the figures in Crome's famous 'Poringland Oak' (National Gallery) but I doubt if the truth of this could be guaranteed.

Henry Jutsum (1816-1869) was London born and educated in Devon but became a pupil of James Stark and a close friend of Henry Bright, his main links with Norwich. Stark's influence clearly shows in his work which, in both oil and watercolour, is in a very traditional but pleasant and comfortable style. He exhibited in the Academy, the British Institute and the Suffolk Street Galleries. His work is represented in the Royal Collection and the Victoria and Albert Museum and now realises quite high prices. His connection with Norwich remains fairly tenuous.

A number of very fine etchings and some drawings by **James William Walker** (1831-1898) are in the Castle Museum but, again, he is late for the Norwich School as generally considered. I mention him out of respect for Dickes. He was born in Norwich and studied at the Norwich School of Design but travelled a great deal and taught in schools in Bolton, London and Southport. His personal work shows good draughtsmanship in the Norwich tradition and a very typical late 19th century style of watercolour.

EPILOGUE

In his *Encyclopaedia of the Arts* published in 1966, Sir Herbert Read defines the Norwich School as an 'English regional school of landscape painting, the only local school in English art history which is comparable with the earlier Italian schools. Its leaders were Old Crome and Cotman and it flourished from 1805 (when Crome founded the Norwich Society of Artists) until c.1830. Minor artists included Joseph Stannard, James Stark, John Berney Crome and George Vincent.'

I have great respect for much of Herbert Read's writing and concur with many of his philosophical views on art and artists. Nevertheless, I take issue with him on the notion that Joseph Stannard was a *minor* artist or indeed, any of the other three that Read mentions. While there is certainly no definite end to the Norwich School era, I have never heard such an early, even approximated, date as 1830.

I have quoted extensively from many earlier historians than Read – Binyon, Dickes, Oppé, Kitson – and from my own contemporaries – Clifford, Day, Hemingway, Rajnai, Moore and others – who have, just as I am doing now, sought to dispel the delusion that the Norwich School consisted of a few Norfolk painters who painted local landscapes in oils over a couple of decades and somehow came to constitute a school. I have added another voice to those who sincerely appreciate the art of the Norwich painters and seek to increase the general awareness not only of the wealth of talent involved but the extent of media used – oil, watercolour, crayon, chalk, mixed media, etching, engraving, pastel, ink and pencil, and the breadth of subject matter – landscape, marine, portraiture, still-life, flowers, architecture and subjects based on classical themes or from the artist's imagination. This is all part of the mystery and the magic of the Norwich School; it has no containing bounds yet it is inexplicably contained. Clifford again: 'The Norwich School did not stand for any special doctrine. It consisted of a body of artists, professional and amateur, centred on the city, who by meeting, working and exhibiting together, acquired a shadowy, corporate sense, and who to some extent came to share a tradition.'

It has often been said that the Norwich painters were all, in some way or another, connected directly or indirectly with Crome or Cotman – pupils, friends, admirers or imitators – or their sons and immediate followers. Yet, to quote Dr Norman Goldberg in his introduction to the Catalogue of the Norwich School Exhibition in Florida in 1967: 'Whenever these artists tried to incorporate the style of Crome and Cotman, they were imitative and weak, but the moment they had the courage to be self reliant, they were more poetic and successful.' I have tried to make this evident in the discussion of several artists' work.

Although the Norwich Society of Artists was undoubtedly the kindling spark, there is no hard and fast connection even here. Many of the Norwich School painters never joined the Society and other Society members came and went without ever being associated with the School. Many professional artists well outside Norwich – Varley, Cox, Mueller and others – exhibited with the Norwich Society but would never for a moment be considered 'of the Norwich School'. Consider that, before 1828, 323 artists* had exhibited 4,600 pictures (which, incidentally, sold better when later exhibited in London, Leeds, Manchester, Edinburgh, Liverpool and Newcastle than in Norwich – perhaps a matter of starvation versus saturation!) and the chosen few seem very few indeed.

We are back to Laurence Binyon and the 'deep unconscious bond'. No one has come up with a better answer and probably no one ever will.

* Rajnai, 1978.

Appendix I

ARTISTS OF THE NORWICH SCHOOL

Bright, Henry (1810-1873)
Bulwer, Rev. James (1794-1879)

Clint, George (1770-1854)
Clover, Joseph (1779-1854)
Colkett, Samuel David (1806-1863)
Colkett, Victoria Susanna (1840-1926)
Cooper, Edwin (1785-1833)
Coppin, Daniel (1771-1822)
Cotman, Frederick George (1850-1920)
Cotman, John Joseph (1814-1878)
Cotman, John Sell (1782-1842)
Cotman, Miles Edmund (1810-1858)
Crome, Emily (1801-1840)
Crome, Frederick James (1796-1832)
Crome, John (1768-1821)
Crome, John Berney (1794-1842)
Crome, Vivian (fl.1858-1898 d.1926)
Crome, William Henry (1806-1867)

Daniell, Rev. Edward Thomas (1804-1842)
Dixon, Robert (1780-1815)

Freeman, William Barnes (1813-1897)

Geldart, Joseph (1808-1882)

Hodgson, Charles (c.1770-1856)
Hodgson, David (1798-1864)

Joy, John Cantiloe (1806-1866)
Joy, William (1803-1867)
Jutsum, Henry (1816-1869)

Ladbroke, Frederick (1810-1865)
Ladbroke, Henry (1800-1869)
Ladbroke, John Berney (1803-1879)
Ladbroke, Robert (1769-1842)
Leman, Robert (1799-1863)
Lound, Thomas (1802-1861)
Love, Horace Beevor (1800-1838)

Margitson, Maria (1832-1896)
Middleton, John (1827-1856)

Ninham, Henry (1793-1874)
Ninham, John (1754-1817)

Paul, Joseph (1804-1887)

Priest, Alfred (1810-1850)

Sandys, Antony (1806-1883)
Sandys, Frederick (1829-1904)
Sharp, Michael (fl.1801-1840)
Short, Obadiah (1803-1886)
Sillet, Emma (fl.1813-1833)
Sillett, James (1764-1840)
Stannard, Alfred (1806-1889)
Stannard, Alfred George (1828-1885)
Stannard, Eloise Harriet (1829-1915)
Stannard, Emily (Mrs Joseph Stannard) (1803-1885)
Stannard, Emily (1827-1894)
Stannard, Joseph (1797-1830)
Stark, Arthur James (1831-1902)
Stark, James (1794-1859)

Thirtle, John (1777-1839)

Vincent, George (1796-c.1835)

Walker, James William (1831-1898)

Appendix II

FAMILY TREES

(Names in **bold** apply to painting members of the family)

The Cromes

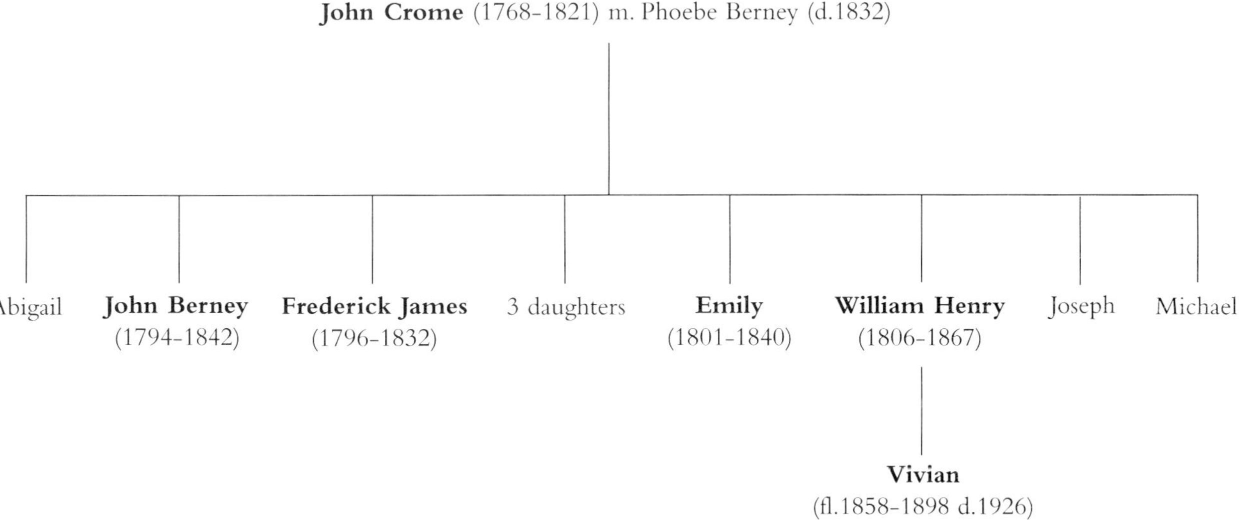

The Ladbrokes

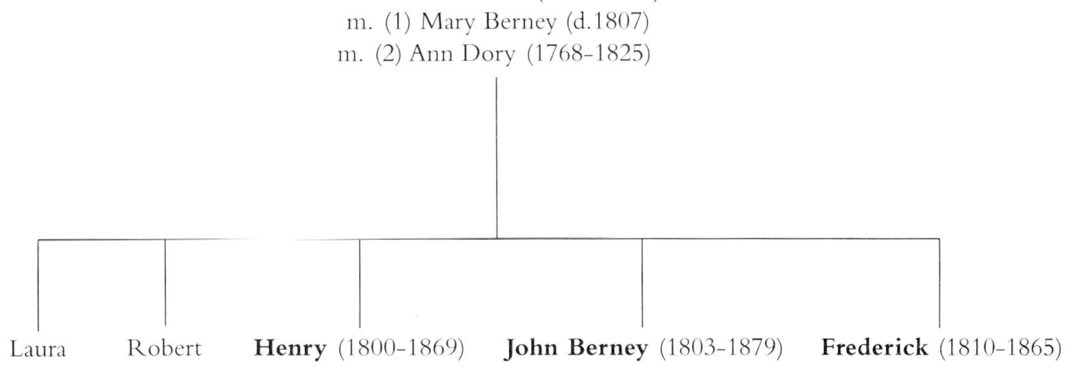

The Stannards

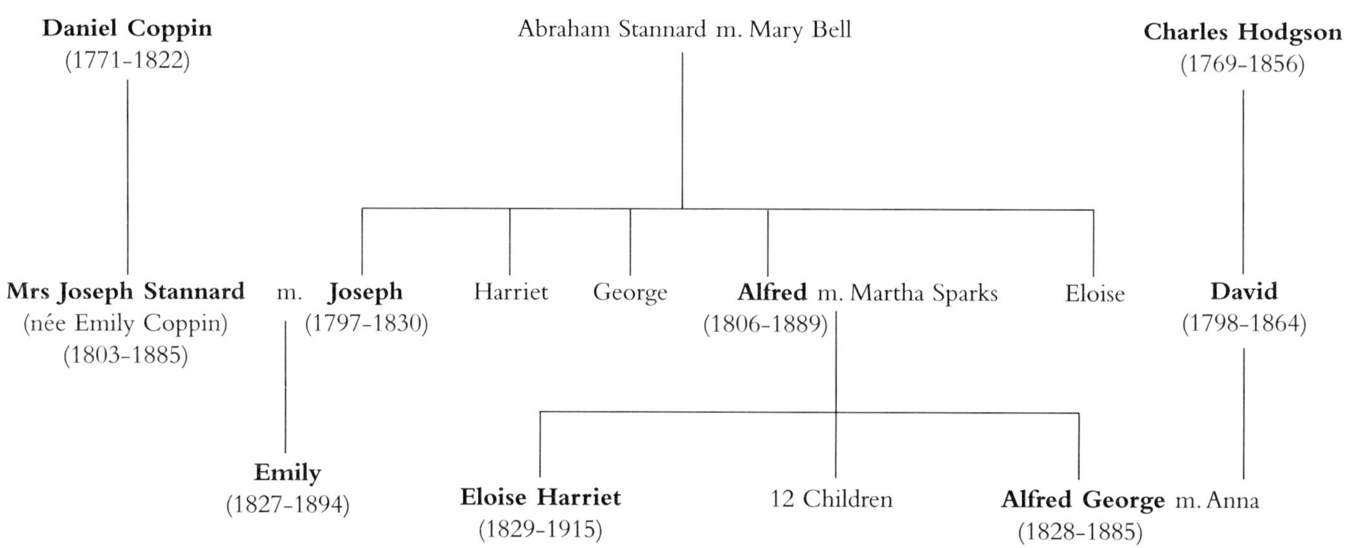

The Cotmans

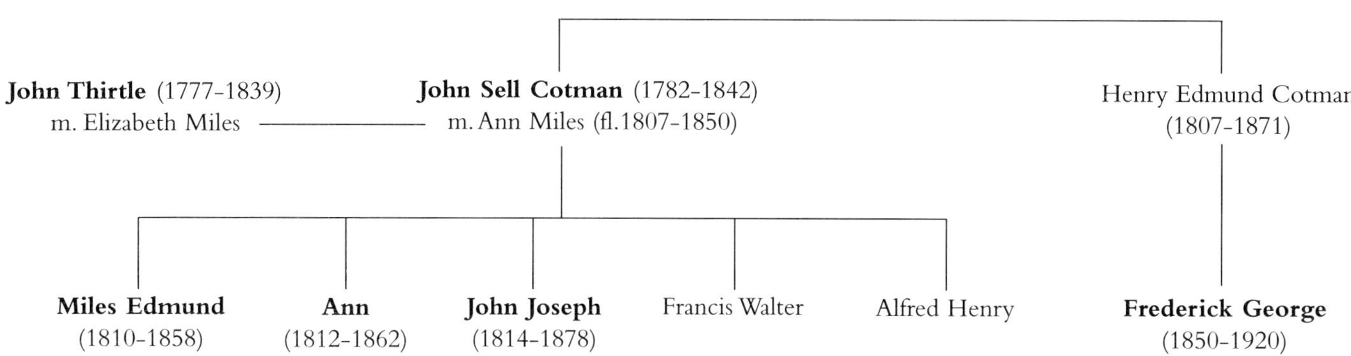

Appendix III

WORKS BY NORWICH SCHOOL ARTISTS IN PUBLIC COLLECTIONS

Needless to say, all the artists of the Norwich School are represented in all relevant media in the vast collection housed in Norwich Castle Museum and almost all by drawings in the British Museum. Their works can, however, be found in many other museums and galleries throughout this country and abroad proving that appreciation of their work is by no means confined to Norwich and London. To give an idea of the breadth of the representation as well as providing a guide for interested viewers, some of the most important venues (other than Norwich Castle and the British Museum) are listed below. There are no doubt other smaller public collections holding paintings and drawings of the Norwich School and certainly many private collections, both in the important historic houses and in the homes of individual collectors. (The work of the two giants, Crome and Cotman, are listed first followed by an alphabetical listing of artists.)

John Crome: the National Gallery, London; the Tate Gallery, London; the Victoria and Albert Museum; the Royal Collection; the National Gallery of Scotland, Edinburgh; the National Gallery of Ireland, Dublin; Glasgow Museum and Art Gallery; Abbot Hall, Kendal, Cumbria; Leeds City Art Gallery; the Lady Lever Art Gallery, Port Sunlight, Wirral; Birmingham Art Gallery; the Iveagh Bequest, Kenwood House; Doncaster Art Gallery; Manchester Art Gallery; the Fitzwilliam Museum, Cambridge; Nottingham Castle Museum; Grundy Art Gallery, Blackpool.

Works formerly attributed to Crome in the Wolverhampton and Bury Art Galleries have now been ascribed to Joseph Paul. Overseas Crome is represented in the Paul Mellon Collection, U.S.A.; the Metropolitan Museum, New York; the Museum of Art, Philadelphia; the National Gallery of Art, Washington, D.C.; and also in galleries in Sydney and Montreal.

John Sell Cotman: the Tate Gallery, London; the Victoria and Albert Museum; the National Gallery of Scotland including one of the Greta watercolours, 'A Shady Pool where the Greta joins the Trees,' 1805; the National Gallery of Ireland, Dublin; Leeds City Art Gallery, which has the major collection from the Sidney Kitson bequest including some 600 watercolours and drawings covering every period and aspect of his work; the Ashmolean Museum, Oxford, which holds an extensive collection of drawings some of which are also from the Kitson bequest; the Fitzwilliam Museum, Cambridge; Abbot Hall, Kendal, including the famous 'The Market Place, Norwich', 1807, one of Cotman's finest Norwich watercolour drawings; York City Art Gallery; the Castle Museum, Nottingham; Manchester Art Gallery; Walker Art Gallery, Liverpool; Birmingham Art Gallery who have the rare *Liber Studiorum;* Glasgow Art Gallery and Museum; Rochdale Art Gallery; Great Yarmouth Art Gallery; Bolton Art Gallery; Bury (Lancashire) Art Gallery; Bristol Museum and Art Gallery (early pencil portraits of the Norton family); the Cecil Higgins Art Gallery, Bedford; the Museum of Art, Philadelphia; the National Gallery of Art, Washington, D.C.; the Municipal Art Gallery, Pietermaritzburg, South Africa.

Henry Bright: the Victoria and Albert Museum; the National Gallery of Scotland, Edinburgh; the National Gallery of Ireland, Dublin; Glasgow Art Gallery and Museum; Leeds City Art Gallery; Castle Museum, Nottingham; Great Yarmouth Art Gallery; the Fitzwilliam Museum,

Cambridge; Birmingham Museum and Art Gallery; York City Art Gallery; Walker Art Gallery, Liverpool; Abbot Hall, Kendal; the Ashmolean Museum, Oxford; Rochdale Art Gallery; Bury (Lancashire) Art Gallery; Bolton Museum and Art Gallery; Ipswich Museums; Leicester Art Gallery; Sheffield Art Gallery; Salford Art Gallery and (with J.F. Herring) the Guildhall Gallery, Aldermanbury, London; the National Gallery of Art, Washington; Montreal, Canada.

Rev. James Bulwer: Birmingham Museum and Art Gallery; Bristol Museum and Art Gallery; the National Gallery of Art, Washington, D.C.; Ottawa.

George Clint: the National Portrait Gallery, London, by his self-portrait and other subjects; the Castle Museum, Nottingham; Guildhall Gallery, Aldermanbury, London.

Samuel David Colkett: Leeds City Art Gallery; Castle Museum, Nottingham; Manchester Art Gallery; Wolverhampton Art Gallery.

Edwin Cooper: Leeds City Art Gallery, several equine collections, and in the Mellon Collection, U.S.A.

Frederick George Cotman: the Ashmolean Museum, Oxford; the Victoria Art Gallery, Bath; Ipswich Museums; Walker Art Gallery, Liverpool.

John Joseph Cotman: the Fitzwilliam Museum, Cambridge; Leeds City Art Gallery; Birmingham Museum and Art Gallery; Great Yarmouth Art Gallery; National Portrait Gallery, London, by a portrait of his father, John Sell Cotman.

Miles Edmund Cotman: the National Gallery of Scotland, Edinburgh; the Ashmolean Museum, Oxford; Rochdale Art Gallery; Birmingham Museum and Art Gallery; the Fitzwilliam Museum, Cambridge; Manchester Art Gallery; Great Yarmouth Art Gallery; Leeds City Art Gallery; Southampton Art Gallery.

John Berney Crome: the National Gallery, London; the Fitzwilliam Museum, Cambridge; Great Yarmouth Museums and Art Gallery; Ipswich Museums; the Iveagh Bequest, Kenwood House, by 'The Yarmouth Water Frolic', shared with his father.

William Henry Crome: the Castle Museum Nottingham; Manchester Art Gallery.

Rev. Edward Thomas Daniell: the Victoria and Albert Museum; the Ashmolean Museum, Oxford; the Fitzwilliam Museum, Cambridge; Leeds City Art Gallery; Bristol Museums and Art Gallery.

Robert Dixon: Leeds City Art Gallery; the National Gallery of Art, Washington, D.C.

William Barnes Freeman: Great Yarmouth Museums and Art Gallery.

William and John Cantiloe Joy: the National Gallery of Ireland, Dublin; the Victoria and Albert Museum; Great Yarmouth Museums and Art Gallery; Birmingham Art Gallery.

Henry Jutsum: the Victoria and Albert Museum; the Royal Collection; Birmingham Art Gallery; Leeds City Art Gallery.

John Berney Ladbroke: Bolton Museum and Art Gallery.

Robert Ladbroke: Leeds City Art Gallery; Great Yarmouth Museums and Art Gallery; Doncaster Art Gallery; by attribution in Wolverhampton Art Gallery.

Thomas Lound: the Ashmolean Museum, Oxford; the Fitzwilliam Museum, Cambridge; Great Yarmouth Museums and Art Gallery; Leeds City Art Gallery; Doncaster Art Gallery.

Horace Beevor Love: the National Portrait Gallery, London, by portraits of John Sell Cotman and James Stark

John Middleton: Abbot Hall, Kendal; Leeds City Art Gallery.

Henry Ninham: Leeds City Art Gallery.

Alfred Stannard: Great Yarmouth Museums and Art Gallery; Derby Museum and Art Gallery.

Joseph Stannard: the Victoria and Albert Museum; the Fitzwilliam Museum, Cambridge; Great Yarmouth Museums and Art Gallery; Leeds City Art Gallery; Paul Mellon Collection, U.S.A.

Arthur James Stark: the Victoria and Albert Museum; Art Gallery and Museum, Glasgow; Exeter Art Gallery

James Stark: the Victoria and Albert Museum; the National Gallery of Scotland, Edinburgh; the Lady Lever Art Gallery, Port Sunlight, Wirral; Art Gallery and Museum, Glasgow; the Ashmolean Museum, Oxford; the Fitzwilliam Museum, Cambridge; Walker Art Gallery, Liverpool; Wolverhampton Art Gallery; Birmingham Museum and Art Gallery; Manchester Art Gallery; Castle Museum, Nottingham; Leeds City Art Gallery; the Paul Mellon Collection, U.S.A.; the Metropolitan Museum of Art, New York; the Philadelphia Museum of Art.

John Thirtle: the Ashmolean Museum, Oxford; Walker Art Gallery, Liverpool; York City Art Gallery; Leeds City Art Gallery.

George Vincent: the Fitzwilliam Museum, Cambridge; Manchester Art Gallery; Birmingham Museum and Art Gallery; Castle Museum, Nottingham; Great Yarmouth Museums and Art Gallery; Wolverhampton Art Gallery; Bolton Museum and Art Gallery; Ipswich Museums; Leeds City Art Gallery; Southampton Art Gallery; the Paul Mellon Collection, U.S.A.; the Philadelphia Museum of Art; the Metropolitan Museum of Art, New York.

Appendix IV

NORWICH SCHOOL ARTISTS REPRESENTED IN THE WITT LIBRARY (COURTAULD INSTITUTE)

Bright, Henry
Bulwer, Rev. James

Clover, Joseph
Colkett, Samuel David
Colkett, Victoria Susanna
Cooper, Edwin
Cotman, Ann
Cotman, Frederick George
Cotman, John Joseph
Cotman, John Sell
Cotman, Miles Edmund
Crome, John
Crome, John Berney
Crome, William Henry
Crome, Vivian

Freeman, William Barnes

Geldart, Joseph
Hodgson, Charles
Hodgson, David

Joy, John Cantiloe
Joy, William

Ladbroke, Frederick
Ladbroke, John Berney
Ladbroke, Henry
Ladbroke, Robert
Leman, Robert
Lound, Thomas
Love, Horace Beevor

Margitson, Maria
Middleton, John

Ninham, Henry

Ninham, John

Priest, Alfred

Sandys, Antony
Sandys, Frederick
Short, Obadiah
Sillett, James
Stannard, Alfred
Stannard, Alfred George
Stannard, Emily
Stannard, Eloise Harriet
Stannard, Joseph
Stark, Arthur James
Stark, James

Thirtle, John

Vincent, George

SELECT BIBLIOGRAPHY

Allthorpe-Guyton, Marjorie, *John Thirtle 1777-1839,* catalogue of drawings in Norwich Castle Museum, Norfolk Museums Service 1977.

Allthorpe-Guyton, Marjorie, *Henry Bright 1810-1873,* catalogue of paintings and drawings in Norwich Castle Museum, Norfolk Museums Service 1986.

Barnard, G.V., *Paintings of the Norwich School,* Jarrolds *c.*1950.

Bennett, Chlöe, *Suffolk Artists 1750-1930*, Images Publications & Ipswich Borough Council 1991.

Binyon, Laurence, *John Crome and John Sell Cotman*, Seeley & Co. Ltd., London 1897.

Boswell, David, and Miller, Corinne, *Cotmania & Mr Kitson*, Leeds City Art Gallery 1992.

Bury, Adrian, *The Fitzwilliam, Cambridge*, Journal of the Old Watercolour Society 31st Annual Volume 1956.

Clifford, Derek, *Watercolours of The Norwich School*, Cory, Adams & Mackay Ltd. 1965.

Clifford, Derek, *The Norwich School of Watercolourists*, Journal of the Old Watercolour Society 41st Annual Volume 1966.

Clifford, Derek, *A Personal Choice*, Journal of the Old Watercolour Society 48th Annual Volume 1973.

Cotman, Alec M., and Hawcroft, Francis, *Old Norwich, A Collection of Paintings, Prints & Drawings*, Jarrolds 1961.

Day, Harold A.E., *The Life and Work of Joseph Stannard*, Eastbourne Fine Art 1967.

Day, Harold A.E., *East Anglian Painters Vols.II & III*, Eastbourne Fine Art 1968, 1969.

Day, Harold A.E., *The Norwich School of Painters*, Eastbourne Fine Art 1979.

Dickes, W.F., *The Norwich School of Painting*, Dickes 1905.

Hardie, Martin, *Watercolour Painting in Britain Vols. I, II, III*, Batsford 1966, 1967, 1968.

Hawcroft, Francis W., *Watercolours in Norwich Castle Museum*, Journal of the Old Watercolour Society 39th Annual Volume 1964.

Hemingway, Andrew, *The Norwich School of Painters 1803-1833*, Phaidon Press 1979.

Kitson, Sidney D., *The Life of John Sell Cotman*, Faber & Faber 1937.

Mallalieu, Huon, *The Norwich School: Crome, Cotman and their Followers*, Academy 1974.

Moore, Andrew, *John Sell Cotman 1782-1842*, Norfolk Museums Service 1982.

Moore, Andrew, *The Norwich School of Artists*, Norfolk Museums Service 1985.

Moore, Andrew, *The Norwich School of Artists*, Norfolk Museums Service and H.M.S.O. 1996.

Mottram, R.H., *East Anglia*, Chapman & Hall 1933.

Oppé, Paul, *The Watercolour Drawings of John Sell Cotman*, Studio 1923.

Rajnai, Miklos, *The Norwich Society of Artists 1805-1833: Members and Exhibitors*, extracts from *Norfolk Archaeology*, XXXIV Pt.IV 1969 (Amended) and XXXV Pt.II 1971.

Rajnai, Miklos, *The Norwich Society of Artists 1805-1833: A Dictionary of Contributors and their Work*, Norfolk Museums Service 1976 in the Paul Mellon Centre.

Rajnai, Miklos, *The Norwich School of Painters*, Jarrolds 1978.

Rajnai, Miklos, and Allthorpe-Guyton, Marjorie, *John Sell Cotman*, catalogue of drawings in Norwich Castle Museum, Norfolk Museums Service 1975.

Reynolds, Graham, *English Watercolours*, Herbert 1950.

Rothenstein, John, *An Introduction to English Painting*, Cassell & Co. 1965.

Walpole, Josephine, *Leonard Squirrell, R.W. S., R.E.: The last of the Norwich School?*, Antique Collectors' Club 1993.

Walpole, Josephine, and Pleasance, Geoffrey, *Suffolk Lives*, Richard Castell Publishing 1993.

Watt, Norma, 'The Struggle of John Joseph Cotman', *Norfolk Fair,* December 1978.

INDEX

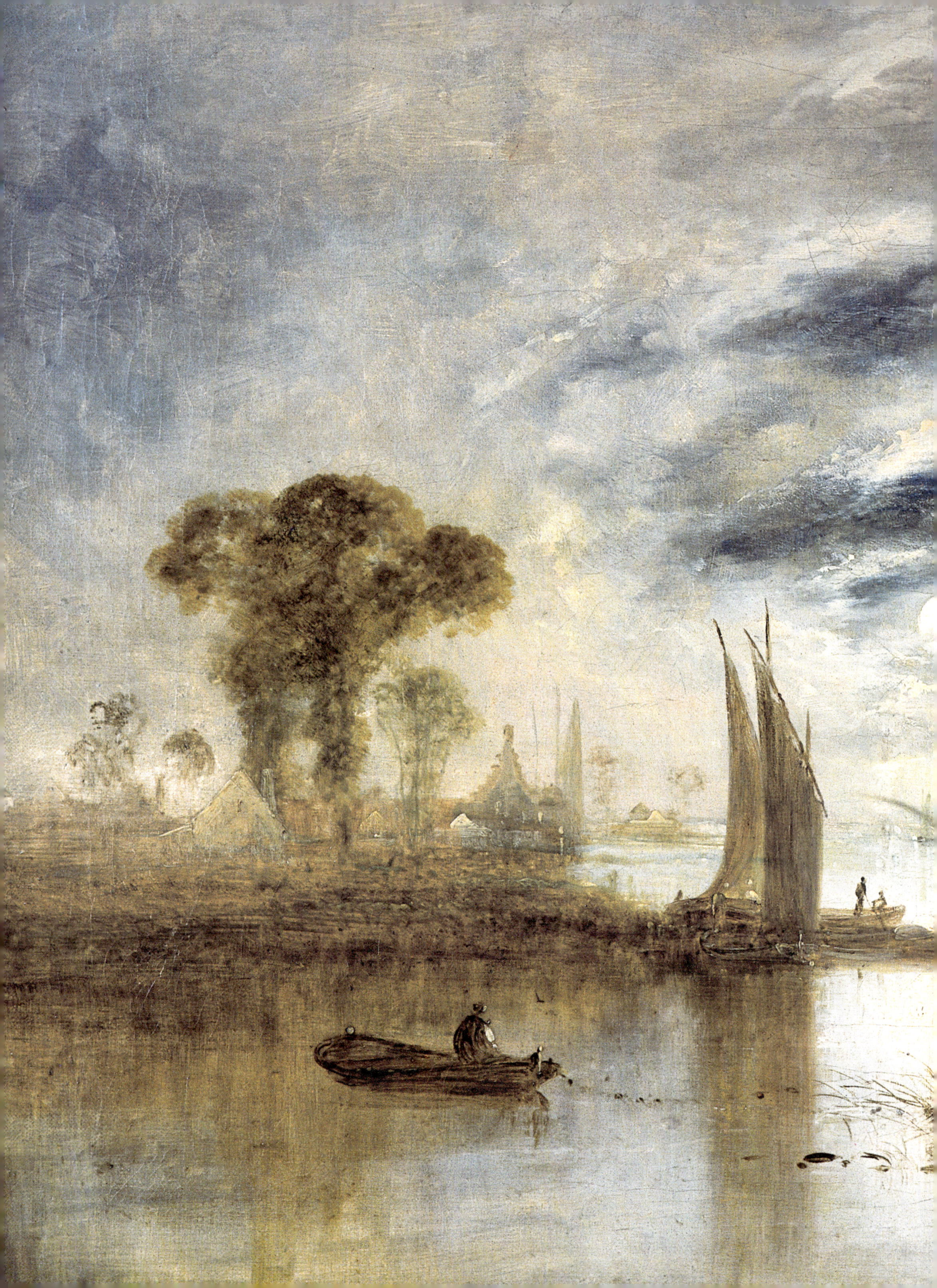